"James Tully's 'public philosophy' aspires to empower transformative change through dialogues in which each of us – as citizens of local, global, and Earth communities – has a say and a hand in governance. *James Tully: To Think and Act Differently* skilfully renders a much-needed service in its thoughtful exploration and framing of the development of Tully's public philosophy from animating ideas and experiences, to mature articulation, to ongoing reconsideration, expansion and application. Along the journey, this carefully edited volume effectively makes the case that you have a vital role in transforming injustices today. Anyone concerned to be part of the change needed by a world governed by elites and by autocrats, a world at once drowning and on fire, should read this book."

Aaron Mills, *Faculty of Law, McGill University Research Chair in Indigenous Constitutionalism and Philosophy*

"This important book introduces the reader to the influential scholarship of James Tully by combining previously published with entirely new material. Beyond mere collection, however, Livingston's thorough introduction and concluding interview provide a fascinating engagement with some of Tully's most important innovations in the field. Together, Livingston and Tully 'travel' with Tully's theory, from his evolving dialogical approach, to his thinking on colonialism, to his transformative account of political philosophy as political practice. *James Tully: To Think and Act Differently* is thus a powerful reflection on the essential themes of Tully's career and a tribute to the hopeful multiplicity of his vision."

Jeanne Morefield, *New College, University of Oxford*

"This volume brings together both classical and unpublished contributions by James Tully that exemplify how political theory can respond in deeply dialogical and transformative ways to the challenges and struggles of our time. It offers an excellent overview of the eminently practical and genuinely political public philosophy Tully has developed over the last decades and documents the pathbreaking force of his continuous efforts to straddle the gaps between theory and practice as well as between diverse traditions of acting and thinking politically. The result is a less parochial, more expansive and profoundly democratic vision of the world we both inescapably share and need to learn to inhabit together."

Robin Celikates, *Institute of Philosophy, Free University Berlin*

"This collection offers a superbly curated selection of, and guide to, the work of James Tully. Alexander Livingston expertly charts the evolving trajectory of one of the most creative political theorists of the twenty-first century from the exploration of imperialism in support of Indigenous struggles to engagement with global climate change, democratic sustainability, and the ethics of non-violence. This is a landmark volume for understanding the past, present and future of Tully's public philosophy and the transformation of political theory it accomplishes."

David Owen, *Department of Politics and International Relations, University of Southampton*

James Tully

James Tully's scholarship has profoundly transformed the study of political thought by reconstructing the practice of political theory as a democratising and diversifying dialogue between scholars and citizens. Across his writings on topics ranging from the historical origins of property, constitutionalism in diverse societies, imperialism and globalisation, and global citizenship in an era of climate crisis, Tully has developed a participatory mode of political theorising and political change called public philosophy. This practice-oriented approach to political thought and its active role in the struggles of citizens has posed fundamental challenges to modern political thought and launched new lines of inquiry in the study of constitutionalism, democracy and citizenship, settler colonialism, comparative political theory, nonviolence, and ecological sustainability. *James Tully: To Think and Act Differently* collects classic, contemporary, and previously unpublished writings from across Tully's four decades of scholarship to shed new light on these dialogues of reciprocal elucidation with citizens, scholars, and the history of political thought, and the ways Tully has enlarged our understanding of democracy, diversity, and the task of political theory.

Alexander Livingston is Associate Professor in the Department of Government at Cornell University. His research addresses social movements, civil disobedience, democratic theory, and the history of twentieth-century political thought. He is the author of *Damn Great Empires! William James and the Politics of Pragmatism* (2016).

Routledge Innovators in Political Theory
Edited by Terrell Carver, *University of Bristol and*
Samuel A. Chambers, *Johns Hopkins University*

Routledge Innovators in Political Theory focuses on leading contemporary thinkers in political theory, highlighting the major innovations in their thought that have reshaped the field. Each volume collects both published and unpublished texts, and combines them with an interview with the thinker. The editorial introduction articulates the innovator's key contributions in relation to political theory, and contextualises the writer's work. Volumes in the series will be required reading for both students and scholars of 21st century politics.

Fred Dallmayr
Critical Phenomenology, Cross-cultural Theory, Cosmopolitanism
Edited by Farah Godrej

Jane Mansbridge
Participation, Deliberation, Coercion
Edited by Melissa S. Williams

Michael Paul Rogin
Derangement and Liberalism
Edited by Alyson Cole and George Shulman

Iris Marion Young
Gender, Justice, and the Politics of Difference
Michaele Ferguson and Andrew Valls

James Tully
To Think and Act Differently
Edited by Alexander Livingston

For more information about this series, please visit: www.routledge.com/ Routledge-Innovators-in-Political-Theory/book-series/RIPT

James Tully
To Think and Act Differently

Edited by
Alexander Livingston

Routledge
Taylor & Francis Group

LONDON AND NEW YORK

First published 2022
by Routledge
4 Park Square, Milton Park, Abingdon, Oxon OX14 4RN

and by Routledge
605 Third Avenue, New York, NY 10158

Routledge is an imprint of the Taylor & Francis Group, an informa business

British Library Cataloguing-in-Publication Data
A catalogue record for this book is available from the British Library

Library of Congress Cataloging-in-Publication Data
A catalog record has been requested for this book

ISBN: 9781032130460 (hbk)
ISBN: 9781032130484 (pbk)
ISBN: 9781003227403 (ebk)

DOI: 10.4324/9781003227403

Typeset in Times New Roman
by Newgen Publishing UK

Contents

Series Editor Foreword

James Tully's scholarship has profoundly transformed the study of political thought by reconstructing the practice of political theory as a democratising and diversifying dialogue between scholars and citizens. Across his writings on topics ranging from the historical origins of property, constitutionalism in diverse societies, imperialism and globalisation, and global citizenship in an era of climate crisis, Tully has developed a participatory mode of political theorising and political change called public philosophy. This practice-oriented approach to political thought and its active role in the struggles of citizens has posed fundamental challenges to modern political thought and launched new lines of inquiry in the study of constitutionalism, democracy and citizenship, settler colonialism, comparative political theory, nonviolence, and ecological sustainability. Through dialogues of reciprocal elucidation with citizens, scholars, and the history of political thought, Tully has enlarged our understanding of democracy, diversity, and the task of political theory.

The editor has focused on work in three key areas:

The Practice of Public Philosophy

The chapters in this section examine the sources of Tully's dialogical approach as a critical alternative to monological or "elite" approaches to political theory, and the interpretive and ethical challenges of sustaining genuine dialogues of reciprocal elucidation across political traditions.

Modes of Citizenship and Practices of Freedom

Public philosophy advances a particular vision of democratic freedom as the civic practice of citizens to question, contest, and democratize practices of government. Chapters in this section examine Tully's agonistic conception of freedom and its contributions to understanding citizen struggles over constitutionalism, citizenship, mutual aid, and human rights in imperial and neo-imperial contexts.

Sustaining Civic Freedom

Tully's most recent work addresses the global crisis of sustainability and the need to reembed politics and economy in the biosphere. These chapters consider sources and implications of Tully's proposed ecosocial reorientation for topics including globalisation and modernisation, Indigenous resurgence and reconciliation, nonviolence and sustainable social change, and the role of law in the climate crisis.

James Tully: To Think and Act Differently is essential reading for anyone interested in approaches to the history of political thought, constitutionalism, democratic theory, Indigenous political thought, settler colonialism and imperialism, comparative political theory, climate change and sustainability, and the politics of nonviolence.

Acknowledgements

The editor would like to thank Terrell Carver, Sam Chamber, Robert Sorsby, Claire Maloney, and two anonymous reviewers for their guidance and support. Conversations with Melissa Williams and Inder Marwah helped bring the volume's editorial vision into sharper focus. Val Napoleon, Hadley Friedland, and Jessica Asch generously shared insights about community-directed research. Jacob Swanson diligently assisted with preparing the manuscript for publication. Judy Dunlop prepared the index. Jim Tully proved an "exemplary examplar" of the public philosopher's generosity, dialogical engagement, and reciprocal elucidation throughout the process of editing this volume. I owe him a profound debt of gratitude for this gift. This volume was supported by grants from the Society for the Humanities at Cornell University, the Cornell Center for Social Sciences, and the University of Victoria.

We are grateful to publishers for permission to reprint the following chapters:

J-Stage for Chapter 1, "Political Theory as a Critical Activity: The Emergence of Public Philosophy," *Japanese Journal of Political Thought* 17 (2017): 498–514.

Cambridge University Press for Chapter 2 "Public Philosophy and Civic Freedom: A Guide to the Two Volumes," in *Public Philosophy in a New Key*, Vol. 1, 3–12. Cambridge: Cambridge University Press, 2008; Chapter 5 "The Historical Formation of Common Constitutionalism: The Rediscovery of Cultural Diversity, Part 1," in *Strange Multiplicity: Constitutionalism in an Age of Diversity*, 99–139. Cambridge: Cambridge University Press, 1995; Chapter 9 "Introducing Global Integral Constitutionalism," *Global Constitutionalism* 5, no. 1 (2016): 1–15.

Indiana University Press for Chapter 3 "Deparochializing Political Theory and Beyond: A Dialogue Approach to Comparative Political Thought," *Journal of World Philosophies* 1, no. 1 (2016): 51–74.

Taylor & Francis for Chapter 4 "The Agonistic Freedom of Citizens," *Economy and Society* 28, no. 2 (1999): 161–82.

Springer Nature for Chapter 6 "Two Meanings of Global Citizenship: Global and Diverse," in *Global Citizenship Education: Philosophy, Theory and*

Pedagogy, edited by Michael A. Peters, Harry Blee & Alan Britton, 15–39. Rotterdam: Sense Publications, 2008.

Bloomsbury for Chapter 7 "Rethinking Human Rights and Enlightenment: A View from the Twenty-First Century," in *Self-Evident Truths? Human Rights and the Enlightenment*, edited by Kate Tunstall, 3–34. London: Bloomsbury, 2012.

Royal Society of Canada for Chapter 8 "Progress and Scepticism 1789–1989," *Transactions of the Royal Society of Canada* 4 (1989): 21–33.

Columbia University Press for Chapter 10 "Life Sustains Life 2: The Ways of Reengagement with the Living Earth," in *Nature and Culture*, edited by Akeel Bilgrami, 181–204. New York, NY: Columbia University Press, 2020.

McGill Law Journal for Chapter 13 "Sustainable Democratic Constitutionalism and Climate Crisis," *McGill Law Journal* 65, no. 3 (2020): 1–28.

Introduction

An Approach to Public Philosophy: James Tully in Contexts

Alexander Livingston

It begins with listening. Participants gathered around the table are asked to share moments when they faced experiences of racism, oppression, or injustice. Each writes a brief note and posts it on the board at the front of the room. They listen to one another and honour the pain and courage it takes to speak. The moderators then ask the participants to share ways they acted in response to these experiences: did you stay within the rules of the game? Follow them differently? Seek to renegotiate their terms? Refuse to play along? Or turn away? Listening, dialogue, and trust shift understandings as participants find themselves moving from silence to agency. Private testimonies become something larger as they are made public around the common table. Perceptions of powerlessness break down as everyday acts of survival are redisclosed as moments in ongoing struggles of and for freedom.

This exercise developed by legal scholars Val Napoleon and Hadley Friedland in their community-directed research with Indigenous communities is called the Tully Wheel (Napoleon and Friedland 2014; Jobin et al. 2021). Inspired by the work of James Tully, the exercise exemplifies his decades-long project of reconceiving political theory as a transformative practice of public philosophy. Public philosophy aims to democratise the practice of political theory itself by centring the practices of citizens challenging the undemocratic ways they are governed and engaging them as equals from whom there is something to be learned. The "we" of its practitioners extends beyond scholars alone to put an enlarged "us" front and centre (Laden 2011, 114). As Tully explains in "Political Theory as a Critical Activity," the practice of public philosophy "starts from the present struggles and problems of politics and seeks to clarify and transform the normal understanding of them so as to open up the field of possible ways of thinking and acting freely in response" (2008a, 37). This is political theory as an ongoing dialogue with scholars, citizens, and the history of political thought where the theorist serves as an apprentice, not a master.[1] Its animating principle is the Roman legal maxim *audi alteram partem*, always listen to the other side, for there is always something new to be learned.

In the *Philosophical Investigations'* discussion of family resemblances, Ludwig Wittgenstein observes that the strength of a rope is not an effect of

DOI: 10.4324/9781003227403-1

one single thread running through it but of many threads woven together. Tully's place as an innovator in political theory likewise lies in no single contribution but in the diverse ways his work has pursued deparochialising dialogues across multiple traditions in pursuit of perspectives adequate to local and global problems of our times (Wittgenstein 2009, §67; cf. Kirloskar-Steinbach 2019; Tully 2022b). Tully's interlocutors range from Hannah Arendt to Edward Said to Peter Kropotkin but a career-long dialogue with three traditions in particular has tuned public philosophy's distinctive new key: Wittgenstein's philosophy of language and its application to the study of the history of political thought by Quentin Skinner and John Dunn (Tully 2008a, 39–70; 1988a; Temelini 2015), Michel Foucault's genealogies of the modern subject and analytics of power (Tully 2008a, 71–131; Owen 2012), and the ways of knowing and being of Indigenous peoples from across Great Turtle Island (Tully 2018b; Asch, Borrows, and Tully 2018). Situated in this way both within and beyond the boundaries of the academy, the power of public philosophy to disclose and transform understandings lies in its continuity with the everyday talk of ordinary citizens (2011, 147–50). Public philosophy is not a system of first principles or normative procedures but "a methodological extension and clarification of historically situated practical reasoning" (2008a, 29).

James Tully: To Think and Act Differently collects classic, contemporary, and previously unpublished examples of public philosophy in action from across Tully's four decades of scholarship. The chapters collected in this volume provide readers with a perspicuous representation of public philosophy as an ongoing experiment with reconstructing the practice of political theory as a democratising and diversifying dialogue between scholars and citizens. It aims to introduce readers to this participatory mode of political philosophy and political change by placing the arc of Tully's intellectual trajectory in contexts, illuminating moments of clarification and transformation, and considering the ways it continues to shed new insights into contemporary challenges of citizenship.

Two Approaches to Political Philosophy

The task of public philosophy, Tully writes, "is to address public affairs" (Chapter 2, 37). This is philosophy made public in a double sense. The first is as a philosophical engagement with what John Dewey called the problems of the public, the pressing political controversies of the day. The second is in addressing the public as its audience. Public philosophers forego the technical jargon of academic debate to speak with ordinary citizens in a plain and accessible style. To paraphrase Dewey again, philosophy becomes public in Tully's sense when it ceases "to be a device for dealing with the problems of philosophers" and becomes a method for dealing with the problems of *citizens* (Dewey 1980, 46).[2] This way of presenting the role of political philosophy bears a certain resemblance to what John Rawls calls the "practical" role of political philosophy – "to focus on deeply disputed questions and see whether, despite appearances, some underlying basis of philosophical and moral agreement can be uncovered" (2001, 2). Yet this apparent agreement obscures the distinctive dialogical style of Tully's public philosophy.

Rawls' approach to the task of public philosophy as the pursuit of shared principles and procedures to impartially litigate political disputes exemplifies what Tully calls the monological or "elite" style of political theory. This is political theory "elevated above the *demos*" and claiming authoritative knowledge *over* the public (Chapter 2, 39). Elite political theory presents its insights into foundational normative principles, inevitable trajectories of political development, and historical preconditions of democratic self-rule as invaluable wisdom citizens and policy makers ought to heed. Tully's approach, by contrast, aims to bring "philosophy 'down' into the world of the *demos*" (ibid.). This is political theory as the pursuit of knowledge *with* the public. Through mutual dialogue, listening, and critical redescription this style of public philosophy aims to strengthen the capacity of citizens to democratise the relations of power and domination they find themselves subject to. In other words, a public philosopher does not speak down to citizens from the lectern; she sits amongst them as both partner and student to generate insights collaboratively as "an interlocutory intervention on the side of the oppressed" (2008a, 17).

The path to this dialogical approach begins in Tully's inaugural studies in the history of political thought as a graduate student at Trinity College at the University of Cambridge. An early statement is "The Pen is a Mighty Sword: Quentin Skinner's Analysis of Politics" (1983a). The essay offers a careful reconstruction of Skinner's theory of language and ideology, and its implications for articulating a "genuinely historical" approach to the study of political thought (Skinner 1978, xi). Drawing insights from post-positivist philosophy of language Skinner proposes to conceptualise texts as speech acts, that is, linguistically mediated modes of social action. The meaning of a text lies in its strategic relationship to the political and discursive context in which it is performed. As Tully explains, understanding a work historically means understanding it as an "ideological manoeuvre" in the political controversies of its age that strategically manipulates shared linguistic conventions to legitimate or subvert specific modes of political conduct (1983a, 493). In contrast to monological political theory's self-presentation as an impartial perspective above the fray, Skinner rediscloses political theory as a mode of political action itself. Discursive interventions in a dynamic field of power, not the force of the better argument alone, are critical for explaining ideological persistence and change. From this insight into the interaction of relations of power and relations of meaning, the essay draws another into the continuity between Skinner's contextualism and a different approach to historical inquiry, the genealogical method of Michel Foucault. With their mutual attention to the nexus of discourse and power, Tully argues that Skinner and Foucault show how contextual study of the past can serve the present as a critical and potentially transformative practice of redescription. This simultaneously forwards and backwards looking approach to the history of political thought will go on to distinguish Tully's version of a "genuinely" historical approach from the narrower contextualisms marking later generations of Cambridge school scholarship (Nichols 2020a).

This integration of contextualism and critique animates Tully's seminal early studies of John Locke. *A Discourse on Property: John Locke and His Adversaries* (1980) is a contextual study of Locke's theory of property as an ideological intervention in the language games of seventeenth-century British political economy. In response to C.B. Macpherson's influential argument concerning Locke's ideological contributions to the origins of capitalism, Tully aimed to show how the reigning interpretations of Locke reflected the language games of post-war political theory more often than the concerns of seventeenth-century readers and their distinctive understanding of categories like "property" (1993, 71–95). Placing Locke's arguments in context corrects for the misunderstanding of the past that such anachronisms produce. And the scholarly rescue of the past from such distortions is an urgent task if citizens hope to rescue themselves from distorted understandings of where they stand in the present. As he summarises this orientation to the history of political thought in *An Approach to Political Philosophy*, "I have sought to develop an approach to political philosophy that throws light on the problems of present age through contextual studies of the history of modern political thought" (1993, 1).

The light study of the past throws on the present is not a source of solutions to current *problems* but critical histories of what Foucault calls contemporary *problematics*: the categories, conventions, and discourses citizens and scholars understand their political problems from within (Foucault 1997, 111–20). Central amongst the problematics shaping and constraining political understanding is the hegemonic "juridical ideology" of modern political thought (Tully 1983a, 500; cf. 1993, 6–68). The critical examinations of the "great juridical edifice" constructed over the course of the modern era—one enshrining the sovereign modern state, its monopoly on violence, and a system of rights, natural law, and constitutional liberty—and the ways it endures in our political language as a picture holding contemporary citizens captive lies at the centre of Tully's early writings on modern political thought.

His editorial introduction to Locke's *A Letter Concerning Toleration* (1982) illustrates a range of contemporary problems Tully viewed as unresolvable within a juridical framework: ecological devastation, nuclear disarmament, the struggles of Eastern European dissidents, and the consolidation of new forms of militarism in the Global North and South (Chapter 8; Tully 1983b). The path leading from this critical redescription of the juridical tradition to the central political questions that would define Tully's work over the following decades – Aboriginal self-government and the politics of empire – unfolded slowly then all at once, as the saying goes. Two events in the summer of 1990 thrust both to the forefront of his research and teaching. The first was the collapse of the Meech Lake Accord, a series of negotiations over the terms of Canadian federalism meant to secure Quebec's consent to the 1982 constitution. The dramatic moment of collapse came when Oji-Cree politician Elijah Harper raised a single feather to signal Aboriginal peoples' refusal of consent to the proposed constitutional amendments for failing to recognise their right to self-government (Webber 2021, 42–52, 225–42). The second was the Oka Crisis, a land dispute in Kanesatake resulting in a seventy-eight day armed standoff between Canadian armed forces and Mohawk warriors (Simpson and Ladner 2010). These twin crises drew Tully into an ever-closer dialogue with Indigenous scholars, students, and Elders. An important inflection point in this learning process was the invitation to serve as an advisor to the Royal Commission on Aboriginal Peoples (RCAP) from 1993 to 1996. Dialogues with Indigenous peoples through RCAP offered an opportunity to deepen his engagement with Indigenous legal systems, claims to self-government, and relations to the living earth, as well as his thinking about the role of political theory in a settler-colonial context.[3]

The "practical" task of political philosophy Tully took from these events was not, as Rawls would have it, establishing shared terms to resolve these disputes. It was rather the task of empowering Indigenous peoples and settlers to come to genuine agreements amongst themselves and in their own voices. To draw again on a Wittgensteinian metaphor, dialogical political theory does not aim to fix the rules of the game but empowers players themselves to raise questions about the rules they are given, challenge them, revise them, and so transform the game as they go along together. The Oka Crisis and the collapse of the Canadian constitutional deliberations disclosed the ways the claims of Indigenous peoples for self-government are rendered illegible within the rules of the game articulated by the juridical language of modern European political thought. As he put this insight in a lecture delivered on the three-hundredth anniversary of Locke's *Second Treatise*, "Rediscovering America," subjecting Indigenous political forms to "the sovereignty of European concepts of politics and property" denied the reality of diversity and so laid the ideological foundations of dispossession and extermination (1993, 139).[4] Such *diversity blindness* – the drive to assimilate or exclude difference – is not simply a convention of early modern thought, although it was often a purposeful tactic of de-legitimating Indigenous claims to sovereignty and property; it is an inevitable consequence of approaching politics in a top-down monological manner. Diversity blindness marks a parochialising style of "false" dialogue found in Locke just as much as contemporaries operating in a juridical framework like Rawls and Jürgen Habermas (2018c).[5]

Re-examining the ways modern political thought remains entangled with these colonial legacies and learning to listen to the voices its silences can begin to loosen the hold of these sedimented ways of thinking and acting. As Skinner argues, the foundations of modern political thought reside in the ongoing struggle between a dominant juridical ideology and competing counter-ideologies from which insights into the present can be gleaned

(Skinner 1978; Tully, 1983: 498–502; 2003; Armitage 2011). Tully similarly argues that our languages of politics are more pluralistic than monological political theory acknowledges. The first practical step the public philosopher takes in addressing the claims of the oppressed is cultivating and sustaining *diversity awareness*. Understanding requires learning from others, exchanging partial perspectives, and drawing analogies between them through dialogue. As Tully explains this point in his 1989 essay "Wittgenstein and Political Philosophy," a dialogical approach to political theory must begin from diversity awareness "because any practice of critical reflection is itself already founded in the popular sovereignty of our multiple humdrum ways of acting with words" (2008a, 70). Diversity blindness, by contrast, undermines the oldest convention of democratic legitimacy shared by multiple political traditions: that what touches all must be agreed to by all (the "all affected" principle). Cultivating and sustaining diversity awareness reorients relations between citizens from one of *power-over* to the dialogical relation of *power-with* on which democratic legitimacy depends (2022c). A second and related step is to deparochialise the practice of political theory itself through greater awareness of the diversity of ideological sources and languages available for critical reflection and comparison (Chapter 3). Learning to shift perspectives and see common problems in new ways liberates citizens from the pictures holding them captive, and in so doing it shifts the problem of politics. A monological approach takes up the problems of politics as questions of *justice*; a dialogical approach engages them as questions of *freedom* (2008a, 38–9).

Democratising Democratic Theory

One way to characterise this shift is as extending the principle of democracy to the practice of philosophy itself (Rorty 1991). Public philosophy is democratising in at least three senses. The first is its dialogical ethos. The public philosopher genuinely *listens* to citizens engaged in practical struggles as equals in hopes of learning something new. In reciprocity for these gifts, she offers her skills as a critical historian of the present to shine new light on the problems citizens face. Reconceiving political theory as a democratic practice of reciprocal elucidation goes hand in hand with a second sense of what it means to democratise philosophy. Public philosophy advances a particular vision of democratic freedom as an ongoing *practical activity* of democratising the relations of government citizens find themselves subject to. These two senses converge in a third: public philosophy's "critical and practice-oriented" insistence that "philosophical inquiry be reciprocally related to practice through mutually enlightening dialogues and aimed at enhancing democratic freedom" (2008b, 109).

As Tully explains in a lecture on the emergence of public philosophy delivered in Tokyo in 2016 (Chapter 1), this agonistic conception of democratic freedom emerged from the confluence of multiple sources. One was Locke's innovations in the language of popular sovereignty. Where his contemporaries drew on medieval arguments justifying resistance to abuses of authority in terms of a right to self-defence, Locke reframed the right of resistance as an expression of popular sovereignty (1993, 15–29, 318–20). Even as essays like "Rediscovering America" detail the ways Locke's *Second Treatise* directly contributed to the colonial project of Indigenous dispossession, Tully shows the ways a dialogical recovery of Lockean arguments can elucidate Indigenous resistance as expressions of democratic freedom (1993, 171–6). Related are his landmark studies of the politics of "government" in seventeenth-century thought. In "Governing Conduct: Locke on the Reform of Thought and Behaviour" and "Rights in Abilities," Tully broke new ground by examining the ways Locke's political thought mobilised technologies of disciplinary power to produce free subjects of liberty (1993, 179–241; 242–61; Ivison 1997). This line of inquiry reflects the influence of Foucault's genealogical studies of the modern subject. Its full impact would mature over the course of the decade as Tully discovered the ways Foucault's notion of "practices of governance" and "practices of freedom" converged with Wittgenstein's account of rule-following to develop his distinctive account of contextual agency (Foucault 1997, 281–301). Reconceiving citizen practices vis-à-vis the myriad of ways they are governed as struggles *of* and *for* freedom marks the core of Tully's agonistic conception of freedom (Chapter 4).

Strange Multiplicity: Constitutionalism in an Age of Diversity (1995; Chapter 5) brings this innovative approach to bear on questions of constitutionalism and civic belonging raised by the "two great Canadian problems" of the decade: the challenge of deep diversity and multinational pluralism, and the struggles of Indigenous peoples for self-determination (Chapter 1, 27). Extending the breakthrough analysis of diversity blindness first outlined in "Diversity's Gambit Declined" (1994a) and lessons learned through RCAP, *Strange Multiplicity* argues that the central obstacle facing diverse citizens seeking agreements on constitutional questions is the juridical language of modern constitutionalism itself. Through a survey of the history of constitutional theory and practice in England and North America, Tully examines modern constitutionalism's claim to supplant the common law tradition of ancient constitutionalism. Rejecting the customary, informal, and open character of ancient constitutionalism, modern constitutionalism aims to fix clear and binding terms of democratic association consonant with the juridical institutions of the modern Euro-American nation state. This language codified in modern constitutional documents and articulated in works of political theory from Hobbes' *Leviathan* to Rawls' *A Theory of Justice* is inadequate to the challenges of a multicultural polity, Tully argues, because its central concepts and conventions exclude or assimilate difference by design. A craving for uniformity and fear of diversity mark its conceptions of popular sovereignty, rule of law, and political order. Re-examining this diversity blindness in the context of European conquest of the New World, Tully argues that the historical triumph of modern constitutionalism carries with it a "residual imperialism" that undercuts the democratic freedom it claims to secure (2008b, 31).

The first step to democratising contemporary constitutionalism is learning to "listen to the voice of the other in their own terms" (1995, 24). As a top-down representation, modern constitutionalism is a "partial forgery" (1995, 96). Unseen in the penumbra surrounding its idealised vision of political order lies a vast and diverse landscape of constitution-making practices. Reorienting political theory's approach towards these "hidden constitutions of contemporary societies" can offer insights for sustaining a genuinely post-imperial constitutional dialogue in the present (Chapter 5, 76). In *Strange Multiplicity* this takes the form of examining conventions shared by European ancient constitutionalism and Aboriginal legal systems exemplified in the nation-to-nation treaties forged between the Crown and Indigenous peoples. The gift political philosophy receives from listening to these histories and attending to elements of ancient constitutionalism living on in contemporary constitutional law is the redisclosure of popular sovereignty as an "intercultural dialogue" (1995, 190). Common identities, principles, and institutions are not the preconditions for democratic dialogue, as modern constitutionalism presumes; they are goods diverse citizens realise through practical participation in the negotiation and renegotiation of the terms of co-existence. Citizens become genuinely self-governing through the practice of self-government itself (2008a, 281–3).

This approach to popular sovereignty as equiprimordial with the rule of law (democratic constitutionalism), rather than a secondary good to be contained by law and liberal principles (constitutional democracy), locates Tully's scholarship in the wake of *Strange Multiplicity* within political theory's agonistic turn (Wenman 2013; Stears and Honig, 2014; Paxton 2019). Theorists of agonistic democracy like William E. Connolly, Chantal Mouffe, and Bonnie Honig foreground the irreducibly partisan, contentious, and adversarial nature of democratic politics as a challenge to the depoliticising pursuit of consensus animating liberal and deliberative theories of democracy. "The Unfreedom of the Moderns in Relation to the Ideal of Constitutional Democracy" summarises the field of agonistic democracy as such: its major contribution lays in its stress on

> the manifest reality of partisanship, dissent, disagreement, contestation, and adversarial reasoning in the history and present of democratic societies and the positive role in exposing and overcoming structures of inequality and justice, fostering critical ethos, and *eo ipso*, creating autonomous citizens with bonds of solidarity across real difference.
>
> (Tully 2008b, 110)

Tully embraced public philosophy's participation in this wider field of agonistic approaches to democracy as he pursued a distinctive path within it. One distinctive element is his emphasis on the priority of practice. Contestation and conflict are not simply means in citizens' struggles *for* freedom but transformative ends in themselves as struggles *of* freedom. Agonistic citizens become citizens in a practical sense by *civicising* the ways they are governed (2008a, 311). This bottom-up focus reorients the research programme of public philosophy away from representative institutions and courts, as the primary sites theory seeks to legitimate or subvert, and towards the diverse and improvised ways citizens practice freedom vis-à-vis local and global practices of government (2008a, 112).[6]

Informal Imperialism and Practices of Civic Citizenship

Most distinctive of Tully's innovations in the field of agonistic democracy, however, is his attention to the global and imperial contexts of democratic citizenship (Nichols and Singh 2014). Critical political theories, no less than the liberal and conservative theories they challenge, often "conceal and overlook the imperialism of the present" (2008b, 127). Listening to and learning from struggles against neo-liberal globalisation, the consolidation of the post-9/11 security state and its global "War on Terror," theorists of neo-colonialism and underdevelopment, as well as cooperative counter-traditions around the globe, Tully developed an expanded analysis of the continuity of imperial rule from modern constitutional theory to contemporary institutions of global governance. At a moment where normative theories of cosmopolitan citizenship and global justice were ascendent within monological political theory, Tully's writings in the 2000s focused on historical surveys of the development of "postcolonial" or "informal" imperialism in the modern international state system, and the ways presumptively non-imperial institutions and discourses of international law participated in the articulation and reproduction of imperial rule (2008a, 153, 132; 2009b; Simpson and Tully 2012; cf. Mommsen 1977; Mignolo 2000).

Essays collected in the second volume of *Public Philosophy in a New Key* portray contemporary imperialism as "much more pervasive than usually thought" and modes of resistance against it as more diverse "than usually appreciated" (Ivison 2011, 131). Keeping both aspects in focus, these studies disclose a broad understanding of informal imperialism defining the modern global order. Informal imperialism refers not simply to the colonial origins of post-war institutions of global governance, their functional roles in sustaining global hierarchy, and their containment of democratic contestation but also to the wider vision of modern developmentalism these institutions presume and enforce. Tully accordingly conceives of contemporary modes of imperialism capaciously as "a contrapuntal ensemble of violent modern power politics": an assemblage of legal, political, economic, and military institutions along with the historical languages of politics through which their governance is articulated, legitimated, and contested (2014b, 246; cf. 2009b). As Tully explains the significance of the account of imperialism laid out in *Public Philosophy in a New Key*

I offer a critique of the historically layered relationships between forms of political, legal, and economic reason and the violence and deceit of Western modernization and expansion, and the forms of reason, violence, and deceit that have been deployed by imperialised peoples in response.

(Tully 2014b, 246)

Reframing imperialism contrapuntally in this way reorients political theory's focus away from the perspective of global institutions towards the practices of citizens they govern.[7] *Public Philosophy in a New Key* concludes with a comparative study of the field of citizenship providing a critical redescription of the "globally dominant language of citizenship" legitimating the basic institutional structure of the global system (Chapter 6). Modern or *civil* citizenship is a juridical mode of citizenship that locates democratic agency squarely within the confines of representative nation states, the capitalist economy, and international institutions of the global order. The civil citizen is the modern rights-bearing subject presumed by monological theories of global justice, human rights, and cosmopolitanism seeking to legitimate and reform modern institutions from within. Yet civil citizenship's claim to universality masks the violent means of its universalisation: namely, dispossession, colonisation, and exploitation. The modern capitalist world system developed through these violent means and depends on their ongoing brutality for its reproduction. Civil citizenship's hegemony keeps citizens and scholars captured within visions of low-intensity democracy where political agency is delegated, market competition is enshrined as the privileged site of freedom, and economic and social inequalities remain shielded from contestation.

Like modern constitutionalism, however, the language of modern citizenship is a partial forgery. Its claim to universality displaces alternative living traditions of citizenship and democracy around the globe. Through critical genealogies of the contemporary global order and its theoretical representations, *Public Philosophy in a New Key* aimed to provincialise civil citizenship and recover democratic lessons from improvised repertoires of citizen practice falling outside its purview (2014a, 10). Just as there is no one way of following the rules of a language game, citizens find ways to think and act differently within, and against, the institutions of civil citizens. Tully calls these alternative modes diverse or *civic* practices of citizenship. Civic citizenship does not name a single language, tradition, or discourse but rather the diversity of "negotiated practices" through which networks of peoples rework their political orders by contesting, renegotiating, and sometimes refusing the undemocratic ways they are governed (2008b, 248). A research programme refocusing democratic theory around the diverse praxes of participatory democracy taking place below the radar of modern citizenship is a dialogical contribution to these struggles. Like Napoleon and Friedland's Tully Wheel exercise, it serves to remind citizens "we are always and everywhere proto-civic citizens, engaged in practices of negotiating the fields of possibilities in the relationships in which we find our feet and learn to walk" (2008b, 279).

Between *Public Philosophy in a New Key*'s critical account of the persistence of imperialism in almost every institution of global governance and its positive vision of bringing these structures under participatory democratic control through negotiated practices of civic citizenship, some readers have found a stark and unsurmountable asymmetry (Ivison 2011; Vasquez-Arroyo 2014;

Bell 2014). The spaces available to civic citizens to practice freedom differently within the institutions of global governance are structured by relations of dependence and profound asymmetries of power. Global institutions, legal regimes, and market mechanisms can be understood as rules of a game but ones considerably less flexible and mutable than the language games Tully analogises them to. Describing his project as tracking "the remaining possibilities for freedom in the rifts and fissures of modern subject constitution," Bonnie Honig questions whether this asymmetry reveals an unreconciled tension between public philosophy's realism and its humanism, a "fingers on the edge of a cliff clinging to some resemblance of human life against all odds humanism" (2011, 142). Tully himself in *Public Philosophy in a New Key* admits concerns that civic contestation within imperial relationships may often only manage to modify the ways citizens are governed without substantially transforming them (2008b, 162–3, 208–9). His response, however, is neither to replot the drama of civic freedom nor blindly embrace a pessimism of the intellect and an optimism of the will. The years following *Public Philosophy in a New Key* show Tully delving ever more deeply into the strange multiplicity of civic practices taking place in these rifts and fissures for a fuller understanding of how citizens are not simply modifying the rules of the game but already transforming the system itself.

On Global Citizenship (2014a) and other writings in the early 2010s mark an important development in public philosophy's evolving research programme (Chapter 7; 2009a, 2012a, 2013b). Learning from the rough ground of mutual aid and fair trade movements, the history of utopian socialism and anarchist political thought, and in dialogue with scholars like Boaventura de Sousa Santos (2005) recentring the study of participatory democracy around institutional innovations in the Global South, Tully's work has focused more directly on the diversity of cooperative practices taking place outside the agonistic field of citizen-governor relations studied in *Public Philosophy in a New Key*. Cooperative citizens respond to the democratic closures of civil citizenship in a direct manner to "work around, rather than within, the basic institutional structure" (2013a, 223). This is civic citizenship as a citizen-citizen relationship where people practice democracy "by bringing the organization of economic activities under democratic cooperation and relationships of mutual aid" (2013a, 228). These are civic practices that more fully "co-articulate" the relationship between popular sovereignty and the rule of law than acting within representative institutions permits (Chapter 7). Cooperative citizens exercise democracy directly. Tully's studies of the field of cooperative citizenship might be misunderstood as sliding into a monological mode of handing down yet another model of citizenship for the *demos* to emulate. Public philosophy, however, does not aim to adjudicate between competing theories of citizenship; it seeks to create the conditions for a possible dialogue of reciprocal elucidation between them. Learning to "join hands" dialogically across traditions of representative and cooperative citizenship is urgent as each negotiates the crises of the twenty-first century, in particular the planetary crisis of unsustainability animating Tully's current research (Tully et al. 2022).

Sustaining Civic Freedom and Transformative Regeneration

"The question for me today," Tully explains in this volume's concluding interview, "is how can we overcome alienation and dis-integration by transforming and co-generating dialogical relationships that co-sustain and enhance the well-being of all interdependent lifeforms in these complex relationships?" (Chapter 14, 268). This question reflects an important further development in the decade since *Public Philosophy in a New Key*. Tully's recent work on the contemporary crisis of sustainability takes a step back from the critical analysis of imperial governance to develop a deeper and wider account of the pictures of modernity, progress, and development holding citizens and scholars captive. The difficulties global citizens face, he now writes, are not "'problems' solvable *within* modernization," they are instead "interconnected crises of sustainability *of* the dominant, gridlocked, anthropocentric, and contested relationships, systems and processes of modern development" (ibid.).

Concern with the democratic and ecological costs of modern development is already evident in Tully's early writings on property and informs his genealogies of civil citizenship but it takes on an expanded significance in his current work. Illustrative of this expanded approach is 2016s "Introducing Global Integral Constitutionalism" (Chapter 9). The chapter offers a grim account of globalisation as a market-driven process of disseminating "anti-contestatory" modes of constitutionalism. Modern political institutions and human rights regimes are artefacts of a history of conquest and expropriation. This history of violence continues to shape them in insulating market freedoms and capital accumulation from democratic interference. Global constitutional institutions accordingly leave democratic citizens politically incapacitated and increasingly unable to respond to crises sustained by these very neo-liberal institutions: global inequality, military-industrial consolidation, and refugee displacement. These are interconnected crises, each accelerating and intensifying the other in a deadly feedback loop proving increasingly unresolvable from within the terms of the political and economic institutions of civil citizenship. The result is not only a global state of political crisis in democratic institutions but more profoundly an existential crisis of global sustainability pressing against the carrying capacity of the planet to sustain life. "Hence, the choice here and now," Tully wagers, "appears to be either unsustainable economic constitutionalism and much harder and catastrophic times or a sustainable alternative paradigm of economics, law, and governance" (Chapter 9, 176).

Pursuing sustainable alternatives demands a radical reorientation in political theory's conception of the relationship between politics and the biosphere. Tully's two-part essay "Life Sustains Life" offers an ambitious overview of just such a reorientation (2020b; Chapter 10). Drawing insight and inspiration from sources as diverse as sustainable food security practices, Indigenous lifeways, and recent developments in earth and ocean sciences, Tully calls on political theory to re-embed political society within the dynamic systems of ecological interdependence and sustainability. A beacon orienting this project is the uptake of James Lovelock's Gaia hypothesis in the climate sciences and their convergence with traditional Indigenous ecological knowledge (Lovelock 2000; Margulis 1998; Turner 2005; Kimmerer 2013). The Gaia hypothesis proposes that the earth is one self-sustaining and self-regulating system of life bound by complex and dynamic relations of interdependence, feedback, and diversification. Formal social systems of law, politics, and economy are embedded within a wider informal background of ecological systems sustaining basic biological functioning of the species and its reproduction. Yet precisely because social and ecological systems are interconnected, disequilibrium in one can create imbalance in the other, and reciprocal feedback loops can drive a cascading system's crisis towards collapse. The global crisis of sustainability driven by modern development and globalisation illustrates such a scenario of interaction between social and ecological forces tipping a *virtuous* system sustaining life on earth into a *vicious* unsustainable system spiralling out of control. From the perspective of public philosophy, creating sustainable alternative paradigms is not a question of how to modify the rules *en passant*; it is how to genuinely transform the system by *regenerating* conditions of systemic sustainability from within a super-predatory world system.

This expanded engagement with sustainability reflects a radicalisation of the pursuit of diversity awareness animating *Strange Multiplicity* and other earlier writings on democratic constitutionalism. The global crisis of unsustainability reflects a deeper mode of diversity blindness. No small part of this crisis turns on the ways participants in vicious systems too readily exclude or assimilate perceptual evidence of crisis before their eyes. In dialogue with philosopher Akeel Bilgrami (2014) and his account of modern subjectivity's blindness to non-human sources of value, Tully writes "that our alienated way of life causes us to overlook the living earth and to represent it as resources for production and consumption, whether capitalist or Marxist" (2020b, 169). What goes misperceived from within a vicious system are the myriad ways life on earth evolves and self-regulates through vibrant relations of interconnection and cooperation rather than antagonism and competition. The juridical tradition's presumption of natural human antagonism and the need for coercive state control reflects a misrecognition of the human species' place on earth. They are perceptions of a *disembedded* subject. Drawing on economist Karl Polanyi's classic study (2001 [1944]) of the rise of market societies, Tully argues that the cost of embedding modern citizens in abstract market relations of competition, antagonism, and coercion is violently disembedding them from their prior relationship to land, to one another, and to themselves. From within these abstract social relations, citizens misperceive the crisis of sustainability because they have been made over into active participants within a parasitical system devouring the informal systems of co-sustainability they depend on.

Like modern constitutionalism and civil citizenship, however, this "fatal illusion of independence" sustaining vicious systems is a partial forgery

(Chapter 10, 190–191). Only partial because perceiving nature through the lens of competition and coercion correctly represents the social relationship enforced by the institutions, norms, and practices of our vicious political-economic system. But a forgery nonetheless because perceptions that naturalise competition and domination overlook the diverse everyday forms of mutual aid, care, and reciprocity human beings rely on to survive. This is what Tully means when he says that modern subjects are not only disembedded but *disintegrated*: always implicitly operating on competing logics of conflict and cooperation—what Richard Gregg calls "dual loyalty" (Chapter 12)—in different social interactions without grasping their self-destructive contradiction. Drawing on Haida stories of the raven trickster who plucks a single eye from villagers while they sleep, Tully describes modern subjects and their extractive relations to nature as lacking the depth of vision to see beyond themselves to future generations. After taking the villagers' eyes, the raven returns their sight so they can see anew their interdependence to the living earth sustaining them (2018b, 111–12; Davidson 1992). How can citizens and scholars regenerate this ability to see life on earth in its corrected fullness and learn to keep both eyes open?

Like the rediscovery of the hidden transcripts of diverse constitutionalism, there is ethical and political knowledge to be gleaned from studying the ways ecological systems flourish through sustaining one another (symbiosis) and increasing diversity and complexity (symbiogenesis). Life is not sustained "through relations of conquest or command and control," as the juridical tradition of modern political thought maintains, "but through relations of cooperation and non-exterminating competition within and amongst species and their ecosystems" (2020b, 173). "Learning from Gaia" – engaging in perceptual dialogues with the living earth, listening to stories shared by Indigenous knowledge keepers, and drawing insight from biological sciences – is critical if citizens are to learn how to live on the planet as caretakers of ecological systems and design alternative economic, legal, and political institutions capable of sustaining the continued existence of life on earth (Chapter 11). However, this deeper kind of diversity awareness is not something that can be offered by the theorist. The ability to engage in perceptual dialogue with ecosocial systems is a function of disengaging from practices intensifying the vicious system and reengaging in practices of connection with the living earth.

Recontextualising *Public Philosophy in a New Key*'s study of civic citizenship and agonistic freedom in the Anthropocene therefore begins by listening and learning from the myriad ways citizens are already acting within vicious systems to expand participatory practices of mutual aid, cooperation, and co-sustaining care. Ecosocial systems are neither totally consistent nor closed. The reason virtuous sustainable systems sometimes become vicious and collapse is because dynamic systems are often far from equilibrium and subject to tipping. It is the same reason why points of resilience and transformation by members within vicious systems can set *regenerative* dynamics in motion that become autotelic or self-sustaining. Drawing an analogy to the ability of forest systems to regenerate in the wake of fires and clear cutting, Tully stresses that regeneration is not restoration of the status quo; it is a transformative process of creating more sustainable and resilient systems. Acts of contestation, refusal, cooperation, and renegotiation across networks of civic citizens thinking and acting differently work to regenerate damaged democratic permaculture and create bottom-up conditions of sustainable transformation. The obstacle to becoming sustainable by living sustainably is not the incapacity to act otherwise nor the overwhelming power of governing institutions. It is the unsustainable representations of modern political thought keeping citizens alienated from their capacities, disintegrated as subjects, and blind to diversity. Just as citizens civicise practices of government by acting democratically within them, they create conditions for sustainability by "being the change."

This renewed approach to cooperation as a basic human capacity, and its prioritisation of doing over knowing in social change, informs Tully's turn towards the modern tradition of nonviolence (Chapter 12; 2018a; 2019). Looking back on his prior work, he writes, "*Strange Multiplicity* and *PPNK* are journals of a long and involved journey in search for and discovery of a nonviolent alternative to this deadly nexus of reason and violence called power politics" (2014b, 247). For Tully, Mohandas Gandhi and his disciple Richard Gregg remain important interlocutors for contemporary scholars and citizens for the ways their critique of violence captures the disembedded and disintegrated character of modern political thought as well as for how their experiments with integrating thought and practice suggest ways to bring about nonviolent alternatives to modernity's alienated way of life here and now. Nonviolence constitutes an *integral* response to the crisis of vicious systems for the ways it both discloses its roots in modern civilisation's normalisation of violence and power-*over* while offering a repertoire of nonviolent agonistics that work to reintegrate the self and others in sustaining relationship of power-*with*. Stressing the continuity between means and ends, Gandhian *satyagraha* integrates with public philosophy's approach to freedom as an experimental practice of building nonviolent alternatives to modernity's vicious system "step by step, day by day" (2019).

The confluence of sustainability and nonviolence in turn gives shape to an expanded approach to participatory democracy and democratic constitutionalism (Chapter 13; 2012a, 2012b; 2022a). The caretakers of a sustainable democratic permaculture are cooperative movements and civic struggles reclaiming creative capacities from commodification and expanding relationships of mutual aid. Tully calls these situated practices of internalising interdependence and more fully realising the democratic "all affected" principle Gaia citizenship (2022a). Experiments with cooperative and Gaia citizenship are not uncommon but neither are they sufficient on their own to tip a super-predatory system into a sustainable future. Public philosophy offers no cookbook for building a new world but it can serve as a mediator sustaining conversation between civic and civil citizens, helping them discover points of convergence and "join hands" to work both with and against the insufficient but necessary institutions of civil citizenship. Akin to the hidden dialogue between ancient constitutionalism and Indigenous legal systems in *Strange Multiplicity*, civil and Gaia citizens each have something to learn from one another in their pursuit of a sustainable democratic future on earth.

Public philosophy's experiments with shifting understandings by reasoning-*with*-others represent a profound provocation to the discipline of political theory. As wisdom dispensed from on high, elite political theory proves not simply unhelpful to citizens confronting these crises but often serves as an ideological obstacle to their struggles for freedom. "Political contests over the practices of politics are always also over the languages of political thought that are used to describe, evaluate, defend, and contest these practices," he writes in "Deparochialising Political Theory." "Although the contests of political theory appear more abstract, they are responses to them, and contributions that enter into the history of the languages of political thought" (Chapter 3, 48). As a disembedded misperception from within the contours of modernity's vicious system, monological political theory is a repository of the pictures holding citizens and scholars captive. From the juridical ideology of *An Approach to Political Philosophy* to the modern constitutionalism of *Strange Multiplicity* to the field of modern citizenship in *Public Philosophy in a New Key*, to the asocial, disembedded, and disintegrated subjects caught in the vicious feedback loops of modern developmentalism's sustainability crisis, Tully's scholarship has sought to attune readers to the diversity blindness of modern political thought. In its place, public philosophy invites us to return to our own practices as citizens, "the vast landscape where our critically reflective games of freedom have their home" (2008a, 52). Reembedded in dialogical practices of contestation and cooperation with scholars and citizens, and reconnected to the living earth, public philosophy represents not simply a challenge to the discipline but to us, its interlocutors, to rise to the global challenges we face by daring to think and act differently.

Roots and Branches

Understanding, Tully observes, is not a matter of holding a general theory; it involves "surveying and paying careful attention to the examples, and thus acquiring a familiarity with them and their complex relations with one another" (Chapter 8, 165; see also Chapter 5, 82–84). This volume offers readers such a collection of examples, drawn from major works as well as previously unpublished lectures and less readily available writings, to glean a genuine understanding of public philosophy. Its organisation draws on Gandhi's metaphor of *satyagraha* as the force animating the banyan tree's many winding branches. Each section examines a vital root system grounding Tully's innovations. They are the idea of public philosophy (Part I), the contrapuntal relationship practices of freedom and practices of government (Part II), and co-sustainability and regenerative transformation (Part III).

Part I contains a selection of methodological writings on the practice of public philosophy. "Political Theory as a Critical Activity" (Chapter 1) is a lecture delivered at Keio University in 2016 recounting the intellectual sources and political events that gave shape to Tully's distinctive dialogical approach to the study of politics. This lecture serves as a roadmap for the chapters that follow in this volume. "Public Philosophy and Civic Freedom" (Chapter 2) offers an introductory synopsis to the method guiding the studies collected as *Public Philosophy in a New Key* (2008a, 2008b). The chapter characterizes the aim of public philosophy as overcoming democratic theory's alienation from democratic practice by placing the democratic theorist and theory back in dialogue with fellow citizens and their ways of articulating their problems. "Deparochialising Political Theory and Beyond" (Chapter 3) considers the decolonizing challenges of dialogical comparative political thought. It shows how a dialogue approach responds to these challenges and can generates comparative and critical mutual understanding across traditions.

Part II contains key writings on citizenship, constitutionalism, and democratic theory.

"The Agonistic Freedom of Citizens" (Chapter 4) engages with the works of Hannah Arendt, Ludwig Wittgenstein, Michel Foucault and Quentin Skinner to articulate Tully's distinctively contextual and relational view of human agency and democratic citizenship. Against state-centric approaches to democratic theory, Tully argues that the challenges of citizenship today need to be understood in terms of games of freedom within and against the diverse ways citizens find themselves governed. "The Historical Formation of Common Constitutionalism" (Chapter 5), drawn from *Strange Multiplicity*, explores the living history of "hidden" constitutions of contemporary societies to recover a dialogical approach to struggles over cultural, legal, and governmental diversity. Engaging both the works of Wittgenstein and the history of nation-to-nation treaty making between Aboriginal peoples and European settlers, Tully reconstructs a set of dialogical conventions shared by Aboriginal and common law traditions more aware of diversity than modern constitutionalism, and better suited to guide contemporary struggles for recognition in a genuinely post-imperial polity.

"Two Meanings of Global Citizenship: Modern and Diverse" (Chapter 6) takes a global perspective on these questions of constitutionalism, democracy, and diversity from the perspectives civic and civil conceptions of citizenship. Connecting ideology and institutions, Tully shows how the language of civil citizenship developed in tandem with informal imperialism and the institutions of global governance. It then contrasts this hegemonic picture with the history of diverse or civic citizenship, first within Europe, and then globally (glocal civic citizenship). "Rethinking Human Rights and Enlightenment" (Chapter 7) marks a further development in Tully's exploration of civic citizenship as it relates to the cooperative tradition. The first part describes the history of the high Enlightenment view that human rights are prior to democracy, the four types of institutionalized human rights it promotes, and their development at the United Nations and during decolonization. The second part describes the civic or cooperative tradition in which human rights are "co-articulated" with and by the exercise of democratic freedom of those subject to them.

Part III looks forward to Tully's most recent work since *Public Philosophy in a New Key* while tracing these newest branches back to roots in his early writing. These chapters capture the development and refinement of Tully's integral ecosocial perspective as it developed iteratively through a series of intersecting dialogues over the past decade.

"Progress and Scepticism 1789-1989" (Chapter 8) offers an important early statement of Tully's critique of modern developmentalism. Tracing the ways Enlightenment and post-Enlightenment languages of progress have left modern citizens trapped within a vicious "global military-scientific-industrial complex" Tully calls for a new approach to reclaiming the tradition of critical thought that begins with "wonder" at the world's diversity and recovering "a sense of our appropriate place *in* the universe" displaced by the Enlightenment picture of humanity as master *over* it. "Introducing Global Integral Constitutionalism" (Chapter 9), an annual editorial for the journal *Global Constitutionalism,* takes up similar themes a quarter century later in the context of struggles over global governance. Tully introduces a neo-Polanyian perspective on four major global crises threatening sustainability and well-being of all life on earth (global inequality, militarism, climate change, and forced migration), to consider how the modern languages and institutions of global constitutionalism are inadequate to respond to them, and proposes an ecosocial vision of "contestatory" global constitutionalism as a critical alternative.

"Life Sustains Life 2" (Chapter 10) marks Tully's deepening engagement with earth sciences in reconceiving the project of civic freedom in the context of climate crisis. It contrasts two distinct ways of relating to the living earth. The first way is to see humans as independent of the living earth and gradually acquiring the knowledge to dominate, control, and exploit it. The second is to see humans as plain members and citizens within and with the biodiverse relations that comprise the living earth. In a dialogue of reciprocal elucidation with Jonathan Schell and Akeel Bilgrami, Tully advocates for the urgency as well as the challenges of reembedding civic practices and perceptions in the second view where life itself sustains life on earth by means of the symbiotic relationships among all life forms. The challenge of Gaia citizenship is to reengage with this living earth and become co-sustaining partners in and of these relationships. "A View of Transformative Reconciliation" (Chapter 11) is a lecture delivered at a symposium marking the twentieth anniversary of *Strange Multiplicity*. Tully reflects on the book's significance in his intellectual development to explore the convergence of earth systems theories with Indigenous traditions of ecological wisdom as responses to the vicious systems accelerating crises of sustainability. Two fundamental themes are highlighted. For many Indigenous people, first, the earth does not belong to humans (as property), but, rather, humans belong to and within the living earth (as their mother); and, second, the relationships of interdependency among humans and all life forms that co-sustain life are best understood as gift-gratitude-reciprocity relationships. Reconnecting and reengagement with these kinship relationship, Tully argues, offers a pathway for transforming our violent relationships to nature and one another he calls "double decolonisation."

The next two chapters extend these inquiries into sustainable ecosocial practices to questions of social and legal transformation. "Integral Nonviolence" (Chapter 12) makes the case for the continuing relevancy of the Gandhian tradition of nonviolence in the face of climate crisis. This lecture offers an introduction to the work of Richard Gregg and his account of nonviolence as a comprehensive way of life in *The Power of Nonviolence*, reissued by Tully in 2018 (2018a). Central to Gandhi and Gregg's lessons for contemporary readers is their concern with the ways the centrality of violence to our languages of politics discloses how we have been embedded in the vicious and self-destructive dynamics of modern civilization. For Gregg, nonviolence represents a transformative way of life. Through agonistic practices of contestation and collective and individual experiments with cooperation exemplified by Gandhi's "constructive programmes" citizens can reconnect with their democratic capacities and re-embed themselves in a sustainable nonviolent counter-modernity by "being the change." "Sustainable Democratic Constitutionalism and Climate Crisis" (Chapter 13) examines the role of law as, on the one hand, a major enabler of the human activities causing climate change, bio-diversity destruction, and related ecosocial crises, and, on the other, a means to regulate, mitigate, and attempt to transform these unsustainable human activities and systems. Returning to themes from *Strange Multiplicity*, the chapter explores how the convergence of common law and Indigenous legal orders point to ways law can become a force of transformative ecosocial succession and regeneration.

The volume closes with an interview with Tully (Chapter 14) where he discusses the origins and evolution of public philosophy, and the ecosocial trajectory of his work since the publication of *Public Philosophy in a New Key*.

Notes

1 Laden (2012) helpfully captures this dimension of the practice of public philosophy in his analysis of the difference between "reasoning with" and "reasoning over."
2 On the influence of American pragmatism on Tully's political thought, see Chin (2018).

3 Through his participation in RCAP Tully drafted a series of exploratory papers and presentations on Aboriginal government and the history of political thought that laid the foundation for the account of democratic constitutionalism in *Strange Multiplicity* and public philosophy in *Public Philosophy in a New Key* (Tully 1994b, 1994c, 1996).

4 Willinsky (2017, 291–5) offers a thoughtful study of the ethos of public philosophy where he argues that Tully's turn to examining the ways Locke's treatise served to legitimate colonial dispassion reflects his sense of the public philosopher's responsibility to make public use of scholarly knowledge.

5 On Tully's ongoing reciprocal and critical engagement with Habermas' dialogical critical theory, see (2008a 39–70, 71–131; 2008b, 91–123; 2012b).

6 Another innovation within the language of agonistic democracy is – *pace* Chantal Mouffe – Tully's reluctance to collapse the critique of consensus into a repudiation of the democratic debate and dialogue as needful practices of democratic citizenship (Volk 2021).

7 Edward Said's notion of a "contrapuntal" approach to empire (1993) has been an enduring influence on Tully's work since at least *Strange Multiplicity* (1995). See Morefield (2022).

Part I

The Practice of Public Philosophy

1 Political Theory as a Critical Activity

The Emergence of Public Philosophy in a New Key (2017)

Introduction

I would like to express my gratitude to the Japanese Conference for the Study of Political Thought for inviting me to visit Japan and to give this lecture.[1] I am also immensely grateful to Professor Yasuo Tsuji for suggesting the topic of my lecture. He asked if I would lecture on my approach to the study of political thought, and the major writers who have influenced me. This invitation thus gave me the opportunity to reflect on my work over many years and to try to articulate its development in a way that I hope is easy to understand. My approach has always been experimental and open to revision after each application of it. So, this invitation gave me the opportunity to reflect on my recent work and attempt to integrate it into a revised picture of my approach as a whole at this stage. This has been edifying for me and I hope it will be for you as well.

I would like to start with my work as a graduate student because this early period in one's career often has a long-term influence on a student's whole career. But, before I do, I will just give you a very brief description of my approach as I now see it: that is, as a type of "public philosophy":

> *Public Philosophy in a New Key* is a new approach to the study of politics. The role of a public philosophy is to address public affairs. This civic task can be done in many different ways. The type of public philosophy I practise carries on this task by trying to enter into the dialogues with citizens engaged in struggles against various forms of injustice and oppression. The aim is to establish pedagogical relationships of *reciprocal elucidation* between academic research and the civic activities of fellow citizens. The specific role of this public philosophy is to throw a critical light on the broad field of *practices of governance* in which civic struggles take place and the *practices of civic freedom* available to change them. It does this by means of historical and critical studies of the field and the given forms of representation (or languages) of it. Reciprocally, this critical ethos learns from citizens and the successes and failures of their civic activities how to improve the historical and critical studies and begin again.

> (Chapter 2, 37 emphasis added)

DOI: 10.4324/9781003227403-3

So, in brief, this is how I see my approach today. Now, I would like to go over the main steps in the path to this approach. I will mention the authors who have influenced me as I go along. However, I would like to say at the outset that the major influence on my work has always been the creative dialogues of mutual learning I have had with students and colleagues over many years.

Cambridge University: The Cambridge School and the Discovery of Practices of Governance and Practices of Civic Freedom

The problem for me and my generation was the division of the world into capitalist and communist states and the decolonisation struggles of the Third World and the Non-Aligned Movement. In the West, and especially on the west coast of North America, there was a very strong anti-war movement against the Vietnam War, which was seen as a continuation of Western imperialism. Moreover, on the west coast of North America there was a strong tradition of a third way, which was not based on either capitalist or communist views of property, but, rather, a third tradition of property: that is, the traditions of the democratically governed commons or "cooperatives" around the world.

I went to Cambridge to work with Quentin Skinner and John Dunn to learn the Cambridge school method of the history of political thought. My objective was to study the rise of capitalist forms of property by studying John Locke and other early modern theories of property. The standard view at the time was that Locke was the first theorist of capitalist forms of property, liberal government, and the spread of capitalist property by means of colonisation of North America. John Dunn, the great Locke scholar, taught me how to interpret Locke textually, contextually, and biographically – and much else for which I am immensely grateful.

I learned that the rise and global spread of capitalist forms of property was a lot more complicated than it is usually portrayed. Indeed, I have continued to research and write on Western imperialism from the 1990s to my book on *Imperialism and Civic Freedom* (2008b). Moreover, I learned that Locke's view of property was far more complex than simply a defence of private property. And his account of the "commons" was also more sophisticated than the standard view of the tragedy of the commons. This began my study of the "commons," local "cooperatives," community-based economics, and globalisation from below that has continued throughout my career.

I not only learned about traditions of property from my study of John Locke. I also discovered in Locke a very powerful account of human agency under conditions of oppression, and of the capacity of humans to overthrow unjust relations of power over them, whether these are exploitive property relations or oppressive relations of governance in the family, marriage, workplace, within a state, or among states; and of the capacity of humans to then set up new forms of government "as they see fit," as he famously concludes the *Two Treatises of Government*. The fascinating feature of Locke's view of human agency is that it is not connected to a theory of stages of historical development in which a people can resist successively and legitimately only under specific economic conditions and only with an aim of furthering a liberal or Marxist theory of modernisation or globalisation. For Locke, people resist when and where "the yoke of oppression galls their necks." They are not determined by some allegedly universal theory of historical development. This came like a breath of fresh air to me and to my understanding of the capacity and legitimacy of the resistance of the Vietnamese people against Western and Soviet intervention.

Locke's view of human agency resonated for me in an interesting way with the account of agency I was learning from Quentin Skinner. Skinner's argument was that an author is always constrained in what she or he can do in writing a political theory by the problems that dominate the age on the one hand and the inherited linguistic conventions or languages in which the problems of one's age are written about. These conventions or "languages of politics" constrain what we can say and communicate in any age, but, they nevertheless also enable a certain kind of constrained agency that enables us to call some of these conventions into question, to challenge them, to try to modify them, and thus to enable us and our readers to think and act differently with respect to the problems humans face, and to the deeply sedimented ways of thinking in the present that limit their options.

This for me was a theory of contextual and potentially transformative freedom in the interdependent linguistic relationships of meaning within which we think, write, and act. As a condition of intelligibility, the agent has to think and write within the shared conventions, yet, nevertheless has a range of ways of acting within this field of linguistic meaning.

Now notice that this view of contextual, practice-based, constrained, and enabled ways of thinking and acting applies to both the writers we are studying in the past or present *and* to ourselves as researchers studying them. That is, we too are embedded practitioners in the language games of our own times and their dominant problems and ways of thinking, and constrained to write in accord with them to be intelligible to others. And these "pre-judgments," as Gadamer calls them, pre-judge the way we interpret texts in the past or in other cultures. Yet, we too have the critical and constructive capacities to call these taken-for-granted conventions into question to some extent and to try to think differently: that is, to try to enter into the world of thought and action of the people we are studying.

Moreover, as both Quentin Skinner and Michel Foucault argue, we are able to employ critically the different ways in which the people we are studying use their concepts as "objects of comparison and contrast," to free ourselves from the dominant and habitual forms of thought in the present, and thus to begin to *think and act differently* with respect to our own problems as well. For both Skinner and Foucault, the history of political thought is also a "critical activity" in this sense.

So far, I have been talking about intersubjective linguistic relationships of meaning of the languages humans share with each other. I have not mentioned relationships of power. I now want to turn to show you the way this approach takes up the question of power relations.

The philosopher who taught us to see the way we inhabit the linguistic world in this way was Ludwig Wittgenstein. His philosophy of language dominated Cambridge and the Cambridge school at the time and has been a source of inspiration for me ever since. In addition, Wittgenstein went on to argue that we are not just embedded in pragmatic relations of linguistic meaning; what he called "language games." He also went on to argue that language games are always woven into the human activities in which they are employed by the participants in these activities. It followed from this that we had to study not only the languages of politics but also the practices in which these languages are used.

At the same time as we were studying Skinner and Wittgenstein, we were also studying Michel Foucault. In his later work, Foucault developed a relational view of power and agency that complemented the relational view of linguistic meaning and practice advanced by Wittgenstein and Skinner. That is, for Foucault, the relationships of power that govern our conduct in the practices of life are much like the linguistic relationships of meaning that make sense of these practices. That is, relationships of power constrain what we can say and do, but, at the same time, they enable a constrained range of ways of acting in relationship to these relationships of power: of questioning, challenging, changing, and, at the limit, transforming them.

Hence, this is how I came to develop my *interdependent and relational* view of human agency in terms of "practices of governance and practices of civic freedom within them." A practice of governance consists of the relationships of meaning, power, and normativity by which we govern and are governed in a practice, and the range of ways of acting in these relationships of meaning, power, and normativity: from going along with and affirming and defending the rules of the game, to questioning, challenging, negotiating, reinterpreting, modifying, resisting, transforming, or withdrawing and acting otherwise. Practices of governance and practices of civic freedom in this broad sense range from the smallest practice in, say, family relationships; to systems of culture, law, government, and economics in states; and on to the complex relationships of meaning, power, and normativity that make up regional and global processes and systems historically and today.

We live in an infinitely complex multiplicity of such criss-crossing and overlapping practices of governance and practices of civic freedom within them in our everyday lives.

This way of thinking about the field of politics did not come to me all at once. It developed very slowly and experimentally over the years. And it is still a work in progress. Let me mention two features of this view that I became aware of later just to give you an indication of what is to follow in this lecture.

First, it took me a while to realise that we can say that we inhabit four main types of relationships of this interdependent and interactive kind. The first are the relationships we establish with ourselves when we reflect on our own activity: that is, ethics or the practices of the self. The second are the myriad relationships of interdependence and interaction we, individually and collectively, have with all other human beings who are affected by our interactions (the field of "all affected" relationships). This is of course the main field of political study. The third is the relationships of interdependence and interaction we have with the ecosystems and earth systems in which we live, on which we depend, and which co-sustain all forms of life on earth. The fourth is the relationships of interdependence we have with the spiritual dimension of life.

These four types of relationships are relationships of interdependence and interaction in different ways. For shorthand I will simply call these relationships "dialogical" relationships. Here, "dialogue" refers to the whole diversity of ways we interdepend and interact in these four types of relationships, whether it is linguistic or non-linguistic. They are dialogical in the broad phenomenological sense of this term. I have learned to use "dialogical" in this broad sense from my colleague, Charles Taylor.

Second, I only gradually came to see that this human capacity of civic freedom to have a say in and over the rules to which we are subject is what we normally mean by the term "participatory democracy," and so to study the traditions of participatory democracy.

McGill University: Cultural, Legal, and Political Pluralism, and Indigenous Peoples of Canada

I met Professor Tsuji when I was teaching at McGill University from 1976 to 1995. I had the great pleasure and honour of being his co-supervisor along with my colleague Charles Taylor. Those were wonderful years and I learned an enormous amount from Professor Tsuji and the penetrating questions he asked Professor Taylor and me about the history of political thought and contemporary political thought. It was very much a relationship of mutual learning.

During my time at McGill University, Charles Taylor and I taught courses together and supervised graduate students together. The dialogue with Charles Taylor had a deep influence on my thinking during this period.

During the McGill years, I was swept up in two great Canadian political problems I had not addressed before. I began to address them by adapting and modifying the approach I had begun at Cambridge. These two problems are: first, the struggles over various kinds of diversity or pluralism in Canada: cultural, linguistic, religious, legal, political, economic pluralism in Canada – or what we call "deep diversity." Canada is a complex multicultural and multinational federation. The "struggles" of this period, which continue today, are struggles over the appropriate relationships of mutual recognition and reconciliation of the diverse members of the federation and the corresponding appropriate forms of distribution of political and economic power to both individuals and groups.

The second problem is the struggles of Indigenous peoples of Canada for decolonisation; and for the recognition and resurgence of their inherent rights of self-government over their traditional territories; and how to reconcile this with the non-Indigenous settlers and their complex federal system of law and government.

There have been two dominant approaches to these two problems by Canadian academics, and by academics elsewhere working on similar problems. The first response is to try to work out a theory of rights for individuals, minority groups of various kinds, and for substate nations within multinational states. This has been the great work of my colleague Will Kymlicka and many others.

The second response is to say that it is not the role of the political theorist to work out the appropriate systems of cultural, legal, and political rights for the plurality of individuals and groups. Rather, these should be worked out by the people engaged in these struggles, and the people affected by them, or their trusted representatives, in legal and political negotiations and deliberations: in official public spheres, in the courts, and in legislatures and parliaments. On this view, the role of the political theorist is thus to work out the correct set of rules of negotiation or deliberation in which the people themselves, or their representatives, can reach agreements on binding systems of rights and duties of mutual recognition and distribution. This second approach was deeply influenced by the theories of deliberative democracy developed initially by Jürgen Habermas and John Rawls, and then developed further by more critical and contextual deliberative theorists in Canada and around the world.

I engaged in, learned from, and contributed to both these responses in my teaching, writing, and public engagement. However, Charles Taylor and I, as well as many of our students, came to see that we were doing something different from both these responses: that is, different from the rights-based and deliberative democracy approaches.

The first and most important difference is that we argue that these struggles over recognition and distribution do not admit of definitive resolutions once and for all. Rather, they are permanent and ongoing features of any free and equal democracy with a diverse population. The problem is not to work out definitive solutions to mis-recognition and mis-distribution, but, rather, to establish institutions that always enable citizens to express their public dissatisfaction with oppressive relationships of recognition and distribution of individuals and groups, to present their reasons for thinking the status-quo is oppressive, and to enter into negotiations over reforming the relationships if they are shown to be unjust in some way. Reciprocally, the majority, or their representatives, have a duty to listen to the expression of discontent and to enter into negotiations if good reasons show that the discontents are legitimate. Moreover, they have a duty to listen for voices that have been silenced in one way or another and do not even have a right to speak. This is called the "non-finality" approach in Canada and the European Union. It was first endorsed by the Supreme Court of Canada before the European Union courts.

The second feature of this approach is the realisation that there is not a definitive system of rights that can be handed down from on high, by a theorist, court, or legislature. There is also not a definitive system of rules for negotiation and deliberation that can be handed down from on high. If negotiations and deliberations are to be just, then the people engaged in them and subject to them must have a say both in and over the rules of deliberation if they are to be treated as free and democratic citizens. This condition is what I came to call "democratic constitutionalism" in contrast to "constitutional democracy." Under constitutional democracy, the background constitution lays out a set of rights and rules within which the citizens then exercise their rights of democratic participation in deliberation within the public sphere, in elections, and so on.

But, if the whole background structure of law is to be democratically legitimate, then it too must be open to democratic questioning, negotiation, and revision by the very people who are subject to it as they go along from generation to generation. That is, the two meta-norms of legitimacy in the modern world – the constitutional rule of law and democracy – must always be equiprimordial. If the constitutional rule of law is prior to democratic participation, then it has no democratic legitimacy and is a case of "juridical containment." If, conversely, the undifferentiated will of the majority is prior to the recognition of the diversity of the people, then it has no rule of law legitimacy. So, a political association in the twenty-first century in conditions of deep diversity is legitimate if and only if it is a democratic constitutional order: that is, one which the citizens are not only subject to the rule of law and democratic rights but also have the right to dissent and call into question these conditions of democratic recognition and participation as citizens, and others have the duty to listen and respond.

I set out my account of the equiprimordiality of democracy and constitutionalism in *Strange Multiplicity* (1995). Again, the Supreme Court of Canada was the first court to acknowledge "democratic constitutionalism" shortly afterwards in the case of *Reference re Secession of Quebec* (1998).

One of the central problems I worked on was the struggle of the Quebec nation or people to find appropriate forms of recognition within the Canadian federation, as a multinational federation, or, by secession and becoming an independent or sovereign nation state. At the same time, as a member of the English-speaking minority in Quebec, I was concerned with the rights of minorities within multinational federations and independent nation states. This led to me work on theories of nationalism, self-determination and federalism, and to minority rights. My work became of interest to scholars working on the same problems in the European Union and in international law, and working with them gave rise to my work on the European Union, multinational and multicultural federalism, and global constitutionalism.

You won't be surprised to know that I connected the protection of minority rights to the core democratic right of having a say and a hand in the way individuals and minorities are governed in larger associations, and thus with the Roman law maxim of *audi alteram partem* (always listen to the other side), which has become a norm of complex societies around the world.

However, the second problem, the struggles of Indigenous peoples of Canada for decolonisation and self-determination, had an equally profound influence on my thinking. The Kanesatake Mohawks near Montreal defended their land from appropriation in a lengthy standoff against the Canadian armed forces in 1990. This important struggle over land and self-government, and other similar struggles, led to the federal government setting up a Royal Commission on Aboriginal Peoples, 1991–1996. The commissioners invited me to participate by listening to what Indigenous people were saying to the Commission and by writing up what they said in a way acceptable to Indigenous people and understandable to Canadians. I also began to teach courses on the history of the relationships of European settlers and Indigenous peoples throughout North American from 1492 to the present, and to teach Indigenous students.

What I learned by working with Indigenous people is, first, that it is not enough to enter into negotiations with them. To meet the conditions of democratic justice, Indigenous people have to be able to speak in their own voices and ways; to negotiate in their traditional ways; and, often, to hold the negotiations on their traditional territories, since their ways of knowing and being are place-based. That is, to force them to enter into the institutions of liberal democracy and follow the rules of deliberation in them is to re-colonise and assimilate them. These reinforced my view that the participants themselves have to work out the conditions of negotiation if they are to be non-imperial and democratically legitimate.

Listening to and learning from Indigenous people across Canada also made me realise the imperial foundations of Canada and the United States. I wrote a second book on John Locke and how his theory of property was used to dispossess Indigenous peoples of their traditional territories. I also learned from them that there is a way to decolonise the relationship with Indigenous people and work out a just relationship between free and equal peoples. This is the nation-to-nation treaty relationship between the Canadian government (the Crown) and the First Nations that was widely used in the early modern period. The Indigenous peoples of North America have called for a renewal of this form of recognition and negotiation among equal peoples. It was adopted by the Royal Commission on Aboriginal Peoples in their final report. Moreover, after decades of nonviolent struggle and negotiation, it was adopted in the United Nations Declaration on the Rights of Indigenous Peoples in 2007 and ratified by Canada in 2010 and 2016.

Thus, as you can see, I have not been interested in working out definitive theories as solutions to the problems we face. Rather, my aim has been to write critical and constructive histories of the problems so those engaged in them can see them in a different way from the representation of them in the dominant languages of contemporary politics. My aim is also to show ways in which people engaged in and affected by struggles over recognition and distribution can resolve their disputes through nonviolent democratic negotiations that are respectful of the customs and ways of the different participants, and also always leave their resolutions open to revision by those who have to live with them in the future.

This is an extension of my earlier view of limited, interdependent, relational freedom in practices of governance, but now extended to struggles over recognition, distribution, and the environment. I came to call this form of freedom "civic freedom" and "civic or diverse citizenship" because it takes a diversity of forms and because it is oriented to making people aware of human diversity.

University of Victoria 1: From Political Theory as Critical Activity or Ethos to a Public Philosophy

In 1996, I moved from McGill University in Montreal, Quebec, to the University of Victoria, in Victoria, British Columbia. Victoria is on Vancouver Island and is the capital city of British Columbia. This is where I was born and brought up. With the exception of two years at the University of Toronto, I have remained at the University of Victoria. At the University of Victoria I have continued my work with Indigenous people. In addition, I have expanded my approach in a number of ways.

The first change is methodological. In 2001, the journal *Political Theory* invited me to describe my approach up to that point in time. In my article, I described my approach as seeing political theory as one type of "critical activity" or "critical ethos." That is, I located my work in the tradition of critical and historical reflection on problems in the present represented by such thinkers as Hannah Arendt, Foucault, Taylor, and Skinner. As we have seen, the aim of this tradition is to study a contemporary struggle and its problem by showing its historical emergence and development; and, thereby redescribing it in ways that show its contingency; freeing us from customary contemporary ways of thinking about it; and thus opening up the possibility of thinking and acting differently.

I came to realise that this description of my approach as a "critical activity" captured a lot of what I was doing. However, it did not express an additional and important dimension of what I was trying to do. It did not capture the dimension of my work that seeks to engage in reciprocal dialogues with the citizens who are engaged in the political problems and struggles that we are writing about as academics. I call these dialogues between academic researchers and engaged citizens dialogues of "reciprocal elucidation."

Consequently, I had to redescribe my own work in a way that included this dialogical dimension, while, at the same time, preserving, and indeed expanding, the "critical attitude" dimension. I did this in 2008 by redescribing my work as "public philosophy in a new key." That is, I went back to the older tradition of "public philosophy" in the West and asked how I can reformulate the tradition of public philosophy in a way that gives expression to what I am trying to do with the dialogical dimension of my work.

This was a difficult task because the dominant view of "public philosophy" is the idea of a public intellectual who knows something about public affairs that citizens do not know and who then "speaks to citizens" about this special knowledge. His or her knowledge is usually framed in terms of an abstract or universal theory of politics, expressed in a language different from the everyday langue of politics. In contrast, what I was trying to do was not to speak *to* citizens in some arcane theoretical language, but, rather, to speak-*with*-citizens in reciprocal dialogues and in the everyday languages they use to articulate the problems we are both addressing. This is why I decided to describe my approach as "public philosophy *in a new key*": that is, in the key of *speaking-critically-with* and in the everyday inherited languages of problems and struggles in which we are entangled.

With this dialogical dimension, I was attempting to "democratise" academic research by putting the researcher in critical relationships of mutual learning *with* their fellow citizens. Here, the researcher learns how the people engaged in the problems understand them, and, in reciprocity, the researcher offers them the insights derived from academic research and from the dialogues we have with our fellow academics.

In doing this, I was influenced by contemporary public philosophers, such as John Borrows, Cressida Heyes, Anthony Laden, Edward Said, Boaventura de Sousa Santos, Charles Taylor, Antje Wiener, and Iris Marion Young. But the deepest influence was still Wittgenstein, who always wrote in dialogical form and in the language of everyday practices and lived experiences. Indeed, he argued that philosophers often simply bypass the problems that they try to address by reformulating them in esoteric languages of description that are disconnected from the language of lived experience of the problems of our times.

I was certainly not alone in taking this dialogical turn. At the University of Victoria and at universities around the world, academics in almost every field have turned to what is called "community-based research" or "community-engaged research," where academics and the subjects they study enter into dialogues of mutual learning. The University of Victoria is a leader in this field in Canada. This approach also changes the way you teach. You want to introduce your students to the problems you are discussing and to the ways that the people engaged in them are talking about them. This means sometimes taking the class out of the classroom or bringing the participants in the struggles you are studying into the classroom.

In Victoria, I began to explore the ways in which people around the world are engaging in practices of civic freedom in response to a range of contemporary problems. I discuss these in *Public Philosophy in a New Key* (2008a,b) and in the two volumes of dialogue with other academics: *On Global Citizenship* (2014a) and *Freedom and Democracy in an Imperial Context* (2014b). In addition, Antje Wiener in Hamburg and I set up a new journal in 2012 to bring scholars together who work on global issues in this way, *Global Constitutionalism*.

In these research projects, I discuss participatory democratic forms of civic freedom such as responses to the new forms of imperialism, local social and economic cooperatives, environmental movements, and fair trade. What interests me here is the astonishing ways in which people act creatively and constructively in response to injustices in the practices of governance in which they find themselves. I realised that I could classify the diverse examples of practices of freedom in practices of governance into two very general classes or types of citizen engagement. I call these two types of citizen participation "civil" and "civic" citizenship or "representative" and "direct" citizenship. Civil or representative citizenship refers to the institutionalised forms of participation available to citizens under modern representative government. Civic or direct citizenship refers to the practices of civic freedom we have been discussing under civic freedom.

Civic citizenship discloses the field of global citizenship in a broad and pluralistic manner. From the civic perspective, citizenship comes into being whenever and wherever people who are subject to or affected by practices of governance become active co-agents within them: exercising the powers of having a say (negotiating) and having a hand (exercising the powers of self-organisation and self-government) in and over the relationships that govern their interaction. "Civic freedom" is the situated, relational freedom manifest in the countless activities of bringing the relationships of disputation and resolution, of recognition and distribution, and of action-coordination that comprise practices of governance in this broad sense under the shared democratic agency and authority of those subject to and affected by them.

The primary examples of civic citizenship are everyday practices of grassroots political, social, economic, and ecological democracy where the members discuss and exercise powers of self-organisation and self-government themselves (citizen-with-citizen relations) prior to any separation of ruler and ruled, or governor and citizen, in the representative institutions of civil citizenship. They become citizens by democratising or "co-operating" their relationships of living and working together.

University of Victoria 2: Peaceful Relationships with Each Other and the Living Earth

I would like to conclude by mentioning my most recent work. I have focused on nonviolence and deep ecology movements as "civic freedom" responses to the problems of war and the ecological crisis.

After I published *Public Philosophy in a New Key*, I realised that at the centre of my work is a focus on two types of human capabilities: the capabilities of participatory democracy (that is, the exercise of the capacities of self-organisation and self-governance), and the capabilities of resolving and reconciling differences, disputes, and conflicts of all kinds by nonviolent means. The exercise of these two sets of intersubjective and relational capabilities (of self-government and nonviolent dispute resolution) is much more common than our major traditions of political theory recognise. Our dominant traditions are based on the premise of coercively imposed and state-centred representative government, on the one hand, and the coercive establishment of political order out of a background of natural disorder, antagonism, war of all against all, struggles for existence, class war, and so on, on the other.

Yet, despite these dominant modern traditions, there is another tradition that stems from Peter Kropotkin's *Mutual Aid* of 1902 to the most recent work on the multiplicity of ways in which humans self-organise, even in the most difficult of situations of war, devastation, and forced migration. This tradition argues that informal relationships of mutual aid, democratic self-government, and nonviolent dispute resolution exist all around us in our everyday activities and institutions and provide the social basis of them; despite the dominant, institutionalised relations of power-over, aggressive competition, and coercion.

That is, this tradition argues that conciliatory relationships of interdependency and mutual support (or *being-with* relations) are prior to the competitive and aggressive relationships of independence.

In her book *On Violence*, in 1970, Hannah Arendt agreed with this. She argued that the continuation of war and violence as the means to resolve conflicts is irrational because "violence begets violence" and because it is leading to the destruction of much of the human species and the ecosystems on which all species depend. Yet, she concluded, humans continue because they have not found a substitute for war and violence as the means to resolve disputes.

Yet, at the same time, Richard Gregg, an American philosopher and activist who worked with Mahatma Gandhi, argued that Gandhi had developed a substitute for war and for coercive, power-over relationships, in his book entitled *The Power of Nonviolence*. The "power of nonviolence," which Gandhi called *satyagraha*, is the power of individual and collective agents to act together to transform violent and unjust relationships of any kind into just and democratic relationships by nonviolent means. Richard Gregg argued that the practices of nonviolence that Gandhi developed in India could spread around the world and gradually displace violent and exploitive relationships; gradually substituting nonviolent means of conflict resolution for the recourse to war and substituting democratic relationships for command-obedience relationships.

This line of argument resonated with what I had discovered in my own work on peace and ecology movements since Gandhi. The important feature of Gandhi's version of nonviolence is that nonviolence is seen as a comprehensive, nonviolent way of life, or nonviolent counter-modernity. It involves acting nonviolently in all four types of relationships I mentioned earlier: in relationships to oneself (ethical practices of the self); relationships with others; relationships within the ecosystems that sustain all life; and relationships with the spiritual dimension of life. It thus includes working on nonviolent relationships with other human beings and with the living earth; that is, nonviolent response to the ecological crisis and climate change. It provides nonviolent, democratic ways of addressing both social and ecological justice: what Gandhi called *swaraj* and *swadeshi*.

At the heart of Gandhi's practice is the famous mantra of "being the change and enacting it in your everyday relations." That is, you can bring about a peaceful and democratic world only by peaceful and democratic means, because means shape the ends. It is the exact opposite of the dominant view that peace can be brought about by war and democracy can be brought about by authoritarian rule.

So, this discovery has opened up a new phase in my work in which I am focusing on nonviolent practices of civic freedom in response to both social and ecological injustice. Here again, it has opened up a conversation with Indigenous peoples on the Northwest coast. They have long traditions of nonviolent dispute resolution. They describe nonviolent relationships with each other and the living earth in the terms of gift-reciprocity relationships of mutual aid. They say that they learn how to live in and sustain gift-reciprocity social relationships from the way plants, animals, and biotic communities co-sustain each other in analogous symbiotic ecological relationships. For Indigenous peoples, humans are citizens of ecological relationships that sustain all life on earth with responsibilities to act accordingly in their social relationships.

This view of traditional Indigenous knowledge is similar to the view advanced over the last thirty years in the life and ecological sciences and earth systems theory – that humans are plain members and citizens of the symbiotic ecological relationships and systems that sustain all life. Thus, the great question of ecological justice is the same as the question of social justice: how do we act virtuously in the ecological relationships on which we depend so as to sustain them and all the interdependent forms of life that sustain us? That is, what are our *ecological practices of civic freedom* as citizens of the ecosystems we inhabit and on which we depend, yet which we are destroying, as the Intergovernmental Panel on Climate Change tells us?

So, thank you very much for listening to this narrative. I hope it has been interesting and edifying for you. I hope it is the beginning of a dialogue with Japanese colleagues. In this spirit, I look forward to your questions and comments.

Note

1 Lecture delivered at the Japanese Conference for the Study of Political Thought, Keio University, October 2016.

2 Public Philosophy and Civic Freedom

A Guide to the Two Volumes (2008)

Public Philosophy in a New Key is a new approach to the study of politics.[1] The role of a public philosophy is to address public affairs. This civic task can be done in many different ways. The type of public philosophy I practise carries on this task by trying to enter into the dialogues with citizens engaged in struggles against various forms of injustice and oppression. The aim is to establish pedagogical relationships of reciprocal elucidation between academic research and the civic activities of fellow citizens. The specific role of this public philosophy is to throw a critical light on the field of practices in which civic struggles take place and the practices of civic freedom available to change them. It does this by means of historical and critical studies of the field and the given theoretical forms of representation of it. Reciprocally, this critical ethos learns from citizens and the successes and failures of their civic activities how to improve the historical and critical studies and begin again.

In the studies that follow, I use the term "citizen" to refer to a person who is subject to a relationship of governance (that is to say, governed) *and*, simultaneously and primarily, is an active agent in the field of a governance relationship. While this includes the official sense of "citizen" as a recognised member of a state, it is obviously broader and deeper, and more appropriate and effective for that reason. By a "relationship of governance," I refer not only to the official sense of the institutional governments of states but also to the broad sense of any relationship of knowledge, power, and subjection that governs the conduct of those subject to it, from the local to the global. Governance relationships in this ordinary sense range from the complex ways individuals and groups are governed in their producing and consuming activities to the ways peoples and subalternised states are subject to global imperial relationships of inequality, dependency, and exploitation. They comprise the relationships of normativity, power, and subjectivity in which humans find themselves constrained to recognise themselves and each other, coordinate interaction, distribute goods, act on the environment, and relate to the spiritual realm. "Practices of civic freedom" comprise the vast repertoire of ways of citizens acting together on the field of governance relationships and against the oppressive and unjust dimensions of them. These range from ways of "acting otherwise" within the space of governance relationships to contesting,

DOI: 10.4324/9781003227403-4

negotiating, confronting, and seeking to transform them. The general aim of these diverse civic activities is to bring oppressive and unjust governance relationships under the on-going shared authority of the citizenry subject to them; namely, to civicise and democratise them from below.

What is distinctively "democratic" about public philosophy in a new key is that it does not enter into dialogues with fellow citizens under the horizon of a political theory that frames the exchange and places the theorist above the *demos*. It rejects this traditional approach. Rather, it enters into the relationships of normativity and power in which academic researchers and civic citizens find themselves, and it works historically and critically on bringing them into the light of public scrutiny with the particular academic skills available to the researchers. Every reflective and engaged citizen is a public philosopher in this sense, and every academic public philosopher is a fellow citizen working within the same broad dialogue with his or her specific skills. Studies in public philosophy are thus specific toolkits offered to civic activists and civic-minded academics working on the pressing political problems of our times.

I first developed this approach in *Strange Multiplicity: Constitutionalism in an Age of Diversity* (1995). By means of a series of historical studies, I argued that constitutional democracies could respond to contemporary struggles over recognition by reconceiving constitutions as open to continuing contestation and negotiation by those subject to them. This would be a transition from constitutional democracy (where the constitution is conceived as founding and standing behind democratic activity) to democratic constitutionalism (where the constitution and the democratic negotiation of it are conceived as equally basic). In the decade since it was published, I have come to see that this approach can be improved and applied to a broader range of contemporary struggles: over diverse forms of recognition, social justice, the environment, and imperialism.

There are many public philosophers from whom I have drawn inspiration. John Locke, Mary Wollstonecraft, Emma Goldman, Antonio Gramsci, Sojourner Truth, Paulo Freire, Bertrand Russell, Maude Barlow, Edward Said, Noam Chomsky, Vandana Shiva, Bonaventura de Sousa Santos, Iris Marion Young, and Gandhi are exemplary. And, as I mentioned, every engaged and reflective citizen is an inspirational public philosopher in this democratic sense. But I have always questioned why more political philosophers and political theorists are not also *public philosophers*. What stops many of them from seeing their work as a discussion with their fellow citizens as equals? I think the answer is that many tend to enter into a relationship with citizens under the horizon of a political theory that sets them above the situated civic discourses of the societies in which they live. This presumptive elevation is standardly based on four types of assumptions.

The first assumption is that there are causal processes of historical development (globalisation) that act behind the backs of citizens and determine their field of activity. It is the role of the theorist of modernisation to study these conditions of possibility of civic activity. The second is that there are universal normative principles that determine how citizens ought to act. It is the role of the theorist of global justice to study these unchanging principles that prescribe the limits of democracy. The third is that there are background norms and goods implicit within democratic practices that constrain and enable the field of democratic activity of citizens in the foreground. It is the role of the interpretative and phenomenological theorists to make these background conditions explicit. The fourth is that there are canonical institutional preconditions that provide the foundations of democratic activity, and it is the role of political scientists to study these legal and political institutions.

In each of these four cases, the theorist is elevated above the *demos* by the assumption that there are background conditions of possibility of democracy that are separate from democratic activity and it is his or her role to study them, not what takes places within them. In the course of the studies in the two volumes, each pillar of elite political theory falls to the ground. Each of the four conditions of possibility is shown to be internally related to and reciprocally shaped by the everyday activities of democratic citizens, not separate from and determinative of their field of freedom. It is this revolutionary discovery that brings political philosophy "down" into the world of the *demos* and renders it a situated public philosophy in conversation with fellow citizens. Equally important, it enables us to see that we are much freer and our problems more tractable than the grand theories of the four pillars make it seem. For while we are still *entangled* in conditions that constrain and enable, and are difficult to change, we are no longer *entrapped* in background conditions that determine the limits of our foreground activities, for none is permanently off limits. I associate this revolutionary insight with the late Richard Rorty (Chapter 4). Others will associate it with other writers and their own experiences of human freedom and agency where they were told it was impossible.

I would like to say a few words about the phrase "in a new key." Just as a jazz musician plays a composition in a new key relative to the classic performances of it, so too a specific public philosopher plays the role in his or her own new *style* in relation to the classic public philosophers in his or her field. The *style* of these studies is a new key in that it combines historical studies and a reciprocal civic relationship in what I hope is a distinctive way. Jazz musicians play in a new key in the course of improvising with other musicians and in dialogue with classic performances and present audiences. Analogously, public philosophers improvise in dialogues with contemporary theorists, the classics, engaged citizens, and in response to the political problems that confront and move them. This is the situated freedom of a public philosopher. I see the studies in these volumes as improvisations in this sense (Benson 2003).

Finally, I would like to respond to a common objection to this style of public philosophy. Radical critics often say, given the radical character of your particular public philosophy, why do you engage in the "mainstream" academic debates and use the conservative language of citizenship, public philosophy, governance, democracy, and civic freedom? Your work will be co-opted by the mainstream you disagree with and alienated from the civic activists you hope to reach. You should write in a language of radical politics.

I acknowledge that my views are somewhat radical relative to much of the literature I discuss. However, there are three reasons for the approach I take. Firstly, the alternative language of radical politics often involves a kind of self-marginalisation and an attitude of self-righteousness that I find incompatible with a democratic ethos. Moreover, there are already many excellent public philosophers, such as Chomsky, who write directly to civic activists and bypass the theoretical debates, and they too write in the same plain and simple language of citizens, public goods, and freedom. Secondly, the economic, political, and military elites and their ideologists have inherited not only much of the earth and its resources but also many of its languages, including the manipulable language of citizenship, democracy, civic goods, and freedom. Yet, it is precisely this ordinary language that the oppressed and exploited of the world have always used to express their outrage at the injustices of the present and their hopes and dreams of another world. Like Edward Said (2004), I refuse to surrender it to our adversaries without a fight and abandon the repository of the history of struggles from which we derive. Moreover, the fall of the four pillars of the *ancien régime* also brings down the fiction of an alternative, pure language of freedom (radical or otherwise) that stands above the fray of politics and is impervious to unpredictable redescription by one's fellow adversaries. Thirdly, I have deep respect for the elaborate Western and non-Western traditions of critical political reflection, the great yet partial insights they can bring, and the people who carry them on today in this public language. While I disagree with the dominant theories that legitimate the status quo in these terms, engagement with them forces dissenters like myself constantly to test our own views against them and, in so doing, to try to move the academic debate in another direction. As we will see, I am far from the first or only one to take this agonistic stance. Furthermore, is it not presumptuous to assume that these debates are alien and of no interest to citizens? The following chapters were written in conversations with engaged citizens. Academic debates are not as far from and unrelated to the public debates as they are often portrayed from the perspectives of the four pillars. They are a historically integral part of the complex field of practical discourses on which public philosophy is inescapably thrown and in which it can find its voice and make a distinctive difference.

Note

1   This chapter is a slightly abridged version of Tully (2008a, 3–11).

3 Deparochialising Political Theory and Beyond

A Dialogue Approach to Comparative Political Thought (2016)

On Understanding Engagement in Genuine Dialogues Among Traditions

If we wish to deepen our understanding of engagement in meaningful or genuine dialogue among and across different traditions of political thought then we should enquire into the conditions of meaningful or "genuine" dialogue.[1] These conditions include the ethical practices of openness and receptivity to the otherness of others that enable participants to understand one another in their own traditions (mutual understanding) and to appreciate the concerns of one another regarding globalisation and the injustices and suffering it causes (mutual concern). The participants may discuss moral standards of judgement and moral bases of political relationship at times in the dialogue, but these are meaningless unless and until through deep listening each comes to understand and appreciate the concerns of others as they experience and articulate them in the terms of their own traditions without inclusion, assimilation, or subordination.

The problem of the "meaninglessness" of abstracted moral principles is even worse than this. Abstract moral principles can literally mean anything the user wishes them to mean unless they are grounded and articulated in relation to the experiential self-understanding of those to whom they are applied. Take these dominant moral standards as examples: treat each other as free and equal; as ends in themselves, never only as means; and the difference principle of organising politics to the benefit of the least well-off. These moral principles have been and continue to be used to justify the greatest inequalities in human history; modern wars of intervention, conquest, subjugation, and modernisation; and environmental destruction and climate change. They also have been and continue to be used to criticise these injustices of globalisation by equally elaborate and well-defended critiques of the dominant justificatory theories.

This is one of the contemporary problems to which the turn to the understanding of the grounded ethical practices of engagement in multi-tradition dialogue is the response. If we can explicate the conditions of genuine dialogues, then the participants themselves will work out their understanding

DOI: 10.4324/9781003227403-5

of and responses to globalisation themselves. That is, a genuine dialogue is not prescriptive: the participants co-articulate their own scripts democratically.

Six Obstacles to Deparochialisation and Genuine Dialogue[2]

I propose that the project of deparochialising political theory can be seen as the work of creating genuine dialogues among and across traditions of political thought and practice. Engagement in genuine dialogues can accomplish much more than deparochialising political theory, as we will see, but it must achieve this first if the other benefits of genuine dialogue are to be achieved.

Deparochialising conversations are exceptionally difficult to engage in yet exceptionally rewarding if we do so.[3] The conditions of a genuine conversation or dialogue are difficult to explicate because it is so easy to finesse the demands of such a dialogue: that is, to appear to engage in them while all the time remaining within one's own tradition (as much of the global dialogue literature does today). Engagement in what we can call non-genuine or "false" dialogues is as common as rain and it conceals the demanding conditions of genuine dialogue from view. Like Gadamer (1999), I distinguish genuine dialogue (mutual or reciprocal understanding) from two main types of false dialogue that fail to live up to the demands of genuine dialogue: strategic-instrumental (strategic) and deliberative-imperative (legislative). Also like him, I discuss both face-to-face dialogues and dialogues between interpreter and the texts of other traditions of political thought, although I place more emphasis on the first.[4] Allow me to mention six ways in which genuine dialogue is suppressed by false dialogue.

First, it is often simply a matter of a person or a dominant tradition being aware that they are pretending to engage in a genuine dialogue with people from other traditions but continue to do so to get the upper hand (strategic dialogues). However, the problem of false dialogue is much deeper than this.

Second, in other cases, the individual or collective agents who engage in a false dialogue deceive themselves into believing that they are engaged in a genuine dialogue, so there is the psychological problem of self-deception to overcome. This problem is common in many of the participatory dialogues employed in the World Bank and IMF policies of democratisation and transitional justice, and, indeed, it is seen by many as a deeply embedded feature of Western traditions of dialogue with non-Westerners, brought to awareness only in times of crises, such as after world war, decolonisation, 9/11, and the war on Iraq, and then quickly forgotten. Yet, the difficulty of false dialogue is more fundamental.

Third, the fundamental reason we get off on the wrong foot is that the very condition of being in a meaningful world with others in any tradition is that humans always and pre-emptively project over, interpret, and try to understand the other in the terms and ways of their own tradition. This is an ontological condition of sense-making. Our living traditions disclose the world to us as an actually and potentially meaningful world. Unless there is some awareness that the horizon of understanding of one's own tradition, which discloses the other and their way of life as meaningful in its terms, has to be called into question in the course of dialogue with others, who, as a matter of course, enter dialogue under the horizon of their tradition, then the dialogue, by definition, will remain a false dialogue in which each misunderstands the other and responds to this misunderstanding by re-imposing – often unconsciously – their traditional understanding over others. Unless there is a critical practice within a tradition or within the course of the dialogue that brings this problem to self-awareness and addresses it by bringing aspects of one's background horizon of disclosure into the space of questions at the centre of the dialogue, genuine dialogue cannot begin.[5]

In addition, this disclosure and projection of our form of pre-understanding over the world (and interpreting and acting under its sway) is not only true with respect to human beings but also over all living beings, including the earth itself. We must somehow learn to listen to and understand the norms of self-organisation of all forms of life and of the animate earth as a whole if we are not to destroy it by disclosing and acting on them under our traditions that disclose them as externalities or resources for the use and abuse of one species (Capra and Luisi 2014; Esbjorn-Hargens and Zimmerman 2009).

Fourth, even when tradition-critical practices are present in traditions or dialogues among them, there is a multiplicity of factors that override or undermine them: psychological, military, economic, religious, rationalistic, political, face-saving, and so on. Fifth, these weighty factors are in turn legitimated by a multiplicity of "secondary explanations" that, as Franz Boas (1911) argued, every tradition gives to itself, such as the grand theories of civilisation, modernisation, and globalisation generated by the West over the last half millennium of global expansion.[6] These are called "secondary" explanations because they often redescribe and conceal what is really going on in false dialogues and the escalating struggles that result from them in the terms of acceptability and approval of that tradition; terms such as progress, modernisation, liberty, necessary means to world peace and justice. For example, Rousseau (1994) pointed out that "slavery" and "subordination" are often redescribed as "liberty." These secondary explanations give us a false picture of our histories of interactions with other traditions.

The demand that global dialogues follow certain allegedly universal rules and be oriented to allegedly universal ends is often said to be a kind of textbook example of this failure to see what one's traditional form of representation conceals from view and of the failure to call the form of representation into the space of questions, even though it has a critical dimension within it. The reason this occurs is that the juridical language of representation of the tradition presents itself as meta-traditional from the outset, conceptually and historically, giving rise to "legislative" rather than genuine dialogues.[7]

As a result of these five factors (and a sixth below), a natural disposition to see the world in the terms of one's own tradition in the first instance is continually finessed, rather than faced and addressed, at each stage of interaction, as false dialogues escalate to the submission of one participant to another, or to conflict. These escalating misunderstandings and conflicts in turn are then legitimated by the secondary explanations of modern politics: namely, that peace cannot be brought about by peaceful means and democracy cannot be brought about democratic means: both require violence and authoritarian rule to bring less-advanced others to see the superiority or universality of the particular form of peace and democracy on offer.

These secondary explanations and their effects in practice lend credence to a global norm of modern politics: in time of peace prepare for war. Once this becomes the norm, even those traditions that are disposed to peaceful means of dispute resolution through genuine dialogue see that it is strategically rational to prepare for war in response to the others who have already done so. This security dilemma at the centre of modern politics discredits genuine dialogue and undercuts the mutual trust on which it depends because it becomes rational to enter into dialogue in a distrustful way: that is, pretending to engage in genuine dialogue, in hopes it might work out, yet openly preparing for conflict if it does not. The dialogical effect of the open hand on the other – the nonviolent power of genuine dialogue – is undermined by the hidden fist in the background, affecting others to do the same in response. As Nietzsche argued in "The Means to Real Peace" (1986, 284, 380–1), and generations of IR scholars and game theorists ever since, this logic leads to the security dilemma and ever-escalating arms races, world without end.

Accordingly, it is not difficult to see that if the logic of finessing genuine dialogue by means of the secondary explanations that comprise the language of development and globalisation is not confronted, it will lead to the destruction of billions of *Homo sapiens* and other forms of life on earth, as Hannah Arendt (1970) forewarned in the 1960s and many others have since substantiated (cf. Dilworth 2010).

Thus, in conclusion to this section, if this analysis is even partially accurate, there is no way to address the multiple crises of globalisation that does not pass through engagement in genuine dialogues among and across the traditions of political thought present on this small planet.[8] Moreover, as these five obstacles show, engagement in deparochialising dialogues is not a simple task that we can do in a year or two. Many have failed, not only for the five reasons given above, but also for the sixth reason. The long, slow, intergenerational crafts of teaching, acquiring, and exercising the ethical practices of engagement in genuine, deparochialising dialogues have been ignored, and fast-time teaching, dialogues, negotiations, bargaining, and pre-scripted, transitional processes have proliferated (Bohm 2014; Mountz et al. 2015).

Given these six obstacles, the cultivation of genuine conversations and dialogues is one of the most important yet difficult tasks in the world. It requires learning and acquiring the ethical practices of genuine dialogue in despite of our human, all-too-human, dispositions to overlook the requisite critical work on our self-understandings and the self-understandings of others, and on all the factors piled up to dispose us to finesse these ethical practices of mutual understanding and concern. But, if genuine dialogue were to succeed in some future generation of people educated and proficient in the requisite ethical practices of engagement (the students of our students' students perhaps), then, in virtue of their sustained engagement in these dialogical relationships, they just might be able to bring into being another world of possible ways of living together peacefully and democratically that we can scarcely even imagine today. We can scarcely imagine these possibilities because our imaginations are constrained by the traditions and false dialogues we inhabit and the factors that hold them in place. Nevertheless, we can begin to explore some of the first steps of engagement, and teaching engagement in genuine dialogues of deparochialising, mutual understanding and concern, and critical comparison.[9]

Reciprocal Elucidation and Transformation

All concepts in which an entire process is semiotically concentrated elude definition: only that which has no history is definable.
— Nietzsche, *On the Genealogy of Morals*

The previous sections survey the complex conditions or stage-setting of the central activity of dialogical comparative political thought: translation. Translation brings with it an additional set of conditions that need to be borne in mind by participants along with the previous ones. Translators today are situated in the dense relationships of translation constituted by the last five hundred years of translation across traditions among translators from hegemonic societies and the counter-translations of translators from subalternised societies ("writing-back"). That is, relationships of translation and counter-translation are located within the larger global "contrapuntal ensemble," as Edward Said (1993) called it.

These are not simple self/other relationships of translation. Translators are situated within an ensemble of different ways of using the language of political thought in their own societies along intersectional lines of inequality and difference: class, gender, ethnicity, race, region, language, sexual orientation, settler-indigeneity, and, as the same time, they are translating spoken and written texts from similarly complex societies (Dhamoon 2009; Tuck and Yang 2012). These inequalities and differences are now so great that there is often little communication or understanding across them. The interweaving of political thought and traditions is yet more complex, due to the vast increase in "diffusion" since Boas and brought about by immigration from former colonies to metropole societies under postcolonial conditions, and *vice versa*, and the deeper penetration of settler-colonial societies, such as Canada and the United States, into the still colonised Indigenous Fourth World. Furthermore, the networkisation of global communication; the global spread of capitalist modes of production, commodification, strategic-instrumental forms of thought, subjectivity, and dialogue; the rise of institutions of global governance; the spread of international law and its presumptively universal language of commerce, human rights, and the good life; and the militarisation of conflict and conflict resolution all bring with them complex relationships of communication (Tully 2012b).

The great dangers in this situation are not only incomprehension and misunderstanding due to inequality and difference. They also include the ever-present danger of the reign of a global network Esperanto that brings about, at best, a fast-time listening and superficial communication, but not understanding. Interlocutors often use the same words, and so presume they understand each other, but, as we have seen, they understand the words differently because they interpret them in light of their own background form, or forms, of life. Or, they can barely cling to a meaningful form of life, as in the massive cases of impoverishment, forced migration, war refugees, climate refugees, and genocide. In addition to the proliferation of strategic-instrumental and legislative dialogues, another danger is what might be called the dialogue of hegemonic ventriloquism, in which the more powerful partners consult with and listen to the less-powerful others and then translate what they hear into the presumptively universal or higher language of their hegemonic discourses.[10] Yet another danger is the influence neoliberal universities that promote many of these trends have on academic research (Mountz et al. 2015).

Bearing all these conditions and dangers of translation in mind, what are the distinctive features of translation dialogues of transformative reciprocal elucidation?

First, participation in translation dialogues of reciprocal elucidation "elucidates" or clarifies texts being translated in light of their contexts. In so doing, participants "enlighten" or bring enlightenment to each other.[11] This is a transformative experience consisting of the following six steps. Through dialogue they: (1) free each other partially from deep attachment to their worldviews; (2) move each other around to see the phenomenon (text) in question from each other's perspectives as much as humanly possible; (3) from these other perspectives each sees their own and others' perspectives as limited perspectives (mutual deparochialisation); (4) through further dialogue they come to see similarities or commonalities, as well as dissimilarities, in the different ways they disclose the phenomenon from different perspectives; (5) they then go on to exchange critical and comparative judgements, and to see if these too share commonalities through negotiation or deliberation; and (6) thus, participation in this dialogical work of translation transforms and transposes the participants into its nonviolent, conciliatory mode of being-in-the-world-with-others, and, *eo ipso*, into the pluriverse that participation both brings to light and teaches them how to be its enlightened citizens. This is the dialogical deparochialisation of, and alternative to, the monological tradition of enlightenment and cosmopolitanism (Tully 2003; Buber 1970, 1993).

The most important set of capabilities that participants acquire through participation – in addition to deep listening, empathy, and, eventually, compassion – is called the intersubjective virtue of the courage of truthfulness: *parrhesia* and *satyagraha*.[12] The first and best known feature is the disciplined capacity to speak as truthfully as possible to others in the dialogue. This is not to speak "the truth," as it is commonly translated, for the obvious reason that participation in dialogue teaches the partners that no one person or tradition knows the whole truth, but only a limited perspective on it. Each participant *needs* the participation of all others, also speaking truthfully, to get as close to the truth as is humanly possible by sharing perspectives. They are interdependent in this radical sense. The second, less-known yet equally crucial, reciprocal feature is the courage to listen truthfully to what the others are saying no matter how difficult this is: that is, deeply and openly by means of non-attachment. When speakers and listeners exercise these reciprocal kinds of courage of truthfulness in taking turns, a third feature comes into being: a "parrhesiastic pact" (Foucault 2001, 11–20).

This is just the term for a genuine dialogical relationship among them. Being reciprocally truthful binds the parrhesiastic partners together in the search for truth. Each dialogue with others who see the situation differently is an "experiment in truth" in Gandhi's famous phrase (Gandhi 2011).

Next, how do truth-seeking participants proceed to bring about mutual understanding? The translating participants elucidate the phenomena (texts) in question (Q) by drawing analogies and dis-analogies to other phenomena with which the listeners are already familiar (F). They suggest, for example, that Q is similar to F in their tradition in the following aspects, yet dissimilar in other aspects. The two phenomena Q and F share what Wittgenstein calls one or more "family resemblances," just as members of families share different characteristics, but none is common to all members. A similarity is a criterion, or set of criteria, for identifying Q and F among the whole cluster of contestable criteria used to identify Q and F.

The dialogue continues with other analogies and dis-analogies, similarities and dissimilarities, with different phenomena of comparison and contrast, until a whole web of criss-crossing and overlapping similarities and dissimilarities between Q and series of Fs comes to light. Each similarity and dissimilarity forms an "intermediate step" that enables listeners and questioners to begin to get a sense of the meaning of Q in its traditional contexts relative to their own. These intermediate steps enable these partners to "see connections" between the phenomenon in question and the phenomena invoked in comparison and contrast. That is, they begin to see how Q is used in various contexts and shades of meaning, and so begin to acquire the ability to use the concept themselves: that is, to understand it in its context. These are steps one and two in reciprocal elucidation.

The reason why participants are able to acquire this kind of participatory ability and mutual understanding of other texts and traditions of political thought is that, *mutatis mutandis*, this is how humans acquire the ability to use and understand language in general. According to this view, humans acquire these abilities through examples and practice, not through the acquisition of a rule stating the necessary and sufficient criteria for the application of the concept in every case, because there is no such essential set of criteria. Wittgenstein illustrates this thesis by taking his readers through various examples of games, showing that there is no one criterion common to all of them, but similar and dissimilar criteria are invoked in different instances of games. He concludes: "we see a complicated network of similarities overlapping and criss-crossing: sometimes overall similarities, sometimes similarities of detail" (Wittgenstein 2009, §66). He then goes on to show how participants learn meaning-in-use through examples and practice. They not only learn how concepts are used in different contexts by invoking criss-crossing and overlapping criteria but also go on to learn how to give contextual reasons to contest habitual uses and to present novel uses. The dialogical work of translation is the extension of this ability to learn meaning-in-use by means of examples and practice in different traditions of political thought and to present translations of them that bring understanding to others. Wittgenstein calls such a translation "surveyable representation" (*übersichtliche Darstellung*) that brings understanding in the sense of "diversity-awareness" or "seeing-as" (2009, §122).[13]

As we have seen, interpretation and translation of particular "texts" has to include interpretation and translation of the contexts in which they make sense. This is especially important in comparative political thought. Political contests over the practices of politics are always also over the languages of political thought that are used to describe, evaluate, defend, and contest these practices. Although the contests of political theories appear more abstract, they are responses to them, and contributions that enter into the history of the languages of political thought. This ongoing contestedness of political concepts explains why Nietzsche says they have histories, not definitions.[14] Translation dialogues of reciprocal elucidation are no exception. They too are in these relations of contestation, of agreement and disagreement, of understanding and misunderstanding, of the languages of politics (Owen 2016). They bring to this field a distinctive nonviolent *way* of contestation.

The acquisition of the abilities of mutual judgement is much the same as mutual understanding. Practitioners of languages of political thought are always already involved in judgements because political concepts are never purely descriptive. They are terms that describe and evaluate at the same time: they "characterise" the phenomena. Think of "democracy," "freedom," "oppression," and so on. In addition, in learning how to use a concept in various contexts, they learn judgements of correct and incorrect uses, and how to give reasons to contest, criticise, and legitimate dominate uses, as well as to extend the use of concepts in new ways and give reasons *pro* and *contra*.

Moreover, in dialogues of reciprocal elucidation, standards and ways of judging are placed in the intersubjective space of translation and compared and contrasted, as in mutual understanding. Standards and ways of judgement are judged and counter-judged, critiqued and counter-critiqued, from various perspectives, without this being second order.[15] Comparative insights and limits and strengths and weaknesses of various types are brought to light from various perspectives and the family resemblances and dissimilarities among them explored. When people learn a language or tradition of political thought they learn how to make judgements and counter-judgements, critique and counter-critique within a background structure of prejudgements that constitutes a worldview or form of representation.[16] As participants move through the six steps of translation dialogues of reciprocal elucidation, they free each other from their background prejudgements to varying degrees and draw them into the foreground of comparison and critique.

The revolutionary feature of mutual understanding and mutual judgement is that they are not oriented to transcending the multiplicity of traditions and languages of political thought in order to understand and judge them from a universal viewpoint. They aim to deparochialise and de-transcendentalise this imperious disposition and place it in the field where it belongs, with other limited viewpoints. They orient the participants to learn how to understand and judge multi-perspectivally from within the lifeworld of living theories, traditions, practices, and places of comparative political thought by learning their way around within them, and with each other. It is the practice of a worldly, *immanent* critique.

The practice of translation dialogues of reciprocal elucidation can be illustrated by three examples. Boaventura de Sousa Santos sees the "work of translation" as the disclosure of the political world as a pluriverse capable of being disclosed from multiple modes of disclosure in comparison with each other. He uses the example of the work of translating concerns over human dignity in terms of the Western concept of human rights, the Islamic concept of *umma*, and the Hindu concept of *dharma*[17]:

> In this case, the work of translation will reveal the reciprocal shortcomings or weaknesses of each one of these conceptions of human dignity once viewed from the perspective of any other conception. Thereby, a space is open in the contact zone for dialogue, mutual understanding and for iden-tification, over and above conceptual and terminological differences, of commonalities from which practical combinations for action can emerge.
>
> (Santos 2005, 17)

The lifelong work of Dennis Dalton in translating Gandhi's political thought is an exemplar of the reciprocal elucidation approach. He carefully situates Gandhi's political thought and practice in the historical context of Indian traditions and shows what is traditional and novel. He then compares and contrasts these translations and interpretations of Gandhi's thought and practice with equally careful, contextual interpretations of similar and dis-similar political thought and practice in the West. Readers are thus able to come to understand such complex concepts and practices as *swaraj* and *swa-deshi* by way of their similarities and dissimilarities with freedom and eco-nomic self-reliance in Western traditions and thus go on to make comparative judgements themselves (McDermott et al. 2013; Dalton 2016). Last but not least, the most famous example of a decolonising dialogue of reciprocal elucidation of comparative political thought is Gandhi's *Hind Swaraj* of 1909 (2009).

In summary, mutual understanding and judgement that can be achieved in dialogues of reciprocal elucidation is neither a comprehensive view nor a consensus. It consists in bringing to light background forms and ways of thought and being from various traditions and becoming able to view and discuss them comparatively from different limited perspectives. They become meaningful for the participants. This is what Gadamer (1999) calls the "fusion of horizons" and Bohm (2014, 29–31) describes as exposing and sharing of tacit meanings in common in dialogue.[18] The diverse forms and ways of thought and being are no longer isolated and foreign. They are *meaningful* precisely because the participants have elucidated the webs of similarities and dissimilarities (family resemblances) that connect them in their diversity.

To borrow a metaphor from Wittgenstein, the languages of comparative political thought compose a "labyrinth of paths. You approach from *one* side and know your way about; you approach the same place from another side and no longer know your way about" (Wittgenstein 2009, §203). The participants in a dialogue of reciprocal elucidation learn their way around the places and connecting paths and the labyrinth becomes full of meaning to them. Thus, a "genuine dialogue" of reciprocal elucidation is meaningful in this sense.[19] The *dia* in "dialogue" does not mean "two." It means to partake in and of *logos* (meaning) with others (Bohm 2014, 6–7).

Dialogues of reciprocal enlightenment exist in many cultures and they too exhibit webs of family resemblances and dissimilarities. For example, in many Indigenous North American traditions, there are somewhat similar practices of dialogue that bring about similar transformative meaningfulness among participants. This is often called "being of one mind." To begin, they usually give thanks in reciprocity to Mother Earth for all the interdependent ecological relationships of gift-reciprocity (symbiosis) that sustain life. Then they listen carefully and quietly to each other's stories of where they come from and how they see from their different perspectives the situation that has brought them together. They understand these dialogue relationships as gift-reciprocity relationships, derived from dialogues with the living earth. The Nootka word for participation in such dialogues on the Northwest coast is "*Pa-chitle*" (tr. Potlatch), the verb "to give" (Clutesi 1969, 9–10).

Moreover, within stories, there is usually a character, such as Raven on the Northwest Coast, who has the ability to transform him or herself in the ways of thought and being of other living beings, human and more-than-human. The gift exchange of stories and mask dances transform the listeners into the ways of life narrated in the stories. Through engagement in these dialogues, they become able to understand and share all the different meanings of their situation in common. This is to be of one mind. It lays the groundwork for negotiating and acting together in response to the situation they share.[20]

Finally, dialogues of reciprocal elucidation have a telos beyond mutual understanding and mutual judgement. First, the intersubjective world of shared meanings brings to light ways of thinking, judging, deliberating, and acting together in response to the situation they share that were *unimaginable and unthinkable* prior to the dialogue. This is often the practical reason for the dialogue. According to Aeschylus and Protagoras, the democratic system of justice in the West was founded on this insight.[21] Even more importantly, the complex repertoire of nonviolent, contestatory, and conciliatory ways of being-with-each-other that the participants acquire in dialogue prefigure and dispose the participants to relate to others in similar ways when they respond to suffering, disagreement, and conflict in the lifeworlds they inhabit. In taking this further, compassionate step, they become the change they experience in dialogue. They extend nonviolent practices of deparochialising political thought into the world of nonviolent practices of deparochialising and transforming unjust political action.[22]

Notes

1 This chapter is an abridged version of Tully (2016) originally presented at the conference De-Parochializing Political Theory: East Asian Perspectives on Politics; Advancing Research in Comparative Political Theory, University of Victoria, August 2012. I borrow the term "genuine" dialogue from the conference agenda. I mean by this term the type of dialogue I describe in this chapter. The participants engage in genuinely trying to understand each other and their concerns. I take this to mean what most people mean by a "meaningful" dialogue.

2 I discuss the points in this and the following section in more detail in Tully (2008a, 2008b, 2014a, 2014b).

3 I sometimes use "conversation" and "dialogue" interchangeably to emphasise that these conversations occur in everyday interactions. However, "conversation" is the broader term, including everyday dialogues that include some but not all of the conditions of genuine dialogue, yet are the intersubjective ground of genuine dialogue. For this type of distinction, see Laden (2012).

4 For interpretations of Gadamer close to my own, see Davey (2006) and Benson (2003).

5 This is the central insight of Martin Heidegger's early *Being and Time* (2008) and it became the starting point for Edmund Husserl, Maurice Merleau-Ponty, and the field of phenomenology, as well as for Gadamer. Ludwig Wittgenstein states that it is the central problem he addresses in the *Philosophical Investigations* (2009). He uses the terms "picture" and "form of representation" for mode of disclosure.

6 In his classic text *The Mind of Primitive Man* (1911) and his methodological articles, Boas used the example of how the unjust treatment of Indigenous peoples of the Northwest coast of North America by Europeans was redescribed by them in ways that legitimated it to explain how secondary explanations function. See Tully (2018c).

7 This is a central problem of the Kantian tradition. See Allen (2016).

8 The anthropologist Wade Davis (2009) estimates that there are roughly seven thousand traditions around the world.

9 One of the best known examples of an attempt at dialogues across traditions as a worldwide educational project is the United Nation's *Alliance of Civilizations*. It was set up by Turkey and Spain after 9/11 to replace the military clash of civilisations with a dialogue of civilisations through cross-civilisation education in dialogue from an early age. I was involved in the early drafting and I draw on this experience. See the United Nations Alliance of Civilizations (2006).

10 This is perhaps the most common form of colonising translation, which includes only to subordinate assimilate, while allowing a patina of multicultural differences to be recognised and celebrated. See Tully (2008a, 291–316). Media panels of talking heads after protests are classic examples of this danger.

11 Enlightenment in French, *l'éclaircissement*, has these two senses as well and Foucault probably had this in mind when he coined the phrase "reciprocal elucidation" (1997, 111–20).

12 *Parrhesia* is the Greek term for this virtue. See Foucault (2001, 2011; cf. Hénaff 2010, 101–55). *Satyagraha* is the term Gandhi invented to characterise holding on to and being moved by (*graha*) truthfulness (*satya*) in everything one says and does. See Gandhi (1961), Dalton (2012, 12–30).

13 This is Wittgenstein's knowing-with alternative to Socrates's knowing-over. Temelini (2015) explicates Wittgenstein's account and shows how Charles Taylor uses it to explain cross-cultural understanding and judgement and Quentin Skinner to contextualise the history of political thought.

14 This internal relationship between political theory and political practice is the basis of the contextual schools of political thought since Nietzsche.

15 Wittgenstein compares this to the way orthographers deal with the word "orthography among others, without being second-order" (2009, §121).

16 Wittgenstein explores the learning and questioning of judgements in *On Certainty*: "We do not learn the practice of making empirical judgements by learning rules: we are taught *judgements* and their connection with other judgements. A *totality* of judgements is made plausible to us" (1974, §140; cf. §§104–52).

17 He suggests that this kind of translation dialogue takes place at the World Social Forum.

18 For a careful analysis of this "limit experience" in the case of Foucault (and Max Weber), see Szakolczai (1998).

19 This answers the question in note 1.

20 See Borrows (2010a), Kimmerer (2013), Atleo (2004), Wilner (2013), Napoleon (2009a), Wilson (2015).

21 Athenians introduced the jury system when they realised that a single agent could not judge justly and devolved judgement to the *demos* in the form of juries. Aeschylus (2009) and Manderson (2019) for this interpretation. This background makes sense of Meletus's disagreement with Socrates in the *Apology* (Plato 1956).

22 Gandhi's nonviolent mode of contesting and transforming violent oppressors, *satyagraha*, for example, is interpreted in this way by Gandhi's good friend, Richard Gregg (2018, 49–72). For an enlightening example of how to take dialogues of reciprocal elucidation into the world of cooperative responses to neoliberal globalisation, see Ouziel (2015).

Part II

Modes of Citizenship and Practices of Freedom

4 The Agonistic Freedom of Citizens (1999)

> There is something happening here. What it is ain't exactly clear.
>
> It might feel good, it might sound a little sumpun, but damn the game if it don't mean nothin'.
>
> What is game? Who got game? Where's the game in life behind the game behind the game? I got game.
>
> She's got game. We got game. They got game. He got game.
>
> It might feel good, Or sound a little sumpun', But f-- the game if it ain't saying nothin'.
>
>   – Public Enemy and Stephen Stills, *He Got Game*

"What Is Game? Who Got Game?"

In the 1950s, Hannah Arendt began to focus on a specific aspect of politics.[1] Instead of looking on the institutions, routines and policies of governance on the one hand, or on the great political theories on the other, she aimed to concentrate on or "confront" the activity of politics itself. In doing this, she drew attention to a specific kind of game-like activity which occasionally emerges in the broader field of politics and government. She associated it with the Greeks and certain moments in the history of Western politics, especially but not exclusively revolutionary times, and claimed that it is the very "*raison d'être* of politics" (Arendt 1977, 146).[2]

For Arendt, four characteristics of this unique political game are of paramount importance. First, the activity consists in interaction among equal citizens with different viewpoints on their common world and who engage in agonic activities for recognition and rule in public space. Second, like players in most games, humans take on their identities *as* citizens and peoples in virtue of participation in this intersubjective activity and, *eo ipso,* bring into being and sustain the "field of action" of the game, the "public realm" in which they interact (Arendt 1977, 145, 148–9). Third, this activity is political freedom. Political freedom is not a matter of the will or the intellect, or of background constitutions, laws, and rights, but a form of activity with others in public that is liberated from the "automatic processes" to which humans are subject

DOI: 10.4324/9781003227403-7

and "within and against which" free citizens "assert" themselves. Freedom is the practice of freedom. It is neither the motive nor the goal of this kind of activity that renders it free but its spirit or character: the "principles," "virtuosity," or *ethos* (such as love of equality) the action manifests (Arendt 1977, 152, 163, 168). Fourth, this unique form of speaking and acting together is free because it embodies two aspects of "action": *agere*, to begin, lead and rule, and *gerere*, to carry something through together, a *task*. It is "a beginning" because the participants always bring something "miraculous" – new, contingent, singular, and unpredictable – into the world, breaking with routine and changing the game to some extent, and they seek to carry it through, to sustain the practice over time. In virtue of the miraculous appearance of practices of freedom, the time of humans is not completely in the realm of necessity or universality but partakes of the unpredictable "deeds and events we call historical" (Arendt 1977, 165, 169).

Modern political theorists tend to overlook this realm of free action, according to Arendt, because they associate freedom with sovereignty: either the sovereign individual will in the Kantian tradition or the sovereign general will of a group in the Rousseauian tradition. "If men wish to be free," she famously concluded two decades before Michel Foucault came to a similar conclusion, "it is precisely sovereignty they must renounce" (Arendt 1977, 165).[3]

Arendt's turn away from the routines, institutions, conditions, explanations, and theories of politics to the activity or game of politics itself – what citizens do and the way they do it – seems to me to be part of a general reorientation in Western thinking in the twentieth century. It might be described as a move away from the search for an essence hidden behind human activities to the surface aspects that give them meaning and significance. In Nietzsche's famous formulation, the more profound attitude is "to stop courageously at the surface, the fold, the skin, to adore appearance, to believe in forms, tones and words, in the whole Olympus of appearance" (Nietzsche 1974, 38). Recall as well that in the 1930s, Wittgenstein rejected theories and explanations of language as a formal system of representation and began to look on it as a multiplicity of activities, of "language-games." As he put it, "look on the language-game as the *primary* thing." Do not look for an "explanation" but simply investigate how the "*language-game is played*" (Wittgenstein 2009, §654, §656). I think he meant by this roughly what Arendt meant: concentrate on the ways language-users use words and the activities in which the uses of words are woven (Wittgenstein 2009, §10; 1974, §204). What is needed is neither a theory of the game in question (which is another game with signs) nor an explanation of an underlying structure that determines the play, but a perspicuous representation of the physiognomy of the game itself: what the players do and how they do it (just as Arendt does in her characterisation of free political activity) (Monk 1990, 302–8). Also like Arendt, he saw this "*Weltanschauung*" as immensely important, as heralding, he occasionally hoped, a general change in Western cultural outlook (Hilmy 1987, 190–226).

Another example of this change in perspective is the influential historical study of the play element of cultures by the great historian Johan Huizinga, *Homo Ludens* (humans, the game-playing animals), published in 1938. Do not look on human activity through the lens of *"homo faber,"* as the Marxists do, Huizinga enjoined, nor through the lens of *"homo sapiens,"* as the rationalists and system-builders do, but, rather, under the aspect of game-playing (Huizinga 1955, foreword). Like Arendt he was concerned to argue that game playing "is free, is in fact freedom." It is a higher form of human activity that liberates us from the routines of everyday life, and, following Burkhardt and Nietzsche, it involves an "agonal" or contestatory element (Huizinga 1955, 8, 71–4, 152). Indeed, many of the themes in Arendt's work are present in Huizinga's classic study, including the general cultural pessimism they share with Wittgenstein that the play element in Western culture is declining in the face of scientism, administration, routine, and the professionalisation of sports and politics (Huizinga 1955, 195–213).

Perhaps the writer who has done the most in the latter half of the twentieth century to disseminate and defend a broad cultural reorientation towards practice and away from theory and structure is Richard Rorty. He has encouraged us to dispense with the great metaphysical and post-metaphysical theories associated with different forms of human organisation and value spheres and to abandon the attempts to discover large-scale underlying processes or conditions of possibility that determine our thought and action behind our backs. Look instead on forms of human organisation, from science to politics, as intersubjective activities of exchanging reasons and redescriptions among the players involved (Rorty 1989). The significance of this change, he writes, is "on a par with the shift from a Christian and Aristotelian outlook to an atheist and Galilean outlook" (Rorty 1998, 289). In short, activity is prior to theory (Rorty 1991). Rorty also suggests that several others have taken this general turn to some extent: for example, Habermas' shift from "subject-centred" reason to "communicative" reason and Rawls' focus on the "political not metaphysical" games of exchanging public reasons among free and equal citizens (Rorty 1989, 289).

I would like to draw distinctions within the broad picture Rorty sketches, for it is possible "to look on the language game as the *primary* thing" in a variety of ways. One approach is to focus on the implicit or explicit rules of the game in question and develop an ideal set of rules. Habermas and other neo-Kantians exemplify this approach (Habermas 1995; Linklater 1998). Another is to study the motives and goals that are said to determine the strategies of the players, as for example in the proliferation of game theoretic approaches in the last thirty years. As Arendt cautioned, although these approaches start from practice, they end in theory or explanation, thereby bypassing the spatial-temporal forms of activity she and Wittgenstein sought to elucidate. One of the main reasons these approaches fail to understand the phenomenon they purport to study, according to both Arendt and Wittgenstein, is that they disregard one of its central characteristics, one which always exceeds the grasp of theory and explanation: the freedom of speaking and acting differently in the course of the game and so modifying the rules or even transforming the game itself.

For Arendt, as we have seen, this sense of freedom is associated with new players and new ways of playing coming into being, so political activity is never closed by a frontier. It is never "rule governed" in the normative or causal sense required by theory or explanation. Indeed, if it were so rule-governed, by definition, it would be unfree, an "automatic process" in the realm of labour or work, not action. Now, this is often taken as a highly idio-syncratic view, rendering her account of politics largely irrelevant to the great concerns of modern politics. But this line of criticism misses the broad significance and application of her insight. To see this, let us return to Wittgenstein for a moment.

Although Arendt and Wittgenstein share an orientation to activity, the obvious difference is that Arendt concentrated on one specific kind of game-like activity, whereas Wittgenstein stressed their multiplicity and investigated the most routine of language games, such as counting, naming, and giving and taking orders, which Arendt would categorise as labour or work. Wittgenstein discovered that Arendt's "freedom to call something into being, which did not exist before, which was not given, not even as a cognition or imagination, and which therefore, strictly speaking, could not be known" can irrupt in almost any organised form of human activity, no matter how routine (Arendt 1977, 151). The reason for this freedom of speaking and acting differently is two-fold according to Wittgenstein: the games humans play with concepts are not everywhere bounded by rules and the rules themselves are not fixed uncon-ditionally. As a result, the condition of being "rule-bound," the requirement for normative and predictive theory being *about* actual games over time, is constantly subverted in practice.

Wittgenstein explains these two features of language use by starting with what appears to be one of the hardest cases, the concept of number:

> I *can* give the concept "number" rigid limits ... use the word "number" for a rigidly limited concept, but I can also use it so that the extension of the concept is *not* closed by a frontier. And this is how we do use the word "game." For how is the concept of a game bounded? What still counts as a game and what no longer does? Can you give the boundary? No. You can *draw* one; for none has so far been drawn. (But that never troubled you before when you used the word "game")
>
> (Wittgenstein 2009, §68)

His interlocutor replies in the same section, "then the use of the word is unregulated, the 'game' we play with it is unregulated." Wittgenstein responds no, not at all. "It is not everywhere circumscribed by rules; but no more are there any rules for how high one throws the ball in tennis, or how hard; yet tennis is a game for all that and has rules too."

We "cannot say," Wittgenstein roundly concludes, "that someone who is using language must be...operating a calculus according to definite rules" (2009, §81). He then immediately criticises those philosophers who not only "compare the use of words with games and calculi which have fixed rules," but who also assume that "using language must be playing such a game" and search for an ideal set of rules. Consequently, they "predicate" of the game what lies in their "method of representation" (a theoretical drawing of the rules at any given time or for a limited set of cases) and thus misrepresent the actual activity they are trying to understand, for it may always involve the extension of the rules in unpredictable ways (2009, §81, §104). The following dialogue summarises the difference between the two orientations to practice:

> "But still, it isn't a game, if there is some vagueness *in the rules.*" – But *does* this prevent its being a game? – "Perhaps you'll call it a game, but at any rate it certainly isn't a perfect game." This means: it has impurities, and what I am interested in at present is the pure article. – But I want to say: we misunderstand the role of the ideal in our language. That is to say: we too should call it a game, only we are dazzled by the ideal and therefore fail to see the actual use of the word "game" clearly.
>
> (Wittgenstein 2009, §100)

When one examines how a concept such as "game" is used (or "freedom," "equality," etc.), it is not by applying the same rule in every case, for, although a rule can be drawn for a limited purpose, there is no unconditional rule. Rather, a concept such as "game" is used in the present case and justified to others by pointing out its similarity or dissimilarity to other cases, "by describing examples of various kinds of games; shewing how all sorts of other games can be constructed on the analogy of these; saying that I should scarcely include this or this among games; and so on" (2009, §75). Through such exchanges of reasons and redescriptions pro and con from different points of view, drawing attention to different aspects of the uses in question relative to others, agreement or disagreement is negotiated on how to go on. This will often reasonably involve extending the concept in a way that modifies a rule which may have well been drawn around a limited number of cases or from a particular perspective before, and often presented as a comprehensive rule in some theory or other (2009, §66–7, §71, §83).

Two writers who have extended this understanding of rules and of freedom in relation to them to the study of politics are Quentin Skinner and Michel Foucault. Drawing on Wittgenstein, Skinner has brought about a revolution in the history of political thought. Somewhat like traditional historians of ideologies, he is concerned to map as carefully as possible the intersubjective conventions that normally govern political thought in a particular period and in relation to a shared set of political problems in practice. However, for Skinner, this is only the stage-setting in order to go on to his primary task: to investigate how individual political theorists in the past have freed themselves from, challenged, and sought to modify the reigning conventions from within, thereby changing the dominant political vocabulary. As he underscores in *Liberty before Liberalism*, one of the primary reasons for engaging in such a historical exercise is to enable his readers to exercise the same intellectual freedom today: to free themselves from and modify the conventions governing political thought and action in the present. Furthermore, the freedom to modify the conventions of political games through the exchange of arguments and redescriptions is not a discovery of the twentieth century but a rediscovery of a major theme of classical humanism (Tully 1998a; Skinner 1996, 15–16, 138–80, 1998, 101–20).

In a complementary manner, Michel Foucault came to describe his work as studies of the multiplicity of human activities or practices – "what they do and the way they do it" – rather than "the conditions that determine them without their knowledge" or the "representations [theories] that men give of themselves" (Foucault 1997, 317). He described these practices as "games," including, like Wittgenstein, the languages and forms of action in which they are woven and, unlike Wittgenstein, the relations of power that govern to some extent the conduct of the participants. "I have tried to find out," he explains

> how the human subject fits into certain games of truth, whether they were truth games that take the form of a science or refer to a scientific model, or truth games such as those one may encounter in institutions or practices of control.
>
> (Foucault 1997, 281)

Like Arendt, Wittgenstein, and Skinner, he argues that the games in which moderns are participants are "not closed by a frontier." Yet, the prevailing modern theories of politics (modern "humanism") disregard this feature, universalise a certain state of play and so obscure rather than illuminate how we constitute and are constituted by the games or practices in which we think and act:

> Through these different practices – [such as] psychological, medical, penitential, educational – a certain idea or model of humanity was developed, and now this idea of man has become normative, self-evident, and is supposed to be universal. Humanism may not be universal but may be quite relative to a certain situation. This does not mean that we have to get rid of what we call human rights or freedom, but that we can't say that freedom or human rights has to be limited at certain frontiers. What I am afraid of about humanism is that it presents a certain form of our ethics as a universal model for any kind of freedom.
>
> (Foucault 1988, 15)

Moreover, he went on to affirm the freedom to negotiate the rules of the game made possible by this understanding of limits:

With regard to these multiple games of truth, one can see that ever since the age of the Greeks our society has been marked by the lack of a precise and imperative definition of the games of truth which are permitted to the exclusion of all others. In a given game of truth, it is always possible to discover something different and to more or less modify this or that rule, and sometimes even the game of truth.

(Foucault 1997, 297)

According to Foucault, the study of any game will involve, first, the analysis of the rules in accordance with which the game is routinely played and the techniques of government or relations of power that hold them in place. Second, it will involve the "strategies of freedom" in which some participants refuse to be governed in this way, dispute and seek to modify the rules, and thus think and act differently to some extent. "That is," he summarises, "the forms of rationality that organize their way of doing things ... and the freedom with which they act in these practical systems [games], reacting to what others do, modifying the rules of the game, up to a certain point" (1997, 317).

Foucault, like Arendt, calls this activity "freedom." The difference from Arendt, and the similarity to Skinner, is that it can emerge in any form of organised human activity, even the most sedimented and rule-governed, such as a prison, mental institution, government ministry, or university. It is potentially an aspect of any practice of governance. Finally, Foucault, like Nietzsche, sees this freedom of problematising the rules of any game by raising objections to them in the field of knowledge or dissenting from them in the realm of conduct as an "agonic" game:

Rather than speaking of an essential freedom, it would be better to speak of an "agonism" – of a relationship which is at the same time reciprocal incitation and struggle; less of a face-to-face confrontation which paralyzes both sides than a permanent provocation.

(Foucault 2000, 342)

This agonic dimension of games separates Foucault, Arendt, Huizinga, and Wittgenstein from theorists such as Habermas who look on the games of politics under the ideal of consensus. For Arendt, Wittgenstein, and Foucault, no agreement will be closed at a frontier; it will always be open to question, to an element of non-consensus, and so to reciprocal question and answer, demand and response, and negotiation. However, the way Foucault conceives the agonic element is slightly different from Arendt and Huizinga. For Arendt and Huizinga, political activity involves agonic contests for recognition and rule, but the agonic element of the game has nothing to do with modifying the rules. It has to do with challenging an opponent and gaining recognition in accord with the rules. Neither Arendt nor Huizinga associates a change in the rules with agonism. Although Arendt suggests that free political action as a whole is "against" the habitual routines of everyday life, the struggles among equals for recognition and rule, which bring something new into the world, appear to take place within the rules of this unique political game. Or, at the least, her interest appears to be the principles the interaction manifests, not whether these constitute a challenge to the prevailing rules.

Foucault's unique contribution to this reorientation in the twentieth century is to link together the following three elements: the practice of freedom, the modification of the rules in the course of a game, and agonic activity. He sees the modification of the rules of any game as itself an agonic game of freedom: precisely the freedom of speaking and acting differently. He asks us to regard human activities as games with rules and techniques of governance to be sure, and these are often agonic games, but also, and more importantly, to look on the ways the players modify the rules by what they say and do as they carry on, and, in so doing, modify their identities *as* players: that is, the games of freedom within and against the rules of the games of governance (Foucault 1997, 291–3).

He brings these three elements together by broadening considerably the concept of agonism. Rather than restricting "agonism" to formal games and face-to-face contests, he extends its application to any form of activity or language game in which the coordination of action is potentially open to dispute, as a "permanent provocation," and, within these manifold games, to any form of reciprocal interplay, or "incitation and struggle," disputation takes, from sedimented games of domination where free play is reduced to a minimum at one end, through all the forms of negotiation and provisional agreements and disagreements, up to direct confrontations that break up game at the other end (Foucault 2000, 342, 346–8).

The reason for this focus is obvious enough. If Foucault, Wittgenstein, and Skinner are correct in believing that no game is completely circumscribed by rules, if it is always possible to go on differently, if a consensus on the rules has an element of "non-consensuality," then an important aspect of concrete human freedom will be "testing" the rules and purported meta-rules of the current game, of ensuring that they are open to question and challenge with as little rigidity or domination as possible, and of experimenting with their modification in practice, so humans are able to think and act differently. In an interview, Foucault explained this element of non-consensuality in apparent contrast to Arendt's conception of the consensus of citizens as presented by the interviewer (Charles Taylor), but I am not convinced that Arendt would disagree with Foucault (Foucault 1984, 374–8).

Let this stand as a brief and no doubt provocative account of an orientation to politics opened up by a redescription of Arendt's conception of freedom in comparison with the similar work of others.[4] I would now like to test its usefulness by applying it to two current political games of great importance: struggles for recognition and new, dispute-specific sites of citizen activity. Rather than approaching from the side of the motives of the citizens or groups involved, the authentic or autonomous identities they aim to have recognised, the rules that should determine which demands are worthy of recognition and those that should govern new sites of "post-Westphalian" democracy, or the changes in sovereignty that these bring about, I would like to examine the ways in which the citizens engaged in these struggles call into question and modify the rules of the game in which they are engaged, the game of citizen participation in constitutional and federal democracies.[5]

Of course, these two forms of current politics have modified the "rules" in the sense of the principles that ought to govern citizen participation: freedom, equality, mutual respect, due process, and consent. In accepting and appealing to these principles in contests to legitimate and delegitimate demands for recognition and for new sites of democratic practice, citizens, legislators, and courts have modified their use and application in unexpected ways, thereby lending credence to the orientation I have laid out above (Tully 1995).

What is less widely recognised is the way another type of rule is questioned and modified in the course of these games. This type of rule is closer to what Arendt, following Montesquieu, means by "principles" and "virtuosity." These are the immanent norms that characterise the ethos of the activity or way of being citizens and peoples. This distinction between democratic, constitutional principles (the mainstay of political theory), and political ethos (modes of civic conduct) is analogous to the distinction between moral principles and ethics, or ethos (Foucault 1985, 25–30, 1997; Connolly 1995). By examining these two kinds of political struggle from the orientation of the free activity of citizen participation (see next section), it is possible to see what other approaches tend to notice only obliquely; that these struggles modify the ethos of citizen participation: the *form* of citizen participation ("Diverse Forms ..." below) and the *practices* of governance in which participation takes place ("Diverse Practices ..." below).

Citizen Participation as the Practice of Freedom

Citizenship in a democracy consists in the participation of citizens in the ways in which their conduct is governed by the exercise of political power in any system or practice of governance. Citizens participate by "having a say" and "negotiating" how power is exercised and who exercises it. This kind of government is "democratic" just because it involves a "dialogue" between those who exercise power and those over whom it is exercised, as opposed to nondemocratic forms of governance, which coordinate human action without the say of those affected, "behind their backs," as in market and bureaucratic organisations. A dialogue is any form of reciprocal to-and-fro encounter with others whose perspectives, from their specific positions on the issue at hand to their most general background understandings, are not completely reducible to one's own. Their opinions, judgements, reasons, or understandings evince some contentious element of otherness and so of resistance. In virtue of this feature, political dialogues are agonic in the broad sense employed by Foucault (Falzon 1998, 36–56). The interplay of reasons and redescriptions in political dialogues can take any of the six basic types of reasoning together: persuasion dialogue, the inquiry, negotiation, information-seeking dialogue, deliberation, and eristic dialogue (Walton 1998).

Participation in dialogues and negotiations over how and by whom power is exercised over us constitutes our identities as "citizens" and generates bonds of solidarity and a sense of belonging to the political association (the "people") that comes into being and is sustained by this (game-like) activity. As in games more generally, the abilities to think and act in the ways definitive of the identity or "form of subjectivity" of a player are acquired through their exercise with others in the game itself. Citizen identity is not generated by the possession of rights and duties, or by agreement on substantive or comprehensive common goods, fundamental principles of justice, constitutional essentials, shared values, understandings or national, multicultural, or cosmopolitan identities, or, finally, by consensus on a set of universal procedures of validation.

It is not that these conditions and constituents of constitutional democracy are unimportant or that they are not illuminated by the theories that reflect on them. Quite the contrary. But, first, these rules are, as Arendt puts it, the "elaborate framework," not the activity of citizenship, of being a free people (Arendt 1977, 164). To concentrate on them is to mistake the stage-setting for the play. Second, and more importantly, citizens (and theorists) disagree about them. They are always open to question, disagreement, contestation, deliberation, negotiation, and change over time in the course of citizen participation, from discussing a municipal by-law to revolution. Principles, rights, goods, and identities are thus constituents of the "framework" in a special sense. Politics is the type of game in which the framework – the rules of the game – can come up for deliberation and amendment in the course of the game. At any one time, some constituents are held firm and provide the ground for questioning others, but which elements constitute the shared "background" sufficient for politics to emerge and which constitute the disputed "foreground" vary. There is not a distinction between the two that stands outside the game, beyond question for all time. Consequently, what citizens share is nothing more or less than being in on the dialogues over how and by whom power is exercised which take place both within and over the rules of the dialogues.

Agreement, when it occurs, is always non-consensual to some extent. At its best, free individuals and groups establish a certain provisional overlapping consensus as the result of a critical dialogue within and on the spatial-temporal field of power and norms in which they find themselves. But, for any number of reasons, the best of agreements remains potentially open to reasonable disagreement and dissent.[6] Hence, participation is a strategic-communicative game in which citizens struggle for recognition and rule, negotiate within and sometimes over the rules, bargain, compromise, take two steps back, start over again, reach a provisional agreement or agree to disagree, and learn to govern and be governed in the context of relatively stable irresolution where the possibility of dissent is an implicit "permanent provocation" which affects the negotiations. What shapes and holds individuals and groups together as "citizens" and "peoples" is not this or that agreement but the free agonic activities of participation themselves.

When these activities are unavailable or arbitrarily restricted, the members of a political association remain "subjects" rather than "citizens" because power is exercised over them without their say, non-democratically. As a result, the political association is experienced as alien and imposed, as a structure of domination that is "unfree" and "illegitimate." Subjects turn to other loci of democratic participation that are available to them, and in these forums they debate how they can reform the larger political association so they can "get in" or how they can secede from it. The larger political association tends to instability and disintegration, and it is held together by force and fraud.

In a well-ordered constitutional democracy, many *ways* of participation are readily available. Citizens can participate both directly and indirectly in political dialogues: directly in public spheres, local initiatives, referenda, consultative meetings, political parties, elections, public service, interest groups, dissent, protest, civil disobedience, and the occasional rebellion; and indirectly, through relations of critical trust with their elected representatives, public servants, courts, "intermediary" organisations, and, especially, media-facilitated discussions. Second, in constitutional democratic federations such as the United Kingdom and the European Union, citizen participation is even more multifaceted. Citizens can participate in these direct and indirect ways in a range of overlapping structures of governance through which political power is exercised: in supranational, federal, national, provincial, regional, and municipal governments, as well as occasionally indirectly in constitutional negotiations. Third, over the last two decades, citizens of constitutional democracies have been positively encouraged to see themselves as the bearers of popular sovereignty and their governments as citizen-centred, and to exercise their rights of citizen participation.

In seeking to engage in the seeming plenitude of ways and broad range of institutions, citizens have come up against two quite different kinds of arbitrary constraints or blockages in the very practices of governance in which they have been encouraged to participate directly and indirectly. These constraints subject them to a form of citizen identity or self-knowledge and a mode of citizen conduct or control, with regard to both the form and loci of participation, without their say. They find themselves unfree in the very activities in which they are supposed to constitute themselves as free citizens and peoples. It is these two types of non-democratic constraints or "forms of subjection" that have been called into question by struggles for recognition and the search for new political space.[7]

Diverse Forms of Citizen Participation

In any game of governance, there are what Habermas calls "relations of inter-subjective recognition" under which the actors involved recognise each other as citizens and governors and in accordance with which they are constrained to conduct themselves in order to be counted as players. These rules of recognition as participants include types of knowledge, standard forms of conduct, and relations of power that govern the negotiations between citizens and governors. These involve such things as who is included and excluded, the language used, cultural ways affirmed or disregarded, religious holidays and practices taken into account and those ignored, genres of argumentation, times and places of political activity, overt and covert behaviour, and so on (Young 1996). In many cases, as Habermas puts it, political dialogues and negotiations cannot avoid upsetting, either intentionally or not, the prevailing relations of recognition:

> Practical discourses [political dialogues] cannot be relieved of the burden of social conflicts to the degree that theoretical and explicative discourses can. They are less free of the burdens of action because contested norms tend to upset the balance of relations of intersubjective recognition. Even if it is conducted with discursive means, a dispute about norms is still rooted in the struggle for recognition.
>
> (Habermas 1995, 106)

When the multicultural citizens of contemporary democracies came forward to participate in the direct and indirect *ways* and in the *range* of structures of governance, they found that the forms of recognition under which they had to act in order to be acknowledged as "citizens" placed arbitrary constraints on the diverse, identity-related forms of thought and action that matter to them, and by which they engage in citizen activities. The prevailing forms of recognition that block these diverse modes of being citizens are experienced as "structures of domination" because they are not readily open to question and the free exchange of reasons. They are presented as the background conditions of free and equal participation. Moreover, they are "arbitrary" in the sense that, while they are often put forward as neutral or universal, they favour the forms of participation appropriate to the practical identities of those groups who have dominated the public institutions for decades: the well-to-do, the able, heterosexuals, males, members of the dominant linguistic, cultural, ethnic, national and religious groups, and so on, and they discriminate against and often exclude others (Taylor 1994). If citizens wish to participate, and so *become* citizens, they have two strategic choices: either to participate within and assimilate to the given structures of recognition, and so perpetuate the biased system, or to challenge and negotiate the prevailing forms of recognition so they can participate on a par with the others: that is, to negotiate the rules of intersubjective recognition.

In the struggles for "mutual" recognition that follow from the clash of these two strategies, women, gays and lesbians, linguistic minorities, immigrants and refugees, religious and cultural groups, suppressed nations within larger multinational associations, and Indigenous peoples have demanded that they be able to participate in ways that recognise and respect, rather than assimilate and demean, their diverse forms of identity-related conduct (including their practices of reflecting on and changing their identity-related conduct), such as gender-related differences, sexual orientation, languages, cultures, religions, nationalities, and indigeneity. These struggles to negotiate the dominant forms of citizen participation so that they accommodate those practical identities that withstand the test of the critical exchange of public reasons pro and con can be classified into three main types, according to the demands they make on the direct and indirect ways of democratic participation, and the range of forms of governance in which citizens can participate. The three types of demand are for the recognition and accommodation of cultural diversity, participatory diversity, and federal diversity.

First, cultural diversity. All these struggles for recognition involve demands to negotiate the ways in which some citizens are currently disrespected and misrecognised or not recognised in the broad sphere of cultures and values where citizens first learn their dialogue attitudes. The aim is to expose and overcome racism, sexism, ableism, ethnocentrism, sexual harassment, linguistic and cultural stereotypes, and other forms of overt and covert diversity-blind speech and behaviour, and to foster an awareness of and respect for cultural diversity in all areas of society, so all citizens can participate in accord with the constitutional democratic principle of mutual respect.

Second, participatory diversity. Some demands are to participate in the existing public institutions of democratic societies in different ways from the members of the dominant groups. The women's movements, gays and lesbians, linguistic, and cultural and religious minorities wish to participate in the dominant practices of governance but to modify them so they can participate in ways that protect and respect their identity-related differences: to be able to speak and hear a minority language in schools, in the media, in political institutions and elections, to have daycare facilities so that women and single parents can participate on a par with heterosexual males, same sex benefits, to have participation-enhancing facilities for the disabled and unemployed so their concerns can be heard, to observe a religious or cultural practice in public and public service without disadvantage, for charters of rights to be interpreted in a diversity-sensitive manner, and so on, so that they can participate equally, but not identically, with others.[8]

Third, federal diversity. Some demands are not to participate in the same institutions in different ways, as in participatory diversity, but to participate in different democratic institutions. For example, provinces, regions, and states within constitutional, democratic federations demand to take part in federal-provincial negotiations and policy formulation in ways that respect their provincial and regional differences and enable them to govern, or share governance, in areas that affect them in a distinct way. In Spain, Belgium, the United Kingdom, the European Union, Canada, and Australia, for example, nationalists and Indigenous peoples argue that citizen participation in a way that protects and enhances their identity-related differences – their nationhood and Indigenous self-determination – requires that they exercise those powers of self-rule that affect these characteristics in their own democratic institutions, on their own territories, and in their own languages and ways. For, if they try to exercise them in the dominant institutions of the larger constitutional associations, they will be overwhelmed by the majority, and forced to participate and be governed in an assimilative and alien manner; that is, non-democratically, with the consequences noted above of disintegration and secession.

Throughout the world, this type of demand is met by the "federalization" of practices of governance: by forms of regional autonomy, subsidiarity, dispersed and shared sovereignty, and types of federal and confederal arrangements. Since federalisation is given in recognition of demands for one type of diverse form of citizen participation (federal), it follows from the reciprocal commitments immanent in political dialogues that the democratic federal institutions established to accommodate nations and Indigenous peoples should in turn be open to the consideration of demands for the recognition of the cultural and participatory diversity of their internal minorities (Gagnon and Tully 2001).

I would like to point out four features of these three types of struggle for diverse forms of citizen participation. First, although they have been extensively analysed in a number of descriptive and normative ways by liberals, communitarians, nationalists, feminists, and post-moderns, these forms of interpretation have tended to overlook the rather obvious point that they are democratic struggles to negotiate the prevailing and biased ethos of citizen participation, and that they can be analysed, both descriptively and normatively, in these terms. As a result, the processes through which members of constitutional democracies are constituted and constitute themselves as citizens are shifting in ways that the standard theories have failed to illuminate.

Second, demands for diverse forms of citizen participation involve agonic dialogues and negotiations in which *audi alteram partem* (always listen to the other side) is the immanent rule of reciprocity. They are struggles *against* the prevailing structures of recognition that subject some citizens to a non-democratic form of identity and mode of governance, with the aim of modifying these, and they are demands *to* other citizens who defend the current forms of recognition or who also seek to modify them, but in different ways, to whom one must listen and with whom one must negotiate. That is, in any demand for recognition, citizens need to listen to other cultural, participatory, or federal demands that may be silenced and ensure that they are empowered to participate in the negotiations if any kind of agreement is to be free and democratic: that is, where all those affected have a direct or indirect say. From this perspective, the demands are all of a piece. They are that the rules of intersubjective recognition be open to question and subject to the interplay of reasons and redescriptions among free and equal citizens. The identity politics of multicultural citizens and the struggles for recognition of suppressed nations and Indigenous peoples in multinational associations are not different in kind or necessarily incompatible, as is often assumed.

Third, the struggles over diverse forms of citizen participation cannot be settled once and for all. It is a game of politics that aims not at an end-state or final goal but, rather, at the free activity of citizen dialogues on the conditions of citizenship over time and generations. It is unfortunate that the Hegelian term "recognition" has been used to characterise and study them, for it suggests that there is an end-state: namely, getting the form of mutual recognition all those concerned demand. But this is a dangerous illusion, as Hegel himself realised. What these different struggles for recognition are about is not achieving an ideal consensus on some definitive recognition of an "authentic" communitarian or "autonomous" liberal identity, as the two standard approaches assume (Cooke 1997). As Arendt and Wittgenstein would surely say, these approaches look for a goal beyond the game on the one hand or a sovereign will behind it on the other and overlook the free concrete activity of the political game itself.

Identity politics and struggles for recognition are agonic games in which the contestants seek to modify and often reverse the rules of recognition of the game, not once and for all, but as their identities and diverse ways of being themselves change over time and generations, often as the result of participation in dialogues with diverse others. Nothing has changed more, for example, than the identities of men and women, of diverse citizens, over the last twenty years as a result of their participation in the three types of negotiation for and against diverse forms of citizen participation.[9] The identities up for recognition are shaped and formed not only by the interplay of the dialogues in which they are presented to recalcitrant and equally demanding others but also by the three types of institutional arrangements in which their mutual accommodation is experimented with, reviewed, and contested again. The game is to ensure that the rules of recognition do not become sedimented but are themselves open to the practices of freedom, so citizens are able to amend them *en passant,* and, in so doing, modify their identities, with as little unnecessary domination as possible. They are paradigmatic struggles *for* and *of* democratic participation in their own right. This is to say that we can gain a better grasp of what is happening in these disputes if we approach them more from a Nietzschean than a Hegelian viewpoint, as Foucault suggests:

I do not think that a society can exist without power relations, if by that one means the strategies by which individuals try to direct and control the conduct of others. The problem, then, is not to try to dissolve them in the utopia of completely transparent communication but to acquire the rules of law, the management techniques, and so the morality, the *ethos,* the practice of the self, that will allow us to play these games of power with as little domination as possible.

(Foucault 1997, 298)

Fourth, struggles for recognition are not simply symbolic or restricted to the cultural sphere, as opposed to struggles for the redistribution of wealth, as critics attached to the model of a unified and uniform class struggle often charge (Young 1997; Phillips 1997). As we have seen, the first kind of diversity of citizen participation, cultural diversity, comes closest to being a purely cultural phenomenon. However, even here, to rid democracies of racism, sexism, and ethnocentrism and foster respect for cultural diversity would itself have substantive effects in redistributing education, jobs, and income. Second, participatory diversity involves the redistribution of access to political power so that oppressed and excluded minorities and women may participate equally. If the proposed equity policies in the public and private sectors, the proposals for proportional representation, electoral reform, and a host of other recommendations to modify the forms of participation in the institutions of contemporary societies were enacted, they would bring about an enormous shift in the present unjust concentration of and access to political and economic power. Third, the demands for federal diversity by regions and nations within multinational associations effect not only symbolic change, but a more equitable distribution of political and economic power. Struggles for diversity of forms of citizen participation, therefore, should be analysed along three axes: their effects on cultural relations of intersubjective recognition, on relations of political power, and on the distribution of economic power (Foucault 2000, 344–5; Dean 1999).

Diverse Practices of Governance in Which Citizens Participate

Let us now turn to the second aspect of the ethos of contemporary politics that is brought to light by the reorientation to the concrete practices of freedom: the diverse practices or sites where citizens demand to participate. These illustrate the point I attributed to Wittgenstein and Foucault: democratic games of modifying the rules of governance are not restricted to the formal institutions of constitutional democracy but can occur in any practice of governance.

The direct and indirect ways of participation and the range of formal practices of governance in which citizens can participate have been expanded in the last two decades, mostly under the pressure of the three types of struggle for diverse forms of participation. However, there is a different kind of diversification of practices of governance and citizenship that needs to be treated separately, even though the two are connected in various ways. Today, citizens assemble, provoke dialogue, negotiate, and contest forms of governance outside the formal institutions of representative democracy. They participate directly at a multiplicity of sites: the local and international sites of resource industries to challenge the way the environment is governed, workplaces throughout the world, shareholders' meetings, gatherings of global regulatory agencies, the United Nations, struggles concerning human rights and cultural differences, through non-governmental and volunteer organisations, the delivery of public services and contracted-out daycare facilities, and at a host of other locations that were formerly said to be in the private sector or beyond democratic control. Citizens demand here and now that the stakeholders sit down and negotiate the way the game in dispute is being governed both locally and globally (Magnusson 1996).

These diverse informal practices of citizens thinking globally and acting locally to contest non-democratic forms of governance can be analysed of course as social movements or as proto-struggles for the eventual extension and establishment of formal institutions of "cosmopolitan" or "post-Westphalian" democracy in the very long run (Held 1995; Linklater 1998). However, from the vantage point opened up by Arendt and Foucault, they can also be seen as novel and relatively enduring practices of free, democratic activity in the present, of what Richard Bellamy and Dario Castiglione call multiple *demoi* (Bellamy and Castiglione 1998). The proof of both their novelty and their relative permanence is the proliferation of new disciplines of dispute resolution, mediation, and negotiation, distinct from the traditional disciplines of the political sciences, to educate professionals to take part in these practices, and to monitor and reform them.

To see this, recall that any form of human organisation is a practice of governance, involving relations of intersubjective recognition, power, modes of conduct, and strategies of freedom, whether it is an educational institution, bureaucracy, firm, a ministry, regulatory regime, or government in the formal sense. As Foucault puts it:

> The forms and the specific situations of the government of men [and women] by one another in a given society are multiple: they are superimposed, they cross, impose their own limits, sometimes cancel one another out, sometimes reinforce one another.
>
> (Foucault 2000, 345)

Any practice of governance will be "democratic" and involve freedom on our definition just insofar as the members of the organisation have some say and the opportunity to negotiate the way and by whom the power to govern their conduct is exercised in the organisation.

Although the term "government" was used in this non-restricted sense in early-modern Europe to refer to any practice of governance, in the development of European nation states, "government" came to be associated with and restricted to the formal institutions of representative constitutional democracies (Foucault 2000, 341). Additionally, the term "democracy," which formerly stood for any *ad hoc* assembly of people in negotiation, came to be associated with "representative democracy" in the late eighteenth century by "ingrafting," as Thomas Paine classically argued, "representation upon democracy" (1987, 281). Moreover, as modern nation states have consolidated, the multiplicity of practices of governance throughout society have tended to come under the "auspices" of the formal central governmental institutions of representative democracies in one way or another (Foucault 2000, 345). As long as this trend held, citizen participation tended to concentrate on the formal institutions of government and the public sphere and political scientists and theorists tended to restrict their study of citizenship to these institutions of formal representative democracy.

What is now occurring under the historical processes of "globalisation" is that the multiplicity of forms of governance no longer tends to be gathered together only or predominantly under the auspices of the formal governmental institutions. There is in addition a widely noted counter-tendency towards the dispersion or diversification of practices of government. Practices of governance without formal government are expanding, not only within constitutional democracies, as Foucault has shown in his historical studies, but also in the international realm, as James Rosenau (1998) has argued. Effective political power can no longer be assumed to be located in representative governments alone. It is dispersed – shared, negotiated, and contested by diverse agencies at the local, regional, national, and international levels. The systems of formal representative democratic government persist, of course, but they are crossed by complex economic, organisational, administrative, legal, and cultural processes and structures that limit and escape their efficacy and grasp (Held 1998).

Most of the dispersed practices of governance from local workplaces to global regulatory regimes are non-democratic. They coordinate the forms of self-consciousness and activities of those subject to them behind their backs, through unelected bureaucracies or market mechanisms. Nevertheless, as we have seen, it is always possible to contest and negotiate the form of governance of any organisation: to graft democratic practice on to it. If the terms "democracy" and "participation" are used to refer only to the formal institutions of representative government, then these local and global struggles to democratise decision making in dispersed practices of governance will not be seen as democratic practices. However, the boundary drawn around the use of "democracy" in the eighteenth century can be contested and its use can be extended (or re-extended) to refer to any activity in which people assemble and negotiate the way and by whom power is exercised over them, on the ground that these too are games of "governance" (in the non-restrictive sense). In this light, then, the struggles around dispersed practices of governance can be seen and analysed as the democratic forms of citizen participation that accompany globalisation.

The trend to the dispersion of governance has increased during the current period of neo-liberalism. A number of regimes of governance which were under the auspices of representative institutions during the earlier period of welfare liberalism have been contracted out or devolved to quasi-public and private organisations. The regulatory regimes of NAFTA, private arbitration in international law, the gutting of environmental regulation and monitoring, and the downsizing of public services are well-known examples. According to neo-liberal theorists, these would be shielded from democratic control and citizens would not be interested in participating in them. However, citizens have not been as apathetic as predicted. They have demanded to participate democratically in the exercise of these so-called privatised regimes of governance in two distinct ways.

First, they have sought to democratise public services wherever they take place. In response to the downsizing of the public services, citizens have demanded engagement in the formulation and the delivery of public services, whether they are contracted out to quasi-public bodies or devolved to the volunteer sector. That is, they have demanded to be treated as "agents" or "citizens" rather than as "subjects" or passive recipients of services, as under welfare liberalism, or as non-recipients, as under neo-liberalism. They have responded in novel ways to the contracting out and downsizing of public services, creating various kinds of partnerships and "associative" democratic practices. The emergence of these so-called citizen-centred governments around the determination and delivery of "public services" is changing the face of the public service in Europe, Australia, and Canada in a way that cannot be explained in terms of either the welfare liberal or the neo-liberal models (Dean 1999).

The second way citizens have responded to the dispersion of practices of governance is to participate directly at specific sites of struggle in order to democratise the global processes that the formal democratic institutions fail to govern. This has taken two forms. The first is to try to reconnect decision making over global processes to formal democratic institutions (partly through the three types of democratic reform discussed above). This is not always possible, either because the economic elites who block democratic reform of the forms of participation are too powerful or because the global processes in question can escape even responsive formal representative institutions. In this case, citizens act directly on the site where the global processes affect them.

These *ad hoc* assemblies of democratic dialogue over the governance of the workplace, environment, gender roles, refugees, and so on are strategic and communicative. They provoke dialogue, set up consultation procedures, bring in local and regional stakeholders, set up inquiries, connect electronically with a global network of similar sites and similar non-democratic practices, call on experts near and far, invent campaigns to hold their governors to the negotiating table, coordinate and negotiate across cultural, gender and class differences, use some aspects of globalisation (such as media and international law) to contest others, find ways to hold their adversaries to their agreements and implementations or bring them back to the table, try to interest municipal, regional and national governments in their struggle, bargain and compromise, and start all over again if necessary. Such games are surely democratic practices of citizen freedom in their own right. They have a validity on their own terms, whether or not they cross a boundary or two in the vocabulary of democracy drawn in the eighteenth century and placed in the framework, and whether or not they may lead to the establishment of more formal institutions in some cosmopolitan future. There is something happening *here* which is not exactly clear, but it will not be clarified by predicating of it what lies in these ideal forms of representation, for the activity takes precisely "the form of a possible crossing-over *(franchissement)*" of one or other of these boundaries (Foucault 1997, 315). In so doing, the participants call "something into being, which did not exist before, which was not given, not even as a cognition or imagination, and which therefore, strictly speaking, could not be known" (Arendt 1977, 151).

Consequently, the concrete practices of freedom are not only modifying the forms and loci of democratic citizenship in novel ways. They are also modifying the rules of political studies. These forms of governance and strategies of freedom require political research and analysis tied closely to the specific systems in which the disputes and resolutions occur: what the contestants do and how they do it. They require a form of analysis which delineates the types of expert knowledge and relations of power employed locally and globally, the strategic possibilities of their modification, and the actual practices of negotiation and implementation that are brought into being and carried through by the citizens involved. As we have seen, both Arendt and Foucault hoped for this sort of change in political studies.

In summary, two types of political struggle are changing in fundamental ways the ethos of citizenship and democracy. These changes are poorly understood when they are viewed from the formal institutions of constitutional democracy and the theoretical approaches that have developed around them since the eighteenth century. The changes in citizenship and democracy can be understood and analysed more perspicuously if they are viewed from the perspective of the free activities of the citizens engaged in them, as struggles of and for more democratic forms and practices of participation in the games in which we are governed. And these struggles can be seen in turn as manifestations of an impatience for what Arendt and many other citizens call freedom.

Notes

1 This is a revised version of the Hannah Arendt Memorial Lecture presented at the University of Southampton, June 9, 1998. I would like to thank the members and students of the Department of Politics and especially Dr. David Owen for inviting me to give this distinguished lecture and for their hospitality during my stay. I also wish to express my debt to the outstanding scholarship of Dr. David Owen (see Owen 1994, 1995, 1999).
2 See Arendt (1998, 1990).
3 See Foucault (2000, 95). He first sketched his non-sovereign account of freedom in (2000, 326–48).
4 I discussed this orientation in more detail in Tully (2008a, 71–131).
5 For the alternative approaches mentioned in this paragraph, see Gutmann (1994), Held (1995), Honneth (1995), Benhabib (1996).
6 Foucault (1984, 374–80) mentions two reasons. Rawls (1993, 54–8) mentions six.

7 Foucault (2000, 332) argues that these general sorts of struggle against imposed forms of subjectivity are "becoming more and more important" in our time but they are not new. They can be traced back to the Reformation and the emergence of pastoral power.

8 As with the principle of mutual respect in the first type of case, the principle of equality is not contested but interpreted in a way that permits changes in the political ethos: culturally diverse forms of participation (Tully 1995, 2008b, 15–42; Taylor 1994).

9 These are precisely the sorts of change in identity and conduct that Foucault suggests should be studied (1997, 316).

5 The Historical Formation of Common Constitutionalism

The Rediscovery of Cultural Diversity, Part 1 (1995)

The Hidden Constitutions of Contemporary Societies

In this chapter, I approach the labyrinth of contemporary constitutionalism by another path; from the perspective of the struggles to gain recognition of diverse cultures over the last four centuries.* In the course of these intercultural encounters, contemporary constitutionalism has been shaped in various aspects to recognise and accommodate cultural diversity. Specifically, the three conventions of the common language of constitutionalism arose in these contests. Of course, modern constitutionalism continues to reign in its imperial splendour, but the aspects I will now sketch are not simply minor disturbances on the frontier of modern constitutionalism, destined to disappear as it progresses. They only appear that way from its perspective. That is "the thing about progress," Nestroy discerned over a century ago, "it appears much greater than it actually is" (1962, 695).[1]

The recognition and accommodation of cultural diversity in the broader language of contemporary constitutionalism discloses what might be called the "hidden constitutions of contemporary societies." They are hidden by the rule of modern constitutionalism and the narrow range of uses of its central terms. As contemporary societies begin to enter a post-imperial age, a vast undergrowth of cultural diversity and its partial recognition in constitutions has begun to come to light as the shadow of the imperial epoch begins to recede. This discovery flies in the face of the seven features of modern constitutionalism: diversity is not a thing of the past, it does not conform to the stages view of historical development, and modern constitutionalism did not trickle down unchanged from the European centre to the non-European periphery.

The first sites where hidden constitutions appear are in the writings and constitutional arrangements of the agents of justice who have sought to come to terms with powerful, non-European cultures, immigrants, women, and linguistic and national minorities fighting for cultural survival. On the intercultural common grounds between the relentless momentum of modern

* Editor's note: All chapter citations refer to Tully (1995).

DOI: 10.4324/9781003227403-8

constitutionalism and the tenacity of other cultures one finds "contrapuntal ensembles" of three conventions which facilitate the recognition and accommodation of cultural diversity. No doubt, these grounds are deeply distorted by relations of domination and inequality and shot through with broken promises and fraudulent designs. Yet for all that, they are places where ancient reluctant conscripts have said "enough," stood their ground or taken the ruins of their culture with them in exile, and so bent the yoke of constitutionalism to fit their diverse necks.

The second places where hidden constitutions have been discovered are in the applications of constitutional law in particular cases, especially but not exclusively in the common law of Commonwealth countries and international law. This "casuistry" of cultural differences and similarities is a remarkable aspect of contemporary jurisprudence. Rather than forcing citizens and institutions to fit the uniform of modern constitutionalism, the language of constitutionalism has been shaped to fit the cultural diversity of citizens and institutions in practice. To put this in a slightly different way, the genres or forms of reasoning developed in the common law to deal with the customary diversity of the ancient constitutions of pre-modern European societies did not disappear with the rise of modern constitutionalism. They have continued to evolve in practice, and others have been added, despite the official view in theory that they should have been replaced by the more abstract form of reasoning typical of the modern theorists.

The discovery of these two aspects of contemporary constitutionalism was marked by the establishment in the 1980s of a new interdisciplinary field of anthropology, history, law, and political philosophy called legal pluralism. Legal pluralism is the study of the variety of ways contemporary constitutions recognise and accommodate cultural diversity. It began with the discovery by Clifford Geertz, Sally Falk Moore, and others that post-colonial societies are constituted by a wide variety of legal and customary systems of authority that cannot be accurately represented in the language of modern constitutionalism. Scholars such as Roderick MacDonald, Jon Elster, and John Griffiths then turned their attention to modern European societies and discovered a variety of normative orders and ways of accommodating struggles for recognition that exist in practice despite the reign of modern constitutionalism. As a result, Clifford Geertz and the many scholars who have been moved by his long and involved journeys have begun to explore the post-imperial landscape of cultures and constitutions which I introduced in the first chapter.

Permit me to frame my survey of the hidden constitutions with two images of constitutionalism. The first comes from René Descartes at the beginning of modern constitutionalism. Descartes is often thought of, especially in this century, as almost the founder of the kind of reform and rationalisation that drives the classic vision of modern constitutionalism. Yet nothing could be further from the truth. In the *Discourse on the Method*, he goes out of the way to show that the kind of radical reform he advocates for his own thoughts should be contrasted with his attitude towards constitutional change. He writes that, at first sight, thorough and systematic reform in accord with a central plan appears more reasonable than adjustment and accommodation to the assemblage of customs and laws that already exist:

> Thus we see that buildings undertaken and completed by a single architect are usually more attractive and better planned than those which several have tried to patch up by adapting old walls built for different purposes. Again, ancient cities which have gradually grown from mere villages into large towns are usually ill-proportioned, compared with those orderly towns which planners lay out as they fancy on level ground. Looking at the buildings of the former individually, you will often find as much art in them, if not more than in those of the latter; but in view of their arrangement – a tall one here, a small one there – and the way they make the streets crooked and irregular, you would say it is chance, rather than the will of men using reason, that placed them so.
>
> (Descartes 1985, 116)

The presumption of reform and regularisation in accord with a single plan is further enforced by the vision of Christianity, for "the constitution of the true religion, whose articles have been made by God alone, must be incomparably better ordered than all the others." Furthermore, he writes, we tend to favour reform and uniformity because we have the image of classical political philosophy before our eyes, in which "the basic laws [are] laid down by some wise law-giver." Moreover, this classical ideal is further reinforced by the image of Sparta, which is admired "because [all the laws] were devised by a single man and hence all tended to the same end." Yet, for all that, "we never see people pulling down all the houses of a city for the sole purpose of rebuilding them in a different style to make the streets more attractive." And, Descartes goes on to infer that it would be "unreasonable for an individual to plan to reform a state by changing it from the foundations up and overturning it in order to set it up again." He therefore concludes that in politics it is better to accommodate the assemblage of customs and ways of the people than to radically reform them:

> Any imperfections [political associations] may possess – and their very diversity suffices to ensure that many do possess them – have doubtless been much smoothed over by custom; and custom has even prevented or imperceptibly corrected many imperfections that prudence could not so well provide against. Finally, it is almost always easier to put up with their imperfections than to change them, just as it is much better to follow the main roads that wind through mountains, which have gradually become smooth and convenient through frequent use, than to try to take a more direct route by clambering over rocks and descending to the foot of precipices.
>
> (1985, 118)

You will say that these are "reactionary" reasons for accommodating diversity, whereas my first chapter made the politics of cultural recognition look "progressive." My response is to say that the uses of the terms "reactionary" and "progressive" here are fixed by the seven features of the language of modern constitutionalism I am trying to question in this book. In chapter 6, I will discuss ways of conceiving diversity and reasons for affirming it other than those advanced by Descartes.

What would Descartes' picture of the constitution of a city look like after three hundred years of modern constitutionalism? The answer is given, I believe, by Wittgenstein, who is often taken to be Descartes' greatest philosophical opponent. In one of the most famous passages of the *Philosophical Investigations*, Wittgenstein, thinking of his two homes, Vienna and Cambridge, compares language to an ancient city:

> Our language can be seen as an ancient city: a maze of little streets and squares, of old and new houses, and of houses with additions from various periods; and this surrounded by a multitude of new boroughs with straight and regular streets and uniform houses.
>
> (Wittgenstein 2009, §18)

This picture of the constitution of a city is strikingly similar to Descartes'. The difference is that, after three hundred years, constitutional reform has made its inroads. The ancient city, with its multiplicity of old, new, and overlapping additions, is now surrounded by "a multitude of new boroughs with straight and regular streets and uniform houses." Constitutional uniformity is not the "soul" of the city, as Pufendorf and other modern theorists suggested it should be. Neither Kant's nor Paine's republican constitution determines every aspect of the whole. Rather, the newer uniformity and regularity of modern constitutions forms a surrounding multitude of new boroughs around a maze of old and new formations and patchwork arrangements from many periods.

Understanding Constitutionalism: Wittgenstein and Hale

Wittgenstein introduces the analogy between language and an ancient city to illustrate the understanding of language one comes to acquire by working through all the examples carefully assembled in the *Philosophical Investigations*. Since this concept of understanding will enable us to understand the language of constitutionalism, let me review his main points. Language, like a city, has grown up in a variety of forms through long use and practice, interacting and overlapping in many ways in the endless diversity and strife of human activities. Like a city, it does not have a uniform constitution imposed by a single lawgiver, although, of course, areas of it have been made regular by reforms, just like some newer neighbourhoods of a city. Wittgenstein often just lists examples of "the multiplicity of language games" played with even the most seemingly univocal concepts to make his point, just as a civic guide would point to different boroughs, then to the diverse styles within each borough, then to the overlapping additions from various periods to make the analogous point (2009, §23). Consequently, the grammar of words is too multiform to be represented in a theory or comprehensive rule that stipulates the essential conditions for the correct application of words in every instance, just as there is no such comprehensive view of the constitution of a city. "We do not *command a clear view* of the use of our words," not because the definitive theory has yet to arrive, but because language "is lacking in this sort of perspicuity" (2009, §122). Like *The Spirit of Haida Gwaii* or a constitutional association, language is aspectival: "a labyrinth of paths. You approach from *one* side and know your way about; you approach the same place from another side and no longer know your way about" (2009, §203).

The analogy holds for the language of constitutionalism that is woven into the practices and institutions of contemporary societies. It is a labyrinth of terms and their uses from various periods, including the surrounding regular ways and uniform institutions of modern constitutionalism surveyed in chapter 3. The theorists and citizens who inhabit these modern suburbs are accustomed to their straight and narrow ways, characteristic forms of thought and relatively stable uses, and they tend to presume that their ways should determine the whole. The presumption is that the identity of modern constitutions consists of some combination of seven essential features. These features provide the comprehensive rule by which all political associations and their institutions are identified and ranked on a scale of historical development. This form of representation is not taken as one arrangement of the data of constitutionalism from the parochial perspective of a few members of one neighbourhood, to be compared and negotiated in dialogue with others, but the way the data are arranged by historical processes of modernisation. The only range of disagreement in understanding constitutionalism is over the interpretation and application of this great map by the three authoritative schools. This map is then projected over the whole, hiding the diversity beneath.

Wittgenstein calls the presumption of such a comprehensive theory "the craving for generality." The craving has its source partly in "our preoccupation with the method of science." It is accompanied by a "contemptuous attitude towards the particular case." The idea that "to get clear about the meaning of a general term" it is necessary "to find the common element in all its applications" has "shackled" philosophy: "for it has not only led to no result, but also made the philosopher dismiss as irrelevant the concrete cases, which alone could have helped him to understand the usage of the general term" (1972, 17–20). The image of an ancient city graphically illustrates the way that the craving for generality overlooks and generates a contemptuous attitude towards the irreducible multiplicity of concrete usage that defeats its aspiration. This illustration is backed up with two lines of argument in the

Philosophical Investigations that expose the mistake in the presumption and present the correct way to understand general terms.

The first argument shows that understanding a general term is not the theoretical activity of interpreting and applying a general theory or rule in particular cases. By using examples of signposts and maps, Wittgenstein shows that such a general rule fails to account for precisely the phenomenon we associate with understanding the meaning of a general term: the ability to use a general term, as well as to question its accepted use, in various circumstances without recursive doubts. No matter how elaborate such a rule might be, it is always possible to interpret and apply it in various ways. "Does the sign-post leave no doubt open about the way I have to go? Does it shew which direction I am to take when I have passed it; whether along the road or the footpath or cross-country?" (2009, §85).

If I am in doubt about how to interpret and follow the rule, or if I can interpret it in endless ways, then the rule and its interpretation "do not determine meaning." So, even if a theorist could provide a theory which specified the exhaustive conditions for the interpretation and application of the general terms of constitutionalism in every case, as modern theorists from Hobbes to Rawls have sought to do, this would not enable us to understand constitutionalism. For interpretative disagreements would arise over how to apply and follow the conditions, as indeed they do over the interpretation of the classic and contemporary theories, thereby pragmatically proving Wittgenstein's point.

Rather, understanding a general term is nothing more than the practical activity of being able to use it in various circumstances: "there is a way of grasping a rule which is *not* an *interpretation*, but which is exhibited in what we call 'obeying the rule' and 'going against it' in actual cases." Such a grasp is not the possession of a theory, but the manifestation of a repertoire of practical, normative abilities, acquired through long use and practice, to use the term and go against customary use in actual cases. The uses of general terms, he concludes, are intersubjective "practices" or "customs," like tennis or the "practice" of law. Our understanding of them consists in the "mastery" of a "technique" or practical skill "exhibited" in being proficient players in the particular cases or "language games" in which they are used (2009, §§198–201).

As Charles Taylor summarises in his article, "To Follow a Rule," Wittgenstein's argument has led to a revolution in philosophy and the human sciences. Nevertheless, some theorists, such as Peter Winch, have gone on to infer that people using general terms in the everyday activities of life are still following rules. The rules are said to be "implicit" or background "understandings" embedded in practice and shared by all members of a culture or community. The role of the theorist is then to make explicit the implicit rules embodied in practice in a culture or community. We have seen Rawls take this turn in his recent work, and many of the communitarians and nationalists mentioned in chapter 2 have done the same in order to try to resurrect grand theory from the ashes left by Wittgenstein's first argument. In so doing, these theorists of practice have uncritically retained the older assumption of cultures and communities as homogeneous wholes and insouciantly carried on with a contemptuous attitude towards particular cases. They have neglected Wittgenstein's second argument that the "grasp" exhibited in "obeying" or "going against" a rule in actual cases cannot be accounted for in terms of following general rules implicit in practice because the multiplicity of uses is too various, tangled, contested, and creative to be governed by rules.

Wittgenstein introduces this second line of argument with the example of the general term "game" in sections 65 and 66. He runs through various examples of games, showing that there is no one feature or set of features, such as "amusement," "skill," or "winning and losing," common to all, but various "similarities" and "relationships" among them. Some features are shared by a number of games, such as board games, but then pass to card games, where "the common features drop out and others appear." "I am saying," he writes, "that these phenomena have no one thing in common which makes us use the same word for all." As he moves through many examples, the upshot is not the discovery of a comprehensive rule implicitly followed in all cases, but "a complicated network of similarities overlapping and criss-crossing: sometimes overall similarities, sometimes similarities of detail," like the constitution of an ancient city.

If, Wittgenstein asks his interlocutor, "observation does not enable us to see any clear rule," and the person using a general term "does not know it himself," then what "meaning is the expression 'the rule by which he proceeds' supposed to have left to it here?" (2009, §82) "The application of a word," he roundly concludes, "is not everywhere bounded by rules." If the freedom of language use still must be described in terms of rules, then, he suggests, it is like a game "where we play and – make up the rules as we go along," or "one where we alter them – as we go along" (2009, §84).

Accordingly, the way to understand a general term is not to look in vain for implicit rules but, like tennis or law, to acquire the complex abilities to use it correctly in practice by working through and becoming proficient in various examples until one is able to go on oneself. Is the knowledge of a general term like "game," he asks, "somehow equivalent to an unformulated definition," as the theorists of practice presume? He then presents his revolutionary reply:

> Isn't my knowledge, my concept of a game, completely expressed in... my describing examples of various kinds of game; shewing how all sorts of other games can be constructed on the analogy of these; saying that I should scarcely include this or this among games; and so on.
>
> (Wittgenstein 2009, §75)

Hence, like many practical activities that are mastered by examples more than by rules, understanding a general concept consists in being able to give reasons why it should or should not be used in any particular case by describing examples with similar or related aspects, drawing analogies or disanalogies of various kinds, finding precedents and drawing attention to intermediate cases so that one can pass easily from familiar cases to the unfamiliar and see the relation between them. For example, in the first chapter I arranged the six examples of the politics of recognition so you could see three similarities among them. Section 66 on the general term "game" illustrates the technique and Wittgenstein then employs it throughout the *Philosophical Investigations* to solve philosophical problems.

The aim of this sort of language game with the general term in question – "the language game with the word 'game'" in Wittgenstein's example – is to employ intermediate examples which make manifest a connection with other cases so that a person understands why or why not the term should be used in this case. As the game proceeds and examples are assembled in various ways, the players come "to regard a particular case differently," to "compare it with *this* rather than *that* set of pictures" and hence to change their "way of looking at things," so they notice the aspects which render the case an instance of the general term or not (2009, §71, §144). Wittgenstein explains, "if I correct a philosophical mistake," I "must always point to an analogy according to which one had been thinking, but which one did not recognize as an analogy" (1993, 163). He calls the analogical activity of finding intermediate cases the giving of "further descriptions" and compares it to the way reasons are given in a court of law for and against a particular case (1993, 106).

Wittgenstein does not mean that the exchange of descriptions and redescriptions of examples to illuminate similarities and differences is some sort of preliminary exercise to the formulation of a general rule under which the concrete case can be subsumed, for, as we have seen, there is none:

> One gives examples and intends them to be taken in a particular way. – I do not, however, mean by this that he is supposed to see in those examples the common thing which I – for some reason – was unable to express; but that he is now to *employ* those examples in a particular way. Here giving examples is not an *indirect* means of explaining – in default of a better.
>
> (Wittgenstein 2009, §71)

> "The work of the philosopher," he simply states, "consists in assembling reminders for a particular purpose."
>
> (2009, §127)

The final aspect of Wittgenstein's two arguments I wish to draw to your attention is that his examples of understanding a general term by assembling examples always take place in dialogue with others who see things differently. The dialogical character of understanding is one of the many things he wishes to convey by calling the activity of understanding a "language game," for, like playing tennis, we grasp a concept by serving, returning, and rallying it back and forth with other players in conversations. Indeed, it is precisely the analogy between the use of words in dialogue and games like tennis that Wittgenstein thought of emphasising by selecting as a possible motto for the *Philosophical Investigations*, the line "I'll teach you differences" uttered by Kent to Oswald in *King Lear*, for the dialogue between them, in which the differences are taught and learned, is based on the analogy between word play and tennis play (Drury 1984, 157).

Since there is no comprehensive view of the uses of a general term, any monological view is always partial to some degree – noticing some aspects of usage at the expense of overlooking others. Any one description of examples, no matter how elaborate, will always be one heuristic way of characterising the case in question among others, not a "preconceived idea to which reality *must* correspond" (Wittgenstein 2009, §131). This is the point of his dictum that you approach from one side and know your way about; you approach the same place from another side and no longer know your way about. To understand a general term, and so know your way around its maze of uses, it is always necessary to enter into a dialogue with interlocutors from other regions of the city, to listen to their "further descriptions" and come to recognise the aspects of the phenomenon in question that they bring to light, aspect which go unnoticed from one's own familiar set of examples. Since there is always more than one side to a case, one must always consult those on the other side. As a result of exchanges of views by denizens from various neighbourhoods and the finding of examples which mediate their differences, a grasp of the multiplicity of cases is gradually acquired. Understanding, like the *Philosophical Investigations* itself, is dialogical.

These two lines of argument are presented in condensed form in section 122. After stating that a single, comprehensive view of the meaning of a general term is unobtainable, he introduces his alternative philosophy of the dialogical comparison and contrast of examples in actual cases as a *übersichtliche Darstellung* – a "perspicuous representation" or "survey" – that "produces just that understanding which consists in 'seeing connexions'." "Hence the importance," he continues, "of finding and inventing *intermediate cases*." He then underlines the importance of his discovery in an exceptionally direct remark:

> The concept of a perspicuous representation is of fundamental significance for us. It earmarks the form of account we give, the way we look at things. (Is this a "Weltanschauung"?).
>
> (Wittgenstein 2009, §122)

Wittgenstein's philosophy is an alternative worldview to the one that informs modern constitutionalism. First, contrary to the imperial concept of understanding in modern constitutionalism discussed at the end of the second chapter, it provides a way of understanding others that does not entail comprehending what they say within one's own language of redescription, for this is now seen for what it is: one heuristic description of examples among others; one interlocution among others in the dialogue of humankind. Second, it furnishes a philosophical account of the way in which exchanges of views in intercultural dialogues nurture the attitude of "diversity awareness" by enabling the interlocutors to regard cases differently and change their way of looking at things.

Finally, it is a view of how understanding occurs in the real world of overlapping, interacting, and negotiated cultural diversity in which we speak, act, and associate together. As a result, if we care to understand *The Spirit of Haida Gwaii*, Wittgenstein's philosophy explains why we must listen to the description of each member of the crew, and indeed enter the conversation ourselves, in order to find redescriptions acceptable to all which mediate the differences we wish each other to recognise. This is a way of doing philosophy and reaching mutual understanding fit for a post-imperial age of cultural diversity.

The general terms of the language of contemporary constitutionalism – constitutions, nations, societies, cultures, recognition, citizens, rights, sovereignty, justice, institutions, the common good, ancient and modern – are like games. David Kahane has corroborated Wittgenstein's second argument by exposing the poverty of attempts to explain the use of these concepts in particular cases by recourse to implicit rules and shared understandings. They are to be understood by surveying the actual cases of their use and the reasons given for and against their application, not only in the regular and uniform uses of modern constitutionalism, where the arrangement of examples has become fossilised, but also in the much broader range of uses in other neighbourhoods and boroughs. Of special importance will be sites where disputes and struggles have occurred and the dominant uses have been challenged and altered. The dialogues of Baron de Lahontan, the comparisons of Joseph Brant, and the further descriptions of other "marginal" writers will be canonical examples for us. This book is but one example of this form of survey which gradually loosens the grip of the theories of modern constitutionalism and discloses the diversity of contemporary constitutions and cultures that they conceal.

Wittgenstein suggests that the diverse similarities among instances of general concepts like games can be thought of as analogous to "family resemblances," for "the various resemblances between members of a family: build, features, colour of eyes, gait, temperament, etc., etc., overlap and criss-cross in the same way." Games "form a family" (2009, §67). In an analogous fashion, the constitutions and cultures of the world form a family – the criss-crossing Aboriginal and non-Aboriginal constitutions, new and old, provincial and federal, general agreements on trade and tariffs, global codes of human rights and environmental treaties, international laws of Aboriginal peoples, and so on. Moreover, within any constitutional association, the rights, institutions, and laws are not identical in every case, but vary with the interacting cultural diversity of the members, again forming a family; except, of course, in those areas where the overwhelming force of modern constitutionalism has crushed the agonic interplay of law and cultural freedom.

The direct relevance of Wittgenstein's arguments to our topic is confirmed by Wittgenstein himself. He first presented them in his "Remarks on Frazer's *Golden Bough*" (1930). In the early decades of the twentieth century, the anthropologist James George Frazer, like the theorists of modern constitutionalism, sought to understand a number of "primitive" practices of various "savage" societies by arranging them in the progressive scheme of historical development and judging them relative to the scientific practices of contemporary European societies. As a consequence, Wittgenstein remarks, Frazer "is more savage than most of his savages." Much as the African scholar V.Y. Mudimbe was to comment decades later in *The Invention of Africa*, Wittgenstein objects that it is "impossible" for him "to understand a different way of life from the English one of his time!" What Frazer does not realise is that "the explanation" in the form of "a hypothesis of development, is only *one* way of assembling the data." The purpose of this arrangement of the data, or any other, is heuristic and mediatory – "to sharpen our eye for a formal connection" among them. It is not, as Frazer assumes, a preconceived idea to which reality must correspond.

Wittgenstein then presents his alternative approach. The "factual material [the various practices]" can be arranged "so that we can easily pass from one part to another and have a clear view of it – showing it in a perspicuous way." This cryptic remark is immediately followed by the first draft of the passage which became section 122 of the *Philosophical Investigations* seventeen years later. In his notebooks, he is even more insistent that his approach be regarded as an alternative to the progressive and scientific form of thinking typical of modern European civilisation. Therefore, there is no question that he intended his arguments to be employed as I have used them: to question the imperial and monological form of reasoning we have found to be constitutive of modern constitutionalism (1993, 119–55).

Since the practical form of reasoning Wittgenstein describes is akin to the reasoning in individual cases at the common law, as Stephen Toulmin and Albert Jonsen have substantiated, it is not surprising that similar arguments were presented by one of the greatest common lawyers, Chief Justice Matthew Hale, against one of the founding theorists of modern constitutionalism, Thomas Hobbes. As we noticed in chapter 3, Hobbes presents his modern theory as a solution to what he saw as the disunity and irregularity of ancient constitutionalism. The metaphors he employs to persuade his readers are, as we might expect, almost the opposite of Descartes'. If the people expect their association to be anything other than "a crasie building, such as hardly lasting out their own time," then it must be constructed by "the help of a very able Architect." Rather than accommodating the constitution to the cultural diversity of the citizens, as Descartes recommends, *"every man* is to strive to *accommodate himself to the rest."* The architect is to view the diverse subjects he must render "plain" and "sociable" as "stones brought together for building of an Aedifice."

> For as that stone which by the asperity, and irregularity of Figure, takes more room from others, than it selfe fills; and for the hardnesse, cannot be easily made plain, and thereby hindereth the building, is by the builders cast away as unprofitable and troublesome.

Even more revealing is the kind of theoretical knowledge the architect needs and *Leviathan* provides. "The skill of making, and maintaining Commonwealths consisteth in certain Rules, as doth Arithmetique and Geometry; not (as Tennisplay) on Practise onely" (Hobbes 1996, 145).

Hale's trenchant reply is that the skill of making and maintaining a constitutional commonwealth is not a matter of a solitary, clever person deducing general rules from essential definitions. Rather, it is a practical skill that "must be gained by the habituateing and accustomeing and Exercising of that Faculty [of reasoning] by reading, study and observation," as well as by "Conversation between man and man." The reason why it is a practical skill acquired by "use and exercise" is that "actions, and the application of remedyes to them" are "so various," "different," and "diversified from another" that abstract rules are a hindrance rather than a help "when it comes to particulars." A man, like Hobbes, who has "a prospect" of "a few things may with ease enough fitt a Lawe" to "those things." But, he continues,

> the texture of Humane affaires is not unlike the Texture of a diseased bodey labouring under Maladies, it may be of so various natures that such Phisique as may be proper for the Cure of one of the maladies may be destructive in relation to the other.
>
> (Holdsworth 1937, 503–505)

Over three hundred years later, Albert Jonsen and Stephen Toulmin, commenting on the theories of Bentham and Rawls in the course of their history of reasoning by cases, draw much the same conclusion:

> If general, abstract theories in moral philosophy are read against their historical and social backgrounds, they will need to be understood not as making *comprehensive and mutually exclusive* claims but, rather, offering us *limited and complementary* perspectives on the whole broad complex of human conduct and moral experience, personal relations, and ethical reflection. So interpreted, none of these theories tells us the whole truth ... Instead, each of them gives us part of the larger picture.
>
> (Jonsen and Toulmin 1988, 293)

In *Reason and Rhetoric in the Philosophy of Hobbes*, Quentin Skinner shows that Hale's common-law view is typical of the Renaissance humanist culture against which Hobbes constructed his scientific alternative. The reasons that Renaissance humanists give for the practical and dialogical character of moral and political philosophy are similar to Wittgenstein's. One should always, they argue, listen to the other side (*audi alteram partem*) because it is always possible to speak on either side of a case (*in utramque partem*). The reason why this is always possible is that the criteria for the application of moral and philosophical concepts are so various and circumstantial, rather than essential and universal, that any case is always open to more than one description and evaluation, by means of comparisons and contrasts with other cases (what they call *paradiastole*). Therefore, the correct attitude or worldview is a willingness to exchange and negotiate alternative descriptions.

Hobbes sought to overcome the "uncertainty" of humanist moral and political philosophy and put it on a scientific and monological footing by setting out essential definitions and deducing general rules that any rational person would be compelled to accept. He thus initiated, as Quentin Skinner concludes, "the shift from a dialogical to a monological style of moral [and political] reasoning." The theorists of modern constitutionalism followed in Hobbes' footsteps so that "the very idea of presenting a moral or political theory in the form of a dialogue has long since lost any serious place in philosophy" (even though, ironically, the successive monological theories have been accompanied by debate and disagreement that only the humanist approach can explain) (Skinner 1996, 16).

This historical shift from a humanist to a scientific worldview turns on the assumption of essential definitions which Wittgenstein challenged three hundred years later. As a result, although Wittgenstein's arguments can be seen as the progenitor of a shift to post-modern humanism, as Dennis Patterson recommends, they can also be regarded as akin to the earlier common-law humanism that has been, like the trials of Rita Joe, covered over but not cast away by the architects of modern constitutionalism.

The great tragedy of the modern constitutionalism is that most European philosophers followed Hobbes and turned their backs on dialogue just when non-European peoples were encountered and dialogue and mediation were needed to avert the misunderstanding and inhumanity that followed. Let us now turn to examples of those few who listened to and negotiated with the others they encountered.

Examples of the Three Conventions: The Aboriginal and Common-Law System and the Conventions of Mutual Recognition and Consent

The following examples of the recognition and accommodation of cultural diversity illustrate the multiplicity of uses of the concepts of contemporary constitutionalism and disclose the hidden constitutions of contemporary societies. They also bring to light the three conventions of common constitutionalism: mutual recognition, continuity, and consent. Constitutional "conventions" in this common-law sense are norms that come into being and come to be accepted as authoritative in the course of constitutional practice, including criticism and contestation of that practice. They gradually gain their authority by acts in conformity with them and by appeals to them by both sides, as warrants of justification, when they are transgressed. These three conventions form the sturdy fibres of Ariadne's thread through the labyrinth of conflicting claims to cultural recognition which currently block the way to a peaceful twenty-first century. If they guide constitutional negotiations, the negotiations and resulting constitutions will be just with respect to cultural recognition.

The first and most spectacular example is the mutual recognition and accommodation of the Aboriginal peoples of America and the British Crown as equal, self-governing nations. This form of mutual recognition was worked out in the early modern period in a common association of "treaty constitutionalism." I would like to discuss it in some detail because it exhibits clearly the three conventions that ought to guide any diverse constitutional association. Once they are grasped in this case, it is easy to see how they can be applied analogously in different cases.

The problem of mutual recognition is classically formulated by John Marshall, the first Chief Justice of the Supreme Court of the United States, in his final and definitive judgement on US-Aboriginal relations in *Worcester v. the State of Georgia* of 1832 (Samuel Worcester's lawyers presented the case for Cherokee sovereignty):

> America, separated from Europe by a wide ocean, was inhabited by a distinct people, divided into separate nations, independent of each other and the rest of the world, having institutions of their own, and governing themselves by their own laws. It is difficult to comprehend the proposition, that the inhabitants of either quarter of the globe could have rightful original claims of dominion over the inhabitants of the other, or over the lands they occupied; or that the discovery of either by the other should give the discoverer rights in the country discovered, which annulled the pre-existing rights of its ancient possessors.
>
> (Marshall 1839, 426–7)

If the Aboriginal peoples of America are recognised as "independent nations," as Marshall argues, the initial conditions of constitutional theory and practice in North America are not any of the three formulations of popular sovereignty employed by the authoritative schools of modern constitutionalism surveyed in the previous lecture. Rather, the situation is a continent of over five hundred sovereign Aboriginal nations governing themselves by their own institutions and authoritative traditions of interpretation for roughly 20,000 years before Europeans arrive in the seventeenth century. The Europeans refuse to become immigrants of the existing Aboriginal nations, as the US and Canadian governments would certainly insist today in an analogous situation and demand instead that their nationhood be recognised and accommodated so they may govern themselves by their own laws and traditions.

The question is how can the people in this diverse form reach agreement on a constitutional association just to both parties. The answer was worked out through hundreds of treaty negotiations between agents of the Crown and the Aboriginal nations from the 1630s to 1832. In *Worcester*, Marshall reviewed the history of treaty making and presented a synopsis of the customary system of treaty constitutionalism that evolved over the previous two centuries. He took as a major precedent the Royal Proclamation of October 7, 1763, in which the Crown set out its understanding of the relations between British North America and the Aboriginal nations. The Proclamation, in turn, was based on a review of treaties since 1664, Royal Commissions on Indian Affairs since 1665, Royal Instructions to colonial administrators since 1670, the Board of Trade's recognition of Aboriginal sovereignty in 1696 (when Locke was a member) and in the case of the Mohegan nation versus Connecticut of 1705 (which John Bulkley attacked with Locke's arguments), and the advice of the Superintendent of Indian Affairs in North America, Sir William Johnson (Joseph Brant's step father). In addition, similar accounts of the treaty system were written by participants in treaty negotiations, such as Samuel Wharton, *Plain Facts: Being an Examination into the Rights of the Indian Nations of America to their Respective Territories* (1781), which Paine attacked in *The Public Good*, Cadwallader Colden, *The History of the Five Indian Nations of Canada* (1747), and Benjamin Franklin's collection of treaties (1762). The oral accounts of the treaties by members of the *Haudenosaunee* or Iroquois Confederation are partially recorded in *The Redman's Appeal for Justice: The Position the Six Nations that they Constitute an Independent State* (1924). Despite the efforts of the builders of modern constitutionalism to extinguish it, this ancient constitution is part of US constitutional law and Commonwealth common law, and remnants of it endure in practice down to this day.

The first convention of constitutional negotiations is to agree on a form of mutual recognition. In this case, it involves the mutual recognition of both parties as independent and self-governing nations. The initial reason Crown negotiators recognised the Aboriginal peoples as nations is that they did not redescribe the Aboriginal peoples in the forms of recognition constructed by the armchair European theorists. Instead, they simply listened to how the Aboriginal negotiators presented themselves in countless meetings. As William Johnson, the chief Crown negotiator, explained to the Lords of Trade in 1763:

> The Indians of the Ottawa Confederacy ... and also the Six Nations, however their sentiments may seem misrepresented, all along considered the Northern parts of North America, as their sole property from the beginning; and although the conveniency of Trade, (with fair speeches and

promises) induced them to afford both us and the French settlements in their Country, yet they never understood such settlement as a Dominion, especially as neither we, nor the French ever made a conquest of them.

(Johnson 1853, 575)

"They have even repeatedly said at several conferences in my presence," Johnson goes on to recount, that

> they were amused by both parties [the British and French] with stories of their upright intentions, and that they made War for the protection of the Indians rights, but that they plainly found, it was carried on to see who would become masters of what was the property of neither the one nor the other.
>
> (1853, 665)

The "Indians," Johnson summarises, are not "subject to" "our Laws" and they "consider themselves as a free people" (ibid.). In 1761, the Chippewa leader Minivavana enlightened the English trader Alexander Harvey at Michilimackinace in the following typical manner:

> Englishman, although you have conquered the French, you have not yet conquered us. We are not your slaves. These lakes, these woods and mountains, were left to us by our ancestors. They are our inheritances; and we will part with them to none.
>
> (Henry 1809, 44)

The second reason why Crown negotiators applied the term "nation" and "republic" to the Aboriginal peoples is that the forms of Aboriginal political organisation they observed, while not identical, were similar in a number of respects to European nations. They did not apply criteria that only seventeenth-century European nations met and conclude that Aboriginal peoples were savages at the lowest stage of development. As the terms of Marshall's description neatly illustrate, they were able to see the cross-cultural family resemblances between Aboriginal and European forms of political association. Whereas long use and occupation of a territory gave them jurisdiction, as the 1665 Royal Commission had ruled, the ability to govern themselves in accord with their own laws and ways for a long time and to have their independence recognised by other similarly organised peoples gave them nationhood.

The very term "nation," Marshall explains, "so generally applied to them, means 'a people distinct from others'." "The constitution" of the United States, "by declaring treaties" to be "the supreme law of the land," admits "their rank among those powers who are 'capable of making treaties'":

> The words "treaty" and "nations" are words of our own language, selected in our diplomatic and legislative proceedings by ourselves, having

each a definite and well understood meaning. We have applied them to Indians, as we have applied them to the other nations of the earth. They are applied to all in the same sense.

(Marshall 1839, 445)

For emphasis, he states that the United States stands to the Aboriginal nations just as it does to "the crowned heads of Europe" (1839, 435).

The reason why the agents of justice applied these looser criteria of nationhood, rather than the biased criteria of modern constitutionalism, is that they are the customary criteria used to recognise nationhood throughout Europe ever since Bartolus of Sassoferrato employed them to bring the Holy Roman Empire to recognise the independence of the Italian city states in the early fourteenth century. Marshall, for instance, was able to draw connections with intermediate examples of European nationhood and treaty making to make his case. In recognising the sovereignty of Aboriginal nations, therefore, the Crown was doing no more than applying to them the same standards European nations applied to each other. These common criteria of nationhood have persisted in the great struggles for national liberation in the nineteenth and twentieth centuries, against the attempts of existing nations to apply the restrictive criteria of modern constitutionalism, and they have regained currency in recent international law and the proposed law of Indigenous peoples.

The negotiators were quite aware that the Aboriginal peoples did not have European-style states, representative institutions, formalised legal systems, prisons, and independent executives. They observed the conciliar and confederal forms of government, consensus decision making, rule by authority rather than coercion, and customary law. Yet this did not cause them to situate the Aboriginal peoples in a lower stage of development. Quite the contrary. They were constantly instructed by the Privy Council to study and respect their constitutions and forms of government, ensure that they "not be molested or disturbed," and punish the "great frauds and abuses" committed against them by the settlers. Observers such as Cadwallader Colden, Benjamin Franklin, Baron de Lahontan, and Joseph-Francois Lafitau repudiated the judgement of the modern theorists and sided with Joseph Brant. They suggested that Europeans were at a lower and more corrupt stage of development and that Aboriginal nations, with their participatory governments, service to the public good and great diplomacy, were similar in stature to the classical republics.

The reasons why the Aboriginal nations reciprocally recognised the Europeans as nations are similar. The Aboriginal peoples who encountered Europeans in the first two centuries had long traditions of recognising each other as nations and entering into various forms of treaty alliances and confederations. This is especially true of the *Haudenosaunee* confederacy, whose constitution, the Great Law of Peace (*Gayaneshakgowa*), dates from the 1450s. It is nonetheless true of the Cherokee, Shawnee, Delaware,

Mohegan, Pequot, Ottawa, Huron, Mi'kmaq, and many others. When Europeans demanded recognition as nations and sought accommodation, Aboriginal peoples took up the demand in their customary forms of nation to nation recognition and adapted them, in the course of the negotiations, to the peculiarities of the case. Francis Jennings and his former students have shown in *The History and Culture of Iroquois Diplomacy* that the Europeans in turn accommodated their ways to the elaborate diplomatic practices of negotiation the Aboriginal leaders insisted on following. Like the European negotiators, Aboriginal peoples did not view this as a great founding moment, marking a transition from the state of nature to constitutional society, but as one link in a chain of multinational constitutional agreements that stretched back long before the newcomers arrived on Great Turtle Island and would long outlast their transgressions and disruptions of it. Aboriginal scholars Gerald Alfred and Mark Dockstator have shown that this continues to be the attitude of many Aboriginal people today.

Although both parties are recognised as nations, the Aboriginal nations are prior or "First Nations," as they are called in Canada, since they were in North America when the Europeans arrived. Once this form of mutual recognition was worked out, the only just way that the Crown could acquire land and establish its sovereignty in North America was to gain the consent of the Aboriginal nations. The convention of consent is the very one we have seen Locke and his followers finesse: *quod omnes tangit ab omnibus comprobetur*, "what touches all should be agreed to by all." Enshrined in the codex of Roman law, *q.o.t.* is the most fundamental constitutional convention. It applies to any form of constitutional association, ensuring that a constitution or an amendment to it rests on the consent of the people, or the representatives of the people who are touched by it. The way it should be applied depends on how the "people" are recognised.

Marshall rejects the anti-constitutional arguments of Locke and Kant that consent is unnecessary, as well as the questionbegging view of other modern theorists that the Aboriginal people could be treated as individuals or cultural minorities within sovereign European institutions and traditions of interpretation. The right of the "discovery" of a part of America by a European government did not give that European nation any rights over the Indigenous people, but only an exclusive right against other European nations to settle and acquire land from the Aboriginal occupants. It was simply a right that the European powers had agreed to among themselves. Applying *q.o.t.*, Marshall infers that it "could not affect the rights of those who had not agreed to it"; that is, "those already in possession, either as aboriginal occupants, or as occupants by virtue of a discovery before the memory of man" (1839, 427). Repudiating his earlier judgement in *Johnson and Graham's Lessee v. M'Intosh* (1823) that the Crown gained title by conquest, he states that the wars against the Indians were defensive and did not convey title.

Moreover, he mockingly asks, did "sailing along the coast," or "occasionally landing on it" give "property in the soil, from the Atlantic to the Pacific;

or rightful dominion over the numerous people who occupied it?" Or, ridiculing Locke and Vattel, "has nature," or "the Great Creator of all things, conferred these rights over hunters and fisherman, on agriculturalists and manufacturers?" (1839, 433).

The form of consent should always be tailored to the form of mutual recognition of the people involved. In this case, Marshall concludes, this is the form of "mutual consent" the Crown established in the treaty system and the United States inherited after the war of independence. In this system, the Crown negotiated, and continues to negotiate, with the First Nations to purchase territory from them, to gain their recognition of Crown government in America, and to work out various relations of protection and cooperation over time. In one of the most generous acts of recognition and accommodation in history, the Aboriginal nations in turn negotiated, and continue to negotiate, to cede land and settle boundaries, recognise the legitimacy of Crown governments, and work out relations of protection and cooperation. However, they consent to this on the condition that the Crown governments and their successors always respect the equal and prior sovereignty of the Aboriginal nations on the territories they reserve to themselves.

In treaty negotiations, Marshall notes, a "boundary is described, between nation and nation by mutual consent. The national character of each, the ability of each to establish this boundary, is acknowledged by the other" (1839, 441). The treaties "manifestly consider the several Indian nations as distinct political communities, having territorial boundaries, within which their authority is exclusive" (1839, 442). Hence, the treaty system is expressly designed not only to recognise and treat the Aboriginal people as equal, self-governing nations, but also to continue, rather than extinguish, this form of recognition through all treaty arrangements over time. Indeed, the legitimacy of *non*-Aboriginal governments in America depends on this continuity, for it is the condition of Aboriginal consent to recognise them. The proof of the Crown's commitment to continuity, Marshall claims (presumably in one of his more idealistic moods), is in the examples of its practice. Following closely the authoritative exposition of the Royal Proclamation by Superintendent Stuart of Indian Affairs for the southern division of British North America in Mobile in 1763, he writes:

> Certain it is that our history furnishes no example, from the first settlement of our country, of any attempt on the part of the crown to interfere with the internal affairs of the Indians, farther than to keep out the agents of foreign powers, who, as traders or otherwise, might seduce them into foreign alliances. The king purchased their lands, when they were willing to sell, at a price they were willing to take; but never coerced a surrender of them. He also purchased their alliance and dependency by subsidies; but never intruded into the interior of their affairs, or interfered with their self-government, so far as respected themselves only.
>
> (Marshall 1839, 431)

The Aboriginal and Common-Law System and the Convention of Continuity

The continuity of both parties' independent nationhood illustrates the third and final constitutional convention. The mutually recognised cultural identities of the parties continue through the constitutional negotiations and associations agreed to unless they explicitly consent to amend them. The convention of the continuity of a people's customary ways and forms of government into new forms of constitutional associations with others is the oldest in Western jurisprudence. As we discussed in chapter 3, it is the spirit of ancient constitutionalism, expressing the view that customs and ways of peoples are the manifestation of their free agreement. To discontinue them without their explicit consent would thus breach the convention of consent.

In the early modern law of nations, the convention holds even in the case of conquest. The customs and ways of a conquered people continue until the conqueror expressly discontinues them. If the conqueror recognises them, either expressly or by long acceptance, then his imperial right to discontinue them must yield to continuity. As Marshall knew and we shall see in chapter 5, the convention was applied in many of the most important constitutional agreements of the eighteenth century. The protection of Aboriginal governments in Royal Instructions and the Royal Proclamation is an example of the convention in practice.

The convention of continuity stands in opposition to the doctrine of discontinuity in, for example, Norman law. On this view, a new constitutional association, whether it is based on conquest or consent, discontinues or "extinguishes" the preexisting customs and ways of the people, and they are, as Marshall explains in *Johnson v. M'Intosh*, not "governed as a distinct people," but "incorporated with the victorious nation" and "blended with the conquerors," so "they make one people" (1839, 275). Hobbes presented the classic theory of constitutional discontinuity in *Leviathan* and many modern theorists followed suit in order to trump the resulting irregularity and assemblage of peoples and their ways the convention protects.

Therefore, no matter how many relations of protection and interdependency the Crown (and later, the US and Canadian governments) and Aboriginal governments enter into as a result of treaty making over the centuries, the identity of both parties as equal and sovereign nations continues, just as it does in other cases of international treaties. "The very fact of repeated treaties with them," Marshall writes, "recognises it." For example, the Aboriginal governments consent from time to time to delegate conditionally certain powers of self-government and to share powers of resource development. Neither of these complex constitutional arrangements, which now span over one thousand agreements across Great Turtle Island, affects their status as equal self-governing nations. Marshall explains how the convention of continuity applies to Aboriginal sovereignty throughout the treaties with the United States in the following way:

[T]he settled doctrine of the law of nations is, that a weaker power does not surrender its independence, its right of self-government, by associating with a stronger, and taking its protection. A weak state, in order to provide for its safety, may place itself under the protection of one more powerful, without stripping itself of the right of self-government, and ceasing to be a state. Examples of this kind are not wanting in Europe. "Tributary and feudatory states," says Vattel, "do not thereby cease to be sovereign and independent states, so long as sovereign and independent authority are left in the administration of the state."

(Marshall 1839, 446)

In this remarkable passage, the modern view that a constitutional association must give rise to one uniform sovereign state that is unlimited by external and internal interdependency is unceremoniously shown to be inadequate to the concrete cases of constitutionalism. The treaties give rise to a constitutional association of interdependence and protection, but not to discontinuity or subordination to a single sovereign. Marshall makes his point first by citing the convention of continuity then, surely with intended irony, by citing examples drawn from Emeric de Vattel, one of the advocates of the discontinuity of Aboriginal governments whom Marshall repudiated earlier. It does not bother him that the examples he cites are selected from "ancient" constitutionalism. Indeed, his point seems to be that feudal constitutions, in recognising forms of constitutional association that accommodate types of self-rule, are more liberal than the modern theories of liberal heroes like Vattel.

Seen in this unfamiliar light, the decision by the Crown and its representatives to recognise and continue the cultures of the Aboriginal nations appears as one of the most enlightened acts of the eighteenth century. The contrary tendency to discontinue and extinguish their cultural ways, justified in the imperial language of modern constitutionalism, appears regressive – the application of the doctrine of the Norman conquest. Yet the axis of this reversal of vision is not the post-modern deconstruction of constitutionalism, but the ancient convention of continuity. The convention continues the so-called ancient constitutions into the modern world, thereby rendering the constitutions of contemporary societies different from modern constitutional representations of them.

Let us now try to approach the treaty system from an Aboriginal point of view. Of course, the descriptions of the conventions will differ from Marshall's and mine, for there is no universal language of description, but if we can see family resemblances among them, then we are on the common ground.

The Two Row Wampum Treaty of the *Haudenosaunee* confederacy is one of the most famous exemplars of treaty constitutionalism between Aboriginal and non-Aboriginal peoples in America. The constitutional negotiations and relations between them are symbolised by belts of wampum beads exchanged at treaty discussions from 1664 to the negotiations between the *Haudenosaunee* confederacy and the Canadian and Quebec governments at Kanehsatake, Quebec, in 1990. The Two Row Wampum belt is the diplomatic *lingua franca* of Aboriginal and non-Aboriginal constitutionalism, recording the form of agreement reached and expressing the good will the agreement embodies.

A background of white wampum beads symbolises the purity of the agreement; that is, the convention of consent. Two rows of purple beads represent the nations involved in the dialogue. Three beads separating the two rows stand for peace, friendship, and respect; the values necessary to an uncoerced and lasting agreement. The two parallel rows of purple beads, Chief Michael Mitchell explicates,

> symbolize two paths or two vessels, travelling down the same river together. One, a birch bark canoe, will be for the Indian people, their laws, their customs, and their ways. The other, a ship, will be for the white people and their laws, their customs, and their ways. We shall each travel the same river together, side by side, but in our own boats. Neither of us will try to steer the other's vessel.
>
> (Mitchell 1989, 109–110)

Aboriginal peoples and European Americans are recognised as equal and coexisting nations, each with their own forms of government, traditions of interpretation and ways. This is the convention of *kahswentha*, the mutual recognition of equality. While not in the same canoe, as in the Haida symbol, the people are in the same river. They agree to cooperate in various ways – travelling "together," presumably mentioned twice for emphasis. But, notwithstanding the agreements they reach, their status as equal and coexisting nations continues. It is never part of the agreement to try "to steer the other's vessel," or, in Marshall's description, "to interfere with the internal affairs" of the other. For example, the treaty signed at Canandaigua, New York, in 1794 between President George Washington's official agent, Colonel Timothy Pickering, and the six chiefs of the *Haudenosaunee* recognises the confederacy as a sovereign nation and guarantees that the United States will never encroach on their remaining lands in western and central New York (Maybury-Lewis 1992, 260–1).

The capacity to delegate to or share various powers of self-government with the protecting government (either the United States or Canada) while retaining their sovereignty is extremely important to the Aboriginal peoples. It enables each Aboriginal nation to work out by mutual consent the degree of self-government appropriate to their population, land base and particular circumstances, without fear of subordination or discontinuity.

The convention of continuity through relations of protection and interdependency is also a common feature of Aboriginal constitutionalism. Article 84 of the constitution of the *Haudenosaunee* confederacy of six nations, for example, states that, whenever a foreign nation has been conquered or has by their own will accepted the Great Peace [confederated with the other nations], their own system of internal government may continue, but they must cease all warfare against other nations.

(Parker and Newhouse 1916, 53)

True to form, each of the six nations of the confederacy has its own language, customs, and government. The confederation itself was founded by the mediation of Deganawidah, who brought the original five warring nations together and guided them to reach agreement through dialogue on a form of association to protect their differences and similarities.

The Aboriginal and Common-Law System of Constitutional Dialogue

The concluding aspect of this example is the way in which the constitutional dialogue itself is guided by the three conventions. As the Royal Proclamation states, the negotiations take place in public, to minimise force and fraud, between representatives of the Crown and Aboriginal nations, thereby instantiating their mutual recognition as nations, and without pressure, so that the agreement will be uncoerced. The negotiations are intercultural. Each negotiator participates in his or her language, mode of speaking and listening, form of reaching agreement, and way of representing the people, or peoples, for whom they speak. These features are simply the application of the convention of continuity and the duty of *audi alteram partem* to the dialogue itself.

Over the last three hundred years, elaborate genres of presentation, speaking in French, English, and Aboriginal languages, exchanging narratives, stories, and arguments, translating back and forth, breaking off and starting again, striking new treaties and redressing violations of old ones have been developed to ensure that each speaker speaks in her or his cultural voice and listens to the others in theirs. The negotiations can be very diverse, such as the multinational and multilingual Great Peace of 1701, which brought over twenty nations together. In the Charlottetown constitutional negotiations of 1992, four Aboriginal negotiators (two women and two men), representing six hundred First Nations, the Métis, Inuit, and Aboriginal people living off reserves, along with a national association of native women on the sidelines, met ten provincial premiers, two territorial leaders and a prime minister, all on equal footing.

When the multicultural negotiations end for the day and transcripts and translations are checked, this is only the beginning of the dialogue. The negotiators must turn to their diverse constituents, explain what has transpired, listen to their objections in their terms, reach agreement in the appropriate way on an acceptable response, and then return to the negotiations. This can take many forms, as the consultation surrounding the multilateral constitutional negotiations in Canada in 1992 illustrated. In the early years of the treaty system, William Johnson, for example, would have to explain his provisional agreement with the Aboriginal nations to Whitehall and fourteen very different colonial governments. The great Aboriginal negotiators, such as Canasatego, Shamokin, Tecumseh, or Pontiac, would in turn have to reach agreement in the appropriate ways with six *Haudenosaunee* nations, the Shawnee, Delaware, Miami, and Ottawa, each with their own internal diversity. In 1992 Ovide Mercredi, the Chief of the First Nations, had to leave the talks and try to reach consensus with the six hundred chiefs for whom he spoke, who, in turn, had to reach agreement with their constituents. Ellen Gabriel, the brave Mohawk negotiator at Kahnesatake, Quebec in 1990, kept a consensus among Mohawk citizens as she negotiated in the face of the force of the Canadian army ranged against her.

As Richard White explains in his fascinating study, *The Middle Ground: Indians, Empires, and Republics in the Great Lakes Region 1650–1815,* the system can deal with issues other than boundaries, military alliances, and commerce. Marriages between catholic *canadiennes,* or *canadiens,* and Cree (which gave rise to the Métis nation), European Americans in Aboriginal nations and vice versa, and a host of other intercultural issues were recognised and conciliated in the common system. He has been unable to find one case where the negotiations were between two internally homogeneous cultures.

The three schools of modern constitutionalism disregard the hidden diversity of actual constitutional dialogue not only by laying down simplistic concepts of popular sovereignty and constitutional association as premises, but also by their corresponding concepts of constitutional dialogue. In recent work (still written in monological form), two concepts of dialogue predominate: the participants aim to reach agreement either on universal principles or on norms implicit in practice and, in both cases, to fashion a constitutional association accordingly. Both concepts are, for example, present in the work of Jürgen Habermas.

The presupposition of shared, implicit norms is manifestly false in this case, as well as in any case of a culturally diverse society. Also, the aim of negotiations over cultural recognition is not to reach agreement on universal principles and institutions, but to bring negotiators to recognise their differences and similarities, so that they can reach agreement on a form of association that accommodates their differences in appropriate institutions and their similarities in shared institutions. (In the case at hand, the appropriate institutions are, respectively, self-government and cooperative arrangements for protection, resource development, health care, and the like.) The presumption of an implicit consensus or a universal goal misidentifies the *telos* of this type of constitutional dialogue, filtering out the diverse similarities and differences the speakers try to voice. Universality is a misleading representation of the aims of constitutional dialogue because, as we have repeatedly seen, the world of constitutionalism is not a universe, but a multiverse: it cannot be represented in universal principles or its citizens in universal institutions.

The responsibility of listening to others is also bypassed by misconceiving the diversity of modes of speaking. In some theories, it is assumed that the claims of various speakers can be framed in a purportedly universal genre of argument. A good illustration of the diversity blindness of this mono-logical assumption is *Delgamuukw v. the Queen* (1991). The Gitskan and Wet'suwet'en nations of the Northwest coast of Great Turtle Island brought forward their claim for recognition of their nations and territories. Gisday Wa and Delgam Uukw carefully outlined Aboriginal concepts of evidence, history, government, and argument, contrasting these with European understandings and finding intermediate examples to help the judge understand. They then explained their claim to territory and self-rule, based on their forms of governance and use long before the Europeans arrived, in their own terms and compared it with analogous European concepts, calling on respected anthropologists to support their claims.

Chief Justice Allan McEachern ruled that their forms of presentation, oral evidence, and title did not measure up to the standards of the court and dismissed their claim. What the court's evidence certainly shows, he fulsomely concluded, is that the

> plaintiffs' ancestors had no written language, no horses or wheeled vehicles, slavery and starvation was [sic] not uncommon, wars with neighbouring people were common, and there is no doubt, to quote Hobbes, that aboriginal life in the territory was, at best, 'nasty, brutish and short.'
>
> *(Delgamuukw v. The Queen* et al. 1991 BCSC 0843;
> cf. Gisday Wa and Delgam Uukw 1992, Cassidy 1992)

Writers such as Seyla Benhabib are critical of the monological theories of dialogue and argue that a democratic constitutional discussion in a culturally diverse society will involve a multiplicity of speech genres. Nevertheless, she goes on optimistically to suggest that we will always be able to put ourselves in the shoes of others and understand things from their point of view, "either by actually listening to all involved or by representing to ourselves imaginatively the many perspectives of those involved" (Benhabib 1992, 54). In her path-breaking paper, "Communication and the Other," Iris Young deepens our understanding of the value of speaking in and listening to a variety of speech modes in such a discussion. "Free and open communication enables different groups each to learn of their own partiality by learning something about other perspectives on their collective problems and on themselves." However, she is sceptical of Benhabib's claim that the participants could reach full reciprocity and symmetry of understanding. There remains "much about the others that they do not understand."[2]

This seems to be an unduly pessimistic view of the possibility of understanding among culturally diverse human beings. It is certainly true that we cannot understand culturally different others simply "by representing to ourselves imaginatively the many perspectives of those involved," any more than I can master tennis by imagining various exchanges. Understanding comes, if it comes at all, only by engaging in the volley of practical dialogue. We need the dialogue itself to become aware of all the aspects of our association that ought to be recognised and accommodated in the constitution. It is also true that the diversity awareness one comes to acquire in dialogue does not consist in being able to replace the other person and speak for him or her. Much remains opaque. However, there is no reason to believe that the participants in the dialogue could not come to "understand" each other.

The reason it is possible to understand one another in intercultural conversations is because this is what we do all the time in culturally diverse societies to some extent. The everyday mastery of the criss-crossing, overlapping, and contested uses of terms is not different in kind (but of course in degree) from the understanding demanded by constitutional dialogue. If one thinks of understanding in the way I presented it in the previous section, the connection becomes clear. The dialogue in such constitutional negotiations usually consists in the back and forth exchange of speech acts of the form, "let me see if I understand what you said," "let me rephrase what you said and see if you agree," "is what you said analogous to this example in my culture," or "I am sorry, let me try another intermediate example that is closer," or "can you acknowledge this analogy?" "Now I think I see what you are saying – let me put it this way for I now see that it complements my view." The participants are gradually able to see the association from the points of view of each other and cobble together an acceptable intercultural language capable of accommodating the truth in each of their limited and complementary views and of setting aside the incompatible ones.

Reading the transcripts, I find it difficult to doubt that Aboriginal negotiators failed to understand William Johnson. The transcript of *Delgamuukw* makes it clear that the Gitskan and Wet'suwet'en understood the concepts that the Chief Justice used to dispossess them under the colour of law and so were able to launch an appeal. Israeli and Palestinian negotiators over self-rule surely understand one another. The Cree, Naskapi, and Inuit negotiators understood the Quebec and Canadian participants in the James Bay and Northern Quebec Agreement of 1975 all too well. Those who participated in the constitutional negotiations and broad consultations in Canada from 1991 to 1992 came, as a result, to understand one another fairly well and temper their earlier views. Those who refused to participate, on the contrary, insisted that their own views were comprehensive and exclusive, held the most extreme positions and, consequently, misunderstood the others. Of course, one cannot fully grasp "where the others are coming from" and so cannot speak for them, but one can, by intermediate steps, understand what they are saying about the ancient city we share.

Young may take a sceptical stance towards reciprocal intercultural understanding because she believes that, if it is possible, then dialogue might be reduced to a mere stepping stone to a monological and universal overview of the ensemble. This concern is suggested by her conclusion that only the "preservation of difference and the recognition of asymmetry – the non-reciprocity – of social positions can preserve publicity and the need for continued communication."[3] But this path out of the world of cultural diversity is closed, not by the inability to understand one another, but by the constitution of the phenomenon we are trying to understand. It is lacking in this sort of perspicuity as a result of the three features of cultural diversity. Understanding it consists in being able to move about within the dialogue, passing from one neighbourhood to the next, exchanging stories, and noticing our similarities and differences *en passant*, not by transcending the human condition.

Further evidence for this mundane point is that written constitutions which have arisen out of such constitutional dialogues are intercultural, without even a pretence of trans-cultural status. The "partnership" constitution of Aoretera-New Zealand, the Waitangi treaty, is written in Maori, the language of the *tangata whenua* (the original inhabitants), and in English, the language of the newcomers. Both are authoritative and have distinct traditions of interpretation, with different conceptions of history, evidence, argument, and government. The non-Aboriginal Canadian constitution is written in French and English. Both are authoritative and have distinct traditions of interpretation. The fundamental constitution of North America, the treaties of the Aboriginal and common law system, should be the same.

In modern theories of constitutionalism, the agreement reached in dialogue is seen as foundational, universal, and the fixed background to democracy. This Platonic image reinforces the attitude that the agreement must be comprehensive and exclusive. In the Aboriginal and common-law system, the agreement is seen as one link in an endless chain, stretching back to what one's ancestors have done before and forward to what one's children will do in the future. The present link, while appropriate to the circumstances at hand, is in line with the whole chain as far as one can see. In addition, the link is always open to review and renegotiation in a future dialogue if it is not as fitting as it appeared at the time. As a result of this more flexible and pragmatic image, the concept of "reaching agreement" is different from the modern one and the corresponding attitude of the participants is more open to mutual understanding, accommodation, and conciliation.

Mohawks call the practice of meeting to review how well an agreement fits, either amending or reaffirming it, "repolishing" the chain. They see the periodic reflection on the constitution as a necessary ingredient of a healthy and untarnished association, just as we noted among the members of the black canoe. This democratic constitutionalism does not, as one might object from the modern viewpoint, lessen the veneration with which they hold an agreement. Each one is sacred and sworn to last "as long as the sun shines and the waters flow," unless a new agreement is reached in accordance with the three conventions. It is, after all, not they who have broken the chain innumerable times and allowed it to tarnish but, rather, those who swore that "peace and friendship" would subsist "through all succeeding generations" (Getty and Lussier 1983; Marshall 1839, 434).

As the settlers gained the upper hand in the nineteenth century, the Aboriginal and common-law system was overwhelmed by the theory and practice of modern constitutionalism. Within its horizons, the relationship of protection, which continued Aboriginal self-government according to Marshall, was reinterpreted. Treaties were said to be mere private contracts and Aboriginal rights mere individual rights to hunt and fish on Crown land. The European-American governments were unilaterally recognised as superior guardians whose burden it was to protect Aboriginal people who were recognised as inferior wards incapable of consent and whose primitive ways had to be discontinued and reformed for their own good. When the wards resisted, they were depicted as "obstacles to progress" and removed to disappear, by neglect, starvation or, as at Wounded Knee, by slaughter.

Although the Aboriginal nations protested throughout this century of the "gradual civilisation of the Indian tribes," it is only in recent decades that their claims for recognition have started to be effectively heard. They have revived the Aboriginal and common-law system hidden beneath the empire of modern constitutionalism to reclaim self-government and control of their territories. From 1972 to 1975, the first contemporary treaty constitution was negotiated between the Cree, Naskapi, and Inuit nations and the Quebec and Canadian governments. The James Bay and Northern Quebec Agreement, while far from ideal, is a precedent that has helped to set the "world reversal" in motion. Since then, the justice of Aboriginal claims for recognition has begun to be acknowledged in the courts of common-law countries and in the United Nations draft Declaration on the Rights of Indigenous Peoples. In this post-imperial dawn, treaties and agreements have begun to take on some of their former lustre and the Crown has started to discern its fiduciary responsibility in the relationship of protection. Even the mighty leviathans who have extended their empire of modern constitutionalism over "stolen continents" are being instructed once again by Royal Commissions to see themselves as the Royal Commission of 1664 recommended: as equal "partners in confederation" with the Aboriginal nations who have survived and continued through the usurpation (RCAP 1993).

These partnerships will take many forms, depending on the arrangements the partners reach in discussions guided by the three conventions. By calling these agreements "treaty constitutionalism" and using the example of the Two Row Wampum Treaty, I do not mean to imply that only one form is possible. This would be another kind of imperialism. The appropriate degree of interdependency and the best sort of agreement vary with the very different circumstances of Aboriginal and non-Aboriginal partners on this earth. Even in Canada, the differences within and among First Nations, Inuit, and Métis are legion. As Augie Fleras and Jean Elliot suggest in *The Nations Within*, a new discipline, the comparative politics of Aboriginal nations, is needed to study the variety of appalling social, economic, and political conditions of Aboriginal nations and to assist the negotiators.

Of course, one might object, only a rough balance of power in the early modern period among the Aboriginal nations, France, England, and the colonial governments caused the Crown to enter into treaty constitutionalism and occasionally abide by it. As constitutional scholars such as Milner S. Ball, Patrick Macklem, Brian Slattery, and Joseph Singer, as well as historians such as John Tobias, Vine Deloria Jr., and Russell Barsh, have shown, the three conventions have been abused many times over the centuries. The treaty of Canandaigua, for example, has never been honoured, despite two centuries of protest. In addition, the Crown has imperiously proclaimed, in the language of Hobbes, the treaties to be a "burden" tolerated solely at its "pleasure." As a result, Aboriginal peoples, as Oren Lyons and John Mohawk protest, have been "exiled in the land of the free."

The practice of treaty constitutionalism is not the ideal speech-situation or the heteroglossia of the scholars. The "kind of scrubbed, disinfected interlocutor" in these theoretical models of dialogue, Edward Said writes, "is a laboratory creation, with suppressed, and therefore falsified, connections to the urgent situation of crisis and conflict that brought him or her to attention in the first place" (1989, 210). The treaty system is a living human practice in which, by great effort, the battle for recognition by arms has been transformed into the conflict of words. This does not end the strategies of fraud and deceit humans play under the colour of the conventions. It only stops the killing, and this only as long as the participants continue to listen to each other.

Nevertheless, the point of this book is that when Aboriginal peoples claim injustice has been done and demand redress, they appeal to the three conventions to justify their case, arguing that their status as nations has been misrecognised, their powers of self-rule discontinued and their consent bypassed. The agents of justice on the other side appeal to the same norms of justification. They argue that they have recognised Aboriginal people appropriately, that they consented to discontinue their powers or that consent can be ignored in this case. The three conventions of common constitutionalism are immanent in this practice – and in the practices of constitutionalism to follow – as the norms of justification, in spite of the efforts of modern constitutionalists to bury them.

It is possible to expose the biases and specious arguments, and see the justice of the practice, not by creating an ideal model to which reality must correspond but, as we are engaged in doing, by surveying it from Aboriginal and non-Aboriginal perspectives. And this practical activity of critical reflection can be extended by drawing comparisons with other examples of common and modern constitutionalism, gradually acquiring a critical understanding of contemporary constitutionalism as we approach this labyrinth from one path after another. In this way, as Wittgenstein recommends, we extend our concept of constitutionalism, as "in spinning a thread we twist fibre on fibre.

And the strength of the thread does not reside in the fact that some one fibre runs through its whole length, but in the overlapping of many fibres" (2009, §67).

Notes

1 The quotation is the motto for this book and for Wittgenstein's *Philosophical Investigations*. For a discussion see Barker (1986).
2 Citation refers to unpaged pre-publication manuscript version of Young (1996).
3 Citation refers to unpaged pre-publication manuscript version of Young (1996).

6 Two Meanings of Global Citizenship
Modern and Diverse (2008)

Two Contested Ways of Thinking about Citizenship

"Global citizenship" has emerged as the locus of struggles on the ground and of reflection and contestation in theory. This is scarcely surprising. Many of the central and most enduring struggles in the history of politics have taken place *in* and *over* the language of citizenship and the activities and institutions into which it is woven. One could say that the hopes and dreams and fears and xenophobia of centuries of individual and collective political actors are expressed in the overlapping and conflicting histories of the uses of the language of citizenship and the forms of life in which they have been employed. This motley ensemble of contested languages, activities, and institutions constitutes the inherited *field* of citizenship today.

The language of "global" and "globalisation" and the activities, institutions, and processes to which it refers and in which it is increasingly used, while more recent than citizenship, comprise a similarly central and contested domain. Globalisation has become a shared yet disputed vocabulary in terms of which rival interpretations of the ways humans and their habitats are governed globally are presented and disputed in both practice and theory. It thus constitutes a similarly contested *field* of globalisation.

When "globalisation" and "citizenship" are combined they not only bring their contested histories of meanings with them. Their conjunction brings into being a complex new field that raises new questions and elicits new answers concerning the meaning of, and relationship between, global governance and global citizenship. When we enquire into global citizenship, therefore, we are already thrown into this remarkably complex inherited field of contested languages, activities, institutions, processes, and the environs in which they take place. This conjoint field is the problematisation of global citizenship: the way that formerly disparate activities, institutions, and processes have been gathered together under the rubric of "global citizenship," become the site of contestation in practice and formulated as a problem in research, policy, and theory, and to which diverse solutions are presented and debated.[1]

Among the many contested meanings of global citizenship I will focus on two. Many of the most important struggles around the globe today are *over*

DOI: 10.4324/9781003227403-9

these two types and the struggles themselves consist in the enactment of these two modes of citizenship in two corresponding practices of global citizenship. They have been interpreted in different ways under different names in a variety of activist and academic literature: for example, global citizenship from above *versus* global citizenship from below, low-intensity *versus* high-intensity global citizenship, representative *versus* direct, hegemonic *versus* counter-hegemonic, cosmopolitan *versus* place-based. I call these two families "modern" and "diverse" citizenship. I call modern citizenship in a modern state "civil" citizenship and in a global context "cosmopolitan" citizenship. The corresponding names of diverse citizenship are "civic" and "glocal." "Glocal" and "glocalisation" in the diverse citizenship tradition refer to the global networking of local practices of civic citizenship in contrast to the use of "global" and "globalisation" in modern/cosmopolitan citizenship. I begin with a preliminary sketch of one aspect of the two meanings and practices of citizenship as a way of introducing them.

The most familiar aspect of modern citizenship is its role as the modular form of citizenship associated with the historical processes of modernisation/colonisation: (1) the modernisation of the West into modern nation states with representative governments, a system of international law, decolonisation of European empires, supranational regime formations, and global civil society; and, in tandem, (2) the dependent modernisation and citizenisation of the non-West through colonisation, the Mandate System, post-decolonisation nation-building, and global governance. The language of modern citizenship, in its civil and cosmopolitan forms, presents successive idealisations of this type of citizenship as the uniquely *universal* practice of citizenship for all human societies. This allegedly universal mode of citizenship is also presented as the product of *universal* historical processes or stages of development under successive discourses of progress – civilisation, modernisation, constitutionalisation, democratisation, and now globalisation – that began in Europe and have been spread around the world by Euroamerican expansion and continuing hegemony. These two features of modern citizenship – a universal modular form of citizenship conjoined with a universal set of historical processes that bring it to the non-West under Western tutelage – are articulated and debated in, respectively, modern normative theories of citizenship and social scientific theories of modernisation from the eighteenth century to today.[2]

In contrast, diverse citizenship is associated with a diversity or multiplicity of different practices of citizenship in the West and the non-West. The language of diverse citizenship, both civic and glocal, presents citizenship as a singular or "local" practice that takes countless *forms* in different locales. It is not described in terms of universal institutions and historical processes but, rather, in terms of the grassroots democratic or civic *activities* of the "governed" (the people) in the specific relationships of governance in the environs where they act and of the glocal *activities* of networking with other practices. The local languages of description (stories) of particular citizenship practices are accepted initially and then compared and contrasted critically along various axes and purposes with other practices in dialogues of translation, understanding, and critique. Whereas modern citizenship focuses on citizenship as a universalisable legal *status* underpinned by institutions and processes of rationalisation that enable and circumscribe the possibility of civil activity (an institutional/universal orientation), diverse citizenship focuses on the singular civic activities and improvisations of the governed in any practice of government and the diverse ways these are more or less institutionalised or blocked in different contexts (a civic activity/contextual orientation). Citizenship is not a status given by the institutions of the modern constitutional state and international law, but negotiated practices in which one becomes a citizen through participation.

Modern Citizenship

The tradition of modern citizenship takes as its empirical and normative exemplar, the form of citizenship characteristic of the modern nation state.[3] Citizenship (both civil and cosmopolitan) is defined in relation to two clusters of institutional features of modern nation states: the constitutional rule of law (*nomos*) and representative government (*demos*). The constitutional rule of law is the first condition of citizenship. The "civil" law (a formal legal order) and its enforcement by a coercive authority establishes (literally "constitutes") the conditions of civilisation, the city (*civitas*), citizenship, civil society, civil liberty, and civility (hence "civil" citizenship). By definition, the "outside" is the realm of the uncivilised: barbarism, savagery, the state of nature or war, or the uncertainty of informal, customary law and unenforceable natural law. A person has the status of citizenship in virtue of being *subject* to civil law in two senses: to an established and enforced system of law and to the "civilising," "pacifying," or "socialising" force of the rule of law on the subjectivity of those who are constrained to obey over time. This is why cosmopolitan citizenship and global civil society depend on some form of legalisation or constitutionalisation of the global order analogous (in various ways) to the modern nation state.

Relative to the constitutional rule of law, modern citizenship is defined as a *status* (state or condition). This civil status is usually explicated and defined in terms of the historical development of *four tiers of rights and duties* (liberties) of formally equal individual subjects of an association of constitutional rule of law and representative government. This association is either the modern nation state, including its subordinate provinces and cities, or its analogous associations for cosmopolitan citizenship (international law, the United Nations, and global governance institutions). I will start with the four citizenship rights and duties within modern nation states as these are the basis for modern/cosmopolitan global citizenship.

The *first* and indispensable tier of rights is the set of "civil liberties" (the liberties of the moderns or "private autonomy") of the modern liberal tradition.

This set includes the liberty of the person and of speech, thought and faith, the right to own private property and enter into contracts, and the right to formal equality before the law. In virtue of these civil liberties, citizens are "at liberty" to engage in these activities if they choose (an "opportunity" status) and are protected by the law from "interference" in the spheres where these rights can be exercised: of free speech and voluntary association, the market, and the law, respectively. They are classic "negative" liberties, protecting persons or citizens from interference in these spheres.

At the centre of these civil liberties is the modern liberty to participate in the private economic sphere and not to be interfered with in it – the right to own property and enter into contracts. This is the modern liberty to engage in the capitalist economy (market freedoms and free trade): to sell one's labouring abilities on the market for a wage to a corporation or, for those with the capital, to establish a corporation, hire the labour of others, and sell competitively the products on the free market to consumers. Private corporations gained recognition as "persons" with the corresponding civil liberty of private autonomy (negative liberty) in the late-nineteenth century. Thus, paradoxically from a civic perspective, the first right of modern citizenship is to participate in the private realm and to be protected from interference by the *demos* (the citizenry and its representatives). This form of participation in the economic sphere ("commercial society") *is* primary – the liberty of the moderns.

The modern civil liberty of private property and contracts accordingly *presupposes* the historical dispossession of people from access to land and resources through their local laws and non-capitalist economic organisations; the accumulation of dispossessed workers into a "free" market of wage labourers and consumers; the concentration of the means of production in private corporations; and the imposition of modern legal systems of property law, contract law, labour law, and trade law that constitute and protect the system of free markets and free trade. Modern citizenship, in its basic commitment to the civil liberty of private property and contracts, is grounded in and dependent on the spread of these institutions of capitalism. It is also the major justification for the spread of these economic institutions – they are the basis of modern liberty. Moreover, it is not only the civil law acting alone that is said to civilise the uncivilised or less-developed peoples. "Commerce" or "economic liberalisation" (a synonym for modern globalisation), by rendering every person and society economically interdependent and competitive within an imposed structure of law, pacifies, refines, polishes, makes predictable, and thus – in tandem with representative government – leads humanity to perpetual peace.

The *second* tier of liberties of modern citizenship is defined in relation to the second cluster of modern institutions: representative government. They consist in the rights to participate in these institutions if one chooses. In the language of modern citizenship, "democracy" and "democratic" are equated with and restricted to "representative government" and "democratisation" with and to the historical processes that bring these representative institutions and rights to participate into being. Other forms of democracy, if they are discussed *as* democracies, are described as less-developed forms of the universal and regulative ideal of "democracy" (as in the case of "citizenship" above). These rights of the modern democratic tradition are called public autonomy or the liberties of the ancients. They comprise the ways the *demos* – the citizenry of a nation state as a whole – legally exercise their popular sovereignty. The exercise of these "democratic" rights enables the people to have a say both within and over the laws and constitutions to which they are subject (and from which their citizenship derives) and thereby to balance the constitutional rule of law with the demands of democracy (the rule of the people). These civil rights include such liberties as: the right to vote for representatives in elections, join parties, interest groups, non-governmental organisations (NGOs) and social movements, stand for election, assemble, dissent and demonstrate in the civil or public sphere, freedom of the press, engage in democratic deliberations, litigate in the courts, exchange public reasons over constitutional amendments or participate in a constituent assembly, and, at their fullest, to engage in some forms of civil disobedience and accept the punishment.

Like civil liberties and their institutional preconditions, these democratic liberties *presuppose* historically the dispossession of people from access to political power through pre-existing local forms of government and citizenship and the channelling of democratic citizenship into participation in the official public sphere of modern representative governments and its global analogue of global civil society. These processes are described as freeing people from pre-modern forms of subjection and bringing democratic citizenship to them. Second, participation is equated with activities of public arguing (deliberating), bargaining (organising, negotiating, and protesting), and litigating over changing the laws, since political power is presumed to be exercised through the rule of law. The objective is to ensure that the law is not imposed unilaterally on those subject to it, but, rather, that they have a say, representatively, in making or amending the laws, and thus can see themselves as co-authors or, more accurately, co-articulators, of the laws to which they are subject *en passant*. The activity of participation thus replicates the ground plan of modern citizenship because the people participate *as* legal citizens exercising their democratic rights and within the constraints of modern civil liberties (even when the people act together and exercise the modern right of self-determination they do so within this juridical-representative framework).

The second tier democratic liberties of the moderns are also circumscribed by the first tier civil liberties in three main ways. Their exercise is optional. A member of a modern political association is a citizen and the association is democratic whether or not one exercises rights to participate. Second, the primary use and justification of these rights in the modern tradition is to fight for laws that protect the private liberty of the moderns from too much governmental interference. Third, these rights cannot be extended and exercised in the private sphere (as in economic democracy in the workplace) for this would interfere with tier one liberties. When the leaders of the great powers today (the G8) speak of the spread of "freedom" and "democracy" in Afghanistan, Iraq, and elsewhere, they are referring to the module of tier one (liberties) and tier two (democracy) rights of citizenship and their underlying institutions of the constitutional rule of law, markets, representative government, and the military as the enforcement institution.

The *third* and weakest tier of modern rights of citizenship comprises the social and economic rights of the modern social democratic tradition. These are the citizenship rights won by working-class movements struggling within the historically established priority and constraints of tiers one and two liberties over the last two centuries in nation states and international law. They are a response to the horrendous substantive inequalities in wealth, well-being, living conditions, and social power that go along with the unrestrained formal equality of tier one civil liberties and the limited democratic rights of tier two. The modern social democratic argument for them is that they are the *minimum conditions* of the worst off being able to exercise their civil and democratic liberties. The argument against them is that they violate the economic liberties of the moderns by interfering in the private sphere and economic competition and thus always must be subordinated to tier one civil liberty and the limits of tier two. Under the current economic liberalisation policies of states and institutions of global governance these rights are seen, at best, as means of enabling individuals to exercise their tier one and two rights.

The *fourth* tier of citizenship rights consists of modern minority rights of multiculturalism, religious and ethnic groups, non-state nations, and Indigenous peoples. These rights appear to some modern theorists to violate one of the premises of modern citizenship, the primacy of the individual legal subject. However, minority rights can be defined as rights that, first, protect the *individual members* of minorities from interference or dominance by the majority (and by the powerful within the minority) and, second, empower members of minorities to exercise their civil and democratic liberties in more effective ways than through the institutions of the dominant society. They thus can be designed to enhance, rather than to challenge, the spread of modern citizenship, and this is the major way that they have been implemented under modern nation states and international law. That is, they too presuppose the dispossession of "minorities" of their own forms of legal, governmental, and economic organisation and processes of integrating them into modern forms of citizenship.

Within Europe, this modular form of modern citizenship became the paramount practice of citizenship during the centralisation and consolidation of the modern constitutional representative nation state and the capitalist economy. Diverse local and regional forms of laws, governments, democracy, and citizenship – of village commons and free city communes – where they were not destroyed completely, were marginalised or transformed, and subordinated as they were brought under the rationalisation of the central institutions of the modern nation state. Modern citizenship was nationalised at the same time as local citizenship was subalternised. The people were socialised by education, urbanisation, military duty, industrialisation, and modern citizenisation to see themselves first and foremost, not as citizens of their local communities, but as members of an abstract and "disembedded" imaginary community of nation, demos, and nomos of formally free and equal yet materially unequal citizens, with an equally abstract imaginary of popular sovereignty they mythically embodied and exercised through the individual liberties of modern citizenship attached to the central legal and representative institutions. These dispossessions and transformations, and the countless resistances to them, were described and justified in the social scientific language of modern citizenship as processes and stages of developments of modernisation that freed individuals from the backwardness of pre-modern customary practices and made him and then her free and equal citizens.

Citizens and especially non-citizens – such as the poor, the propertyless, women, immigrants, excluded "races," and others – struggled (and continue to struggle) within-and-against these processes in Europe. When they were not struggling for their local ways, they organised to be included in modern citizenship, to extend the use of political rights beyond the official public sphere, and to gain social and economic rights and minority rights that do more than protect individuals from the majority. These are "civic activities" against the powerful actors who seek to circumscribe citizenship to tier one civil liberties and a limited module of democratic rights. Since these types of struggles are *for* new kinds of citizenship and *by means of* people who are not official citizens or official citizens who often act beyond the official limits of citizenship of their generation, they cannot be called practices of citizenship in the modern tradition. They are acts of "civil disobedience." If these illegal struggles are successful and the extensions institutionalised, then the extensions are redescribed as a stage in the development of modern citizenship (as in the case of working-class struggles giving rise to social and economic rights and suffragette movements giving rise to women's right to vote). Thus, what are seen as two of the fundamental features of citizenship from the civic tradition – the historical struggles for diverse local forms of citizenship and for extensions of national citizenship rights – fall outside of citizenship for the modern tradition with its institutional orientation.

The Globalisation of Modern Citizenship

I want now to examine how the modular form of modern citizenship has been spread around the globe as "global citizenship."[4] It has been and is being globalised in two forms. *First*, the module of a modern nation state and its institutions of modern *civil* citizenship, at some "stage of development" towards its mature form, has been and continues to be spread around the world as the universal form of political association recognised as the bearer of legitimate political authority (sovereignty) under international law. *Second*, a modular form of modern *cosmopolitan* citizenship, also at some stage of development towards its mature form, has been and continues to be spread around the world as the universal form of global citizenship recognised as legitimate under international law and global institutions.

During the long period when Europeans were building modern nation states with institutions of modernising citizenship they were also, and simultaneously, building these states as competing *imperial* modern nation states. As imperial states they built and defended vast overseas empires that colonised (in various ways) 85 percent of the world's population by 1914. The imperial "great game" of competing economically and militarily against other European great powers over the control and exploitation of the resources, labour, and markets of the non-European world *and* the counter-actions of the non-European peoples *co-created* the modern West and the modern colonised non-West. After decolonisation in the twentieth century, this unequal relationship continues between the former imperial powers (renamed the "great eight" or "great twenty") exercising "hegemony" rather than "imperium" through the post–World War II institutions of global governance and the renamed "post-colonial" world of more than 120 nominally free and equal ("sovereign") yet substantively still *dependent* and *unequal* new modernising nation states, constructed on the foundations of the former colonies. The spread of the institutions of modern citizenship beyond Europe can be understood only in the context of this complex contrapuntal ensemble of Western strategies of expansion and non-Western strategies of counteraction (Mignolo 2000).

The institutional conditions of modern citizenship were spread in the course of European expansion by a deceptively simple strategy that linked a right of global citizenship to imperial power in a circular relationship. Initially formulated and exercised in different ways by the European imperial powers, this right of global citizenship for Europeans is called the right of commerce (*ius commercium*) or "cosmopolitan" right. From the earliest phase of European expansion to today the great powers have claimed the cosmopolitan right of *their* citizens, trading companies, monopoly companies, and multinational corporations to travel to other countries and attempt to engage in "commerce" in two senses of this term. The first is to travel the globe freely and converse with the inhabitants of other societies. This covers such activities as the right – and also as the *duty* – of Western explorers, missionaries, religious organisations, voluntary associations, and academics to travel to non-Western countries to, first, study and classify their different customs and ways into developmental stages of different societies and races, and, second, try to free them from their "inferior" ways and teach them the uniquely civilised ways of the West. This cosmopolitan right is the historical antecedent of the right of modern cosmopolitan citizenship of civil society associations (modern NGOs) and Western academics to modernise and democratise people in the post-colonial world today by bringing them the institutional preconditions and forms of subjectivity of modern citizenship. The second sense of this cosmopolitan right is to travel and try to engage in "commerce" (trade) with the inhabitants: to enter into contracts and treaties, gain access to resources, buy slaves, hire and discipline labourers, establish trading posts, and so on. At first it was used by the European powers to establish imperial monopolies over the exploitation of the resources and labour of non-European societies, but monopoly imperialism gradually gave way to "free trade" imperialism in the nineteenth and twentieth century.

This right correlates with the duty of "hospitality" of the host country to open their doors to free commerce in this dual sense. If they close the door to entry, break the contract or expropriate the property of a foreigner who has engaged in commerce, or if they expel the voluntary societies, then the appropriate recognised legal authority – under the old law of nations, or imperial law of the respective empire, or, later, international law – has a reciprocal right to open the door by diplomacy or military intervention, punish the violation of the cosmopolitan right, and demand reparations or compensation (even for damages caused by the intervention). This correlative duty of hospitality – openness to free commerce – holds even if the cosmopolitan right was initially exercised unjustly: that is where a trading company used force and fraud to establish trade relations and contracts in the first place. This early-modern duty of non-European societies to open themselves to commerce dominated by the West continues to be one of the core duties of transnational trade law agreements today.

As with modern civil liberty within a modern state, this cosmopolitan right *presupposes* a number of institutions. The host country must either have or adopt the legal, economic, and cultural institutions that make possible commerce in this broad sense (private property, corporations, contracts, wage labour, markets dominated by the West, openness to cultural conversion, protection of foreigners, and so on). The imperial power must either submit to and modify the local laws and institutions or impose a structure of commercial law that overrides and restructures them, such as Merchant's Law (*lex mercatoria*), a vast system of global trade law that developed in tandem with Western imperialism.

As we can see, this cosmopolitan right is a right of citizens of the civilised states to exercise the first right of modern citizenship (civil liberties) and a version of the second right (to participate) *beyond their nation state*, and to be protected from interference in so doing. The two cosmopolitan rights – of the trading company to trade and the voluntary organisations to converse and convert – also fit together in the same way as within the nation state. The participatory right to converse with and try to convert the natives complements the primary right of commerce since the inhabitants are taught the requisite forms of subjectivity and modes of civil conduct that go along with the commercialisation of their society and its gradual civilisation: from the discipline of slavery and indentured labour at the bottom to the training of dependent elites at the top. From the perspective of the language of modern citizenship, the two rights of cosmopolitan citizenship appear to globalise the civilising institutions of law, commerce, and Western civility across an uncivilised or semi-civilised or less-developed world, thereby laying the foundations for an eventual world of modern civil citizenship in modern nation states. From the perspective of the non-Western civilisations and of diverse citizenship, the two cosmopolitan rights appear as the Trojan horse of Western imperialism (Anghie 2004).

In practice, this strategy was employed to globalise modern citizenship in three main ways. First, settler colonies were established that *replicated* the basic features legal, political, and economic institutions of the imperial country. These "new Europes" were established in the Americas, Australia, New Zealand, and later in Africa by dispossessing Indigenous peoples of their diverse civilisations, territories, resources, and citizenship practices, exterminating 80–90 percent of the population (which was larger than Europe at the time), marginalising those they could not enslave or indenture, importing twelve million slaves from Africa onto plantations in North and South America and the Caribbean, and imposing the civilising institutions of property and contract law and rudimentary representative government (colonial legislatures).

Second, by "indirect" imperial rule, non-Western societies were opened to commerce by establishing a small colonial administration, often run by trading companies, to rule indirectly over a much larger Indigenous population. A centralised system of Western colonial law was used to protect the commercial rights of their citizens and traders, while also preserving and modifying the local customary laws and governments so resources and labour were privatised and subject to trade, labour discipline, and investment dominated by the Western trading companies. Local rulers were recognised as quasi-sovereigns and unequal treaties negotiated. The local elites were made dependent on Western economic and military power, undermining accountability to their local citizens, and employed to introduce modernising techniques of governance and train the local armies to protect the system of property, often against the majority of their own population. This was the major way that the institutional preconditions of modern civil citizenship were introduced in India, Ceylon, Africa, and the Middle East.

The third and most recent way is through "informal" or "free trade" imperialism. Here the imperial powers permits local self-rule, and eventually self-determination, but within a protectorate or sphere of influence over which they exercise informal "paramountcy" (now called "hegemony" or "dominance"). By various informal means they induce the local governments to open their resources, labour, and markets to free trade by establishing the appropriate modern local legal, political, and economic institutions – the foundations for eventual modern citizenship, with civil liberties preceding and circumscribing the other rights. The means include: economic, military, technological, educational, and aid dependency; the modernisation of the population by Western experts and civil society organisations; bribes and threats; and frequent military intervention when local citizens resist. This requires in turn small but effective military bases strategically located around the world and supported by a global navy and (later) air force and satellite surveillance. The informal imperial powers are thus able to intervene whenever the local population tries to take control of their own economy through their own government and citizenship practices and thus violate the duty of openness to free trade. This type of imperialism was introduced by the British in the nineteenth century, but the United States has become the global leader of informal or "open door" imperialism, first in Latin America and then throughout the former colonial world by the end of the Cold War. The United States now has over 760 small military bases around the world and the Pentagon claims to exercise "full spectrum dominance" over an informal global system of commerce and freedom.

The cosmopolitan right and its three modes of imposition were gathered together and formalised as the *standard of civilisation* in the creation of modern international law during the nineteenth century. The European imperial nation states (and the United States after 1895) declared themselves to be "civilised states" in virtue of their institutions of modern statehood and citizenship (modern rule of law, open to commerce, representative government, and modern liberty). As such they were the sole bearers of sovereignty and subject only to the laws they could agree to among themselves: "international" law. Their modern institutions provided a "standard of civilisation" in international law by which they judged all other civilisations in the world as "uncivilised" to varying degrees (depending on their stage of development) and thus not sovereign subjects of international law, but subjects of the sovereign powers through colonies, indirect protectorates, and informal spheres of influence. They asserted a right and duty of civilisation under international law. "Civilisation" referred to the historical process of modernisation and the end-point of a modern state like the European model. The duty to civilise consisted in the consolidation and international legalisation of the imperial processes they began in the earlier period. The opening of non-European societies to European-dominated commerce, exploitation of their resources and labour, and the destruction or marginalisation of "uncivilised" ways that hindered this "progress" were seen as the first steps in the civilising mission. The second and equally important duty was to introduce into the colonies and protectorates more systematic and effective forms of colonial governance (or *governmentalité*) that would shape and form the dependent peoples and "races" into civilised subjects eventually capable of modern self-government.

This global civilising project under international law lacked an enforcement mechanism and the civilising duty was left to the sovereign empires and their voluntary organisations. The destruction, exploitation, despotism, genocide, and wars continued apace and increased after the failure of the Berlin Conference (1884) and the "scramble over Africa," eventually cumulating in the barbarism of World War I (the "great war of civilisation"). In response to these horrors and to control increasing demands for decolonisation, the first concerted attempt to operationalise the civilising duty under international law was the Mandate System under League of Nations. The League classified the "subject" peoples into three categories according to their level of "backwardness" and gave the respective imperial powers the mandate to civilise them as they increased their economic exploitation, especially in the oil-rich Middle East.

This project was interrupted by the decolonisation movements of the mid-century. Although the people fought for freedom from imperial dependency on the West or the Soviet Union and the development of their own forms of self-government and citizenship, the Westernised nationalist elites (subject to economic and military dependency) and the informal means of the great powers ensured the continuation of the civilising and modernising processes. During the Cold War and the phases of post-independence dependency, the nation-building elites were constrained to destroy or subordinate local economies, governments and citizenship practices, entrench or extend the artificial colonial boundaries, centralise, and nationalise governments into the armed nation-state module, open their resources to free trade and promise minimal institutions of modern citizenship, or face military intervention. The result tended to be constitutional and institutional structures that concentrated power at the centre, often entrenching the worst features of colonial administration, or replicating the concentration of power in both urban and rural regions characteristic of the divide and conquer model of indirect imperial rule (as in much of Africa).

During the same period, the great powers set up the institutions of global governance through which informal hegemony and post-colonial subalternity could be continued: the concentration of power in the permanent members of the Security Council of the United Nations, the World Bank (WB), International Monetary Fund (IMF), General Agreement on Tariffs and Trade (GATT), the World Trade Organisation (WTO) after 1995 and its transnational trade agreements such as Trade Related Aspects of Intellectual-Property Rights (TRIPS) and the General Agreement on Trade in Services (GATS), modernising NGOs, North Atlantic Treaty Organization (NATO), and the United States' system of global military dominance.

At the request of the newly independent states, the language of civilisation was removed from international law and the United Nations. However, it was immediately replaced with the language of modernisation, marketisation, democratisation, and globalisation with the same grammatical structure, signifying universal processes of development and a single endpoint of modern citizenship and its institutions. These are now to be brought about, not by the "civilising mission" of the imperial powers, but by the "global governance" of the informal federations or coalitions of the modern (or post-modern) states imposing "good governance" through the global institutions (WB and IMF), their multinational corporations (exercising the cosmopolitan right of commerce), and official NGOs (exercising their cosmopolitan citizenship) building civil societies and civil subjects on the ground. As the leaders of the decolonisation movements recognised after independence, they were thus conscripted into a familiar script, but now in a vocabulary of a world system of free and equal nation states that erased any reference to the imperial construction of this world and the persistence of imperial relations of inequality and exploitation (Ayers 2006; Evans and Ayers 2006).

The difference from the old colonial strategies of spreading the institutional preconditions of modern citizenship is that the formerly colonised peoples are now seen as active, self-governing agents in these processes at home and in the institutions of global governance (the G120) – and thus bearers of modern civil and cosmopolitan citizenship – yet still under the enlightened leadership of the more advanced or developed peoples. International law provides the legal basis for this by promoting a "right to democracy," and democracy is equated with tier one civil liberties (neoliberal marketisation) and a short list of democratic rights (elections). However, if, as often happens, the majority of the people become too democratic and seek to exercise their right of self-determination by taking democratic control of their own government and local economy, and thus violate their duty to open their doors to multinational corporations and subordination to a global economy, one of two strategies of modernisation follows. They are either repressed by their own dependent elites, democratic rights are further reduced or eliminated, and the government becomes more authoritarian. Or, if the people manage to gain power, the repertoire of covert and overt informal means available to the great powers are employed to desta-bilise and undermine the government, bring about regime change, and institute structural adjustment policies that promote tier one civil liberties of individuals and corporations. The coercive imposition of the global market and the market discipline of civil liberty is said to come first and lay the foundation for democratic rights. The result in either case is the suppression or severe restriction of democratic citizenship, the corresponding rise of a militarised authoritarian rule and market freedoms on one side and violent authoritarian resistance movements on the other. The countries that are subject to these horrendous oscillations are said to be "failed states," military intervention follows, resistance intensifies, and instability continues.

The consequence is that a restricted "low-intensity" form of modern civil citizenship at the national level is promoted by an equally low-intensity form of modern cosmopolitan citizenship of NGOs and multinational corporations under global governance and international law. The first wave of international human rights after World War II sought to give protection to the person from the worst effects of these processes (civil liberties) and to elaborate a set of global democratic, social and economic, and minority rights similar to those at the national level. However, these are hostage to implementation by nation states and thus subject to the processes described above. The second wave of international law brought into force a vast array of transnational trade law regimes (under GATT and the WTO) that override and restrict national constitutions and constrain weaker and poorer countries (the majority of the world's population) to open their economies and labour to free trade, unrestrained exploitation, and pollution transfer by the dominant multinational corporations in order to gain loans, aid, and debt relief. The third wave of international law after 9/11 consists of Resolutions of the Security Council of the UN promoting international security. These global securitisation regimes, which are said to protect the security and liberty of modern citizens, often override the first wave international human rights, force national governments to enact security legislation that rolls back hard won democratic rights, thereby circumscribing democratic opposition to the war on terror and neoliberal globalisation, and they secure the tier one civil and cosmopolitan liberty of individual and corporate citizens in national and transnational law (United Nations Security Council 2001; Scheppele 2006). This new formulation of the old cosmopolitan right to civilise is now the major justification for the continuation of Western informal imperialism, as in Iraq and Afghanistan today. The result is not only the continued popular resistance, instability, and escalating militarisation and repression, as above, but also growing global inequalities between the West and the non-West that are worse now than at the height of the ruthless phase of Western imperialism in the late nineteenth century.

A total of 840 million people are malnourished, and six million children under the age of five die each year as a consequence of malnutrition. Over one billion people live on less than $1 a day and half the world's population lives on less than $2 a day. Ninety-one out of every thousand children in the developing world die before five years old. Twelve million die annually from lack of water. Approximately 1.1 billion people have no access to clean water, whereas 2.4 billion people live without proper sanitation. Forty million live with AIDS. One hundred and thirteen million children have no basic education. One in five does not survive past forty years of age. There are one billion non-literate adults, two-thirds are women and 98 percent live in the developing world. In the least developed countries, 45 percent of the children do not attend school. In countries with a literacy rate of less than 55 percent, the per capita income is about $600.

In contrast, the wealth of the richest 1 percent of the world is equal to that of the poorest 57 percent. The assets of the two hundred richest people are worth more than the total income of 41 percent of the world's people. Three families alone have a combined wealth of $135 billion. This equals the annual income of 600 million people living in the world's poorest countries. The richest 20 percent of the world's population receive 150 times the wealth of the poorest 20 percent. In 1960, the share of the global income of the bottom 20 percent was 2.3 percent. By 1991, this had fallen to 1.4 percent. The richest fifth of the world's people consume 45 percent of the world's meat and fish; the poorest fifth consume 5 percent. The richest fifth consume 58 percent of total energy, whereas the poorest fifth consume less than 4 percent. The richest fifth have 75 percent of all telephones, the poorest fifth 1.5 percent. The richest fifth own 87 percent of the world's vehicles, the poorest fifth less than 1 percent. As a result of the globalisation of modern citizenship and its underlying institutions, the majority of world's population of the dispossessed are thus "free" to exercise their modern civil liberty in the growing sweatshops and slums of the planet (Seabrook 2003, 52–3).

In summary, the globalisation of modern citizenship has not tended to democracy, equality, and perpetual peace, but to informal imperialism, dependency, inequality, and resistance. This tendency is a consequence of its basic universal/imperial orientation. From within the perspective of modern citizenship modern citizens see their modular form of citizenship as universal and superior and all others as particular and inferior, and see themselves as having the imperial right and duty to enter into other societies, free them from their inferior ways, impose the institutional preconditions of modern citizenship, which conveniently brings unconscionable profits to their corporations and unconscionable inequality to the people they are modernising, and use violence and military rule against those envious "anti-moderns" who resist. From the alternative perspective of diverse citizenship, this is neither freedom, nor democracy but five hundred years of relentless tyranny against local citizenship and self-reliance, the undemocratic imposition of institutions of low-intensity citizenship over which the majority of the people have little or no effective say and in which they are subject to subordination, exploitation, horrendous inequalities, and repression when they refuse to submit.[5]

Diverse Citizenship

Although modern civil and cosmopolitan citizenship is the predominant form of global citizenship, a multiplicity of other meanings and practices of citizenship coexist and, consequently, the global field of citizenship is considerably more complex and contested than the view from the modern tradition suggests. I want now to turn and examine this field from the standpoint of diverse citizenship. I will mention six general aspects of diverse civic citizenship and contrast these with modern civil citizenship.[6]

Rather than looking on citizenship as a status within an institutional framework backed up by world-historical processes and universal norms, the diverse tradition looks on citizenship as *negotiated practices* – as civic actors and activities in local contexts. The modern tradition in social science and political theory overlooks these activities because it presupposes that rights, rules, institutions, and processes must be primary (the conditions of civilisation), and human actors and activities secondary (what happens within the civil space constituted by the civilising rights, institutions, rules, and processes). The diverse tradition reverses this modernist, institutional orientation and takes the perspective of actual citizens in civic activities in the dwelling places they are enacted and carried on. Institutionalisation of citizenship practices is seen as secondary; coming into being in countless unpredictable and open-ended ways out of, and in interaction with, the *praxis* of citizens – sometimes furthering, strengthening, and formalising these activities; other times dispossessing, channelling, cancelling, downsizing, constraining, limiting, and repressing (as we have seen).

The second way the diverse tradition avoids the prejudice of mistaking one institutionalised form of citizenship as the universal model for all possible forms is always to take any specific civic activity in context as one local citizenship practice among countless others. They start from the local languages and practices of citizens *in* their forms of citizenship and compare and contrast their similarities and dissimilarities critically with each other from various standpoints, either by engaging in other forms of citizenship or by civic dialogues of mutual edification among diverse citizens. There is thus no universal module of citizenship but, rather, a multiplicity of criss-crossing and overlapping practices of citizenship, of which modern citizenship can be seen to be one singular and imperious form masquerading as universal.

Third, since civic activities of citizens are primary, people do not become citizens in virtue of a status defined by rights and guaranteed by the institutions of the modern state and international law. This status is simply to be a "subject" of that system of laws and a "member" of that association. Individual and collective agents *become* citizens only in virtue of actual participation in civic activities. Through apprenticeship in citizenship practices they acquire the linguistic and non-linguistic abilities, modes of conduct and interaction in relationships with others, forms of awareness of self and other, and use of civic equipment that are constitutive of citizenship as a practice. The difference in meaning between "citizenship" as a status and as a negotiated practice is made in European languages by the distinction between "civil" and "civilisation" (law-based) and "civic" and "civicising" (activity-based). Whereas civil citizens have the legally guaranteed opportunity to participate in the civil sphere if they choose, civic citizens engage in and experience "civics" – the activities and practical arts of becoming and being a citizen, referred to as "civicism." Civic citizenry are not seen as bearers of civil rights and duties but of the abilities, competences, character, and conduct acquired in participation, often referred to as "civic virtues." Civil citizens are civilised by the institutional rule of law, commerce, and anonymous processes of civilisation, whereas civic citizens criticise and reject this disempowering picture that conceals the real world of histories of civic struggles. They "civicise" themselves. They transform themselves into citizens and their institutions into civic spaces by civic activities and the arts of citizenship, whether or not these activities are guaranteed by the rule of law or informal customs and ways, or neither. The civic citizen manifests the freedom *of* participation *in* relationships *with* other citizens. The civic citizen is not the juridical citizen of a national or global institution but the "free citizen" of the "free city": that is, any kind of civic "sphere" or "world" that comes into being and is reciprocally sustained by the civic freedom of its citizens, from the deme, village, common, commune, grassroots federation to a global networks of such civic nodes.

Fourth, whereas modern citizenship always exists in institutions, civic citizenship always exists in relationships. There are two major kinds of civic being-with relationships: (1) relationships among roughly equal citizens acting together in relationships of solidarity, civic friendship, and mutual aid (citizen relationships) and relationships between governors and citizens (governance/citizen relationships). Civic citizenship is the *vis-à-vis* of governance. To see the importance of this contrast we have to set aside the institutional language of the civil tradition (constitutions, rights, autonomous rules, jurisdiction, states, and sovereignty) and look at what goes on within, beyond, and often in tension with these institutions. What we see are individual and collective actors in citizen and governance/citizen relationships.

A relationship of governance is a relation of power, knowledge, and mode of subjectification through which one agent or collection of agents (governors or government) tries to govern or conduct the conduct (thoughts and actions) of another agent or agents (the governed or all affected), either directly or indirectly, formally or informally, by innumerable means and strategies. They exist in small groups, families, workplaces, sweatshops, bureaucracies, colonial administrator, and colony, in producing and consuming activities, in our relations to the environment, between multinational corporations and their suppliers and consumers, in the informal global relations of inequality, and so on. As modern states consolidated, the term "government" came to be restricted to the official form of "representative government," "the governed" to the body of individual citizens with rights, the relationship between them as the "rule of law," and "civil democratic citizenship" as the right to participate in the official public sphere in relation to the rule of law and representative government. The diverse citizenship tradition sees this as one important set of representative governance relationships, albeit highly institutionalised and abstracted. However, there are multiple, overlapping and criss-crossing local, national, and global governance relationships in the broader sense that either do not pass through the modern national and global legal and political institutions or, if they do, they are often overlooked by the institutional perspective, to which we are subject, yet over which the governed often have little or no democratic say. This is the field of diverse citizenship.

A governance relationship is the site of citizenship from the civic perspective. In any governance relationship, there is always a more or less restricted field of possible ways of acting, of conducting oneself in the relationship, even in the most tightly controlled cases (such as prisons and military training). As a result of this irreducible element of freedom and free play in a governance relationship, it is always a negotiated practice between the partners to some extent. Governance is not a unilateral phenomenon of subjection, but a much more complicated and open-ended *interplay* and *interaction* between governors and governed over time. This dimension of negotiation is the ground of civic citizenship. The governed begin to become civic citizens and initiate civic activities when they not only negotiate how to act in accord with the governance relationship in which they find themselves but when they negotiate the relationship itself. Hence, from the perspective of civic citizens, a governance relationship is always a governance/citizen relationship. Classically this activity of civic negotiation (the public world of *negotium*) consists in (but is not restricted to): citizens organising and nonviolently calling a governance relationship into question (speaking truth to power), demanding that those who govern enter into negotiations over the acceptability of the relationship, negotiating a modification or transformation of it, implementing the changes, acting in the new relationship, reviewing it over time, and reopening the negotiations again whenever the new relationship becomes unacceptable. In contrast to the institutional distinction between public and private in modern citizenship, this activity of calling any governance relationship anywhere into question and subjecting it to public examination and negotiation brings it out of the private sphere (of not being questioned) and into the public sphere of civic enquiry.

Opening the relationships we bear to the ongoing negotiation and experimentation of the partners (governors-citizens) is to "civicise" them. They are no longer imposed monologically over the governed who are presumed to simply obey as subjects. They are transformed into civic and dialogical relationships under the shared authority of both partners. The partners become mutually subject to and co-authors of the relationship between them. Governors become "civic servants," accountable to those they serve, and subjects become free citizens rather than unfree subjects or slaves (who have no say in their despotic relationships). To civicise governance/citizen relationships is also to "democratize" them; for one ordinary, everyday sense of "democracy" is that the people (*demos*) in their locale (*deme*) rule by exercising an effective say in and over the relationships in which they are both subjects and citizens. Civic citizenship is thus the practice of grass-roots democracy. It civicises and democratises the relationships in which the people find themselves *here and now*. Civil citizenship in contrast imposes a singular institutionalised process of civilisation and democratisation from above, often coercively and often over local forms of civic citizenship, on the imperial premise that institutions precede civic activity, and it restricts democracy to a small island of representative participation in a sea of non-democratic relationships in the private sphere. This is the initial and continuing unjust and anti-democratic foundation of modern citizenship from the civic standpoint. Democratic citizenship practices exist in everyday relationships long before institutionalisation and they can be extended only by the same democratic means of nonviolent civicisation from the ground up.[7]

Fifth, the other general way civic citizenship is manifested is when citizens organise themselves in citizen relationships: that is, relationships among fellow citizens as equals in which there is no governor/citizen distinction. Sometimes this is done in order to enter into negotiations with governors of various kinds (as above), as in cases of collective bargaining, and negotiating NGOs and social movements that are organised civically and democratically. But, in many other cases, citizens organise an activity entirely on the basis of citizen relationships for its own sake. The classic examples are the celebrated practices of direct democracy.

However, another important example is the cooperative. If the private corporation is both the basis and flagship of modern citizenship – the institution in which moderns exercise their civil liberties in competing, working, shopping, and consuming, then the cooperative is the contrastive organisation of the civic tradition. Here citizens ignore the civil division between (non-democratic) private and (representative) public spheres, between civil liberties and democratic rights. They participate as democratic citizens governing themselves directly in the economic sphere (and other spheres), civicising the relations of supplying, hiring, working, managing, and distributing. In contrast to individual and corporate competition in market relations, cooperatives are founded on the ethic of cooperation. In the place of competitive free trade, they practice fair trade: trade relationships based on non-violent democratic negotiations among all affected. In contrast to the goal of profit, coops are "not for profit" but for living democracy and mutual aid. All the human creativity that is channelled into the world of commerce and profit by corporations is poured into experimentation with forms of democratic cooperation by the cooperative movements. The most astonishing feature of the countless cooperatives on the planet is that they manifest, in concrete and practical forms, actual alternative worlds of citizenship *within* the interstices of the dominant national and global institutions of modern citizenship. They do not organise to overthrow the state or the capitalist mode of production, or to confront and negotiate with governors to change this or that regulation. They simply *enact* alternative worlds of citizen relationships around various activities, refusing to abjure their civicism to privatisation or governmentalisation.

Sixth, modern citizenship is "egocentric," oriented towards the protection of the liberty of individuals to be free from interference and to be free to exercise their autonomy in the private sphere (tier one rights) or in the official public sphere (tier two rights). In contrast, diverse citizenship in both citizen and governance/citizen relationships is ecocentric and commune centric. Civic activities are oriented towards *caring for* the public or "civic goods" of the correlative "city" – the community bound together by citizen and/ or governance/citizen relationships in dependency relationships with non-human animals and the environment they bear as inhabitants of the natural habitat. Civic goods are many and they too are subject to negotiation. They include such procedural goods as civicising relationships in many spheres and the character development and conviviality that come from participation, and such substantive goods as caring for the environment, economic self-reliance, mutual aid, fair trade, equality among citizens, and so on. When civic citizens call a particular governance relationship into question, they do so under the general critical ideal that it fails to realise civic goods in some specific way or another. These are goods that make possible and enhance civic forms of life (Tully 2008b, 73–90).

Accordingly, civic citizens are thus caretakers of dwelling "places" in this broad sense that dissolves the modernist distinction between culture and nature, and they care for their relations to the natural world (the ground or mother of their civic life) as carefully as the cultural world. They also take their civic responsibility of caring for the goods of communities and members *in* dwelling places and placeways to be prior to protecting the liberty rights of abstract individuals. They translate the latter back into one important civic good among others (negative freedom) that must vie for attention in our discursive practices. They also reply that, in many cases, what oppressed individuals and minorities say they want is not protection from their own communities by a tier one right enforced by a distant national or international court, but democratic empowerment in their communities (civic freedom). In theories of modernity, this grounded civic ethic is discredited by redescribing it as a pre-modern stage of historical and moral development and as a particular ethos of care in contrast to the allegedly higher and universal theory of morality and justice for abstracted and autonomous individuals. And the "public good" is redescribed as the spread of modern liberties and their underlying institutions. Notwithstanding this peculiarly modern stance, multilayered civic ethics of care in human and natural relationships have been and continue to be the more widely held political and ethical orientation of the world's peoples in their diverse cultures and traditions. Under the dawning awareness of the destruction of local communities, environmental devastation, and climate change caused by the last five hundred years of Western imperialism under the modernising orientation (in which these public bads are "externalities"), not only ecological scientists but even former modernisers and globalisers have come around to see the good of this alternative way of citizenship (Moran 2006; Borrows 2002, 138–59).[8]

The Glocalisation of Diverse Citizenship

Now I want to examine two main ways diverse citizenship has spread around the globe.[9] The first is the persistence and recent renaissance of local forms of civic citizenship practices despite the globalisation of modern citizenship. The second is by the global civic federation and networkisation of local diverse citizenship practices. I call this global networking "glocalisation" and the networkers "glocal citizens" because they are grounded in and hyperextend the civic features of local citizenship.

I will also discuss these two ways of glocalising civic citizenship in relation to the global crisis of citizenship examined in "The Globalisation of Modern Citizenship" section. To recollect, the formal and then informal imperial spread of modern citizenship and the underlying institutions it sends on ahead to clear the way has led in many cases, at best, to a form of global cosmopolitan citizenship for official NGOs and multinational corporations; low-intensity citizenship for dependent elites of the former colonies; the dispossession or marginalisation of local citizenship and governance, the subordination of local economies and polities to global corporations and trade regimes; enormous inequalities; violent cycles of repression and resistance; and increasing environmental destruction. This crisis of modernity/coloniality has coincided with a crisis of democratic deficit in the representative democracies of the hegemonic states. The informal imperial networks of economic, legal, cultural, media, security, and military relationships not only bypass and undercut the diverse citizenship of billions of people who are governed by them, but also manipulate, downsize, and disregard the representative and legal institutions of modern citizenship that are supposed to bring them under representative authority. These trends of globalisation constitute a crisis of global citizenship that, viewed in isolation, is experienced as a pervasive sense of disempowerment and disenchantment. I want now to move around and reinterpret them from the standpoint of glocal citizenship.

First, despite these devastating trends, another world of legal, political, and even economic diversity has survived and continues to be the *loci* of civic activities for millions of people. The reason for this remarkable survival and renaissance in the post-colonial world, unknown to the dominant debate over global citizenship, is that Western imperialism governs through indirect or informal means and thus depends on the active collaboration of imperialised peoples exercising constrained local self-government. Those who are not part of the Westernised elite have been able to keep their diverse local citizenship practices alive to some extent within the broad parameters of informal dependency relationships. One of the most astonishing examples among many is the survival and resurgence of three hundred million Indigenous peoples with their traditions of governance and citizenship after five hundred years of genocide, dispossession, marginalisation, and relentless assimilation. The lived experience of citizenship in the present age is thus different from and more multiplex than it is portrayed through the sweeping generalisations of globalisation theories of both its defenders and critics. Many existing diverse practices of governance have been corrupted into exploitative and despotic relationships by their dependency on indirect rule and others were non-civic from the get go. The point is neither to reject them simply because they are non-modern nor to uncritically accept them because they are different or traditional. It is rather to bring them into critical and comparative discussions with other forms of governance and citizenship and to explore ways citizens can civicise them by speaking and acting within them (Mander and Tauli Corpuz 2004; Mamdani 2001). In the modernised West a vast repertoire of local citizenship practices have also survived within the interstices of state-centric modern citizenship, such as traditional working class organisations and countless new and creative forms of coops and networks linking rural and urban citizens in countless ways and around countless civic goods (the environment, nonviolent dispute resolution, low-cost housing, anti-racism, organic farming, place-based pedagogy, neighbourhood security, and so on). These old and new citizenship practices and improvisations are multiplying rapidly today in the "turn to the local" of a new generation disenchanted with the elite manipulation of representative citizenship.

The second example of glocalising civic citizenship is the array of movements to "democratise democracy." The aim of these movements is to democratise the legal, political, and bureaucratic institutions of modern representative democracy so that the people who are subject to them are consulted and have an effective negotiated say within them *wherever* power is exercised non-democratically and unaccountably, in ad-hoc processes of speaking out and "going public" or in more formal modes of negotiation in which those who govern must listen and give an account. These are thus movements to "civicise" the civil institutions of modern citizenship. Here civic citizens join hands with civil citizens engaged in the same projects from within – such as proportional representation, deliberative democracy, democratic constitutionalism, legal pluralism, civic *versus* civil security, and the various initiatives to democratise the UN and global governance institutions from within (Santos 2007; Loader and Walker 2007).

Third, since decolonisation and the triumph of informal imperialism, millions of the world's poor have been forced to migrate from the colonised world to the imperial countries to find work in a closely controlled global labour market. Despite the hardships of poverty, slavery, exploitation, racism, xenophobia, and second class or non-citizenship, they refuse to be servile subjects and exercise their civic citizenship in new and untoward ways instead, negotiating their diverse cultural ways into the public and private institutions of modern citizenship. This "journey back" or "boomerang effect" of formerly colonised peoples now civicising the imperial countries challenges the dominant imperial, nationalist, and racist cultures encoded in modern citizenship institutions and creates new forms of multiculturalism and multi-civilisationalism, both in the urban centres and the diasporic relationships ("transnational civic scapes") they sustain with their former countries. These deeply multicultural communities in "mongrel cities" generate new kinds of citizen relationships of "conviviality" among their members and with supportive local civic citizens groups.

These three examples and many others similar to them are existing practices of local civic citizenship. These worldwide local sources and resources of civic citizenship are much stronger and resilient than we think. They are the bases of glocal citizenship. Networks such as informal federations, NGOs, social movements, and similar creative improvisations are the means by which glocal citizens link together and so glocalise these local civic bases. These networks are civic and glocal just insofar as they are (1) grounded in and accountable to the local civic nodes, and (2) hyperextend civic relationships (citizen and governance/citizen) and other civic aspects in their own organisation and their relationships with others. If, in contrast, they see themselves as bringing the gifts of civilisation and modern citizenship to the less-developed, then they are "modern" (civil and cosmopolitan) networks. In addition to providing mutual learning and aid to their member civic nodes, they also crucially provide the civic means of democratising the persisting global imperial relationships of inequality, exploitation, and dependency that are the major cause of the crisis of global citizenship. Civic networks do this counter-hegemonic work in two mains ways.

First, as we have seen above, the persisting economic, legal, political, debt, media, educational, and military relationships of informal imperialism are so unequal that, although the elites within the former colonies are able to have a say and negotiate (in global governance institutions and elsewhere), they (the G120) are barely able to modify these governance relationships, let alone transform them into governance/citizen relationships, and they are in turn scarcely in civicised relationships with their own people (the majority of the world's population). Similarly, the hegemonic partners in the relationships – the great powers and their multinational corporations – are not held democratically accountable by their own citizens. Accordingly, the first role of a glocal network is to link together glocally enough local citizenship practices of those who are governed by any of these relationships to single it out and contest it: to call its existence and privacy into the space of public questioning and put enough soft power pressure on the responsible powers-that-be to bring them to negotiations in the most effective place or places. It is thus the glocalisation of the whole practice of civic negotiation discussed in the "Diverse Citizenship" section. Networked contestation and negotiation can take place anywhere and by anybody in the relationships (for example, in sweat shops and/or consumer boycott of sweatshop products, in the WTO or in protest against the WTO). It should not be the burden of the wretched of the earth to refuse to submit and act otherwise, as in the dominant theories of resistance, but of the most powerful and privileged to refuse to comply and engage in the work of glocal citizenship. In doing this, citizens in glocal networks are engaged in civicising and democratising these imperial relationships by bringing them under the shared authority of all those subject to them *in* their local places and ways. If the negotiations take hold, the subaltern partner ceases to be "dependent" but also does *not* become "independent" (as was imagined in the unsuccessful theories of decolonisation). Rather, the partners gradually become "interdependent" on the ongoing democratic relationships between them. These innumerable practices of glocal negotiation comprise one nonviolent path of de-imperialisation and democratisation characteristic of the civic tradition (Escobar 2004).

The second way glocal networks work to transform imperial relationships into democratic ones is through the spread of cooperative relationships between partners in the North and Global South. These cooperative informal federations are not strategies of contestation and negotiation, but of directly acting otherwise; of creating nonviolent civic relationships between partners in the North and the Global South. The relationships among all the partners in the network, and within each partner's local association, are worked out civically and democratically as they go along. Although there are thousands of examples, perhaps the best known are glocal cooperative "fair trade" and self-reliance relationships, such as the specific fair trade case, in contrast to competitive free trade; glocal networks of nonviolent dispute resolution in contrast to war, militarisation, and securitisation; and deep ecology networks in contrast to (oxymoronic) sustainable development. Like their local cooperative partners, these glocal cooperative citizens play within the existing global rules in each case, yet they play a completely different game. They create and live "another world" in their civic and glocal activities.

Third, the World Social Forum has emerged as an important place where civic and glocal citizens can meet each year. It is to diverse citizenship as the

World Economic Forum is to modern citizenship. The forum does not take a position, but, rather, provides a civic space in which participants from diverse citizenship practices can enter into dialogues of translation, comparison, criticism, reciprocal learning, and further networking. They share the knowledge of their different arts of citizenship with each other without granting modern citizenship the universal and superior status it claims for itself and on the presumption that each mode of citizenship is partial and incomplete, so each can learn its limitations from others. The forum also hopes to develop closer links of reciprocal learning between academic research on citizenship and the practices of citizenship we have been discussing, perhaps setting up popular universities of the social movements for this purpose, thereby deepening relationships of mutual aid (Santos 2006; Conway 2004).

If all the millions of examples of civic and glocal citizenship practices could be taken in in a single view, like the tradition of modern citizenship and globalisation presents it inexorable progress, perhaps this would help to dissipate the sense of disempowerment and disenchantment the present crisis induces. But, from the situated standpoint of diverse citizenship, this cannot be done and the attempt would overlook the very diversity that the civic approach aims to disclose and keep in view. Civic empowerment and enchantment come not from grand narratives of universal progress, but from *praxis* – actual participation in civic activities with others where we become the citizens we can be. But this response raises the question of the motive for participation in the first place. The civic answer has always been the motivating force of role models or exemplars of the civic life.

Today, there are millions of exemplars from all walks of life in all locales that move potential citizens of all ages to participate in civic/glocal practices that arguably make up the largest decentralised and diverse movement in the world (Hawken 2007). But perhaps a particularly exemplary exemplar for our dark times of the kind of glocal citizenship I have sketched is Mahatma Gandhi and his lifelong struggle to rid the world of imperialism. His ordinary civic and glocal life continues to move millions of people to begin to act. The reason for this, I believe, is the sheer simplicity of the four citizenship practices his life manifests. The first is active non-cooperation in any imperial (non-civic) relationship and with any corresponding idea of one universal civilisation or cosmopolitanism for all. The second is civic organisation and uncompromising nonviolent confrontation and negotiation with those responsible for imperial relationships with the aim of converting them to nonviolent, democratic relationships. Third, for these two activities to be effective they have to be grounded in the local practice of the alternative world you want to bring about. For Gandhi, this consisted of "constructive work" in local, self-reliant, civically organised villages, and respectful participation in their ways. Fourth, all this has to be grounded in "experiments with truth" – a spiritual relationship to oneself in one's relationship with others and the environing world. This is a relationship of working daily and truthfully on oneself and one's attitude in order to improve how one conducts oneself in these trying yet rewarding civic relationships with others: that is, the daily practice of making oneself an exemplary citizen (Weber 2004).[10]

Notes

1 The endnote at the beginning of each section lists the background scholarship on which the section is based. The few endnotes within each section refer to specific literature that is not referred to in the scholarship list at the beginning or is particularly pertinent. For introductions to this broad field, see Amoore (2005), Brodie (2004), Dower (2003), Dower and Williams (2002), Held and McGrew (2002).

2 I discuss the various theories of modern citizenship from Immanuel Kant to the present in the works listed in notes 3, 4, 6.

3 For the background scholarship to the "Modern Citizenship" section, see Tilly (2007), Held (2006), Ishay (2004), Skinner and Strath (2003), McNally (2006), Tully (2008b, 195–222).

4 For the background scholarship to the "The Globalisation of Modern Citizenship" section, see Tully (2008b, 127–65, 195–222), Potter (1997), Tilly (2007).

5 For the origin of the widely used term "low-intensity democracy," see Gills et al. (1993). For the more recent scholarship see notes 4, 6, and Grandin (2007).

6 For the background scholarship to the "Diverse Citizenship" section, see Tully (2008b, 73–90, 91–123), Pocock (2003, 553-584).

7 For recent critical work in this complex tradition of civic freedom, see Norval (2007), Zerilli (2005), Kompridis (2006).

8 The best known example of this movement is Joseph Stiglitz, the former head of the World Bank (see Stiglitz 2002)). See more generally Rahnewa (2006).

9 For the background scholarship to the "The Glocalisation of Diverse Citizenship" section, see Tully (2008b, 225–42, 166–94, 73–90), Sahle (n.d.), Hawken (2007).

10 I am most grateful to Eunice Sahle and Michael Byers for helpful discussions and Michael Peters for inviting me to participate in this important project.

7 Rethinking Human Rights and Enlightenment

A View from the Twenty-First Century (2012)

The Oxford Amnesty Lecture Series invited "speakers to explore both the historic contexts from which rights emerged, and what an understanding of this history might mean for their relevance and, more importantly, their status as truths today."[1] This is a weighty historical task. I can only begin to explore the surface in my simple historical approach. If we approach rights as tools or equipment for getting things done by individuals and groups in the multiplicity of relationships in which they live and act, then I argue that we can distinguish at least two distinctive traditions of human rights that stem from the European Enlightenment: that is, two ways of thinking and acting with rights in fields of relationships. These traditions overlap and criss-cross in complex ways historically and in the present. Nevertheless, explicating their dissimilarities, and the differences these make in practice, helps in clarifying the struggles both with and over human rights today.

The first tradition is alluded to in the title of the lecture series. It claims that human rights are something that can be unilaterally declared by an authority because they are self-evident universal truths that are beyond debate. These universal human rights presuppose and are exercised in a universal set of modern legal, political, and economic institutions. These universal institutions have to be coercively imposed prior to the exercise of human rights since they are the pre-condition of the exercise of human rights. Among these universal institutions is the modern state, which establishes the basis for human rights and coercively remedies their violations. To declare, project and then spread these institutions around the world; to be socialised into them; and to exercise human rights within them is to be on the universal path of development to a universal endpoint, which is called the modern Enlightenment. This tradition became dominant in the nineteenth century and it remains paramount today. It is the view of human rights from the perspective of a legislator who has the power to project rights and institutions over the world. I call it the Enlightenment project or the high Enlightenment tradition of human rights.[2]

The second tradition claims that human rights are proposals. They need to be *proposed* to fellow citizens by fellow citizens, rather than declared by an authority. The reason for this is that human rights are not self-evident, but, rather, they are always open to question and critical examination by the

DOI: 10.4324/9781003227403-10

humans who are subject to them. They gain their normative force by being reflexively tested, interpreted, and negotiated *en passant*. Moreover, there is not one universal set of institutions in which human rights can be exercised. There is a plurality of political, economic, and legal institutions in which human rights can be realised and these too gain their legitimacy from being open to the contestation of self-determining persons and peoples who are subject to them. Human rights and their institutions are not prior to democratic participation, but, rather, human rights and democracy go together, hand in hand. It follows that human rights and their institutions cannot be coercively imposed. They must be spread by democratic and nonviolent means. Enlightenment does not consist in a developmental and institutional endpoint, but rather in the continuous deepening of the co-articulation of human rights and democratic participation in exercising and improving them, world without end. I call this the democratic or co-articulation human rights tradition. It has come together as a recognisable alternative tradition more slowly and recently than the predominant high Enlightenment tradition. However, I conjecture at the end that this democratic approach to human rights may now be gaining ground.

The first part of the lecture consists in setting out the high Enlightenment view of human rights and its history from the eighteenth century through to international human rights at the United Nations. The second part of the lecture consists in setting out the main features of the democratic approach to human rights in a series of historical and conceptual contrasts with the dominant tradition.[3]

Before I begin I would like to acknowledge my debt to three outstanding exemplars of human rights. The first is Howard Zinn. For me and millions of people in the Global North and South he exemplified the democratic human rights tradition in his writing and his human rights activism (Zinn 2007). The second is Jeremy Seabrook of Oxfam, whose writings on the history of the inequalities between the Global North and South are a constant inspiration (Seabrook 2003). The third is Amnesty International. This organisation is one of the finest global exemplars of the democratic, nonviolent, and pluralistic ways to propose, discuss, and spread human rights (Kahn 2009). As you can see from these three mentors, my lecture is not neutral with respect to the two traditions. My aim is to challenge the common presumption that one must either be for the Enlightenment project, which presents itself as the only way to think about and institutionalise human rights, or reject human rights altogether, and to show that there is another, better way of thinking about and actualising human rights that is alive and well in practice.[4]

Part I: The High Enlightenment Project of Human Rights: The Priority of the Institutions of Human Rights to Democracy

Introduction: Enlightenment Human Rights, Institutions, and Processes

The high Enlightenment project of human rights consists of four main features. First, a person is recognised as having the status of a human being with dignity in virtue of a universal set of rights and correlative duties. Second, the possession, exercise, and security of these fundamental rights presuppose an underlying universal set of legal, political, economic, and military institutions of the modern state. Third, these universal rights and institutions are the product of historical processes of civilisation or modernisation. Fourth, this Enlightenment module of rights, institutions, and processes develops first in Europe. It is then spread to non-European peoples, who are at lower levels of world-historical development, by means of European imperialism: first by colonisation and indirect rule, and then, after decolonisation in the twentieth century, by means of informal imperialism of the modernisation and democratisation projects of the great powers, the institutions of global governance, and the dependent elites in the former colonies.

Such a project makes sense only if we take into account a fifth self-evident truth of the Enlightenment. This is the transition from the pre-Enlightenment view that humans have rights and responsibilities in prior social relationships of cooperation to the Enlightenment view that modern rights are prior to and the condition of civilised relationships of cooperation and sociability. Subjection to and participation in the modern institutions of Western law and private property, commerce, representative government, and the public sphere pacify and socialise pre-modern or pre-civilised human beings. This truth is so self-evident that it does not have to be proposed to humans for their consideration. It can be declared unilaterally. Indeed, human beings reach the stage of sociality and reasonableness sufficient to reflect on and affirm this self-evident truth only once they have been socialised in and by these enlightened rights, institutions, and historical processes.

Four Types of Human Rights and Underlying Institutions

Let's look at four main types of Enlightenment human rights and their underlying institutions. These types of human rights are not exhaustive and I do not mention every specific right within each of the four categories; rather, I focus on the core rights in each category. Other rights are normally subordinate to these high Enlightenment human rights.[5]

The first and most important tier of rights comprises civil rights. These are the negative liberties of modern subjects. These rights consist of: the liberty of the individual or corporate person of free speech, thought, conscience and faith, of formal equality before the law, and of the economic liberty to own property and enter into contracts. At the centre of civil rights is the modern civil liberty to enter into the private economic sphere, to engage in commerce or market freedoms and free trade, and to be protected from interference. This first tier of rights of modern liberty is primary; it is literally *the liberty of the moderns*. It acts as a kind of sheet anchor with respect to other rights.

The first tier of human rights presupposes not only the rule of modern law that underpins it and the modern state that enforces it, but also a set of legal and economic institutions in terms of which it makes sense. That is, for us to be able to exercise our market freedoms in the private sphere there must be capitalist markets, the dispossession of the people from other relationships to their land and resources by means of the often violent and destructive establishment of private property, labour markets and corporations, and the corresponding systems of legal rights.

This first tier of modern civil rights – the liberties of the moderns – is paramount. It is the right not to be interfered with in these activities by the *demos*. In addition, it provides the major justification for the global spread of these legal and economic preconditions and for the opening of societies to free trade, that is, economic modernisation.

The second tier of modern rights comprises the political rights. These are rights to participate in representative elections, the public sphere, and civil society. Like the first tier of modern civil rights, participatory rights presuppose underlying institutions in which they can be exercised: that is, representative governments, political parties, elections, the public sphere and civil societies, and the differentiation between private and public spheres.

The imposition of these modern, centralised institutions presupposes the *processes* that remove the multiplicity of other forms of citizen-participation in other forms of government; and the socialisation of citizens into this modern mode of representative participation. Citizens do not exercise powers of self-government. They are said to "delegate" these to representatives. Citizens exercise communicative powers in elections and public spheres through official channels, and with the hope of influencing voting behaviour and public policy.

The political rights of modern participation in politics are subordinate to the first tier of civil rights of market freedoms in the private sphere in four ways. First, historically, rights of participation in modern representative institutions are said to come along after processes of modernisation set the underlying economic institutions of modern commercial freedom in place. The processes of economic modernisation are said to require more dictatorial forms of rule initially, such as colonisation, slavery, indentured labour discipline, military rule, structural adjustment, military intervention and reconstruction, and so on. Once the modern discipline of labour market competition is established, people can begin to exercise their modern participatory rights; yet under the tutelage of colonial powers, and, after decolonisation, the tutelage of modern advisors, non-governmental organisations and the policies of democratisation of the World Bank and International Monetary Fund.

Second, the rights of modern participation are optional: one is a citizen in virtue of having the right to participate whether or not one actually exercises it. Third, the major justification for political rights, especially in the liberal and neo-liberal traditions, has been to protect individuals from interference or domination by the government or the *demos*: namely, to protect private autonomy. Fourth, the rights of citizen participation are restricted to exercise in the public sphere, not in the private sphere (as in economic democracy).

The third tier of modern rights comprises social and economic rights. These are rights that were won in response to the horrendous inequalities and exploitation of unregulated market freedoms of tier one civil rights and by means of political rights. In this tradition, they are not interpreted as rights of citizens to exercise their social and economic powers themselves, but rights that provide basic social assistance and help to integrate the unemployed back into the market.

This modular form of civil, political, economic, and social rights, with their underlying military, economic, legal, and political institutions of the modern state, was codified in the nineteenth century in the standard of civilisation in modern international law. The modern state-form was recognised as the highest form of political organisation. It alone was recognised as sovereign under international law. Although only European states approximated this norm of human organisation, it was said to be the ideal form for all peoples and societies. All other, non-civilised societies and their institutions were ranked by the new social sciences historically, normatively, and cognitively in accordance with universal stages of historical development, from hunting-gathering societies at the bottom to modern European states at the top.

The Enlightenment project of human rights was not only a project for Europe, but for the world. The European powers gave themselves a fourth human right, *ius commercium* or cosmopolitan right of free commerce and trade. This right is the Trojan Horse of European imperialism because it brings the institutions of tier one economic rights with it (Mommsen 1977, 86–99). It is the right of European traders and missionaries to enter into non-Europe societies and enter into commercial relationships with them. This involved opening their resources and labour to commodification and exploitation by the private and public companies of the competing European state empires. Non-European peoples were said to have a correlative duty of hospitality to open their doors to trade and commerce. If they failed to do so, then the great powers had the right to intervene, open doors, protect foreign investments from expropriation, and so on. Finally, the European powers were said to have a duty not only to exploit the resources and labour of non-European countries, but also gradually to guide them up the stages of historical development to the civilised level.

Just like the other three human rights, this fourth universal right of trade, of exercising one's market freedoms abroad, also presupposes an underlying set of economic institutions in the host country: namely the commodification of land and labour in accordance with Western property and contract law. The coercive spread of the basic economic and legal institutions of private property in land and labour throughout the non-European world has been called primitive accumulation, the second enclosure movement, commodification, privatisation of the commons, and economic globalisation today.

These violent processes of modernisation require the military force sufficient to overcome resistance, to override previous forms of economic organisation, to slaughter the millions who refuse to submit, to impose slavery and severe labour discipline, to protect the whole system of market rights from resistance and expropriation, and to establish colonial despotic rule or support local compliant despotic rule. This enforcement mechanism took various forms: gunboat diplomacy, formal colonies, indirect rule, spheres of influence and, most successful of all, free trade imperialism backed up by garrisons and naval bases around the world in the case of the British Empire. As the United States grew to a world power in the nineteenth and twentieth centuries, it followed the British in exercising free trade imperialism over Latin America and the establishment of small military bases throughout the continent, all under the right to spread civilised institutions under the Monroe Doctrine. The United States now has over 780 military bases around the world to open doors to free trade and to keep them open against the threat of local peoples taking democratic control of their own economies.

The imperial project of civilising the non-European peoples consists first in imposing the basic economic and legal institutions that open resources and labour to rapid exploitation by the companies of the competing European states. Second, as the lower peoples are gradually moved up through the stages of development through authoritarian governance by Western administrators, they can gradually be introduced to degrees of self-government, and this leads eventually to the acquisition of the same four tiers of human rights and underlying institutions as the enlightened modern states already possess.

The coercive projection of modern rights and institutions throughout the world by imperial means, most famously presented by Immanuel Kant and John Stuart Mill, was put into practice in nineteenth-century international law, the Mandate System of the League of Nations, the trustee system of the United Nations, the foreign policy of the United States since the Cold War, and the policies of the institutions of global governance today (Anghie 2004; Wilde 2008). According to Kant, the very existence of a country that does not have rudimentary modern legal and commercial institutions and centralised coercive authority (a legal civil state) is a threat and injury to all civilised states. The civilised states have the right to impose such an order over the people, thereby putting them on the developmental path to civilisation, or remove them (Kant 1991, 98; Anghie 2004, 295–7).

Human Rights at the United Nations and Decolonisation

The development of international human rights at the United Nations by the Commission on Human Rights (CHR) is arguably the most important event in the history of human rights since the eighteenth century. Human rights became part of international law and the United Nations became a forum to discuss, formulate, enact, promote, and monitor human rights. From the CHR, beginning in 1947, to today, a very large catalogue of international human rights has been developed: the Universal Declaration of Human Rights (1948), the International Covenant on Civil and Political Rights (1966), the International Covenant on Economic, Social, and

Cultural Rights (1966), the Declaration on the Granting of Independence to Colonial Countries and Peoples (1960) and, after the CHR, the Declaration on the Right to Development (1986) and the Declaration on the Rights of Indigenous Peoples (2007). These have been complemented by the Universal Declaration of the Rights of Peoples (1976), the African Charter on Human and Peoples' Rights (1977), the expansion of minority rights, the rights of the child, the right to participate in development, and much more. This remarkable achievement has changed the way that the whole world thinks about politics and it has given rise to a global culture of human rights and human rights organisations of various kinds.[6]

Yet if the history of human rights at the United Nations is examined, as Roger Normand and Sarah Zaidi (2008) have recently done, a certain amount of continuity with the earlier period of the spread of the high Enlightenment human rights module is evident. The three main types of human rights, their hierarchical ordering and interpretation, uniform institutional bases, and processes of imposition and monitoring by the powerful states have remained at the centre of the human rights project since 1948.

The United States delegation, with the aid of the British and Canadian delegations, dominated the Commission and crafted the main documents in accordance with US foreign policy in the Cold War. The modern sovereign state remains the enforcer of human rights and the ultimate decision-maker of which human rights are to be protected and violations remedied. One litmus test was the refusal of the Commission to hear complaints of racial discrimination by the African-American delegation on the grounds that individuals and groups do not have a right to petition human rights abuses; only states have the right of petition. As Hersch Lauterpacht famously complained, the lack of individual petitioning power and the devolution of the enforcement of human rights to domestic jurisdiction effectively increased the power of states (Normand and Zaidi 2008, 157–9). Against the wishes of the socialist states, economic and social rights were separated from the civil and political rights and subordinated to them. Yet the socialist states accepted the general Enlightenment project, its underlying institutions and processes of rapid development and centralisation, and the sovereign state as the ultimate authority over human rights. Thus, the three ranked tiers of rights of the Enlightenment module were reproduced in the covenants. The right to private property and the fourth right of corporations to trade freely in any country in the world were also written into the Universal Declaration of Human Rights and almost every international trade law and agreement of the General Agreement on Tariffs and Trade and the World Trade Organisation. Moreover, most of the human rights documents conform to the high Enlightenment premise that human rights and their canonical institutions are the preconditions of human freedom and democracy (Normand and Zaidi 2008, 139–242).

The Third World of decolonising peoples came into the CHR once it was underway. They received recognition of their right to self-determination in Resolution 1514 in 1960 (United Nations General Assembly 1960). The

Non-Aligned Movement of former colonies attempted to free the majority of the world's population in the Third World not only from colonial imperialism, but also from the new form of neo-colonial or post-colonial imperialism after decolonisation, exercised by both the capitalist West and the socialist East. They based their case on the universal right of self-determination, of peoples' right to determine their own interpretation of human rights, their appropriate institutions, and the best processes of development. That is, they argued for political, legal, and economic pluralism in opposition to the imperial imposition of one form of institutionalisation and development of human rights.

Next, the former colonies argued that the right of self-determination gave them the right to renegotiate the deeply unequal power relations between the Global North and South by means of negotiation between free and equal peoples. That is, they used the right of self-determination to try to bring the great powers to address and transform the greatest injustice on the planet: the persistent relationships of massive inequality, exploitation, subordination, environmental destruction, indebtedness, dependency, and forced centralisation and militarisation. This was put forward in the New International Economic Order (1974). It was defeated by the great powers (United Nations General Assembly 1974; Rajagopol 2004, 73–134).

During the Cold War, the United States was able to continue what the centuries of formal imperialism had begun, but now by informal means: the integration and subordination of the Third World into the global economy and the opening of their resources, labour, and markets to free trade dominated by the multinational corporations of the great powers. The great powers and their dependent elites imposed rapid centralisation, dependent development, indebtedness, and militarisation, destroying or marginalising local forms of political, legal, and economic organisation. Free trade prevailed over fair trade; comparative advantage over self-reliance; centralisation over pluralism; armament over nonviolence; dependent elite rule over broad-based democracy from below; huge private corporations and government agencies over democratically run cooperatives. As Wolfgang Mommsen summarised this trend, "the end of empire and the continuity of imperialism" (1976, 332–58; 1977).

There has always been a lively debate and healthy lack of consensus over human rights and institutions at the United Nations. Yet a dominant interpretation emerged early and continues today. The right of self-determination, which initially seemed so promising, is interpreted as the right of a people to determine themselves into a modern Western state form, based on the three rights and their underlying institutions, and open to free trade under international law. This is now argued to be the universally valid form of self-determination (Habermas 1996, 286–7). If a people fail to follow this universal model, they are subject to covert or overt intervention and reconstruction along familiar lines. As Woodrow Wilson explained to the earlier League of Nations, this is simply the application of the Monroe Doctrine to international affairs (Tully 2008b, 3–30; Grandin 2007).

In the 1980s and 1990s, economic and social rights were reinterpreted as rights to participate in capitalist markets. Minority rights were seen as ways of integrating minorities into the three main types of rights of the Enlightenment project. As the Non-Aligned Movement disintegrated in the 1980s, the right to development was read down as the right to be included in global processes of rapid neo-liberal economic development or face intervention and reconstruction. The right of participation of the early 2000s, which looked so promising in the 1980s, has come to mean the right to have a say within, and to be socialised into, the institutions and forms of subjectivity of tier one and two rights and their underlying institutions. The new "right to democracy" of international law entails the duty to accept the basic market and representative institutions of the Enlightenment project. The security resolutions of the Security Council after 9/11 have reinforced these trends and criminalised the widespread popular opposition to them (Normand and Zaidi 2008, 243–342; Rajagopol 2004, 135–232; Scheppele 2006). If this neo-liberal trend continues unopposed, the recognition of the right of Indigenous peoples to a form of internal self-determination in 2007 may serve to integrate 370 million Indigenous peoples into the modern states imposed over their traditional territories by five hundred years of imperial expansion (United Nations General Assembly 2007; Henderson 2007).

The Asocial Sociability Premise and its Consequences

The coercive spread and enforcement of the institutions that are said to underlie universal human rights have always been met with various forms of responses. And outright resistance has been met with counter-insurgency. I do not think we can understand this complex contrapuntal history unless we grasp the underlying premise of both sides.

As we have seen, one of the basic assumptions of the Enlightenment project of human rights is that these rights rest on and presuppose a specific set of modern Western institutions in which the rights are exercised. Humans must have these institutions and be socialised into them before they can participate in the free activities of cooperation and contestation that human rights guarantee. The reason for this coercive and anti-democratic basis of human rights is that humans (individuals, races, peoples, classes) are basically antisocial and antagonistic, and thus untrustworthy. As a consequence of this widely held Enlightenment premise, it is irrational to try to reason with another person or people prior to imposing coercively a secure structure of law on them. Only once their asocial dispositions have been socialised, pacified, civilised, or modernised by subjection to a coercively imposed structure of cooperation of some kind (such as military rule, Western law, primitive accumulation, labour discipline, markets, state structures, restructuring policies) is it reasonable to approach and engage with them as persons and peoples with the dignity of rights-bearing and self-determining agents. Thus the coercive imposition of the basic institutions of human rights is the means to bring about a situation in which we can treat each other as persons with the capacities to exercise rights properly and the democratic capacities to question, negotiate and improve rights over time. Violence, wars, and despotic rule – as authors from Thomas Hobbes and Kant and John Stuart Mill, Charles Darwin, Karl Marx and their many followers argue – are the necessary and irresistible means to peace and a rights-based just world order.[7]

Unfortunately for this dogma of the necessary relation between violence and human rights, the people over whom the allegedly universal institutions of forced cooperation are imposed do not submit. They understandably distrust the intruders, reason in exactly the reciprocal way in response, purchase arms, and resist violence with violence. This familiar outcome is then said by the proponents of violence on both sides to prove the reasonableness of their premise (humans are naturally antagonistic because they are not yet socialised) and of the conclusion (more coercive imposition of the institutional preconditions of socialisation is needed, or more resistance to their imposition is needed).[8] Unremitting wars of imposition and resistance continue apace, but, contrary to Kant's prediction, they do not lead to perpetual peace and the kingdom of ends. The resulting "security dilemma," as it is called in international relations, leads to the spiral of violence, war, and power politics, as everyone can see today who is not blinded by this dogma and the exploitative way of life it serves. Yet we are told again today, by philosophers, world leaders and peace prize recipients, just as Europeans were told in the late eighteenth and nineteenth centuries, that once these "pathological" processes of the Enlightenment project are complete, some future generation will have a just world order of human rights and perpetual peace.

Transition

Whatever its benefits may be, the imperial spread of the high Enlightenment module of ranked human rights and their underlying institutions has led to horrendous economic exploitation, massive inequality and poverty of the majority of the population of the Global South. These processes in turn are the major cause of environmental damage and global warming. The expansion of the United States global military network to protect these institutions and processes has led to wars, spiralling arms races, deepening indebtedness, and the militarisation of politics and dispute resolution. The current profiling and ranking of peoples and their different ways of life and religion as worthy of respect or threatening are also closely related to their conformity or non-conformity to the institutions and forms of subjectivity of the Enlightenment module (Seabrook 2003; Kahn 2009; Johnson 2004; Sahle 2010).

When concerned citizens try to exercise their human rights in response to these global problems they find that the institutions of second- and third-tier human rights are not very effective. Their political, social, and economic rights and institutions are limited by and subordinated to tier one market rights and institutions. Moreover, the limits on democratic human rights shield from public engagement the very processes and institutions that cause the global problems, since they are said to be prior to and the condition of democratic participation. These limitations thus lead to a further global problem. This is the global crisis of restricted or "low intensity" democratic participation, and hence the global protests by concerned yet constrained local and global human rights activists in response (Santos 2006). With this crisis of the paramount tradition of human rights in mind, we can now turn to the alternative democratic tradition of human rights.

Part II: The Democratic Enlightenment: The Co-Articulation of Human Rights and Democratic Freedom

Introduction

Let's now examine the history of human rights from the democratic Enlightenment tradition. This tradition derives from the Quakers in England and America, John Locke, Jean-Jacques Rousseau, Olympe de Gouges, Mary Wollstonecraft, Toussaint Louverture in Haiti, Henry David Thoreau, William Lloyd Garrison, Robert Owen and the great cooperative, enfranchisement, peace and anti-imperial movements of the nineteenth century, to Mahatma Gandhi, Martin Luther King Jr., Amnesty International and non-violent, democratic human rights activists today.[9] At the heart of this tradition, as I see it, is the rejection of the premise that a set of unquestionable human rights and their equally unquestionable institutions and processes of socialisation all precede democratic participation. It stands on the democratic premise that human rights and their institutions must always be co-articulated by the citizens who are subject to them. The individuals and peoples who are governed by and subjects of human rights must be, at the same time, free to call them into question and test them in discursive practices and to contest and reform them in non-discursive practices of various types of democratic cooperation and contestation. They should be both subjects of human rights and co-articulators of them.

Human Rights as Proposals to and by Free and Equal Human Beings and Peoples

First, human rights are not norms that can be unilaterally declared by some authority to be self-evident and binding on subjects and beyond question. Rather, human rights are proposals made by and to free and equal persons and peoples. They are proposed as tools for cooperating and for contesting and changing unjust forms and means of cooperation. No human rights are self-evident. As proposals, they are always questioned by those to whom they are proposed and the proposer has the responsibility to give reasons for them (Forst 2010). Dialogue, negotiation, interpretation, contestation, and revision emerge around human rights and continue forever. Human rights exist and have their meaning and normative force, not in striking us as self-evident, but rather in being proposed and used, and simultaneously being open to continuous questioning, interpretation, and negotiation by the persons and peoples who use them or are entertaining the possibility of using them. Human rights gain their authority from being open to the reflective critical enquiry and testing of the persons and peoples who hold them.[10]

This ideal of the co-articulation of human rights and democracy is manifest in practice. The human rights of the European Enlightenment have not gained their authority from being declared as self-evident truths. They have gained it from being questioned, interpreted, expanded, transformed, and fought over since their inception. And as we have seen, this questioning, testing, and improving has continued at the United Nations and on the ground in the great post-colonial struggles over human rights today.

The Democratic Dignity of Human Rights Holders and Being the Change

This democratic element is not just a basic feature of human rights. It is also a basic feature of the dignity of the person or the people that rights of individual and collective self-determination are designed to recognise and affirm. In the high Enlightenment view, the dignity that human rights embodies is that of a person being the subject of three types of self-evident universal rights and their universal institutions and processes of enlightened modernisation that socialise them into modern forms of subjectivity.

In the democratic view, the dignity that human rights recognise is the dignity of self-determining persons and peoples who have the capacities to work up and revise forms of self-government themselves: to be both subjects and authors of the norms of action coordination. To declare human rights as self-evident and to impose a rights regime unilaterally violates and undermines the dignity of human agency that human rights are supposed to recognise and enable. It robs human rights of their democratic authority. Furthermore, rather than creating free and equal democratic subjects from anti-democratic foundations, this approach tends either to socialise subjects into persisting relationships of master and compliant servant, since this is the relationship through which subjects are governed or, as we have seen, to generate resistance and counter-insurgency.[11]

The democratic approach treats the other to whom rights are proposed as always already a free and equal democratic agent, capable of agreeing to or dissenting from any human right from the first step. That is, humans acquire the abilities to treat each other as free and equal human beings with rights by being treated as such and being drawn into democratic relationships of dialogue and interaction. It follows from this Gandhian premise that human rights can never be spread coercively, by war and despotic rule, but only by means of respecting the dignity of persons and peoples that human rights are designed to affirm, empower, and protect.

This discovery of the peace and nonviolent movements means that human rights promoters and activists have to "be the change" that they wish to bring about. As difficult as it is, they must always act as if the other is already a person or people with democratic dignity. The human rights activist brings a human rights ethos into being by interacting with others in this free and equal democratic manner. Local and global cultures of human rights are *not* brought about by means that violate human rights: that is, by declarations, coercion, violence, and authoritarian forms of government. The effective and lasting way to actualise human rights is by acting and interacting in accordance with democratic human rights. Contrary to the high Enlightenment dogma, pathological means do not lead to moral ends. In the democratic view, means and ends are one and the same.[12]

This is the invaluable lesson that Amnesty International has taught us by the way they conduct themselves. Their nonviolent and democratic promotion of human rights has not only transformed the conduct of rights violators. It has also brought into being and sustained an exemplary culture of human rights cooperation and contestation that has served as a role model with normative force for millions of others.

The Plurality of Ways of Institutionalising Human Rights

Next, there is no single, universal, and uniquely modern or civilised module of institutions that underlie human rights. Rather, there are countless practices, customs, institutions, and relationships in which human rights can be exercised as tools for cooperating and for contesting unjust forms of cooperation. The democratic approach to human rights that I have just laid out entails the recognition and fostering of pluralism in the corresponding legal, political, and economic institutions both locally and globally (Tully 1995; Paley 2002).

Human beings take up human rights in the social relationships in which they find themselves here and now, social relationships that are often thousands of years older than the artificial legal, economic, and political institutions of the high Enlightenment module. Persons and peoples do not require a global project that destroys or marginalises their existing social relationships by military intervention or revolution and implants allegedly universal ones in their place. Rather, human rights are practices that can begin anywhere within everyday relationships, and they are path-dependent in their free and democratic evolution.

Almost all the human rights documents proposed by the Third World and the Fourth World call for this kind of human rights pluralism, and they ground it in the human right to individual and collective self-determination. This democratic ethos of human rights is also manifested in the organisation and proposals of the World Social Forum. The Global North is also beginning to rediscover the diversity of forms of political, legal, and economic life and the roles of human rights within them, and thus to awake from the dogmatic slumber of the imperious presumption that one size fits all (Santos and Rodriguez-Garavito 2005; Walker 2002).

The Democratic Response to Three Dogmas of the High Enlightenment Project

The acknowledgement of political, legal, and economic pluralism of the institutions of human rights involves more than recognising that the Enlightenment project's institutions are not universal, but simply one set of human rights institutions among many. This is of course true, and it is captured in the post-colonial critique of provincializing Eurocentric institutions and their links to imperial power (Chakrabarty 2000). Yet we have to go one step further to see the distinctiveness of the democratic approach to human rights and its challenge to the dominant approach. This step involves criticising three false dogmas in the high Enlightenment project.

The first criticism is of the assumption that the human right to private property in the productive capacities of labour is a commodity that can be treated just like any other commodity in market relations. The commodification of the productive capacities is not like other commodities. Human productive capacities cannot be disembedded from their background social relationships and inserted into the imposed competitive relationships of the global labour market without damaging or destroying the background cooperative social relationships in which labouring persons and peoples exist, and on which competitive market relationships ultimately depend.

This deeply flawed dogma of the Enlightenment project was recognised and criticised immediately, long before Karl Polanyi (2001) formulated it in 1944.[13] The response of the democratic tradition has been to propose and exercise the human right to disengage from the commodification of human productive capacities and the right to exercise them in democratically organised cooperatives, community-based enterprises, peasant communes, microcredit, local and global fair trade networks, and so on. These traditions have given rise to democratically organised political, social, and economic activities with their distinctive regimes of human rights and responsibilities. These have evolved nonviolently around the world and run parallel to the two destructive high Enlightenment alternatives of market liberalism and state-run socialism, and interpret human rights differently.[14] These democratic and cooperative institutions of social and economic human rights treat human productive capacities as embedded in broader local social relationships and exercised under the democratic authority of the producers, consumers, and local communities. This grassroots interpretation of social and economic rights is what Gandhi (2008, 67–105) and E.F. Schumacher (1973) called *swadeshi* and *swaraj:* economic self-reliance and democratic self-government.

The second criticism of the Enlightenment module is of the assumption that the human right to private property in land, in the environment, is a commodity that can be treated just like any other commodity in market relations.

The privatisation of the environment is not like other market commodities. The natural world cannot be transformed into commodifiable resources, and its effects treated as externalities, without destroying the background ecological relationships in which human beings live and breathe and have their being.

This ecological criticism of the commodification of the natural world developed at the same time as the social criticism of the commodification of productive capacities. It gave rise to the deep ecology movements that are now worldwide. The response of the democratic human rights movements to this second dogma of the Enlightenment project is to realise that human rights are not only embedded in and exercised in broader social relationships. They are also, and even more fundamentally, embedded and exercised in cooperative ecological relationships that unite the diversity of all forms of living beings in the world. Rights-bearing persons and peoples are thus Gaia citizens. They are citizens of a commonwealth of all forms of life and thereby have duties to respect and care for the ecological relationships that sustain them. If, on the contrary, modern human rights are taken as the very basis of legal, political, and economic relationships, their exercise destroys both social and ecological relationships, and, eventually, life on earth (Moran 2006; Brown and Garver 2008).

Thanks to the democratic, cooperative and ecological tradition of human rights, we are learning that the drafters of the Universal Declaration of Human Rights were correct in stating that human beings have dignity, human rights, and responsibility, not as abstract individuals, but as "members of the human family."[15] Following Albert Schweitzer, Rachel Carson, and Gandhi, democratic human rights activists have extended this world community to include all forms of life, human and non-human (Shiva 2005).

The third and final criticism is of the basic Enlightenment premise that humans are anti-social and untrustworthy and thus require the coercive imposition of modern institutions before they can exercise human rights. This dogma leads, as we have seen, to the false hypothesis that the unintended consequence of unremitting wars in the name of human rights will lead to the spread and eventual affirmation of human rights. Two hundred years later, we now know what Montesquieu already predicted in 1748: that the premise leads to perpetual distrust, armament, war, and rearmament (Montesquieu 1989, 224–5).

The democratic tradition challenged this premise in the nineteenth century. Classically, Kropotkin (1902) responded to Darwin that ecological and social relationships of cooperation and mutual aid are more pervasive and fundamental than relationships of antagonism and violent struggles for existence. If this were not true, if the basic condition were one of wars of all against all, or wars of classes, races, civilisations, and religions against each other, then the human species, and all other species, would have perished long ago.[16]

It has taken the work of peace and nonviolent activists and scientists the entire twentieth century to bring this cooperative premise to the awareness of the dominant tradition. Ecological scientists, climate scientists, conservation biologists, anthropologists, and even political scientists have substantiated the proposal that cooperation, not antagonism, is the primary factor in human and ecological evolution. This cooperative or Gaia hypothesis has begun, for the first time since the rise of the antagonistic model of human behaviour, to make inroads into the way proponents of modernisation think about human rights (Brown and Garver 2008).

Of course, this is not a self-evident truth but a contested hypothesis in the natural and human sciences. The point of the democratic tradition is that if we wish to realise a world of respect for human rights, we should to act as if other human beings are trustworthy and inclined to cooperation, as the majority of humans evidently do in everyday life, within or outside modern states.

If cooperative relationships are among the basic conditions of life, then institutions of human rights do not need to be violently imposed in order to lay down the basis of sociality. Quite the opposite. This approach disrupts and destroys already existing ecological and social relationships of cooperation. Rather, human rights are tools for conviviality within cooperative relationships; relationships that we have responsibilities to uphold and improve, as well as to remedy violations. Rights-bearers are caretakers of the pre-existing relationships in which they live and evolve, and human rights are tools of cooperation and nonviolent contestation within them.

Next, it is not only that relationships of cooperation and mutual aid are prior to competition in and over them. The democratic view is also that when disputes break out in everyday life, the normal course of action is to resolve them nonviolently rather than violently. Again, if this were not the case, if the violent resolution of disputes were normal rather than abnormal and pathological in everyday life, then the human and non-human world would have perished ages ago. If follows that violence is not a necessary feature of government or of the contestation of unjust forms of government.

This is of course the most contentious claim of the peace and nonviolent human rights movement of the twentieth century – of William James, Leo Tolstoy, Albert Einstein, Aldous Huxley, Bertrand Russell, Mahatma Gandhi, Martin Luther King Jr., and millions of followers. The coercive apparatus of modern states and global military networks, and of violent opposition movements, are unnecessary and counter-productive means in the promotion and protection of human rights, and in remedying their violations.

Human rights can be effectively proposed, adopted, used, abused, and remedied all by the plenitude of nonviolent means of cooperation and contestation that the peace and nonviolence movements have developed in the twentieth century. These countless means of exercising human rights and of alternative dispute resolution techniques are now argued by researchers and human rights activists to be "a force more powerful" than the power politics of the modern world (Ackerman and DuVall 2000).

As we have seen, democratic human rights activists argue that the use of violent means is to treat the other as less than human, a means rather than an end, to sow the seeds of distrust and armament in response, and thus to beget more violence. To employ nonviolent means to promote rights, undermine unjust rulers, resolve disputes, and remedy violations is to treat the other person or people as actors with democratic dignity, as capable of being moved by the normative power of reason and example. This nonviolent and rights-respecting mode of interacting with others brings into being here and now a nonviolent way of life and draws violent or unjust others into it. The way to remedy rights violations in this view is thus to engage in nonviolent forms of non-cooperation and negotiation. This is at the heart of the nonviolent practice of dispute resolution and the practice of transformative justice.

Human rights activists in this tradition neither impose human rights coercively nor submit to or resist violently narrow rights regimes imposed by others. They have developed three main strategies: revolutionary *satyagraha* and non-cooperation with unjust regimes and human rights violators (as with Gandhi); the transformation or modification of narrow rights regimes from within by bringing them under the democratic co-articulation of all those subject to them (as with King and countless human rights struggles today); and the re-appropriation of their own capacities of self-government and the establishment of democratically organised cooperative regimes of political, social, and economic rights (as with cooperatives, community-based organisations, and fair trade networks).[17]

Both Gandhi and King embodied this human rights *ethos* in their struggle for the right of self-determination in India and civil, political, and economic rights in the United States. They held on to it against all the violence mobilised against them. Yes, they were assassinated. Yet, the most powerful empire in the world was defeated in India, the Indian people gained the right of self-determination, and African-Americans gained civil rights in the United States, after the United Nations refused even to hear their petition. Perhaps even more importantly, they set an example that has been followed by millions of nonviolent human rights activists ever since.

The Democratic Relationship Between Human Rights and Duties

The final contrast that I wish to draw is between the role of duties or responsibilities in the two human rights traditions. The Universal Declaration of Human Rights states that rights and duties go hand in hand. In the high Enlightenment tradition, this is taken to mean that rights correlate with duties: (1) with a duty of others to respect the right; or (2) with a duty of government to provide the underlying institutions in which rights can be exercised; or (3) with a duty of governments coercively to remedy violations of rights.

In the democratic tradition, duties are interpreted differently. They precede and enable human rights. The persons and peoples who hold human rights are also the holders of duties to cooperate in providing the social conditions and means by which human rights can be exercised. The internal relationship between human rights and the enabling human duties follows from everything

I have said and from the historical lessons of the self-governing and cooperative movements of the last two centuries. It is based on the premise of popular sovereignty and self-government: we the people, individually and collectively, have to be the change: to embody in our activities the change that we hope to bring about in the world at large.

For example, if humans have a human right to clean water, then they have a duty to protect the commons from privatisation and to participate in governing the water supply for the public good. If they have a right to peace, then they have a duty to act peacefully and for peace in their activities and to refuse to cooperate with war and violence. If they have rights to health, work, shelter, and a decent diet, then they have corresponding duties to work in relationships of mutual service that make the exercise of these rights possible (as in the food sovereignty movement). If someone violates a human right, the remedy is the duty we all have not to cooperate with them, as well as to boycott, protest, strike, and negotiate until the violation is remedied and the violator is converted to nonviolence and human rights.

Like members of the high Enlightenment tradition, democratic human rights movements are proponents of delegating some of these corresponding human duties to representatives, whether the representatives are public governments or responsive private corporations. They also engage in public spheres and courts to try to influence representative governments and hold private corporations and international institutions of global governance accountable. Yet they are opposed to the idea that this delegation model is the only way that human rights can be realised; for, as we have seen, it tends to lead down the slippery and disempowering slope of the unconditional alienation of these responsibilities to coercive institutions that then claim they are the very condition of the possibility of human rights.

The democratic human rights tradition has learned that huge private and public institutions that claim to spread and protect the foundations of human rights will do so by means of human rights if and only if they are held accountable by active and engaged democratic citizens. If citizens sit on their hands and expect governments to provide the public goods and private corporations to provide the meaningful work that human rights require for their exercise, they will not do so. They will be unaccountable to the persons who handed over their responsibilities to them and they will be manipulated by the powers that be.

Moreover, democratic citizens have learned that a culture of active and engaged democratic citizenry, capable of acting in public spheres and holding governments and private corporations accountable, has to be grounded in something even deeper than participating in elections and public sphere discussions. It has to be grounded in an everyday, democratic human rights way of life in which persons and peoples from an early age learn to practice their underlying human responsibilities at the same time as they learn to practice the human rights that these underlying duties of mutual service make possible.

For the entire democratic human rights tradition, the practice of these human responsibilities is the real foundation of the human rights that we have today. These human rights were not declared by the political, economic, and military powers that be and handed down to the people after they had built the underlying institutions for us and spread them around the world by anonymous processes of development. It is a grand narrative that is reiterated by the great powers and legitimated by their great philosophers generation and after generation. Yet from the democratic perspective, it has the world of human rights upside down. We have the imperfect human rights we enjoy today because human beings, individually and collectively, took up the responsibilities of enacting their human duties and rights in every walk of life, from the lowest to the highest. It is the manifestation and normative force of this living democratic ethos of human rights that moves governments and corporations to recognise and support human rights.

In conclusion, to see this underlying human rights ethos is to become aware of another kind of Enlightenment – democratic human rights Enlightenment – that exist all around us and is the real foundation of human rights. It is overlooked, partly because of its familiarity and everydayness, and partly because of the captivating majesty and power of the high Enlightenment alternative. Yet I would like to propose that this lower case human rights Enlightenment is worth your attention and consideration.

Afterword

In 1947 the Secretary General of UNESCO asked the world's leading authorities on human rights to present their views on what a universal declaration of human rights should contain. The Secretary General would then pass their suggestions on to Eleanor Roosevelt, the Chairperson of the CHR. As we all know, Eleanor Roosevelt declined to accept the collection of articles that the Secretary General presented to her. Yet this collection became the most famous and comprehensive philosophical reflection on human rights in the mid-twentieth century. Among the lengthy articles that the great thinkers of the time submitted, there is a short, one-page letter by Mahatma Gandhi, written just before he was murdered. He explains that he does not have time to write a lengthy treatise, but is able to send only a short paragraph. Here is what he says:

> I learnt from my illiterate but wise mother that all rights to be deserved and preserved came from duty well done. Thus the right to live accrues to us only when we do the duty of citizenship of the world. From this one fundamental statement, perhaps it is enough to define the duties of Man and Woman and correlate every right to some corresponding duty to be first performed.

(Gandhi 1949, 18)

And he explains further elsewhere:

> Every man has an equal right to the necessaries of life even as birds and beasts have. And since every right carries with it a corresponding duty and the corresponding remedy for resisting any attack upon it, it is merely a matter of finding out the corresponding duties and remedies to vindicate the elementary fundamental equality. The corresponding duty is to labour with my limbs and the corresponding remedy is non-cooperation with [and conversion of] him who deprives me of the fruit of my labour.
>
> (Gandhi 2008, 97–8)

As you can see, my lecture is just a restatement of Gandhi's homespun view of rights and duties. All I have done is to put his thesis in the form of a proposal for your consideration.

Notes

1 Lecture delivered as the Oxford Amnesty Lecture, University of Oxford, February 2010. I would like to thank the organizers of the Oxford Amnesty Lecture Series for inviting me to present my thoughts. I would especially like to thank Kate Tunstall for being the perfect host. For their indispensable help in improving the lecture for publication, I am most grateful to Annabel Brett, Rainer Forst, Bonnie Honig, Anthony Laden, Quentin Skinner, Kate Tunstall, Jeremy Webber, and Antje Wiener.
2 One of the most influential presentations of this view of human rights is given by Immanuel Kant in two complementary essays: *Idea for a Universal History with a Cosmopolitan Purpose* (1784) and *Perpetual Peace: A Philosophical Sketch* (1795) in Kant (1991).
3 The lecture draws on the more extensive and detailed research and references in Tully (2008b, 243–310).
4 For a complementary defence of rights to which I am indebted, see Ivison (2008).
5 Background arguments and references for this section are in Tully (2008b, 125–310).
6 For United Nations documents see "Documents," accessed January 31, 2022, www.un.org/en/our-work/documents.
7 In *Idea for a Universal History* and *Perpetual Peace*, Kant argued that the unremitting wars and European expansion were the unjust yet necessary and irresistible "pathological" means by which providence spreads the institutional conditions for an eventual global "moral whole" based on his scheme of human rights. See Kant (1991, 45, 47, 108–14). See also Mill (1991, 232–7, 447–70), Pitts (2005), Marx (1853), Darwin (2003, 132–43).
8 For example, Fanon (1963) is the mirror image of the necessity of violence in the high Enlightenment theories.
9 I do not mean to suggest that each of these members endorsed every feature I use to define this tradition. Almost every one of them endorsed features that define the high Enlightenment tradition. This is the overlap. Rather, I mean that each member on the list advanced at least one feature that makes up the democratic tradition. I have retrospectively put these features, and so these members, together to compose a distinct tradition. I doubt if it could have been seen as a distinctive tradition prior to Gandhi.

10 For the philosophical justification of this democratic way of thinking of human rights, and norms of cooperation generally, see Laden (2012). For the contestability of human rights and norms in international law, see Wiener (2008). I am deeply indebted to Forst, Laden, and Wiener for their outstanding work on the internal relation between human rights and democratic contestation.

11 This is the classic argument of Wollstonecraft (2010). For the argument that the imposition of the high Enlightenment rights and institutions (primarily tier one economic rights) has had similar effects on colonized and post-colonial peoples and their governments, see Prashad (2007).

12 Although this idea and its practice were articulated in the nineteenth-century nonviolent suffragette and peace movements, they were brought together in a comprehensive anti-imperial and democratic philosophy by Mahatma Gandhi in *Hind Swaraj* in 1909 (2009) and developed throughout his later life.

13 For an update of the Polanyi hypothesis, see Evans (2008).

14 The classic study is Davidovic (1967). More recently, see Zamagni and Zamagni (2010).

15 The Universal Declaration of Human Rights, Preamble: "Whereas recognition of the inherent dignity and of the equal and inalienable rights of all members of the human family is the foundation of freedom, justice and peace in the world," accessed January 31, 2022, www.un.org/en/about-us/universal-declaration-of-human-rights.

16 Compare with Gandhi (2008, 88–90) and Montagu (1952).

17 The classic manual of nonviolent politics, endorsed by Gandhi and King, is Gregg (2018). See also Powers (1997) and Sharp (2005).

Part III
Sustaining Civic Freedom

8 Progress and Scepticism 1789–1989 (1989)

Many of the great thinkers of the European Enlightenment advanced two closely related beliefs.[1] The first was that the societies in which they lived possessed or were about to possess properties that made them different from all other societies in history and thus distinctively "modern." The second was that these modern features gave rise in turn to a second equally distinctive aspect of their societies: their "progressive" nature. Two hundred years later we continue to believe that we live in societies that are "modern" in roughly the sense given to this word during the Enlightenment. However, we tend to doubt and in fact to be highly sceptical of the belief that modern societies are progressive.

Four deeply troubling characteristics of our century are standardly said to have provided good reasons for the rise of scepticism and disillusionment with respect to progress. The horrors of two world wars shattered the belief advanced by Adam Smith (1723–1790), Immanuel Kant (1724–1804), Marie-Jean Condorcet (1743–1794), and Jeremy Bentham (1748–1832) that modern societies tend to peace. Our experience with war and militarism since 1945 has, if anything, increased scepticism. Over thirty million have died in the hundreds of wars since 1945; enough nuclear, biological, chemical, and conventional weapons have been built and deployed to exterminate most forms of life on the planet many times over; and our militarised international relations sustain an ever-increasing arms trade. The resulting *global* military-scientific-industrial complex is deeply embedded in the fabric of every modern society and, as Charles-Louis de Secondat Montesquieu (1689–1755) forewarned, it seems to be self-sustaining. Further, this complex is not some pre-modern atavism, but a structure that involves our most advanced and modern natural, social, and military sciences.

The second set of problems that has engendered robust scepticism about progress is the wide range of ecological damage, pollution, and destruction caused by the very features of modern societies that were claimed to support the progressive control of nature. In recent years, scientists working in the ecological sciences have done most to draw attention to the way modern societies squander resources and destroy rather than control nature. Third, in the so-called Third World high levels of famine, starvation, and hunger,

DOI: 10.4324/9781003227403-12

coupled with the brazen forms of oppression and exploitation, fly in the face of the predictions of Smith and Kant that the spread of modern markets and European imperialism would lead to "improvement" for non-Europeans. This feature alone has caused much of the world's population to see the belief in progress as an ideology that has served to legitimate the continued exploitation of the Third World by the first. The fourth characteristic is the failure of modern capitalist and socialist societies to cope with the domestic problems that the Enlightenment claimed they were uniquely suited to solve: unemployment and poverty, debt, corruption in politics, lack of political participation, human rights abuses, violence and crime, illiteracy, and the spread of "modern" diseases such as cancer, heart disease, toxic poisoning, stress, and so on.

As Lewis Mumford concluded in his review of Charles Beard's *A Century of Progress* (1932), "progress is the deadest of dead ideas ... thoroughly blasted by the facts of twentieth-century experience." Christopher Lasch (1987) pointed out in his recent lectures on progress that writers who still profess allegiance to progress do so as a matter of faith rather than belief, and out of fear of the consequences of giving it up rather than consideration of the evidence.

These four sets of problems, therefore, have given rise to a sceptical attitude to the belief in progress that has legitimated and secured allegiance to modern civilisation for almost two hundred years. This predicament often leads, as we know, to the degenerative extremes of either a cynical attitude towards the modern societies in which one must live and work but which one no longer respects or admires, or to a blind and dogmatic adherence to progress in the face of our problems. Fortunately, however, it also has ushered in a healthy resistance to and examination of the concept of progress in all areas of modern society. The aim of this examination has been to clarify how our belief in progress has led us to overlook, and so fail to question, those forms of modern thought and action that sustain and reproduce the four sets of problems we need to address.

There is scarcely a university discipline that has not been touched by the sceptical examination of the ways in which its procedures may rest on the uncritical acceptance of progressive assumptions inherited from the Enlightenment. This questioning has been most intense in the social sciences, for many of them were constituted during the Enlightenment and thus the sceptical attack seems to question their basic status as sciences. We have also seen the growth of the philosophy of science and social science as a separate discipline in which these debates are carried on. Further, scepticism itself, as an independent epistemology and moral and political philosophy, has become one of the fastest growing areas of contemporary philosophy. Finally, the broad cultural movement of postmodernism is probably best seen as an attempt to construct an ethos based on a permanent scepticism that would replace the modern ethos of progress. Indeed, post-modern writers argue that in their scepticism towards the present they are more faithful to the spirit of the Enlightenment than the defenders of progress.

The current reflection on progress is not a continuation of the longstanding debate over whether or not modern societies are progressive. This debate is a constitutive feature of modernity, from the debate over the ancients and moderns during the early years of the Royal Society, through the Enlightenment to the views of Thomas Henry Huxley (1825–1895) and Oswald Spengler (1880–1936), and on to Robert Nisbet's *History of the Idea of Progress* (1980). Since the writers in this debate use the procedures of critical reflection that are defining features of modern thought, they do not provide an independent means of questioning these procedures. Within this debate the question marks are not placed far enough down. Therefore, the current discussion of progress seeks to go one step further: to bring to light and call into question the language and forms of thought that both defenders and critics of progress share. These conventions, taken for granted in the course of the debates, are basic constituents of modern thought.

In the following two sections, accordingly, I will survey some of the major conventions of the language of progress that we have inherited from the Enlightenment. Of the many uses of the word "progress," the one that has become most common is closely related to "construction" and its cognates. Progress as construction consists in two parts: types of "development" inherent in modern societies, and forms of thinking and knowing in the natural and human sciences that are said to be characteristically modern. Modern forms of thought in the sciences are related to development in society by the application of the human sciences to administer and govern modern societies and by research, development, and application in the natural sciences. These features make up a picture of progress as the increasingly successful coordination of modern forms of thought and the rational control of natural and social processes.

This is not a comprehensive definition of progress but, rather, one picture of progress that has tended to captivate us and to elbow aside other ways of thinking about progress over the last two hundred years. It captivates us because it informs what we might call the language of progress: that is, the broad range of vocabulary and conventional linguistic usages that we, as children of the Enlightenment, continue to employ in our thinking and acting even when we attempt to take a critical stance to progress. As Ludwig Wittgenstein commented in 1930, "Our civilization is characterized by the word 'progress'. Progress is its form rather than making progress being one of its features. Typically it constructs" (Wittengstein 1980, 7).

To clarify this picture of progress, and so help us to free ourselves from its hold, I shall present synoptic historical sketches of the two sets of conventions the language of progress comprises. The first set of conventions represents progress as reform and gradual improvement. This view of progress was established in the early Enlightenment, from the mid-seventeenth century to the French Revolution. The second, progress as unintended and dialectical, was developed in reaction to the first, from the late eighteenth century to the present. Our current language of progress and the picture of progress sustained by our continued use of this language are an amalgam of these two. As we will see, even the most sceptical critics of progress tend uncritically to employ some of these conventions in their criticisms and so become entangled in the very language of progress they seek to clarify.

Progress as Reform and Gradual Improvement

> A *picture* held us captive. And we could not get outside it for it lay in our language and language seemed to repeat it to use inexorably.
>
> (Wittgenstein 2009, §115)

The early Enlightenment view of progress as reform and gradual improvement was developed in response to the crisis caused by the wars of religion that engulfed Europe from the 1560s to 1648. At the centre of the project of reform and reconstruction was the systematic use of techniques of sceptical doubting (inherited from the ancient sceptics and introduced into European thought by Michel de Montaigne [1533–1592]) to disengage from blind assent to custom, opinion, and the dogma of religious and scholastic authorities. Adherence to these authorities was said to be a major cause of the religious wars and of the blindness to advances being made in the mechanical arts and the new, non-Aristotelian science associated with Galileo Galilei (1564–1642). Once people had suspended their assent to traditional and authoritative beliefs, they would examine them in accordance with criteria of rational assent until they reached ideas that were indubitable. These ideas would provide the foundations of knowledge on which the new natural and moral sciences would be constructed, each step being systematically examined in accordance with the criteria of rational assent. Further, the "ideas" that were assembled in this way were understood to "stand for" or to "represent" their objects. The new way of thinking, accordingly, consisted of three parts: (1) systematic and shared procedures for doubt and examination, (2) the view of rational thought as cumulative construction on foundations that had passed the test of rigorous doubt, and (3) knowledge (or ideas) as representing its object domain. All disagreements of Thomas Hobbes (1588–1679), Pierre Gassendi (1592–1655), René Descartes (1596–1650), John Locke (1632–1704), and Isaac Newton (1642–1727) rest on agreement in these three assumptions.

This tripartite picture was related to the following concept of rational control. Accurate theoretical representations – of the workings of nature, of the human body and its motivational mechanisms, of human interaction, of the circulation of money and the balance of power, and so on – were to be constructed step by step and applied to reform and to improve the "human condition," and the effects of each reform were to be monitored systematically to correct the original projection and to guide the next reform in a cumulative manner. The modern applied sciences and the human sciences of political economy, statistics, demography, education, medicine, ballistics, and psychology emerged within this general framework in the seventeenth and early eighteenth centuries, from Antoine de Montchrétien (1575–1621) and William Petty (1623–1687) to René Louis d'Argenson (1694–1757) and Claude-Adrien Helvetius (1715–1771). These applied sciences were related in turn to the efforts of early modern states to increase their populations and improve their health, and to organise and increase their production and trade. The aim of this new comprehensive government of the basic productive and biological processes of the population was to "strengthen" the state and increase its wealth so it could hold out in the commercial and military rivalry among European states. These states in turn were locked in a balance of power system and in competition for control over the resources and labour of the non-European world. The new comparative political economy, from the analysis of European states by Samuel Pufendorf (1632–1694) to the great *Encyclopédie* edited by Denis Diderot (1713–1784) and Jean d'Alembert (1717–1783), provided ever more accurate and utile knowledge of the global possessions of the European colonial systems.

The last but not least important convention of this picture of progress was the understanding of the person as a malleable *tabula rasa* or blank tablet, without any innate ideas or natural dispositions. The individual was said to acquire dispositions to think and act in habitual ways by a process of continual repetition of the activity itself. The only constant and reliable disposition of human beings was said to be a causal inclination or motive to be concerned for one's self, that is, to seek pleasure and avoid pain. This provided a powerful explanation of human behaviour and a model for reform. Accordingly, by the judicious application of various types of pleasures and pains through rewards and punishment, an individual could be induced to engage in repetitive exercises of modern forms of thinking and behaving until these movements became habitual, and eventually pleasurable in themselves. Educational and legal reform consisted in applying these techniques to break down traditional ways of thought and action, to inculcate the new tripartite way of critical thought and to apply it in different activities. Also included was the systematic reform of work habits in the poorhouses of early modern Europe, so the poor would grow up with settled habits of industriousness and be inured to labour. The moral and political sciences were reconstructed around the individual calculating the pleasures and pains associated with the courses of action open to her or him.

Although these conventional assumptions continue to be deeply lodged in modern thought and action, willy-nilly, they have been shown to be dubious by many of the major philosophers of the twentieth century, including Maurice Merleau-Ponty, Ludwig Wittgenstein, Thomas Kuhn, and Charles Taylor (1986). The three-part account of knowledge rests on a straightforward misunderstanding. Our most critically reflective activity of doubting any proposition rests on the non-reflective uses of innumerable other words which are not doubted in the course of subjecting the proposition in question to doubt. Thus, our knowledge does not rest on foundations that have themselves been grounded by some doubting procedures. Rather, our doubting procedures themselves rest in a nest of judgments that are not doubted at all in the course of our enquiries. As Wittgenstein sums up this point:

> All testing, all confirmation and disconfirmation of a hypothesis takes place already within a system. And this system is not a more or less arbitrary and doubtful point of departure for all our arguments: no, it belongs to the essence of what we call an argument. The system is not so much the point of departure, as the element in which arguments have their life.
>
> (Wittgenstein 1974, §105)

Further, the assumption that language is a representational medium and that knowledge consists in clear and distinct representations of what it represents has been shown to be an overly simplified account of language and knowledge. "Representing" is one thing we do with language, but there are innumerable other things we do with it, even when we are engaged in the specialised and reflective activity of representing.

These criticisms from various quarters help us to see the captivating image of the knowing subject held in place by the three assumptions. It is a subject disengaged from customary and traditional beliefs, from language itself, and standing apart from the world as representer to object represented. The ascetic attraction of this godlike image of disengagement and radical autonomy has been explained in many ways. In addition, the picture reform and improvement has been shown to contain the same view of the acting subject, disengaged from the world and standing in an instrumental relation to it as controller to thing controlled. This too has been shown to be overly simplified and untenable. Even our specialised activities in which we do exercise control always rest in and presuppose a horizon of natural relations that we do not control and on which we depend.

Accordingly, critics have gone on to draw attention to the limits of human knowledge and control, to stress the extent to which we are, in knowing and acting, engaged in and dependent upon language and the world. They have also turned this argument around and shown that many of our problems in theory and practice in the twentieth century derive from continuing to think and act as if we could gain this kind of disengaged knowledge and control (Capra 1983; Mercant 1980).

As important as these criticisms are, they tend to overlook one striking feature of European intellectual history. Almost all the criticisms our contemporaries have advanced were made by the major thinkers of the late eighteenth and nineteenth centuries. However, these thinkers used the very limitations of human knowledge and control they discovered as a basis on which to construct an even more Faustian concept of progress. Many of our contemporary critics, far from criticising this new, dialectical concept of progress, continue to work within and sustain its conventions.

Progress as Unintended and Dialectical

The concepts of knowledge and rational control of the early Enlightenment were criticised in the period from roughly 1780 to 1850. The concept of rational control as comprehensive reform and improvement was associated with enlightened absolutism in France, from Cardinal duc de Richelieu (1585–1642) and Jean-Batiste Colbert (1619–1683) to Simon Linguet (1736–1794) and Louis XVI, and with the mercantile system in England. Adam Smith, Condorcet, Bentham, and Emmanuel Joseph Sièyes (1748–1836) all argued that modern commercial societies with representative political institutions and the division of labour were far too complex to know or to control in this way. Indeed, they argued that the attempt to exercise this type of control failed and also stifled improvement. Progress could be achieved precisely by not attempting to bring it about as a project. Rather, progress and the wealth of nations are the unintended and unplanned consequences of leaving individuals more or less alone to pursue their enlightened self-interest in the constraints of the division of labour in civil society and representative government. On this view, progress occurs behind the backs of the agents involved, by means of a hidden hand or, as G.W.F. Hegel (1770–1831) phrased it, by the cunning of reason. Thus, the three features that most of the earlier thinkers considered essential – comprehensive knowledge, control, and habituating each member of society to work for the common good – were said to be unobtainable, unnecessary, and inimical to progress. The philosophers of the late Enlightenment and of the Age of Reaction disagreed over how much coordination and invigilation was required *of* the autonomous processes in which mankind found itself constrained to live and work, but all agreed these were the natural limits of planning and control.

As we can see in hindsight, these later thinkers simply took for granted the organised forms of thought (the scientific disciplines) and the political, economic, and technical institutions that the earlier reformers had constructed. These appeared to be quasi-autonomous processes that were tending in a progressive direction without an overall director. The political act that symbolised this transition from modern to contemporary thought was the execution of Louis XVI. The absolute monarch, who stood above the law, was replaced by the republic, in which everyone was equally subject to the laws of politics, economics, and science, and to the division of labour, and was moved in a progressive direction by this very subjection.

The theorists went on to show how the conditions over which humans had no control were moving them, in spite of themselves, in a progressive direction. Individuals caught up in the dependency relations of the market – which automatically rewarded economically rational behaviour and punished irrational behaviour – would gradually become disciplined, polished, and enlightened, without the need for moral education. Their selfish pursuit of unlimited wants would bring about the greatest good of the greatest number.

As markets spread around the globe, governments would become economically interdependent and war would no longer be in their self-interest. Even wars would lead unintentionally to peace. Citizens, experiencing the cost and destructiveness of war, and thinking only of their self-interest, would curb military spending and adventurism through a free press and representative government. Thus, as Kant was able to sum up this whole line of thought in *Perpetual Peace* (1795), supposing humans to be devils, the unintended consequences of their dialectical unsocial sociability were leading them to scientific and material progress and to perpetual peace.

These progressive thinkers did not stop at grounding the mechanisms of progress in the institutional structures of modern societies. Charles Darwin (1809–1882) claimed to find such a mechanism in the natural world. Further, all of human history was understood as an unplanned progressive development passing through four stages. Since no other society in recorded history has ever understood itself in the terms of progress, but, rather, usually in the natural cycles of growth and decay, historical progress was said to occur behind the backs of the people involved. This entrenchment of progress in a fundamental historical process proved attractive to the generation of philosophers who grew up in the Age of Reaction after the French Revolution. The failures of the Revolution and the Terror were seen to be the result of sweeping away the traditional structures of French society and the imposition of abstract reform. This enabled critics as diverse as Edmund Burke (1729–1787), Joseph de Maistre (1753–1821), Hegel, Claude-Henri Saint-Simon (1760–1825), Isidore Auguste Comte (1798–1857), and Karl Marx (1818–1883) to interpret the Terror as the consequence of the earlier movement of progress, and to criticise it for its lack of historical and sociological understanding. Moreover, with their new historical and dialectical language of progress, this was an exercise in replacing one concept of progress with another. They could thus criticise the excesses of the Revolution, and indeed the whole "slaughterbench" of history, yet situate it as a necessary step in the progressive development of humanity.

This form of argument was shared by conservative and radical alike. Marx, for example, argued that the immediate unintended consequences of capitalism were regressive rather than progressive but that the consequence of these consequences was the unplanned development of the conditions for the overthrow of capitalism and progression to socialism. In this "master-slave" dialectic, the unintended consequences of human action create and sustain the social and historical conditions that enslave mankind, but the overall tendency of this self-imposed "subjection" is the progressive development of the human species in spite of itself. At its most optimistic, the belief is that the mechanisms of progress will gradually produce a human animal capable of knowing these mechanisms and bringing them under a new and comprehensive form of rational control. From Condorcet's *Esquisse d'un tableau historique des progrès de l'esprit humain* (1795) to the latest cybernetic model of humans' place in society and nature, this utopian rationalisation of present ills in the terms of their alleged future, progressive benefits knows no bounds.

The form of thinking characteristic of this dialectical concept of progress contains, in addition, two features not present in the earlier, tripartite conception. The first or "critical" feature is to ask of any claim to know or to doubt, what are the "conditions of possibility" for making such a claim or exercising such a doubt. This reflective step was employed to criticise the earlier view of knowledge by showing that there are background conditions for our reflexive activities of doubting and representing. The step, however, generates a paradox for two reasons: we are both the knower and the known, the subject and object of knowledge, and we claim both that our knowledge is limited and that we can know these limits. The paradox, or "dialectical of finitude," as it is often called, appears in the sciences that were developed in the nineteenth century on this form of thought: the attempt in the empirical sciences to account empirically for the transcendental conditions of possibility of the empirical field; in hermeneutics to make explicit the implicit horizons of explicit knowledge; and in phenomenology, to grasp conceptually the conditions of embodied or pre-conceptual knowledge (Foucault 1966, 1970, 312–35).

The second feature is the attempt to find some way to overcome the paradox. As we have seen in the new social theories, the sociological and historical conditions of possibility of human action were said to have a progressive bent. In an analogous manner, the solution was to claim that the epistemic conditions of knowing contained a dialectically progressive tendency. From Kant and Hegel through Friedrich Nietzsche (1844–1900) to Jürgen Habermas, this feature has taken a variety of forms. It standardly involves the claim that, due to historical development, the present generation can see more clearly into the underlying conditions of human knowledge. For Habermas, tendencies to truth, rightness, and sincerity are built into the use of language and these are uniquely transparent to moderns. In the hermeneutical or interpretative sciences, we are told that the condition of possibility of interpretation is an underlying inclination to clarity and truth. Even the sceptical Nietzsche posited, as the ground of his hermeneutics of suspicion, a natural drive of self-overcoming (*selbstaufhebung*). Thus, the first step is used to expose and criticise the unclarity, error, immorality, and insincerity of the age, whereas the second step claims to discover an underlying tendency to progress, as one stage or paradigm is typically said to correct and supersede in a more comprehensive form an earlier one.[2]

This language of progress as unintended and dialectical is deeply woven into contemporary ways of thought and action. Rather than replacing or superseding, it has become grafted on to the earlier language of progress as reform and gradual improvement. Thus, positivists and dialecticians from the Vienna Circle and the Frankfurt School, tend to play the conventions of one language of progress against the other in an interminable twentieth-century debate on progress.

Over the last twenty years post-modern critics have subjected dialectical progress to extensive investigation and refutation. The most influential post-modern scholar has been Jacques Derrida, who initially applied his "deconstructive" criticism to the work of one of the most important philosophers of science in the twentieth century, Edmund Husserl (1859–1938). The broad generalisations about the progressive tendencies of the unintended consequences of our scientific, industrial, military, and political institutions have been refuted by the four sets of problems mentioned above. The prevailing belief that knowledge develops in the natural and social sciences by one theory or paradigm superseding and comprehending its predecessor has been shown to be question-begging and inconclusive. Post-modern critics have exposed this dialectic of progress in all areas of our thinking, from the way we conceptualise scientific research and development and the way we organise the world into developed and developing nations to learning theory and the way we think about history. They have gone on to "deconstruct" this last "meta-narrative" of the Enlightenment. The cumulative effect of these criticisms has been to suggest that the progress the dialecticians claim to discover is rather a feature of the language they use.

Conclusion

The new post-modern sceptics have shown how we have become entangled in and bewitched by these two language games of progress over the last two hundred years. However, their way of thinking continues the most destructive features of both conceptions of progress. In criticising the limits imposed on *our* thinking by progressive assumptions, they assume that the only rational response to any limit or convention is to deconstruct and to overcome it. They see themselves as engaged in the endless task of "overcoming" or "overthrowing" self-imposed limits. Thus, any use of the word "natural," "limit," or "foundation" needs to be exposed as something imposed by us and constraining us in what is essentially a wholly contingent universe, self, and society, open to infinite interpretation and manipulation.[3] They thus combine the radical contingency of the first view of progress with the ethics of overcoming of the second (without its progressive faith).

I scarcely need to say that this post-modern way of thought and action is not what we require today. Its activity of deconstruction is simply the reversal of the prevailing picture of progress as construction. We need a way of thinking that continues the best traditions of critical thought, not only from the Enlightenment but also from a much more cosmopolitan range of sources, in order to continue this careful task of self-criticism of our reigning forms of critical thought. Moreover, as ecological and feminist scholars have stressed, we require a way of thinking that is able to recognise and to affirm the limits of our knowledge and action and the extent of our dependency on the natural world. Rather than a mistaken picture of our control *over*, we surely need to recover a sense of our appropriate place *in* the universe, which the Enlightenment swept away as a pre-modern superstition. As an increasing number of people have sought to remind us, we are one species among millions on an interdependent and fragile planet. And we are in a universe that was not made for us and that will long outlast our inevitable passing.

A line of argument that might lead in this direction is the current questioning of two further conventions of both conceptions of progress. These conventions, perhaps more than any others, cause us to overlook the complexity of what we are trying to understand and to assume a disengaged and transcendent viewpoint. The first is the widely held assumption that understanding consists in having a comprehensive theory, which sets forth the essential features of the phenomenon in question. In the *Philosophical Investigations*, Ludwig Wittgenstein showed that this is a mistaken conception of understanding (2009, §§65–97). Any phenomenon we seek to understand is too complex to be grasped in a general schema which purports to lay out its essential features, because instances of a general phenomenon do not have the common and essential features this view presupposes. Rather, to put it negatively, they have complicated and overlapping similarities and relationships. If so, understanding cannot consist in possessing a general theory. It involves, rather, surveying and paying careful attention to the examples, and thus gradually acquiring a familiarity with them and their complex relations with one and another.

Let us take progress as an example. I have presented a brief survey of two examples of progress and drawn your attention to their similarities and dissimilarities. There are numerous other examples of progress and no one could claim to know what progress is until they had become familiar with additional samples. Moreover, a general theory of progress would necessarily overlook the complexity of my two examples, and *a fortiore* the complexity of other examples, by treating a small number of features as if they were essential to and definitive of every instance of progress. A theory, by representing progress in this way, would thus cause us to overlook and therefore misunderstand the very phenomenon we seek to understand.

We can see that many of the sweeping generalisations that the great progressive thinkers put forward about the essential nature of knowledge, reason, science, society, history, and, of course, progress itself, were based on this mistaken view. Unfortunately, many of the critics who have picked out errors in the earlier theories continue to construct even more abstract and misleading theories. Recently, for example, philosophers of science have put forward one theory after another of the essential nature of science. Critics such as Paul Feyerabend have demonstrated that for each theory of the essential rules of any science there is always a decisive counterexample. However, sharing the same assumption as their opponents, some critics (but not Feyerabend) have gone on to conclude that since science conforms to any of the sets of rules or schemata advanced by the philosophers then it is not a rule-governed activity at all: anything goes. If they would abandon their common misconception, as Wittgenstein and Thomas Kuhn recommend, they could go on to survey the numerous examples of science available to them, to become familiar with the various and irreducible ways in which science is a rule-governed and non-anarchic activity, and thereby come to understand what science is.

Of course, we can always construct a theory or a generalisation if we wish as long as we remember that it serves the limited and heuristic purpose of throwing light on a small number of features of the phenomenon at the expense of obscuring all others. Therefore, whereas the misidentification of understanding with theory directs us away from the multiplicity of the world and towards abstract and procrustean representations of it, Wittgenstein's argument directs us towards attention to and wonder at its irreducible diversity and our relations to it. Wittgenstein complemented this with a second line of argument that I have used in my analysis of the two concepts of progress. All our enquiries, no matter how reflective and critical, always take place within some ways of thinking and acting that are taken for granted and not questioned. Being engaged in these "language games" or "forms of life," as he called them, does not impose some limit that needs to be deconstructed and overcome, nor does it render our knowledge defective in any way. The correct attitude, accordingly, to this prosaic and natural feature of the way we are in the world is acceptance: "what has to be accepted, the given, is – so one could say – *forms of life*" (2009, §226, §23). (He does not mean that we must accept any given form of life, but that questioning a given form of life involves the acceptance of others and not a transcendental standpoint.) As we have seen, the Cartesian activity of radical doubt – of the earlier conception of progress – overlooked the non-reflective and unquestioned forms of thinking and acting with words in which it was indeed grounded. Although the post-Kantian thinkers were able to see this error in their predecessors, they mistakenly claimed that their own reflective activity of making explicit the unquestioned conditions of any claim to know was itself free of such conditions. Yet, their forms of reflection rested on and took for granted a whole range of conventions of the progressive form of life in which they thought and acted. Wittgenstein argued that the progressive forms of expression I have surveyed in this essay caused these great thinkers, and continue to cause us, to overlook and misunderstand the forms of life in which we are naturally engaged in all our reflective activities, and thus to struggle against the natural way we are placed in the world as if it were some limit to be overcome (Hilmy 1987, 190–227).

We are just beginning to appreciate the full significance of these two lines of argument. However, if we are to have a future in which we are able to address the four sets of problems that confront us, we shall need to clarify and to set aside the conventions of the old language of progress that cause us to overlook and to perpetuate the activities that give rise to these problems. Hence, it seems that these two arguments will be as central to such a future as the arguments of Descartes and Kant were to the old age of progress. And, if we are fortunate enough to modify our destructive forms of life in time, there will be a different sense in which it will be right to call this future an age of progress.

Notes

1 Lecture delivered at the Royal Society of Canada symposium on Progress, Université Laval, June 1989. This chapter is dedicated to Professor Charles Taylor, Fellow of the Royal Society of Canada, of McGill University, who was unable to attend the symposium.
2 For a recent example of these two features, see MacIntyre (1988, 349–69).
3 A good example of this line of thought is provided by Rorty (1989, 3–69).

9 Introducing Global Integral Constitutionalism (2016)

Jeffery L. Dunoff, Anthony F. Lang Jr.,
Mattias Kumm, and Antje Wiener

Introduction

As we stated in our 2012 and 2014 editorials, *Global Constitutionalism* is a scholarly arena of critical reflection on the contested field of global law and governance. Although there is a long history of global interaction among peoples, empires, and colonies, the field was re-articulated as global and globalising after World War II and, with even more and widespread insistence, after the end of the Cold War. The field includes the law and politics of states and state-centred international law, but it situates these in the dense, global legal and governmental relationships, institutions, and processes within, around, and beyond the state and state-centred systems (that is, globalisation from above, in between, and below).

We emphasised in our 2013 editorial that this is an inherently contested field in both practice and theory. We invited scholars from multiple disciplines to submit articles on the contested practical problems of law, governance, and ethics of the field from their different methodological and normative perspectives, whether these are empirical case studies, historical interpretations, or middle- and high-level theoretical contributions. Our objective was and remains to bring to life an ongoing critical dialogue among contributors and readers around the world from their diverse perspectives. This *Global Constitutionalism* dialogue is not based on a pre-emptive editorial consensus or an implicit orientation towards consensus as the end point. Rather, it is an attempt to instantiate the kind of critical and problem-oriented dialogue that David Bohm (2014), the great scientist and philosopher, argued is necessary if we are to clarify and address effectively the crises we face today. This is a form of dialogue that takes into account the fact that all perspectives are limited (perspectival) and, therefore, all disclosures of the problem and proposed solution are also limited. Thus, they always require the reciprocal enlightenment of engagement with alternative perspectives to bring each other's explicit claims and implicit presuppositions (limits) into the space of questions and create a genuinely multi-perspectival critical dialogue.

The contributors to *Global Constitutionalism* have been remarkably successful in initiating this kind of dialogue in the journal and the events,

DOI: 10.4324/9781003227403-13

courses, and discussions that have grown around it. We look forward to its continuation and especially to contributions from perspectives that have not yet entered the arena. To facilitate this enlargement of the dialogue, in the 2015 editorial we argued that the global crises of the "hard times" of the present call into question the globalisation of the trinity of human rights, democracy, and rule of law, as well as the progressive narrative that underlies it. We suggested in response that human rights, democracy, and rule of law should be seen as historically contingent and contested phenomena that should be studied contextually from a plurality of perspectives outside of the progressive framework in which they are normally situated. Furthermore, we welcomed submissions that not only critique the progressive narrative, but also the colonial and post-colonial imperial project of international law that it is said to legitimate by its critics. We would now like to take this suggestion a step further by sketching one such critical and contestable perspective and the alternative understanding of global constitutionalism that it discloses. We are not endorsing this perspective, but, rather, bringing it into the arena for critical consideration.

The Development Paradigm and Human Rights, Democracy, and Rule of Law

Global constitutionalism refers to the global field of diverse, formal, and informal assemblages of laws and governance, norms and actors that exhibit *constitutional qualities*. Although they are contested, constitutional qualities include features such as the distribution and separation of powers, responsibilities, rights, and offices; secondary rules that constitute and limit primary rules, courts, and governments; bindingness and compliance mechanisms; degrees and types of institutionalisation; intergenerational persistence; publicity, non-arbitrariness, and contestedness; and widely accepted norms of legitimation. A sufficient number of such features constitute assemblages of governance and laws as "systems." Different systems of laws and governance around the globe exhibit various subsets of these constitutional qualities and, accordingly, are called constitutions, constitutional systems, and "processes of constitutionalisation" to that extent.

In the modern West, constitutions and constitutional processes are standardly seen as the basic constitutional qualities or structure of a state and state system under international law that *coordinates* the domains of law, representative governance, foreign policy, economy, technology, military-industrial complexes, public and private, human rights, citizen participation, and popular sovereignty (or constituent power). The well-known, unattained yet enduring immanent ideal of this modern form of constitutionalism is that the constitutional qualities coordinate the constituent power of the people (or peoples) and the rule of law across these domains so that they are always equally basic or equiprimordial: the people and peoples who are subject to the laws are also the ongoing authors of them, directly and/or through delegated and revocable representatives (what we call democratic constitutionalism).

Broadly speaking, the space of questions our journal seeks to open includes questions such as what are the global assemblages of law and governance?, what kinds of constitutional qualities do they exhibit?, what systems of coordination or non-coordination do they bring about, and with what consequences?, do new spaces emerge where constitutional norms are negotiated by a plurality of stakeholders?, and if so, what are the potentially novel organising principles that are forged through these bottom-up practices of constitutionalisation? The objective is to enquire into these sorts of question without disclosing the field in terms of constitutionalisation within states, yet also to learn from the similarities and dissimilarities between state and global constitutionalisation.

In our 2012 editorial, we noted that three norms of legitimation of constitutional states (human rights, democracy, and rule of law) were predicated of processes of globalisation from the founding of the United Nations onward. Much of the contestation of globalisation has been devoted to struggling for their realisation in diverse practices and to critical reflection on the norms and practices of implementation from different perspectives and traditions of interpretation in academic research. Yet, much of this research, in *Global Constitutionalism* articles and elsewhere, shows how poorly these norms represent the real, grim, and violent world of contemporary globalisation. This disconnection between the trinity and the real world of globalisation is the reason we turned in our 2015 editorial to question a fourth norm predicated of globalisation: progressive development. This norm posits a set of global processes that is presumed to bring about the necessary historical conditions for realising democracy, human rights, and rule of law. This supposed relationship between a certain kind of economic and technical development and the realisation of human rights, democracy, and rule of law is the "development paradigm" we wish to examine.

From this modernising and globalising perspective, human rights, democracy, and rule of law are not seen as primary or constitutive constitutional qualities, but, rather, as secondary constitutional qualities that are realised by the gradual spread around the globe of the more basic constitutional qualities of the development paradigm. Economic and technical development move assemblages of law, governance, and forms of subjectivity through stages of development from authoritarianism to modern constitutionalisation, rule of law, social mobilisation, human rights, and democratisation. In 1944, Karl Polanyi (2001) pointed out the three constitutive processes and institutions of economic constitutionalisation that drive development: the privatisation, commodification, and constitutionalisation of the earth (natural resources); human productive capacities (human resources); and money (fiscal resources). That is, private law precedes and sets out the range and limits of regulatory possibilities for public law and its coordination role.

According to the development paradigm, these three processes and institutions of commodification are placed under the control of private corporations and spread around the world and protected by military and financial competition among states during and after colonisation; by profit-driven competition among corporations; and by competition among governments, parties, unions, communities, and individuals for jobs. In time and through the exercise of military and financial power, the more advanced states and corporations establish institutions of global governance and bring the weaker states in line. Once the primary constitutional qualities of economic constitutionalisation are secured by top-down institutions of global law and governance, the realisation of the secondary constitutional qualities of human rights, democracy, and regulatory rule of law will follow by progressive social mobilisation, governments, and civil society actors engaging in reforms or revolutions. Global constitutionalisation thus follows the same general development pattern as state constitutionalisation, yet with specific differences in stages and the much-discussed question of the institutional form of the end state (world state, plurality, hegemony, communism, unlimited growth, endless conflict, and so on).

The central dynamism of development is explained by its mobilisation of competitive freedom and the lack of any overall plan or governance, which would intervene in the private sphere, infringe on freedom, and stifle growth. Hence, establishing the historical conditions for the global realisation of human rights, democracy, and rule of law, and thus global justice and perpetual peace, is the unintended consequence of self-interested competition for wealth and power of the free actors caught up in the modernising processes. Vicious means bring about virtuous ends.

This "hidden-hand" development paradigm became orthodoxy in the nineteenth century. Adam Smith, Immanuel Kant, G.W.F. Hegel, John Stuart Mill, Karl Marx, and Max Weber initiated its major schools of interpretation and legitimation. These schools have continued to dominate the interpretation, legitimation, and debate of globalisation since World War II.

When critics raise doubts about this metanarrative over the last century and in our times, its apparent setbacks and depressions are explained by uneven development or the backwardness of those who resist. Its remarkable capacity to overthrow non-compliant regimes, defeat revolutions, survive wars and crises, and continue to grow is said to be proof of its inevitability and the non-existence of any alternative modernity or globalisation. Moreover, the very idea of progressive development by means qualitatively different from its legitimating ends enables its proponents to locate its norms of legitimation in the realm of the "to come" no matter what happens. Thus, the discontented and impatient are told to become mature, stay the course in the face of hard and seemingly contradictory times, and hold tight to the blind faith that more inequality will lead eventually to equality; war and war preparation to peace and disarmament, authoritarian rule to democracy; competition to cooperation; capitalism to communism, securitisation to liberty, emergency law to rule of law; withholding human rights to human rights; more development to creative technological climate change solutions, and so on.[1]

Sustainability Crises

Despite these sophisticated yet circular defences of the development paradigm in response to recurrent anomalies, critical scholars, and activists remain unpersuaded. They continue to raise objections and offer alternatives (Rist 1997).[2] They point to four global sustainability crises that appear to be brought about by the development paradigm and which fly in the face of its faith in progress.[3]

The first crisis is the systemic, intergenerational inequalities, poverty, starvation, and suffering within the Global South, and, increasingly within the Global North. The second is the expanding military-industrial-intelligence complexes engaged in escalating cycles of violence and counter-violence: war preparation, wars of massive human, infrastructural and environmental destruction, reconstruction, and rearmament. The third is the ecological crisis, including climate change and the onset of a sixth mass extinction. The fourth is the refugee and migrant crisis.

These four global crises are interconnected by the global processes that bring them about and reproduce them. The historical processes of modernisation, industrialisation, Western expansion, economic globalisation, and rapid exploitation and depletion of the world's renewable and non-renewable resources are the major cause of climate change and the ecological crisis. They are also the major cause of the inequalities between the Global North and South, and within the Global North and South. And, one of the primary roles of the escalating global military-industrial complexes of the great powers is to protect and expand the very processes of economic globalisation that are deeply implicated in the ecological and inequality crises. Major factors of the refugee and migrant crisis are the destabilising effects of Western imperialism, the war and arms sales complex, poverty, climate change, and the ethnic and religious differences that these processes transform into armed antagonisms. These four interconnected processes generate resistances of various kinds, and the responses to the resistances in turn often generate complex positive feedback loops that amplify the inequalities, recourse to violence and counter-violence, and ecological damage, pollution, and global warming. Moreover, the interactions of these far-from-equilibrium complex systems produce multiple, ramifying collateral and boomerang effects and tipping points on all life systems on earth that are difficult, if not impossible, to predict and control, as we mentioned in our 2015 editorial (see also Brown 2011).

As a result, these systemic crises are called "sustainability and well-being" crises because their cumulative effects damage and destroy the interdependent social, ecological, and atmospheric networks and cycles that co-sustain the life and well-being of *Homo sapiens* and millions of non-human species and ecosystems. They are damaging and destroying the ecological conditions and living networks that have sustained life on earth for over 3.5 billion years as the successive reports of the Intergovernmental Panel on Climate Change show (2014; Harding 2013). The evidence for the multiple crises of sustainability and well-being was sufficient by the 1980s for a new norm to emerge and be widely accepted in principle across all systems of law and governance: sustainability and well-being.[4]

Global Economic Constitutionalism

Moreover, these four crises take place in the context of a global democratic deficit that severely constrains effective responses. When governments and citizens organise to contest, regulate, and reform the unsustainable development processes, they find that they are severely limited by the global economic constitution of the development paradigm in the following anti-democratic ways. The global processes of development that are the major causes of the crises are driven largely by the transnational corporations (TNCs) that profit from the activities that cause them. They have grown so large on the basis of the three commodifications that they are now more powerful than most governments and citizens' movements. Governments and citizens have become dependent on them for taxes, financing, jobs, and consumer lifestyles that feed the crises. TNCs have become "shadow sovereigns" (George 2015; Cutler 2013).

From the General Agreement on Tariffs and Trade (GATT) to World Trade Organisation (WTO), International Monetary Fund (IMF) and World Bank (WB) to the latest Free Trade Agreements (FTAs), such as Transatlantic Trade and Investment Partnership (TTIP) and Transpacific Trade Partnership (TTP), they put in place global systems of trade laws, agreements, and treaties. These legal regimes function as the constitutional quality of "secondary rules" relative to national constitutions, democracy, human rights, and rule of law. The resulting form of global constitutionalism is often called neoliberal constitutionalism or "economic constitutionalism." (The troika of the IMF, European Central Bank, and European Commission is argued to function in a similar manner in the European Union.)

The institutions associated with global economic constitutionalism possess the authority to limit, restructure, or override the authority of democratically legitimate national constitutions and rule of law. They often prescribe rules and policies that override and roll back well-established civil, social, economic, and environmental rights, impose austerity programmes, and generate chronic unemployment. Similarly, their Investor to State Dispute Settlement (ISDS) institutions supplant the authority of national courts. Democratic governments, implementing the will of their citizens, can be and are sued by the TNCs for millions of dollars for actions intended to advance environmental, health, safety, and other legitimate social interests. Furthermore, there is a deep asymmetry in access to the institutions of global economic constitutionalism. Only foreign investors can initiate a claim process. Thus, the narrow definition of "stakeholder" in these institutions effectively disempowers the vast majority of citizens (and non-human life forms) that are massively affected by global economic treaties and agreements. Moreover,

TNCs' well-paid lobbyists, and a handful of officially recognised non-governmental organisations, exercise non-democratic and disproportionate influence on the world's governments, institutions of global governance, and the United Nations. In these and numerous other ways, the institutions associated with global economic governance violate the basic principle of democratic legitimacy that all subject and all affected should have a say. And, finally, the secret drafting of the agreements violates the basic principles of transparency and justification. The processes that support global economic constitutionalism thus enact an anti-contestatory mode of constitutionalism.

Furthermore, the various international attempts by government and institutions of global governance to cooperate through negotiations, treaties, protocols, and accords in order to reduce poverty and social suffering, reduce war and increase disarmament, and to reduce global warming and repair destruction of ecosystems and biodiversity since the 1960s have been limited at best. These failures and limited successes are not all due to the influence of TNCs. They are also often due to denial, short-term interests trumping long-term consequences, and strategic geopolitical-economic competition among unequal states in the more familiar realist sense. However, even in these more traditional coordination problems TNCs play a significant and non-democratic role.

In these and other ways, global economic constitutionalism protects the development paradigm and TNCs from "interference" (regulation) in the name of the primary rights of corporate persons, free trade, and unlimited growth. In so doing, the development paradigm does not unintentionally lay the groundwork for human rights, democracy, and rule of law to come, as the official narrative has it. Rather, it tends to produce and reproduce the crises of sustainability and well-being, and limit and override democratic and high-level attempts to address them. These are arguably the real unintended consequences of the development paradigm in our time. On this view, the power of the global economic constitutionalisation of the development paradigm and its crises does not begin with neoliberalism, TNCs, and the state-owned enterprises of China. They derive from the global enclosure and commodification of the last three centuries: that is, from the beginning of the Anthropocene age.[5]

The Great Disembedding: Extraction and Externalisation

We can respond effectively to the four sustainability crises only if we understand how the development paradigm generates its unsustainable effects. Much of the academic literature on this points to Karl Polanyi's analysis in 1944 as among the best first-generation explanations under a sustainability and well-being framework and which more recent multidisciplinary and global research has substantiated and improved (Dilworth 2010; Bardi 2011; Evans 2008). Polanyi argued that during the great transformation of the last two centuries the dominant economic system has been disembedded from within the much larger ecological and social systems that sustain all life on earth and inserted in abstract and competitive economic, legal, and governmental relationships that are dependent on, yet destructive of the carrying capacity of the encompassing ecological and social systems. The economic system is then treated as external and autonomous in relation to these two larger life-sustaining systems. The transformation involves four main processes.

First, Indigenous peoples have been dispossessed of and removed from their life ways and ecosystems in which *Homo sapiens* co-evolved for 150 thousand years in the name of development and progress. The genocide and destruction of Indigenous peoples and their cultural systems is treated as external to the economic system imposed over their traditional territories (Hall 2010).

Second, the legal-economic system of privatisation and commodification of the living earth as a storehouse of "natural resources" is imposed first in Europe then throughout the colonised world. This commodification disembeds natural resources from their place and participation in the interdependent and symbiotic ecological relationships and cycles that sustain all life on earth. It inserts them into the abstract and competitive relationships of the global market system. The damage and destruction to the surrounding, life-sustaining ecosystems caused by the extraction, production, transportation, consumption, and disposal of these commodities is treated as external to the economic system.

Third, the productive capabilities of human beings are also treated as commodities for sale on the labour market by the spread of Western contract, labour, and corporate law. This disembeds collective human producing and consuming capabilities and activities from the surrounding interdependent social and community relationships in which they take place. It inserts productive capacities as individual commodities (self-ownership) into abstract, competitive, and non-democratic global labour market relationships. The alienation and exploitation this causes to the well-being of workers and the damage that competition does to the larger social relations in which they live are treated as externalities.

Fourth, the medium of exchange – money – is itself transformed into a commodity in the financial market. Money is disembedded from its role in fair exchange relations in which the partners are constrained to take reciprocal care of the well-being or suffering of each other as a result of the exchange. It is inserted in abstract and competitive financial exchanges in which profit maximisation is the overriding consideration. The marginalisation of gift-reciprocity or mutual-aid exchange relationships among the partners is treated as external to the financial system, leading to the financial crises and austerity programmes of the present. Polanyi predicted that the result of this great transformation would be disastrous for individuals, communities, and the living earth.[6]

The "fatal flaw" of this economic system is that if the costs of the repair to all the damage it does to the externalised life-support systems were "internalised," the system would be unprofitable and would collapse (Brown 2011; Bardi 2011). And, much of the damage is unrepairable. Moreover, it is not simply a matter of transitioning from non-renewable to renewable energy because the system exploits renewable resources at a rate that exceeds the slow temporality of the renewability cycles of renewable resources and their ecosystems (Jevons law) (Heinberg and Lerch 2010). And, the race for what's left of renewable resources is as much the cause of the crises as the exploitation of non-renewable fossil fuels and other non-renewables (Klare 2012). The development paradigm becomes a super-predatory system that eventually destroys the life systems on which it depends and destroys itself. This has happened with many super-predatory species in the past, but not on this scale (Dilworth 2010; Ward 2009).

As these features of the global development paradigm became clear in the 1970s and 1980s, from the limits to growth literature to the Gaia hypothesis, the initial response was to protect the system by grafting sustainability on to development with the elastic phrase "sustainable development." It became the legitimating norm under which global economic constitutionalism expanded and was unsuccessfully contested. But, as the present crises and scientific predictions substantiate, sustaining humans and the living systems that support them is incompatible with the development paradigm. If the precautionary principles were applied on the basis of the latest earth and social science predictions, the economic system would have to be shut down. Hence, the choice here and now appears to be either unsustainable economic constitutionalism and much harder and catastrophic times or a sustainable alternative paradigm of economics, law, and governance.[7]

Eco-Social Constitutionalism

Here is an alternative to this unsustainable global system. It is to create sustaining social systems by learning from the way life systems have sustained and diversified life on earth over 3.5 billion years. The basic principle is that successful life systems sustain themselves and their members in ways that also internalise and co-sustain the interdependent and intra-dependent life systems on which they co-depend: that is, by symbiosis and symbiogenesis. Life systems internalise their environments. Photosynthesis cycles, in which the emissions of each life form are usable or reusable by interdependent others, are the primary co-sustaining life cycles. The now widely accepted Gaia theory of James Lovelock holds that the self-sustaining features of the living earth system as a whole are themselves emergent properties of symbiosis and symbiogenesis of its member systems. Humans can learn from the way life co-sustains life. Accordingly, it is possible to learn or relearn, from the living earth and from contemporary life and earth sciences how to design sustainable social systems that co-sustain the interdependent social and ecological systems on which they reciprocally depend. This is called the great reembedding or reconnection.[8]

This alternative co-sustaining, post-development paradigm already exists in what is called "legal globalisation from below" and "eco-social constitutionalisation."[9] It consists of practices and networks of internalising interdependency, co-sustenance, and well-being of "all affected." These include: ecological footprint analysis of each practice, using renewable energy sources, cyclical steady-state economics rather than the linear growth economics, fair trade rather than free trade, governing the commons rather than the tragedy of privatisation and commodification, democratic cooperatives and community-based businesses rather than TNCs, community-based and networked direct democracy as the basis of representative democracy, co-sustaining "cradle to cradle" recycling technology and industrial planning rather than "cradle to grave" technology of extraction, externalisation and waste, caring for common goods before private interests, nonviolent means rather than violence, learning from and with Indigenous peoples and their earth ways, and the application of the local and global principle that "all affected have a say (or are stakeholders)" with respect to the exercise of any relationship of power.

In contrast to the development paradigm, in eco-social constitutionalism the means are instantiations of the ends in each of these practices: sustainability is pursued by sustainable means; peace by peaceful means; democracy by grassroots democratic organisation: that is, the Gandhian principle of being the change. As a consequence, the modern ideal of coordinating constituent power and rule of law is realised to a greater degree in these practices than in our best representative institutions (Bailey and Mattei 2013). These practitioners strive to realise human rights, democracy, and rule of law, but they do so in a revolutionary way. They reinterpret and reapply these three norms not only in contextual, self-governing ways, but also under the normative framework of sustainability and well-being. Perhaps most important of all, eco-social constitutionalism, following Indigenous peoples' constitutionalism, cognises natural resources, human resources, and human exchanges as always already embedded within the larger life-sustaining social and ecological networks and cycles. Capra and Mattei (2015) call these "ecolegal orders" and see them as the constitution of a new and renewed sustainable, Gaia-centric paradigm (see also Santos 2014).

This vision is hardly utopian or unachievable. There are over 800 million people engaged in these everyday practices of local and global constitutionalism from below and there is a large body of academic research on them (Hawken 2007). This is more people than participate in TNCs (Restakis 2010). Indigenous peoples and the Indigenous Peoples Working Group on Climate Change (IPWGCC) are at the heart and frontlines of this global movement (Grossman 2012).[10] However, by themselves they are unable to dislodge or transform the dominant paradigm, which not only continues, but often either preys on the ecological and social repair and regrowth they generate or brings them down by the force of economic constitutionalism, austerity measures, and emergency law.

Contestatory Constitutionalism

If the participants of eco-social constitutionalism wish to transform the development paradigm, they need to find ways to join hands with those who are striving to contest, reform, and transform it from within its economic, legal, and governance institutions and processes. Many of the articles in *Global Constitutionalism* have been excellent case studies of individual and collective actors engaged in diverse forms of contestation of the development paradigm and economic constitutionalisation by exercising formal human rights, representative democracy, and rule of law available to them in innovative ways. We call these activities agonistic or "contestatory global constitutionalism," using contestation in a broad sense (Wiener 2014). As we have suggested above, while contestatory actors have been able to regulate and reform economic constitutionalism to a limited extent, they have been unable to slow down its rapid pace, let alone transform it.

However, if practitioners of eco-social and contestatory constitutionalism were to find ways to network and coordinate their activities, they just might be able to build up an alternative world with the exemplarity, momentum, and nonviolent means to transform unsustainable constitutionalisation and its development paradigm, thereby proving the doomsayers wrong.[11] There are good reasons why the two types of citizen engagement – often call "horizontality" (power-with organisation) and "verticality" (power-over organisation) – should join hands. They both share the same constitutional norms of sustainability and well-being and the all-affected principle in conjunction with human rights, democracy, and rule of law, yet enact them differently. Eco-social citizens put into practice what contestatory citizens argue for in public spheres, courts, representative institutions, and institutions of global governance. Reciprocally, the gains that contestatory actors make in official institutions protect and support the fragile practices of eco-social actors. Many of their activities overlap in practice; for example, when community-based organisations find it necessary to go to court or elect supportive representatives. Moreover, most citizens responding to the four crises are engaged in practices of both contestatory and eco-social constitutionalism in their daily lives, so the grounds of their coordination and integration already exist.

Yet, these two modes of constitutionalism often are seen as either working separately or eco-social organisations are subordinated to social movements oriented to gaining power in the official vertical institutions by elections or revolutions. Nevertheless, as Boaventura de Sousa Santos was among the first to point out, there are several contemporary attempts to coordinate the two modes of constitutionalism democratically and without subordination so that they are co-sustaining and co-empowering. Well-known examples exist in Spain, Italy, India, and between Indigenous peoples and the government of Bolivia. Participants learn from their successes and failures, and from globally connected academic research and discussions with them and many other examples, and move forward in networks of reciprocal elucidation.[12]

Conclusion: Integral Constitutionalism

In the *Encyclical on Climate Change and Inequality*, Pope Francis (2015) calls the general kind of coordinated thinking and acting together of socio-ecological and contestatory constitutionalism to care for our common home – our communities and the living earth – "integral ecology." The specific version we have put forward thus could be called integral constitutionalism.[13] As we mentioned in the Introduction section, a central role of *Global Constitutionalism* is to disclose and discuss the emergence of constitutional qualities that coordinate law and governance in different ways in the global field. The perspective we have briefly introduced brings to light three distinctive types of global constitutionalism and the important challenge of coordinating two of them into an integral constitutionalism. We are pleased to bring it into the *Global Constitutionalism* arena, invite critical discussion of it, and thereby partake in the larger discussion already underway.

Notes

1 Immanuel Kant, *Idea for a Universal History with a Cosmopolitan Intent* and Karl Marx and Friedrich Engels, *The Communist Manifesto*, presented two of the most influential versions of this structure of argument that vicious means, while unjust, are necessary means to virtuous ends, despite appearances to the contrary. Mahatma Gandhi, *Hind Swaraj* and Hannah Arendt, *On Violence*, presented two of most influential criticisms of it and alternatives to it. They both reasserted the traditional view that vicious means beget vicious ends and virtuous means beget virtuous ends.

2 For a careful analysis of how the unexamined faith in development continues in the contemporary normative literature on globalisation, see Allen (2016).

3 The most comprehensive account is Dilworth (2010). For our disagreement with the doomsaying conclusion he draws, see text accompanying note 11.

4 The Club of Rome Report entitled *The Limits to Growth* was first published in 1972 and is recognised as one of the most influential books of the twentieth century in bringing the crisis of sustainability to the attention of the scientific community and the broader public. See also Bardi (2011) for a survey of its influence. For a careful explication of the norm of sustainability and well-being, see Bandarage (2013).

5 For a critical approach to this neoliberal global constitutionalism, see Gill and Culter (2015).

6

> To allow the market mechanism to be sole director of the fate of human beings and their natural environment ... would result in the demolition of society... Robbed of the protective covering of cultural institutions, human beings would perish from the effects of social exposure; they would die as the victims of acute social dislocation through vice, perversion, crime, and starvation. Nature would be reduced to its elements, neighbourhoods and landscapes defiled, rivers polluted, military safety jeopardized, the power to produce food and raw materials destroyed.

> (Polanyi 2001, 76)

7 Lovelock (2014) sees our situation in this way but does not offer an alternative. However, his former student and co-researcher, Harding (2013), builds on Lovelock's work to present an alternative vision complementary to the one presented below.

8 For the most comprehensive account of this view, see Capra and Luisi (2014). The following summary draws on this synthetic work.

9 For a comprehensive account of eco-social constitutionalism, see Capta and Mattei (2015). Compare Bailey and Mattei (2013) and Santos (2005).

10 For an example of the Indigenous philosophies that underlie Indigenous constitutionalism, see Atleo (2004).

11 The doomsayers who predict the self-destruction of the majority of the world's population due to the three crises standardly overlook socio-ecological and contestatory constitutionalism. See, for example, Dilworth (2010), Ward (2009), Emmott (2013).

12 For an in-depth study of the relation between socio-ecological constitutionalism (15M) and contestatory constitutionalism (Podemos) and the dilemma of non-subordination in Spain see Ouziel (2015). For Italy, see Bailey and Mattei (2013). For India, see Shiva (2005). For Bolivia, see Grossman (2012) and Sahle (2014, 147–74).

13 For critical discussion of aspects of integral constitutionalism, see Nichols and Singh (2014) and Tully (2014a).

10 Life Sustains Life 2

The Ways of Reengagement with the Living Earth (2020)

Over the last five hundred years, the West has developed a social system that is socially and ecologically unsustainable and destructive.[1] It overreaches and undermines the social and ecological conditions that sustain life on earth for *Homo sapiens* and many other species and ecosystems.

This social system has been spread around the world by Western imperialism in the colonial and postcolonial periods and is now the dominant social system on the planet.

It is a "vicious" system in the technical sense that the regular feedback loops within the social system and between the social system and the ecosystems in which it is embedded reproduce and intensify the destructive effects of the system on the social sphere and ecosphere. These effects include such things as global warming, climate change, pollution, and the diseases it causes, acidification of the oceans, desertification of once arable land and the recolonisation of Africa, melting of the polar icecap and the release of methane, the depletion of non-renewable recourses and the military conflicts over what's left, the use of renewable resources and aquifers beyond their cyclical rate of renewal, millions of climate change refugees, global inequalities in life chances, petro-states, a planet of slums and gated enclaves, the domination of democracy by concentrations of private, media, and military power, the concentration of the means of production in a handful of multinational companies, and counterviolences to the system's overt and structural violence that trigger counterinsurgencies and feed an ever-increasing arms race and arms trade, and so on.

We have known that the dominant social system (a historical assemblage of many social systems) is unsustainable and self-destructive socially and ecologically since the 1970s: Rachel Carson (1962), Barry Commoner (1971), the Club of Rome, and *The Limits to Growth* (Meadows et al. 1972). It has been reaffirmed ever since by experts from a wide variety of different fields: *The Limits to Growth Revisited* (Bardi 2011), the Intergovernmental Panel on Climate Change (2014), Lester Brown (2011), and Craig Dilworth (2010).

Yet it continues despite efforts to address it in various ways since the 1970s and in the face of increasing evidence of its destructiveness, such as the sixth mass extinction, global warming and its effects, and the naming of the predicament *as* "peak everything" and the "Anthropocene."[2]

DOI: 10.4324/9781003227403-14

The phenomenon of a life system becoming a vicious system rather than a virtuous and self-sustaining system, and thus overshooting and destroying the social and ecological conditions on which it depends for its sustainability and collapsing, is not unusual in the history of human systems or non-human living systems.

Furthermore, as the resiliency literature argues, it is also not unheard of for a vicious life system tending towards self-destruction to transform itself into a virtuous one and avoid collapse, albeit usually at a qualitatively different dynamic equilibrium.

Thus, while life systems are the most complex systems in the world, they are not predetermined, and it is not impossible for humans to save themselves from self-destruction, for, after all, we are the subjects and agents who reproduce the unsustainable social system by participating in it in our everyday activities, and we have the freedom to act otherwise.

Thus, there are three central questions with regard to sustainability I wish to address:

1   How do we act in such a way as to transform the unsustainable system in which we find ourselves into a sustainable system?
2   How do we become motivated to act in a sustainable way once we know what that is?
3   And, before these two questions can be addressed, a third, prior question needs to be addressed: what are the salient features of sustainable and unsustainable life systems?

I want to address the question of the main features of unsustainable and sustainable life systems through the distinction Akeel Bilgrami makes between alienated and unalienated ways of life (2014, 101–16; Tully 2020b). For his concept of an alienated way of life describes life from within the unsustainable social system we inhabit as moderns and his concept of an unalienated way of life describes life within a sustainable social system.

An alienated or unsustainable way of human life has the following features:

1   A disengaged or disembedded stance of humans vis-à-vis nature;
2   A working relationship of control, mastery, and domination of nature embedded in our working relationship to nature; and
3   The presupposition that nature is devoid of intrinsic value and norms. Values and norms are assumed to derive from the autonomous human mind and are imposed by humans on a non-normative world.
4   If there is a normative dimension to nature then it is a basic, amoral antagonism or struggle for existence among independent living beings (humans and non-humans) in which the fitter gain control over or exterminate the less fit and establish a new order or system that is a higher stage of development than the previous one in an unlimited set of stages of development and progress.

An unalienated or sustainable human way of life has the following features:

1   Humans see themselves *as participants in nature*, in the ecosystems in which they live;
2   From this participatory perspective, when humans act, they *engage with* nature: they interact symbiotically in ecological relationships. They do not stand above and control.
3   When humans act and experience the world in accordance with steps (1) and (2), the world is disclosed to them as interdependent webs of life (comprising living systems) and of value. Nature is seen and experienced to be suffused with values and norms that can be seen to involve responsibilities: that is, norms that are *action-guiding*.

Bilgrami argues that an alienated way of life became dominant over the last five hundred years, from the seventeenth century onward. I agree and I believe that our task today is to begin the long project of reengaging or reconnecting with and within the symbiotic living ecosystems on which our social system is an interdependent subsystem.

We have brought forth and spread around the world a social system within which we see ourselves as disengaged from and independent or autonomous of the interdependent social relationships on which we are interdependent, and we also see ourselves and our entire social systems as independent of the ecosystems in which we and our social systems are embedded and interdependent.

From this independence perspective, the natural, social, and policy sciences see themselves as exercising control and mastery over the living earth.

But the life sciences and earth sciences over the last sixty years have shown this modernist picture to be a false representation or illusion. Our social system is a subsystem deeply embedded in and interdependent upon the ecosystems that compose the living earth for every breath we take. This is how Barry Commoner famously made this fundamental point in 1971:

> To survive on earth, human beings require the stable, continuing existence of a suitable environment. Yet the evidence is overwhelming that the way in which we now live on earth is driving its thin, life-supporting skin, and ourselves with it, to destruction. To understand this calamity, we need to begin with a close look at the nature of the environment itself. Most of us find this a difficult thing to do, for there is a kind of ambiguity in our relation to the environment. Biologically, human beings *participate in* the environmental system as subsidiary parts of the whole. Yet, human society is designed *to exploit* the environment as a whole, to produce wealth. The paradoxical role we play in the natural environment – at once participant and exploiter – distorts our perception of it. . . .
>
> [That is,] all of modern technology leads us to believe that we have made our own environment and no longer depend on the one provided by

nature. We have become enticed into a nearly fatal illusion: that through our machines we have at last escaped from dependence on the natural environment. . . .

[Yet,] every human activity depends on the integrity and proper functioning of the ecosphere. Without the photosynthetic activity of green plants, there would be no oxygen for our engines, smelters, and furnaces, let alone support for human and animal life. Without the action of plants, animals and microorganisms that live in them, we could not have pure water in our lakes and rivers. Without the biological processes that have gone on in the soil for thousands of years, we would have neither food crops, oil nor coal. If we destroy it, our most advanced technology will become useless and any economic and political system that depends on it will founder. The environmental crisis is a signal of this approaching catastrophe.

(Commoner 1971, 14–17)

If this description is accurate, and if we are to respond to the crisis, we need to free ourselves from the alienated way of life and move around and see and experience ourselves and our social system as embedded and ourselves as engaged participants in (damaged) relationships of interdependency and co-sustainability within the ecosystems in which we live and breathe (Korten 2007).

We need to think not of independent social systems and ecosystems but of interdependent social and ecosystems: that is, *ecosocial systems*. Rather than independence we need to think about sustainability in terms of mutually interactive and interdependent co-sustainability of all life systems, human and non-human.

Three more important distinctions between the alienated and unsustainable way of life and the unalienated and sustainable way of life follow:

1   The distinction Anthony Laden (2012) makes between ways of conceptualising reasoning in his workshop presentation and his book on social reasoning maps on to the alienated/unsustainable versus unalienated/sustainable distinction of Bilgrami. Laden's conception of "reasoning and acting *with* others" and "connecting" describes the ways humans interact reasonably in mutually sustainable ways.
2   Spatially, the alienated way of life consists of independent entities in (efficient) causal or consensual relationships; temporally, they are in linear or developmental time.
3   Spatially, the unalienated way of life consists of interdependent beings as always already in relationships of mutual support, networks, or webs of life; temporally, they are in cyclical time.

That is, we need to think of ourselves, as Aldo Leopold put it in *The Land Ethic* (1966 [1949]), as "plain members and participatory citizens" of the "commonwealth of all forms of life on earth" with responsibilities not only to sustain ourselves, but always to sustain ourselves in such a way that we also reciprocally co-sustain all the other forms of life on which we are inter-dependent and which co-sustain us. This is an unalienated way of thinking about our responsible capabilities as sustainabilities (LaConte 2012).

And to do this, we need to learn from the living earth how living systems sustain themselves over billions of years and use this knowledge to transform our unsustainable and destructive social systems into sustainable and symbi-otic systems within systems.

In this view, symbiotic ecosystems are the ground of life and socioecosystems are the ground of human life. That they sustain life on earth is their value and the ground of all human value.

This is how Fritjof Capra puts the challenge:

> The key to an operational definition of ecological sustainability is the realization that we do not need to invent sustainable human communities from scratch but can model them after nature's ecosystems, which are sus-tainable communities of plants, animals, and micro-organisms. Since the outstanding characteristic of the earth household is its inherent ability to sustain life, a sustainable human community is one designed in such a manner that its ways of life, businesses, economies, federations, phys-ical structures, and technologies do not interfere with nature's inherent ability to sustain life. Sustainable communities and networks evolve their patterns of living over time in continual interaction with other living systems, both human and non-human.
>
> (Capra 2002, 230)

I would like to respond to this challenge in the following way. In the "Symbiosis and Interdependency" section, I set out what I take to be four central features of sustainable living systems according to the life and earth sciences. In the "The Hegemonic Unsustainable and Vicious Social System" section, I set out what I take to be the main features of our unsustainable social system that cause damage to the ecosphere on the one hand and give rise to the illusion of independence from it on the other hand. In the "Responses of Reengagement and Reconciliation: Realising Interbeing" section, I then turn to several ways of responding to the sustainability crisis that are informed by this way of thinking about our interdependent relationship in and with ecosocial systems. These are ways of disengaging from our unsustainable practices, beginning to engage in practices of reengaging and reconnecting socially and ecologically, and thus beginning to bring into being unalienated and sustainable ways of life on the earth. If the symbiotic interdependency thesis of the "Symbiosis and Interdependency" section is true, participants in these connecting practices should be empowered in reciprocity by the interdependent relationships they connect with, and thus initiate expanding virtuous cycles. This reciprocal empowerment is discussed in the "Reanimation" section below.

Symbiosis and Interdependency

Let's begin with Commoner's description of how life sustains life:

> There is an important lesson here. In the form in which it first appeared, the earth's system had a fatal fault: the energy it required was derived from the consumption of a *nonrenewable* resource, the geochemical store of organic matter. Had this fault not been remedied, the rapid self-propagated growth of life would have consumed the earth's original "organic soup." Life would have destroyed the condition for its own survival. Survival – a property now so deeply associated with life – became possible because of a timely evolutionary development: the emergence of the first photosynthetic organisms. These new organisms used sunlight to convert carbon dioxide and inorganic materials to fresh organic matter. This crucial event reconverted the first life-form's waste, carbon dioxide, into its food, organic compounds. It closed the loop and transformed what was a fatally linear process into a circular, self-perpetuating one. Since then the perpetuation of life on the earth has been linked to an essentially perpetual source of energy – the sun.
>
> Here in its primitive form we see the grand scheme which has since been the basis of the remarkable continuity of life: the reciprocal interdependence of one life process on another; the mutual, interconnected development of the earth's life system and the nonliving constituents of the environment; the repeated transformation of the materials of life in great cycles, driven by the energy of the sun.
>
> The result of this evolutionary history can be summarised in a series of propositions about the nature of life and its relation to the environment:
>
> Living things, as a whole, emerged from the nonliving skin of the earth. Life is a very powerful form of chemistry, which once on the earth rapidly changed its surface. Every living thing is intimately dependent on its physical and chemical surroundings, so that as these changed, new forms of life suited to new surroundings could emerge. Life begets life, so that once new forms appeared in a favourable environment; they could proliferate and spread until they occupied every suitable environmental niche within physical reach. Every living thing is dependent on many others, either indirectly, through the physical and chemical features of the environment or directly for food or a sheltering place. Within every living thing on earth, indeed within each of its individual cells, is contained another network – on its own scale, as complex as the environmental system – made up of numerous intricate molecules, elaborately interconnected by chemical reactions, on which the life-properties of the whole organism depend.
>
> (Commoner 1971, 20–1)

Of course, there are important differences between human social systems and ecosystems. However, there are similarities as well. We are, after all, earthlings in the first instance. Following the earlier quotation from Capra, there are three kinds of education we can gain from the study of non-human life systems: (1) how they manage to sustain and complexify life over 3.5 billion years; (2) how humans are interdependent participants in ecosystems, and thus how we must design our social systems so that they support rather than undermine them; and (3) how to design or transform social systems so they are similarly self-sustaining. We need to acquire this education to engage in the practices of cultural and ecological reconciliation. Over the last forty years the ecological, life, and earth sciences have advanced three hypotheses concerning the ways life sustains life that are essential for these reconciliation practices.

Interdependency and Symbiosis: Life Sustains Life

First, sustained life is a property of ecological systems rather than of single organisms or species. No individual organism can exist in isolation. Animals depend on the photosynthesis of plants for their energy needs; plants depend on the carbon dioxide produced by animals, as well as on the nitrogen fixed by the bacteria at their roots, and these living entities are interdependently coupled with abiotic rocks, atmosphere, and waters.

The major factor in the coevolution of forms of life is "symbiosis": the ways that organisms and ecosystems "live together." This refers to the way relations of interdependency within and among organisms and ecosystems are *mutually supportive* of the members: for example, the ways that animals depend on photosynthesis of plants, plants depend on carbon dioxide produced by the animals, and so on, in a circular manner.

Here is an example from Michael Simpson, a permaculture expert:

> Living systems do not only reproduce themselves. Their very life processes nourish their habitat and strengthen the conditions of life around them. They thereby create an organism that is larger than themselves or their individual species. When a forest is growing back from a disturbance, herbaceous (non-woody) plants are the first to move in. These plants exude sugars that attract bacteria around their roots. The bacteria in turn exude an alkaline "bioslime" that creates a favorable habitat for themselves as well as for the pioneer plant species. The alkaline condition of the bioslime also allows the bacteria to break down ammonia in the soil into nitrates that are taken up by plants allowing them to grow vegetatively. This cycle of life creating the conditions for more life continues as the forest gradually grows into a rich, biodiverse ecosystem (ecological succession).
>
> In short, living systems are not only self-regulating but they are relational in so far as they build the conditions of life around them. Hence, the organism is not something independent in its own right which then adapts itself to its environment; on the contrary the organism adapts a particular environment into it.[3]

The central point is this: in the activities of sustaining themselves, living systems also co-sustain the conditions of life around them, and vice versa. This symbiotic relationship of reciprocal sustainability among interdependent living systems is how life sustains life.

It is called a "virtuous" cycle because it reproduces itself, becoming more complex. Moreover, it gives rise to symbiogenesis: the emergence of new systems of life out of the background symbiotic relationships and their complex relationships, creating the immense biodiversity of forms of life over billions of years (Margulis 1998).

Thinking about living systems in this symbiotic way brings to awareness Arne Naess' "ecological self" in contrast to the independent, ego-self of the dominant way of life (Naess 2008). We realise that if we wish to live well we should live in such a way that our way of life supports the ways of life of those with whom we are related and that they should do the same in reciprocity.

That is, Gaia citizens gradually come to identify with the interdependent members of the commonwealth of all forms of life. They see themselves as citizens of this commonwealth with reciprocal responsibilities of mutual recognition and sustenance as the condition of sustaining life on earth. They also realise that if they are suffering, it is probably because they are not living in ways that support such mutually supportive networks. This way of life is neither altruistic nor egoistic, for that debilitating distinction rests on the presupposition that organisms are independent and self-sufficient to begin with.

Despite the individualistic and competitive relationships of the dominant economy, we humans are participants in multiple social systems of this symbiotic or gift-reciprocity-gift kind. Relationships within families, neighbourhoods, communities of practice with fellow workers, and an array of social networks are often symbiotic. Many psychologists argue that symbiotic relationships are the bedrock of communities and mutual well-being, unnoticed by the dominant competitive ethos, yet necessary to hold societies together.[4]

Symbiogenesis and Gaia Hypothesis

Second, the evolution of all the complex symbiotic feedback loops among life systems, atmosphere, rocks, and water has symbiogenetically given rise to the biosphere or ecosphere as a whole: that is, the evolving, self-regulating ensemble that has maintained habitable conditions on the surface of the planet over vast stretches of geological time. Earth-systems scientist James Lovelock (2000) named this the Gaia hypothesis in the 1960s. As Lynn Margulis (1998) commented, it is symbiosis and symbiogenesis from a planetary perspective. The Gaia hypothesis has since sustained several tests and is now accepted, in one form or another, by a wide range of scientists and members of the Intergovernmental Panel on Climate Change.

"Gaia" is the Greek term for the earth as a living or animate earth. The idea that the earth is alive (animate) is a view shared by Indigenous cultures and many religious traditions, as well as by the Greeks and early modern Europeans. For the last four hundred years, the dominant Western view was that the earth is inanimate, a mechanism of some kind, and that the animate view was nothing but a premodern primitive superstition. With the Gaia hypothesis, there is now a growing convergence and conversation in theory and practice between leading trends in Western sciences and the complementary fields of Indigenous sciences. For example, Stephen Harding writes:

> The key insight of the Gaia theory is wonderfully holistic and non-hierarchical. It suggests that it is the Gaian system as a whole that does the regulating, that the sum of all the complex feedbacks between life, atmosphere, rocks, and water gives rise to Gaia, the evolving, self-regulating planetary entity that has maintained habitable conditions on the surface of the planet over vast stretches of geological time.
>
> (Harding 2013, 64)

And Lynn Margulis: "Gaia is not an 'organism' but an emergent property of interaction among organisms. Gaia is the series of interacting ecosystems that compose a single huge ecosystem at the earth's surface. Gaia is symbiosis on a planetary scale" (1998, 119). *Homo sapiens* do not control these systems but rather are active participants within and with them, as both subjects and agents (Harding 2013, 62–85).

Dynamic Resilience, Tipping Points, and Responses

Third, complex, overlapping, non-linear systems of symbiotic and symbiogenetic relationships are neither stable nor harmonious. Their interactions are cooperative and competitive, and often far from equilibrium. They change and transform continuously as they interact and readjust to the interactions of their neighbours: that is, living systems are dynamic systems that are resilient – they respond to disturbances in complex ways that systems theorists call positive and negative feedback loops.

In negative feedback, the initial change is counteracted. In positive feedback, the initial change is amplified. Feedback loops are the "circles of participation" by which living systems bring about constancy or change (Harding 2013, 62–85).

Now, it is *always* possible that a positive feedback loop that causes the system to move away from dynamic equilibrium may begin a series of loops that move the system further away until it reaches a tipping point and transforms into an unsustainable system: that is, the system transforms from its conciliatory feedback loops of sustainable interaction (virtuous cycles) into unsustainable relationships by a series of positive feedback loops (vicious cycles) and eventual systemic collapse.

Systems theorists explain the last four centuries of developmental modernisation as the rise of a viciously cyclical global system – the Anthropocene – that is reaching, or has reached, a catastrophic tipping point in our time. They describe the overall crisis in two steps and the appropriate two steps of dealienation and reconnection as follows:

1   The human enterprise is structurally and functionally inseparable from nature: that is, the human enterprise is a fully embedded, totally dependent subsystem of the ecosphere – people live within socioecosystems. Human activities can therefore significantly affect the integrity and behaviour of supportive ecosystems and these changes immediately feedback to affect the state of the human subsystem. We can no longer understand the dynamics of either the natural system or the human subsystem in isolation without understanding the dynamics of the other component.

2   Linked/integrated/interdependent and interactive socioecosystems are constantly changing in response to both internal and external forces – they are dynamic complex adaptive systems. The changes within these systems are not linear, smooth, or predictable, particularly outside the systems' "normal" regime. Indeed, under sufficient pressure, critical systems variables may "flip" (cross a threshold or tipping point) into a different regime or alternative stable state. In other words, like natural ecosystems, socioecosystems also have multiple possible equilibria, some of which may not be amenable to continued human use or existence (remember the collapse of the North Atlantic cod fishery) (Rees 2010, 32).

3   The sustainability of the human enterprise on a crowded and resource-stressed planet depends on our ability to conserve the resilience of socio-ecological systems. In this context, resilience defines the capacity of the system to assimilate disturbances without crossing a threshold into an alternative and possibly "less-friendly" stable state. A desirable socioeco-logical system characterised by high resilience is able to resist external disturbance and continue to provide biophysical goods and services essential for a satisfactory quality of life.

4   For sustainability, resource-management efforts must shift from reshaping nature for the purpose of satisfying human demands to moderating human demands so that they fit within biophysical limits. They must do this in a way that is consistent with both the productive and the assimilative capacities of ecosystems and in a way that enhances the long-term resilience of the integrated socioecosystem (ibid.).

The Hegemonic Unsustainable and Vicious Social System

It is my working hypothesis that the current destructive and unsustainable relationship to the living earth that is causing climate change and the ecological crisis developed in Europe and spread around the globe by European imperial expansion and modernisation. It is the driving force of the Anthropocene age. It is a vicious and unsustainable system.

It is this social system that brings about and reproduces the alienated way of life Akeel Bilgrami describes and sustains the illusionary world view of independence. This "illusion" of independence and linear temporality is grounded in the basic structure of the system, which constantly works to "disembed" humans from the ecosphere.

One way of *seeing* this unsustainable relationship is to reflect on a saying Indigenous people across Canada use to distance themselves from it. Since the 1960s, Indigenous people have been saying the following: "the land does not belong to us; we belong to the land." If our mode of being in the world is one of being engaged participants in living interdependent and symbiotic ecological and sociological relationships that mutually sustain life, then the true expression of this mode of being is "belonging to the land": that is, as we have seen, we belong to this great commonwealth of earthlings and have shared responsibilities to sustain it and our fellow members.

From this orientation, it would be absurd to say that we stand in a *relationship of ownership or property* to the living earth. Ojibway Elder Basil Johnston says this is like having property in your mother: mother earth. Yet, this relationship of the land belonging to humans has displaced the earlier relationship of belonging to the land and has become the basis of our modern way of life and the cause of the crises (Kimmerer 2013).

For 95 percent of their time on earth, *Homo sapiens* lived in predominantly sustainable social systems and understood itself to belong to the ecosystems in which they dwelled. Although things began to change with the sedentary agricultural revolution eleven thousand years ago, the "great transformation" of the world as a whole to the orientation that the earth belongs to humans occurred over the last four hundred years and accelerated exponentially in the twentieth century. There are many accounts of this, but among the best was advanced by Karl Polanyi in *The Great Transformation* (2001 [1944]), and those who have learned from his analysis.

The Great Disembedding and Reembedding in the Global Social System

Polanyi argued that during this great transformation humans have been disembedded from participation in the interdependent ecological and social relationships that sustain life and reembedded in abstract and competitive economic, political, and legal relationships that are dependent on, yet destructive of, the underlying interdependent ecological and social relationships. This "great disembedding" takes place in the following three steps.

First, the peoples who are embedded in symbiotic ecological and social relationships are dispossessed of this way of life and the territories in which it is carried on; first by the enclosure of the commons in England and then by the dispossession of Indigenous peoples throughout the non-European world (the "second enclosure").

The second step is to impose an ownership relation to the land by the spread of Western legal systems of private property and so to transform "earth into property," as Anthony Hall puts it (2010). Polanyi describes the privatisation of land as a "fictitious commodity" because land is not a commodity produced for sale on the market. What we now call commodifiable and exchangeable "natural resources" are, as we have seen, interdependent coparticipants in the symbiotic webs and cycles of life that sustain life on earth.

Relating to the living earth as a storehouse of commodifiable resources disembeds them from these interdependent ecological relationships and reembeds them in the abstract and competitive relations of the global market system. The ecosystems in which resources are embedded are then treated as "external" to the global system of commodification and radically changed. The result of "development" under this system is the destruction of the webs of interdependent ecological relationships that sustain the natural and human world, giving rise to the environmental crisis and climate change.

Once the means of the reproduction of human life are placed under the ownership of independent corporations, the third step is to treat the productive capabilities of human beings as commodities for sale on the labour market by the spread of Western contract, labour, and corporate law. This kind of commodification disembeds human producing and consuming capabilities and activities from the surrounding social and ecological relationships in which they take place and reembeds them in abstract, competitive, and non-democratic global market relationships. Polanyi describes the commodification of the productive capabilities of individual humans as the second "fictitious commodity" of modernisation.

It is fictitious because abilities to work together and sustain ourselves are not commodities made for the market. These capabilities are, as we have seen in the previous section, the cooperative response-abilities and sustain-abilities through which we humans participate in the social and ecological systems that conciliate and sustain life on earth. They are the capabilities through which we "belong to the land" and are grounded in it. Yet, they are now treated as abstract capabilities that we as separate individuals "own" (self-ownership), and by selling the use of these abilities to a corporation, they become the means by which we insert ourselves in the global market system. The underlying social systems that producers and consumers live in and that sustain them – such as families, communities, First Nations, and networks – are treated as "external" to the market system. The result of "development" under this system is the destruction of the webs of interdependent social relations of mutual aid that sustain human communities, giving rise to the well-known forms of social suffering of modern life: alienation and anomie, the horrendous inequalities in life chances, and the planet of slums and gated "communities" in which we find ourselves.

In 1944, Polanyi predicted that the result of this "great transformation" would be disastrous:

> To allow the market mechanism to be sole director of the fate of human beings and their natural environment ... would result in the demolition of society... Robbed of the protective covering of cultural institutions, human beings would perish from the effects of social exposure; they would die as the victims of acute social dislocation through vice, perversion, crime,

and starvation. Nature would be reduced to its elements, neighbourhoods and landscapes defiled, rivers polluted, military safety jeopardized, the power to produce food and raw materials destroyed.

(Polanyi 2001, 76)

The Global Vicious Cycle

Despite Polanyi's warning and hundreds of others, this global system of double commodification in which the human species is reembedded continues to unfold as he predicted. It is now a deeply entrenched *vicious cycle*, what global systems theorists call an "automaton" (Capra 2002, 129–57).

Briefly, they argue that corporations are caught up in a competitive system in which they must continuously extract and exploit natural resources and human resources (capabilities) at the lowest price and at maximum speed in order to make a profit or go under. Any damage to the environment and communities is treated as external and offloaded to governments. Governments and communities are constrained to compete for these corporations, because they fund their campaigns, bring jobs to the electorate, and provide the taxes that enable governments to provide basic services and repair the damage they do to social and ecological systems. If governments try to internalise the externalities and regulate and charge the corporations, corporations move to more compliant countries. Governments are also constrained to give military and economic support to companies that extract resources in foreign countries, giving rise to the huge global military network and the wars over scarce resources that follow. These degrade further once self-sustaining human communities and ecosystems. As non-renewable resources become scarce, it becomes more expensive and destructive to extract and exploit them. And it becomes more difficult to regulate the "race for what's left" that we see today in the North, in fracking, in the Northern Gateway Pipeline, and other examples. Even "renewable" resources, such as fisheries, are exploited to extinction, because the temporality of market competition is faster than the natural cycles that *renew* fish, forests, and oceans.

Finally, in contrast to sustainable cycles, in which the "waste" of one organism is used up by another so there is zero waste or emissions overall, the global market system produces commodities in a linear, non-circular way, so they rapidly become waste, and require new commodities to replace them, as in automobiles or terminator seeds. And new commodities are required to repair the damage they cause during their short life span. It is a cradle-to-grave system of production rather than a cradle-to-cradle system.

If the real costs of this global system were taken into account it would collapse under its own economic irrationality. As Lester Brown points out:

As the world economy expanded some 20-fold over the last century it has revealed a flaw – a flaw so serious that if it is not corrected it will spell the end of civilization as we know it. The market, which sets prices, is not telling the truth. It is omitting indirect costs that in some cases now dwarf direct costs. Consider gasoline. Pumping oil, refining it into gasoline, and delivering the gas to US service stations may cost, say, $3 per gallon. The indirect costs, including climate change, treatment of respiratory illnesses, oil spills, and the US military presence in the Middle East to ensure access to oil, total $12 per gallon. Modern economic thinking and policymaking have created an economy that is so out of sync with the ecosystem on which it depends that it is approaching collapse.

(Brown 2011, 8)

As a result, this is how the dominant system looks from the resiliency perspective of the "Symbiosis and Interdependency" section: contemporary resource-management approaches typically attempt to maximise one or a few desirable systems components at the expense of other species and systems functions – think agricultural or forestry monoculture. Diversity plummets and functions are lost. The managed system becomes inflexibly brittle and vulnerable to unexpected external shocks.

Now, consider the form of contemporary global economic development. The emphasis here is on maximising economic growth by exploiting the efficiency gains conferred by local specialisation and global trade (comparative advantage). The approach tends to maximise resource exploitation and material dissipation (pollution), both of which simplify ecosystems, undermine life-support functions, and erode systems resilience. The global economy becomes dominated by a few global enterprises (and their numbers continue to shrink with each merger or acquisition). The sheer economic power of these monster corporations stifles meaningful competition and blocks new players from entering the market: both local diversity and global diversity plummets. Meanwhile, the economy and society have become dependent on a few declining energy sources (petroleum) and on energy-intensive systems (e.g., the global transportation systems and even the Internet) (Rees 2010).

Moreover, when we participate in this vicious system in our business-as-usual activities we *overlook* the destruction it is causing to the symbiotic social and ecological relationships on which humanity and other forms of life depend. When we can no longer overlook, deny, and discount the problem and must confront the underlying relationship that causes it, the response is to try to regulate the system: to repair damage and compensate stakeholders. Most of these responses take place within and reproduce the vicious system because we continue to see the problem through the lens of the artificial system in which we are reembedded. And it creates the illusion of independence, as Commoner's quotation earlier mentions.

There are three ways in which the crisis is denied or discounted: (1) the boiled frog syndrome: the brain functions so that slow changes, long-term implications, and multiple connections cannot be easily seen; (2) mental apartheid: the psychological barrier between modern humans and the rest of reality: perceptual dualism since Descartes; (3) the idea of the tragedy of the ungoverned commons, from Hobbes' state of nature to Garret Hardin's analysis, makes it appear that the only alternative is privatisation (and this becomes our present tragedy). So, there appears to be no other possibility (Wackernagel and Ress 1996).

I think all three of these strategies can be seen as consequences of the alienated form of life.

However, the really basic one is that our alienated way of life causes us to overlook the living earth and to represent it as resources for production and consumption, whether capitalist or Marxist, and this because of the sense of ourselves as independent and the sense of the only alternative to it as being a kind of servility, dependency, or heteronomy. The third possibility of being agents within and with the living earth disappears from the picture.

Responses of Reengagement and Reconciliation: Realising Interbeing

Aldo Leopold was one of the first people to point out the way in which our modern mode of life diverts our attention from its destructive effects and to suggest an appropriate response:

> One of the penalties of an ecological education is that one lives alone in a world of wounds. Much of the damage inflicted on land is quite invisible to laymen. An ecologist must either harden his shell and make believe that the consequences of science are none of his business, or he must be the doctor who sees the marks of death in a community that believes itself well and does not want to be told otherwise.
>
> (Leopold 1966, 183)

> All ethics so far evolved rest upon a single premise: that the individual is a member of a community of interdependent parts. His instincts prompt him to compete for his place in the community, but his ethics prompts him also to cooperate (perhaps in order that there may be a place to compete for).
>
> The land ethic simply enlarges the boundaries of the community to include soils, waters, plants, and animals, or, collectively: the land ...
>
> In short, a land ethic changes the role of *Homo sapiens* from conqueror of the land-community to plain member and citizen of it. It implies respect for his fellow-members, and also respect for the community as such.
>
> In human history, we have learned (I hope) that the conqueror role is eventually self-defeating. Why? Because it is implicit in such a role that the conqueror knows, *ex cathedra*, just what makes the community clock tick, and just what and who is valuable, and what and who is worthless, in community life. It always turns out that he knows neither, and this is why his conquests eventually defeat themselves.
>
> (1966, 219–20)

> An ethic ... presupposes ... some mental image of land as a biotic system. We can be ethical only in relation to something we can feel, understand, love, or otherwise have faith in.
>
> (1966, 230)

Practices of Dealienation, Reconnection, and Reengagement

Now, let's turn to the practices of freeing ourselves from captivity to the alienated and unsustainable way of life, of beginning to reconnect and engage with the living earth in regenerative rather than extractive-dominative ways, and thereby of beginning to see our place in the world differently and being moved by the animacy of Gaia, as Leopold recommends. There are countless ways in which this transformation can take place in everyday life. Here are several examples.[5]

The most obvious activities of reconnection are those engaged in by citizens and elected officials in the representative institutions and courts. These are indispensable yet insufficient. As we have seen, the social system as a whole places severe limits on what can be done for all the reasons discussed in the previous section. When Gaia citizens run up against these limits they turn to more direct forms of transforming unsustainable and destructive social systems.

In response to five hundred years of dispossession we are witnessing in our time a reclaiming of the local commons as a worldwide phenomenon. From the renaissance of over 350 million Indigenous people, to global movements such as the Food Sovereignty movement, and on to the return to local food production and distribution in the Global North, people are not only repossessing privatised commons. They are also reasserting local knowledges of how to use and sustain the living earth, knowledges that were swept aside as primitive and replaced by modern scientific agribusiness and synthetic fertilisers, yet are grounded in thousands of years of practical knowledge of the renewability conditions of local resources. In Boaventura de Sousa Santos's famous characterisation of this renaissance of local practices and local knowledges, there is no global justice without local epistemic justice (Santos 2014).

In response to the commodification of labour power, democratic, cooperative citizens refuse to comply with this undemocratic mode of production and consumption. As much as possible, they reappropriate their producing and consuming capabilities from commodification and exercise their capabilities "in common," in democratically run cooperatives and community-based organisations' that are reembedded in social and ecological relationships. Such grassroots democracies then produce and distribute the basic public goods that are privatised under the dominant form of democracy: food, shelter, clothing, health care, clean water, security, and so on. These social and economic democracies are linked together by global networks of fair trade relationships that are also under the democratic control of the producers and consumers subject to them.

This famous response to the injustices of the privatisation of labour power has given rise to the tradition of cooperative democracy throughout the world. From Robert Owen, William Thompson, and Peter Kropotkin in Europe, to Gandhi, Richard Gregg, Fritz Schumacher, and the *swaraj* and *swadeshi* movements across Asia and Africa, to food sovereignty in Latin America, there is a turn to local food production, microcredit, democratic cooperatives, and Indigenous and non-Indigenous community-based organisations of diverse scales and types. These are then linked together by global networks of fair trade and self-reliance. These cooperative practices generate social capital and realise social and economic justice directly, by bringing the local and global organisation of economic activities under the democratic cooperation and mutual aid of all subject to and affected by them.

This is the cooperative citizenship response to the global problem of economic inequality and exploitation. It is important to note that despite the global spread of the institutional module of modern representative government and civil citizenship, poverty and hunger persist on this "planet of slums":

963 million people go to bed hungry every night. One billion people live in slums. One woman dies every minute in childbirth. 2.5 billion people have no access to adequate sanitation services and 20,000 children a day die as a result.

(Khan 2009)

Cooperative citizens offer a response to this *glocal* injustice that is more immediate and perhaps more lasting than representative responses because the victims of hunger, starvation, and poverty become the agents of grassroots democracy and economic self-reliance.

Another response is ecological or Gaia citizenship. In response to the third process of the commodification of the living earth, civic citizens withdraw their capacities from activities based on the commodification of the environment and develop a responsible way of relating in and to it. They reembed natural resources and the human uses of them into their place within ecological relationships and cycles of no waste and regeneration. They see the webs of ecological relationships as a living commonwealth of all forms of life. They derive the fundamental duties, responsibility, and rights of democracy in the first instance from their membership in the webs of ecological relationships in which democracy takes place and on which all forms of life depend. This natural gift economy, as Vandana Shiva (2005) puts it, is for them the true mother of democracy. The norms of ecological well-being govern economics not the other way round.

This revolutionary response to the injustice of privatisation of the natural world has given rise to the great cooperative and community-based ecology movements. From Aldo Leopold, Rachel Carson, and Vandana Shiva to the Chipko Movement in India and Asia, and on to Japanese fishing cooperatives, the water justice movement, Food Sovereignty, and everyday ecological footprint initiatives, millions of Gaia citizens are reclaiming the commons and exercising their capabilities democratically in ethical relationships of stewardship in the commonwealth of all forms of life. These experiments in ecodemocracy and cyclical economics are responses and alternatives to the idea of unlimited linear development that gives rise to the ecological crisis.

Finally, two of the foundational premises that justify the imposition and continuation of the unsustainable processes of modernisation are that humans are naturally antagonistic, and thus that they need an authoritarian master who coercively imposes a structure of law over them as a socialising precondition of peace and democracy. These are foundational presuppositions of modernisation in theory and practice since Hobbes. As we can see from the examples I have just given, Gaia citizens reject these premises.

From Kropotkin, through Gandhi and Richard Gregg, to millions today, these citizens argue in contrast that humans are self-organising and self-governing animals. Autopoiesis – self-organisation, cooperation, and nonviolent contestation and dispute resolution – is a more basic condition of human evolution than antagonism, violent conflict, and the hegemonic relationships of command and obedience that violence aims to establish, yet it tends to generate counterviolence. If this were not the case, if Kantian antagonism and Hobbesian war of all against all were primary, the human species would have perished long ago. We overlook this pacific feature of our everyday activities precisely because it is so commonplace and familiar (Gregg 2018; Engler and Engler 2016).

Humans are not unique in this respect. The hypothesis holds for all forms of life and for the ecological relationships in which they all live. This was put on scientific footing in the 1960s by James Lovelock in the Gaia hypothesis. It is widely endorsed by biological, ecological, and climate scientists today (Capra and Luisi 2014). This view that the ground of our being as earthlings is ecological and sociological relationships of mutual interdependence and support is also widely endorsed by many of the spiritual traditions of the world. This helps to explain the powerful attraction of cooperative citizenship to people from such different secular and spiritual traditions.

It follows from this scientific revolution in the way we think about our place and roles in the ecosphere that there are two gift-reciprocity or mutually co-sustaining socioecosystems. The first is the natural ecosystem that sustains all forms of life. The second is that there are informal, and often unnoticed, social networks of mutual sustenance that sustain the day-to-day lives of members in any community of practice. These informal networks of mutual aid underlie the dominant, formal, and unsustainable social systems. The dominant systems are parasitic on these relationships of "social capital," as Polanyi argued, in the sense that they need these symbiotic systems to sustain the members that they simultaneously separate, exploit, place in competition, and disemploy. This is a complex dynamic because the more concerned citizens repair the social and ecological networks that sustain life, the more attractive they become as resources for recommodification (Klare 2012; Dilworth 2010).

Another important local and global initiative is the turn to zero waste and cyclical, non-violent technology, architecture, and urban planning. These movements find their inspiration in Gandhi's constructive programs and Fritz Schumacher's cyclical economics and appropriate technology. More recently, McDonough and Braungart explain their "cradle-to-cradle" version in the following way:

> Nature operates according to a system of nutrients and metabolisms in which there is no such thing as waste. A cherry tree makes many blossoms and fruit to (perhaps) germinate and grow. This is why the tree blooms. They fall to the ground, decompose, feed various organisms and microorganisms, and enrich the soil. Around the world, animals and humans exhale carbon dioxide, which plants take in and use for their own growth. Nitrogen from wastes is transformed into protein by microorganisms, animals, and plants. Horses eat grass and produce dung, which provides both nest and nourishment for the larvae of flies. The earth's major nutrients – carbon, hydrogen, oxygen, nitrogen – are cycled and recycled. Waste equals food.
>
> This cyclical, cradle to cradle biological system has nourished a planet of thriving, diverse abundance for millions of years. Until very recently in the earth's history, it was the only system, and every living thing on the earth belonged to it. Growth was good. It meant more trees, more species, greater diversity, and more complex, resilient ecosystems. Then came industry, which altered the natural equilibrium of materials on the planet. Humans took substances from the earth's crust and concentrated, altered, and synthesised them into vast quantities of materials that cannot be safely returned to soil. Now material flows can be divided into two categories: biological mass and technical – that is, industrial – mass.
>
> From our perspective, these two kinds of material flows on the planet are just biological and technical nutrients. Biological nutrients are useful to the biosphere, while technical nutrients are useful to what we call the technosphere, the systems of industrial processes. Yet somehow we have evolved an industrial infrastructure that ignores the existence of nutrients of either kind.
>
> Humans are the only species that takes from the soil vast quantities of nutrients needed for biological processes but rarely puts them back in usable forms.
>
> (McDonough and Braungart 2010, 92–3, 96;
> cf. Schumacher 1973)

Another important example is the way green legal theory and practice are presenting alternatives to the modern legal commodification of land and labour under national and international law. The role of green legal theory is to develop a way of thinking about law that cognises the cyclical and symbiotic interdependency and co-sustainability of "natural resources" in ecosystems and "human resources," technology, and "communities of practice" (cooperatives and corporations) in socioecosystems (Cullinan 2011).

Finally, one of the most important movements over the last few decades is the attempt to bring together and integrate the various fields of knowledge, research, and teaching that I have drawn on in describing our predicament and responses to it (Capra and Luisi 2014; Esbjorn-Hargens and Zimmerman 2009).

The challenge today is thus not to dream up responses to climate change or seize power. Rather, it is to find ways to democratically coordinate the multiplicity of such practices of dealienation and reconnection around the world so they grow and gradually hollow out, displace, and transform the unsustainable systems. The tragedy of the present is that we who inhabit the dominant social systems and view the world through their theories of transformative change by means of reform or violent revolution do not see this alternative, non-violent way of systemic transformative change from below, yet it is the way damaged life systems repair and regenerate themselves.[6] If it took five hundred years for the dominant system to reach "peak everything," perhaps we should think of this new "great transformation" as also taking centuries of sustained and sustaining practices of regeneration.

Reanimation

Perhaps one of the most important practices of sustainability is the everyday individual and cooperative practices of engaging with the living earth through the primacy of dialogical perception. This consists in disengaging our perception/cognition (senses and synaesthesia) from the built environment and reconnecting with the animate earth sensuously, as our nervous system does naturally. This is how David Abram, following Maurice Merleau-Ponty, describes it:

> The event of perception, experientially considered, is an inherently interactive, participatory event, a reciprocal interplay between the perceiver and the perceived.
> Perceived things are encountered by the perceiving body as animate, living powers that actively draw us into relation. Our spontaneous, preconceptual experience yields no evidence for a dualistic division between animate and inanimate phenomena, only for relative distinctions between diverse forms of animateness.
> The perceptual reciprocity between our sensing bodies and the animate, expressive landscape both engenders and supports our more conscious, linguistic reciprocity with others. The complex interchange we call

"language" is rooted in the non-verbal exchange always already going on between our own flesh and the flesh of the world.

(Abram 1997, 89–90)

Reengaging with the natural world in this way reconnects us with our interdependent "ecological self" and overcomes the separation of culture and nature in our dominant identity formation. Interacting in this way "brings forth the world" cognitively as interdependent and coevolving and, in so doing, brings us into connection with the suffering of the world. It enables us to see our responsibility for and interdependency on the living world. Yet, even more importantly, it connects us with the animacy of life itself (*anima mundi*) that empowers us (Harding 2013). As Joanna Macy and Chris Johnstone argue, the gratitude we experience for the invaluable gifts of the life-sustaining goods and services that the living earth gives us every second motivates and moves us to reciprocate (Macy and Johnstone 2012). It is animacy of life itself that empowers us to continue to act in reciprocally sustaining ways (Kimmerer 2013).

Notes

1 This chapter follows from Tully (2020b) on this theme at the 2013 NOMIS Workshop. I would like to thank the participants in both the 2013 and 2014 workshops for their helpful comments on my presentations, especially the late Jonathan Schell, Akeel Bilgrami, Charles Taylor, Anthony Laden, David Kahane, and Pablo Ouziel. I would also like to thank Michael Carpenter for assistance with editing both chapters. I have discussed the topics in this chapter further in Tully (2018b).
2 For example: Emmott (2013), Deffeyes (2005), Crutzen and Günter Brauch (2016). For a history of sustainability, see Caradonna (2014).
3 Michael Simpson, PhD student, University of British Columbia, personal correspondence with the author.
4 See further the "Responses of Reengagement and Reconciliation: Realising Interbeing" section.
5 I have discussed these in more detail in Tully (2014a, 2008b).
6 See the quotation from Simpson in note 3.

11 A View of Transformative Reconciliation

Strange Multiplicity and the Spirit of Haida Gwaii at Twenty (2015)

Introduction: Gift, Gratitude, Reciprocity

Giving Thanks for the Gift of this Symposium

Thank you to Edward and Dorothy Clarke Kempf Memorial Fund, Yale Group for the Study of Native America, Department of History, and the Department of Political Science.[1]

I would like to thank Logan Mardhani-Bayne for all the work he did in organising this symposium. Moreover, I would like to thank everyone who has come to speak and to discuss the amazing growth of the field of Indigenous studies over the last two decades, where it stands today, and future directions. Most of all, I would like to thank Ned Blackhawk for everything he has done to create the idea of the symposium and to bring it to life.

I would also like to thank Seyla Benhabib and the 2015 Yale Critical Theory Roundtable for including my lecture as part of their roundtable this year. I am most grateful because one of my objectives in *Strange Multiplicity* was to bring Western political theorists and intellectual historians around to see the history of European and Euro-American imperialism, and the traditions of European political and social thought that have served to legitimate them, from the perspective of those who have been subjects of Western imperialism; not only the Third World of the Middle East and the Global South; but, primarily, the Fourth World of four hundred million Indigenous people of the world.

The major objective of the symposium is to attempt to survey the rich field of Indigenous studies since *Strange Multiplicity* in 1995. It is not a symposium on *Strange Multiplicity* but on what has happened since then. As you all know, the field of Indigenous studies has grown immensely since 1995. I look forward to learning from the panels tomorrow about all the developments in the field since 1995 by the amazing group of scholars gathered here.

I see my lecture this afternoon as one small contribution to the exploration of the field of Indigenous studies. I would like to say a few words about the genesis of *Strange Multiplicity* and what I hoped to achieve in giving it as a

DOI: 10.4324/9781003227403-15

Seeley Lecture and publishing it. However, the main theme of my talk is how I am thinking today, in 2015, about two themes I first addressed in *Strange Multiplicity*.

Reciprocal Elucidation Cycles

When I wrote *Strange Multiplicity* there were a number of ways of writing about Indigenous peoples with respect to European expansion, settlement, dispossession, and colonisation. However, my concern was somewhat different. It was *to learn to listen* to what Indigenous people have been saying about two things: (1) their own social and ecological lifeworld and lifeways on the one hand; and (2) how they understand a good relationship with the settlers on their traditional territories on the other hand. I see these two themes as distinct from their forms of resistance to imperialism and cultural genocide; that is, as the normative or generative ground of the forms of Indigenous resistance and resurgence.

Hence, my approach is a kind of educational dialogue of reciprocal elucidation between non-Indigenous and Indigenous interlocutors: where listening to and working with them helps to free myself from my Western prejudgments; then to try to see if I can articulate what I am hearing in terms that would be understandable to a Western audience; and then, *in reciprocity*, to see if I could find a way of relating to Indigenous partners from my own traditions that might be a reciprocal good relationship of peace and friendship in both theory and practice.

Well, this attempt at an ongoing dialogical relationship of reciprocal learning began in the 1980s, then to the Oka Crisis, the setting up of a course at McGill, inviting Ellen Gabriel and others to come and speak, Indigenous students at McGill, and on to the Canadian Royal Commission on Aboriginal Peoples (RCAP).

At the RCAP I was invited to listen and discuss issues with hundreds of Indigenous people from across Canada over a three-year period. This kind of dialogue of reciprocal learning has continued down to today, and I hope will continue for years to come. Thus, the first thing I would like to do is to acknowledge and express my gratitude to the Indigenous and non-Indigenous partners in these relationships of reciprocal elucidation inside and outside the academy. Many of the partners from whom I have learned the most are present today.

I am from Vancouver Island. The Coast Salish peoples on the island always begin a meeting by giving thanks for all the gifts they have received from both human and more-than-human others; so that we all see ourselves located in the social and ecological relationships and life-cycles to which we belong and on which we all depend. So, it is my great honour and pleasure to start by engaging in such a welcoming gift-reciprocity relationship today – of giving thanks to the Indigenous and non-Indigenous interlocutors from whom I have learned so much.

I would like to mention people who helped me during my years at McGill University and the University of Victoria. They include Dale Turner, Ellen Gabriel, Ned Blackhawk, Ardith Walkem, Taiaiake Alfred, Charles Taylor, Tony Laden, Darius Rejali, Bassel Salloukh, the many interlocutors at RCAP, Richard Atleo (Umeek), Nuu-chah-nulth philosopher, Charles Elliott, Elder, Tsartlip First Nation, Audra Simpson, Glen Coulthard, Robert Nichols, Jakeet Singh, Johnny Mack, John Borrows, Val Napoleon, Hadley Friedland, Heidi Stark, Jeremy Webber, Nancy Turner, Aaron Mills, Keith Cherry, Isaiah Wilner, Russ Meyers, Sarah Morales, Rachel Flowers, Deanne LeBlanc, Gina Starblanket, Joshua Nichols, and Ryan Nicholson. International dialogue partners include Boaventura de Sousa Santos, Tony Anghie, Antje Wiener, Amy Allen, Rainer Forst, Jeanne Morefield, Duncan Bell, Akeel Bilgrami, Jonathan Schell, Karuna Mantena, and Dennis Dalton.

I call this kind of engaged research "public philosophy in a new key" or, adapting Foucault's phrase, "reciprocal elucidation": of working up ideas through critical and comparative dialogue and testing them out in practice, and then returning to reflection, correction, and improvement of it through renewed dialogue and renewed application – in what I hope are virtuous cycles of ongoing learning and practice. I think of it as akin to an Indigenous feast on the Northwest coast in which stories are shared and mutual learning achieved. Each brings the gift of their own way of looking at things to the dialogue, each is grateful for the other's gifts, and each reciprocates in turn: it sets in motion a *virtuous learning cycle of gift-gratitude-reciprocity.*

Land and Treaties: 1995 and 2015

Strange Multiplicity grew out of the early stages of this dialogue: of the Oka Crisis, classes on Indigenous rights, the Rare Books Room in the Redpath Library, my own dialogue with the Western tradition at Cambridge, and especially the dialogue of learning at RCAP. The RCAP was set up in response to the Oka crisis. Recall that the Oka Crisis gave a new voice to two major unresolved issues on Great Turtle Island.

The first was *the land question*: the municipality of Oka, Quebec, tried to take unilaterally some of the traditional land of the Kanesatake Mohawk community for the purpose of expanding a golf course. The Mohawks refused to allow this violation of their traditional territory and defended it.

The second was *the treaty question*: how should the relationships between Indigenous peoples and settlers over sharing Great Turtle Island be worked out. As Oren Lyons answered, it is not by stealing Indigenous land and sending in the army but by nation-to-nation treaty relations. These issues of land and treaties were taken up and responded to by RCAP in terms of four basic questions:

1   What is a sustainable relationship to the living earth?
2   What is a sustainable relationship to each other – Indigenous and settler – in sharing the land?

3   What is the internal relation between the way we relate to the earth and to each other?
4   How do we transform the present destructive and unsustainable relationships to the living earth and each other (double decolonisation) into sustainable relationships?

These are what I call *transformative reconciliation* questions. We are still working on them today.

In response to the land question, Indigenous people from across the continent said that the land question is not simply one of dispossession without consent. Rather, and more fundamentally, it is a question of a whole different way of relating to the land from the Western way of Crown sovereignty and capitalist private property (the commodification of the earth) that the settlers brought with them. Indigenous knowledge keepers said that "the land does not belong to them" as either private property or eminent domain. Rather, "they belong to the land." That is, they belong to the living earth in the sense that they are participants in lifeways that are carefully woven into the ecological lifeworlds or ecosystems that sustain life on Turtle Island. This is Traditional ecological knowledge and wisdom (TEKW)

In response to the treaty question, Indigenous people from across the continent said that the way of establishing good relationships between Indigenous peoples and settlers is through *Kaswentha* – the form of treaty relationship embodied in the Two Row Wampum belts of peace and friendship exchanged with the settlers since 1623, recognised in the Royal Proclamation of 1763, affirmed in the Treaty of Niagara in 1764, and referred to ever since. This is the fundamental constitution of Indigenous-settler relations of North America.

Moreover, in response to the third question, traditional elders explained that the relationships to the living earth and to human beings are internally related; the latter grows out of the former. And, in response to the fourth question, that these two relationships hold the key to the means of transformation of the current colonial relationships into sustainable relationships of peace and friendship with mother earth and each other: that is, of transformative reconciliation.

Strange Multiplicity and the Spirit of Haida Gwaii

Strange Multiplicity was my first sustained attempt to try to understand these great ideas and to articulate them in ways that are true to what I was being told and also might be understandable to an academic audience in my field of political thought and its history.

Strange Multiplicity is a story of Indigenous peoples of America prior to European settlement; of an early period of treaty relationships, of the gradual dispossession, internal colonisation, cultural genocide, and assimilation of Indigenous peoples by the settler states erected over their traditional territories or lifeworlds. It is also a story not only of resistance against monumental odds. It is also a story of intergenerational efforts to sustain and regenerate

Indigenous lifeways and traditional ecological knowledge and wisdom in grounded practices on traditional territories. It is also a story of Indigenous peoples' countless attempts to transform the colonial relationship into a peace and friendship relationship of reconciliation between equal yet different partners. Most of all, it is an attempt to bring non-Indigenous readers around to see the importance of learning to listen carefully to what Indigenous knowledge keepers are saying about treaty relations and relations to the land – without translating what they were saying into a Western modernisation framework.

Finally, although I did not see this at all clearly at the time, it is also a story of how the regeneration of Indigenous lifeways and lifeworlds provides the reciprocal ground of genuinely transformative treaty negotiations of reconciliation. I think I have a better view of the transformative power of treaty negotiations of reconciliation grounded in Indigenous lifeways in practice today. I have this better view today thanks to the ongoing dialogue with many interlocutors that I mentioned earlier.

I began to see that my understanding of what Indigenous knowledge keepers were saying was superficial, and thus that my articulation of a renewed and genuinely transformative relationship to the living earth and each other was superficial. And, in our research, we all began to see that the processes of reconciliation set in motion were also superficial – in the sense that they served to integrate Indigenous peoples even further into destructive and unsustainable processes of economic, political, and cultural modernisation. And, this *double neo-colonialism* replicated the history of the earlier twentieth century. Let me explain what I mean here.

Parallel to Indigenous people, Adorno and Horkheimer argued that modern relations of the domination of nature went along with dominating social systems. They and Marcuse argued that some kind of Marxist revolution could bring about a genuinely transformative reconciliation to nature and to each other. However, the Third World violent decolonisation revolutions, the Non-Aligned Movement, and the New International Economic Order in 1974 did not bring about transformative reconciliation, but, rather, heavily armed and indebted states, the primacy of unequal command-obedience relationships among humans (individual and collective), and rapid economic development and exploitation of the living earth. And, the former colonies continued the colonisation of Indigenous peoples.

That is, the former colonies were integrated into the destructive global systems that have given rise to *the global sustainability crisis*: the unsustainability of our dominant destructive relationships to the living earth and living communities. This double tragedy of post-colonial enlightenment led to a whole set of research networks around the continuation of informal imperialism, the ecological and social crisis of globalisation, and *the search for alternative modes of transformation* of the colonisation of the Fourth World after the failure of violent revolution of the Third World and the failure of internal reform since the 1970s. First, it led to the study of nonviolent ways of transforming our destructive relationships to the earth and each other, and so to Gandhi and

Schumacher, and to nonviolent Indigenous traditions. Second, it led to the study of the global sustainability crisis and transformative responses to it.

The work of Glen Coulthard, Johnny Mack, and Robert Nichols has been absolutely fundamental in this regard. But, also, Art Manuel, the son of George Manuel, who attended the Bandung Conference in 1955 and co-authored *The Fourth World,* John Borrows, the great Anishinaabe legal scholar, Russ Meyers, Tsilhqot'in chief, and Richard Atleo Senior (*Umeek*) have been of enormous assistance.

The Indigenous Peoples Working Group on Climate Change (IPWGCC), the Environmental Law Center at University of Victoria, Boaventura de Sousa Santos, Tony Anghie, Akeel Bilgrami, Jonathan Schell, and Karuna Mantena, among many others, helped us to see the depth and scope of the problem we are facing in the twenty-first century: the need to transform the destructive and unsustainable system that the settlers brought with them to Turtle Island and spread around the world. All this intense reciprocal elucidation has helped us to gain a deeper understanding of the four questions I was struggling with inadequately in 1995 – and of their contemporary importance. I will try to set out this clearer view of transformative reconciliation in my talk today.

"We Belong to the Living Earth": Indigenous Understandings of Belonging to the Living Earth and Belonging to Treaty Relationships

Johnny Mack and I are exceptionally fortunate in being able to learn from Nuu-Chah-Nulth elder Richard Atleo (*Umeek*). He explains the mantra that I first heard at RCAP – "The earth does not belong to us. We belong to the earth" – in the following way.

The first part of the mantra refers to the relationship to the living earth that the settler brought to this continent and imposed over their Indigenous social and ecological lifeways. This is the view that the earth belongs to us as our private property; as commodifiable resources. Indigenous knowledge keepers reject this system. It is vicious and unsustainable; the primary cause of the global sustainability crisis all around us. From their perspective it is a relationship of dispossession, alienation, exploitation, and eventual self-destruction of the conditions of life on earth.

Indigenous people could see what is wrong with the settlers' system because they have often generated vicious and unsustainable relationships to their ecosystems and to each other. However, over millennia, they have learned by trial and error how to repair these unsustainable ways and to relate to the earth in sustainable ways. This Indigenous way of being in the world is captured in the mantra: "We belong to the living earth." Umeek explains this in terms of three basic features: (1) *Heshook-ish Tsawalk*: the basic character of creation is (dynamic) unity; (2) the basic logic of this dynamic unity is gift-gratitude-reciprocity relationships and cycles; and (3) we become aware of our life-giving participation in these gift-reciprocity relationships and of our responsibilities to sustain them through practice – engagement in them.

Gift-Reciprocity Ecosystems

To belong to the living earth is to see and experience ourselves as participants within the larger-than-human ecosystems that comprise the living earth. We are plain members and citizens of its webs of ecological relationships and cycles, just like all other forms of life on earth. (Recall that this is also the phrase that Aldo Leopold uses in *Sand County Almanac* [1966].) These ecological relationships are relationships of deep and complex interdependency, intradependency, and interaction of all forms of life on earth. As a result all forms of life, human and non-human, are our relatives.

This is a *kincentric* way of being in the world, as the distinguished Potawatomi biologist Robin Wall Kimmerer puts it in *Braiding Sweetgrass* (2013) and ethno-botanist Nancy Turner in *Earth's Blanket* (2005). The central insight of traditional ecological knowledge is not only that we are embedded in relationships of complex interdependency. It is also that these are relationships of co-sustainability.

The lifeways of the members and their interrelationships have evolved for the most part in ways that are not only self-sustaining, but, they also sustain themselves in ways in that co-sustain the interdependent lifeways of their relatives. (They integrate what we call the "environment" into their lifeways.) To belong to the land is to belong to complex interdependent lifeways and life-cycles that co-sustain all life on earth since time immemorial (3.5 billion years). Hence, the terms "mother earth" or "living earth." When you participate in and experience the sensuous world in this co-sustaining way, the world is brought forth to you as a "kincentric worldview": of all forms of life as our interrelated and co-sustaining kin of various kinds.

Next, life-giving and life-receiving relationships of interdependency and co-sustainability are called gift-reciprocity relationships, networks, and lifecycles. The ways that plants, animals, photosynthesis, fungi, nutrients, ecosystems, sun and rain, soil and rivers interact in giving and receiving the conditions of life from each other appear as complex cycles of gift exchange.

As Kimmerer puts it, *life sustains life* by means of gift-reciprocity systems:

> Reciprocity – returning the gift – is not just good manners; it is how the biophysical world works. Balance in ecological systems arises from negative feedback loops, from cycles of giving and taking. Reciprocity among parts of the living earth produces [dynamic] equilibrium, in which life as we know it can flourish. When the gift is in motion, it can last forever.
>
> (Kimmerer 2014, 4)

The symbiotic gift-reciprocity relationship is thus the common feature or logic of the relationships that sustain life on earth in all its diverse forms. It is the "animacy" or aliveness of the living earth. It is the greatest power on earth since it has sustained and generated life for over three billion years. It is far greater than the forms of power humans have created.

Gift-Reciprocity Social-Ecological Systems

Traditional knowledge keepers have learned how the living earth sustains life through 150 thousand years of trial and error. As John Borrows and Aaron Mills have taught me, the word for "education" in many Indigenous languages, and in Ojibwa in particular, literally means "to look towards and learn from the living earth."

Once humans learn that they are interdependent members of life-sustaining gift-reciprocity relationships and cycles, then they can see what their responsibilities are as citizens who belong to and depend on the living earth. Their responsibilities are to connect (or reconnect) with the animacy of the ecosystems in which they live in self-sustaining and co-sustaining ways: to accept and use with gratitude the gift of clean air, plants, trees, animals, water, and so on to sustain themselves; but, always also in reciprocal gratitude for these life-giving gifts, to use them in such ways that co-sustain the non-human life systems and cycles in which these gifts are embedded and on which we and other forms of life co-depend.

As fellow inhabitants, we design our socio-ecological systems in reciprocal care and synchronicity with the larger gift-reciprocity systems in which they are embedded and on which they depend. That is: not to *take*, but to *caretake*. That is, in general, socio-ecological systems should always be gift-gratitude-reciprocity systems. And, thus, as Val Napoleon has shown in her teaching and research, Indigenous peoples draw on their stories of the larger-than-human world and human interactions with it to derive their laws and forms of self-governance.

For millennia, then, *Homo sapiens* have co-evolved with their bioregions as cooperative apprentices; learning by trial and error. Their lifeways and life cycles are "indigenous" in the precise sense of this term of being in dynamic equilibrium with the place in which we dwell.

Gift-Gratitude-Reciprocity Treaty Relationships

Indigenous knowledge keepers say that the ecological gift-reciprocity relationships that co-sustain all forms of interdependent life are also the model for human social relationships with one another, individually and collectively. They too are countless varieties of gift-gratitude-reciprocity relationships among human kin, as in families, clans, and so on.

Since first contact, Indigenous peoples have been inviting settlers to enter into treaty relationships in order to work out how to live with each other as different yet interdependent relatives in co-sustainable ways. The model for gift-reciprocity treaty relationships has been the *Kaswentha* Two Row

Wampum treaties exchanged between Iroquois and settlers from the seventeenth century to today.

Treaty negotiations begin with ceremonies of giving thanks to mother earth for all her gifts and the exchange of gifts before entering into the exchange of stories and arguments and proposals in the negotiations. The gift exchange at treaty talks reminds the partners that they should see themselves as both embedded in natural cyclical gift relationships and bringing into being new ones in the negotiations. Just as the living earth consists of gift-reciprocity relationships that sustain the living members, so humans should relate to the living earth and each other in their social relationships in the same general way.

That is: a gift is given; the recipient expresses the emotion of gratitude and the giver perceives this; and the emotion of gratitude moves the recipient to reciprocate by giving a gift to the giver or another in reciprocity. In so doing, participants bring into being and continue gift-gratitude-reciprocity networks and cycles that co-sustain all participants: treaty and social networks that mimic self-sustaining ecological networks.

If, conversely, they fail to reciprocate with the living earth or with their treaty partners, appropriate and use the gifts with ingratitude, then they break the cycles that sustain life in both cases, destroy the cyclical networks that are the conditions of life for their neighbours and themselves, and eventually destroy themselves.

Accordingly, the exchange of gifts before and after treaty talks reminds the participants that they have shared responsibilities to connect or "reconnect" the gift-gratitude-reciprocity circle that sustains all forms of life.

As Taiaiake Alfred has taught me, the Haudenosaunee (Iroquois confederacy), for example, explain their "call to consciousness" before treaty negotiations in the following way:

> The original instructions direct that we who walk about on the earth are to express a great respect, and affection, and gratitude towards all the spirits which create and support life. We give a greeting and thanksgiving to the many supporters of our lives – the corn, bean, squash, the winds, the sun, all living beings who work together on this land. When people cease to respect and express gratitude for those many things, then all life will be destroyed, and human life on this planet will come to an end.
>
> Today we have gathered and we see that the cycles of life continue. We have been given the duty to live in balance with each other and all living things. So now we bring our minds together as one as we give greetings and thanks to each other as People.
>
> Now our minds are one.

This is what Indigenous people have been telling settlers at treaty talks for four hundred years. If you wish to settle here, share this beautiful land, and live in peace and friendship with all your relatives, then interact with the living earth and your treaty partners in gift-gratitude-reciprocity ways.

Settlers came with another system; one in which "the land belongs to humans." From within this system, they thought Indigenous people were negotiating the sale of land they owned in the treaty negotiations. Treaty relationships were thus seen as contractual relationships. And treaty negotiators were seen as bargaining to get the best deal for themselves. This still remains the dominant understanding today.

Relationship Among Three Gift-Reciprocity Systems

In summary, to live in such a way as to "belong to the land" is to learn to live within three interdependent living systems that manifest the same basic gift-reciprocity logic: (1) The larger-than-human living world on which we all depend; (2) the socio-ecological systems through which humans interact and co-evolve with the larger-than-human world; (3) the sustaining social relationships among humans; especially treaty relationships among peoples living together in peace and friendship. These three types of life systems make up the living earth to which we belong and in which we live and breathe and have our different modes of being.

Moreover, in response to the initial question of what the internal relations are between these life systems, the answer seems clear. The gift-reciprocity relationships of the living earth are the ground and grounded normativity for the human gift-reciprocity systems (as both Glen Coulthard and Aaron Mills have shown me). The three systems are interdependent and co-sustaining life systems. Coast Salish stories often point out this interdependency by stating that they have treaty relations with the plants and animals of their bio-region.

Motivation

What motivates a person or people to interact with each other and all their human and non-human relatives in these gift-gratitude-reciprocity ways and, thereby, sustaining a global federation of all forms of life?

There are a number of overlapping reasons for living in this way. These are recorded in Indigenous stories and each draw on different features of gift-reciprocity relationships and individual and collective agency within them:

1 The most important is that experiencing being in the world with others in gift-reciprocity ways invokes the emotion of gratitude for these gifts of life and gratitude, informed by traditional ecological and ethical teachings, and moves us to reciprocate in kind. We "realise" that every breath we take, the food we eat, the beauty all around us, and the sustenance that sustains us are given to us by the living earth into which we are born. The feeling of gratitude that washes over us moves us to participate within and sustain the cyclical relationships that sustain them.

2 Next, within this kincentric worldview, we recognise other living members are our family members and the whole earth system as our mother, and

thus we interact as we would normally do with family members; namely, with care and compassion.

3   Next, reflection on the gift-reciprocity cycles makes us realise that if we, individually and collectively, take care of mother earth, she in reciprocity will continue to take care of us.

4   Our primary form of self-awareness and self-formation is not of an independent and separate individual or group, but, rather, our more extensive interdependent self – what Arne Naess called our "ecological self." We identify with, and so care for, all our relations as the background way to care for ourselves in the individual sense.

5   Finally, and perhaps most importantly, the experience of participating in gift-gratitude-reciprocity relationships is just to *be reconnected with and empowered by the animacy of the living earth* – the autopoietic power that has brought life into being, sustained and diversified it for over three billion years.

Three States of Gift-Reciprocity Systems and Transformative Reconciliation

Let me mention one final and crucial feature of this Indigenous worldview that is often misunderstood yet is of fundamental importance. Ecological and social gift-reciprocity systems are dynamic. They can exist in three different states.

In the first state they are what is called conciliatory systems. Here the living members interact virtuously by enacting their responsibilities within gift-reciprocity relationships and cycles. These "circles of participation" (or negative feedback loops as they are called in systems theory) sustain the life of the members, the system as a whole, and co-sustain the social and ecosystems with which it in turn interacts.

Yet, even this so-called "steady state" is not automatic but dynamic and conciliatory, and often far from equilibrium. The members participate reciprocally, yet make mistakes; others fail to reciprocate or become greedy and selfish, violent rather than peaceful, aggressive rather than cooperative and nonviolently contestatory; taking more of renewable resources than the system can renew, and so on. However, through trial and error, the members of the system learn how to correct this behaviour before it gets out of hand, and re-conciliate. That is, bring the members back to relationships of peace and friendship.

Indigenous peoples are evolving apprentices: they learn this knowledge and wisdom by means of trial and error. Even the best virtuous ecosystem, socio-ecosystem, and social system built on the gift-reciprocity model are often far from equilibrium, require continuous "conciliation" by their members, and always open to abuse, the magnification of vicious interactions, tipping points, and the transformation of a virtuous system into vicious system:

Indigenous story traditions are full of cautionary tales about the failure of gratitude. When people forget to honor the gift, the consequences are always material as well as spiritual. The spring dries up, the corn doesn't grow, the animals do not return, and the legions of offended plants and animals and rivers rise up against the ones who neglected gratitude.

(Kimmerer 2014, 20)

If the vicious behaviour is not corrected, it can be self-reinforcing by means of positive feedback loops among the interconnected members that amplify its destructive effects. The system as a whole reaches a tipping point and is transformed into a vicious and unsustainable system. If this dynamic is not stopped, it can lead not only to the destruction of the forms of life and gift-reciprocity relationships on which its members depend, but, as a result, to the self-destruction of the vicious system and its members. This has happened many times in the history of non-human and human life on earth. Many scholars and the Intergovernmental Panel on Climate Change (IPCC) suggest that this is happening in our time, in the global sustainability crisis.

I will suggest in a moment that this global crisis is brought about by the rise to global dominance over the last four hundred years of the unsustainable system that the settlers brought with them: a system in which we act as if the earth belongs to us (as our property). When this occurs, the vicious system cannot be re-conciliated by normal means within the system. It requires means of reconciliation that transform the vicious system into a virtuous system: that is, reconnects and regenerates the members with the animate gift-reciprocity relationships of the living earth and with each other.

The key feature of this third cycle of transformative reconciliation is that it transforms the vicious way of life of the members of the unsustainable system into a virtuous and sustainable way of life by reconnecting them with the larger-than-human gift-reciprocity animacy that sustains all life on earth.

Transformative reconciliation transforms and reconnects by regenerating and enacting here-and-now gift-reciprocity relationships with the living earth and with each other in their everyday practices *within* the vicious system. These everyday activities of reconnecting gradually bring about a tipping point that transforms the dominant vicious way of life into a virtuous and sustainable one. Reconciliation and reconnection are brought about by regenerating gift-reciprocity relationships from the ground up – just as a damaged ecosystem is recovered by the regeneration of permaculture. Accordingly, the means of transformative reconciliation have to be *prefigurative* of the end they are designed to bring about if they are to be effective. They have to manifest the gift-reciprocity logic of the animacy of the great commonwealth of all forms of life.

Indigenous story-telling on Turtle Island is replete with stories of these three great cycles of life earth: virtuous and sustainable dynamic gift-reciprocity systems; the emergence of vicious non-reciprocal behaviour, which is either corrected or continued, tipping the system into a vicious and unsustainable state; and, third, great attempts to transform and reconcile the vicious system into a virtuous and sustainable system by reconnecting its members with the larger gift-reciprocity relationships that sustain life on earth. Indeed, the foundational "sky woman" and "muskrat" stories of how North America itself (Turtle Island) was regenerated after the last interglacial flood is a classic story of transformative reconciliation.

The Raven cycle of stories on the Northwest coast are also replete with stories of these three states of life systems: sustainable, unsustainable, and transformative reconciliation with the living earth and each other.

The Convergence of Western Earth, Life, and Social Sciences

Until recently this animistic worldview of Indigenous peoples was considered to be primitive and superseded by the scientific worldview of the West that was claimed to be at a much higher stage of development. On this modern view, humans were claimed to be independent, separate from the living earth and each other, knowing and controlling the mechanistic natural systems, and moving up through stages of modernisation by means of the unintended consequences of institutionalised competition among self-interested individuals, corporations, and states. However, since the dawning awareness of the global ecological and social crisis of the Anthropocene age in the 1960s, many earth, life, and human scientists have presented hypotheses that are complementary to the traditional ecological worldview I have just summarised.

I will mention briefly nine Western earth sciences, life sciences, and human sciences that have converged on the gift-reciprocity view of the ways life sustains life on this planet in recent decades:

1   Earth systems science: Gaia is a self-generating and self-regulating system that sustains the conditions of life on earth by means of negative and positive feedback loops (Sir James Lovelock [2000] and endorsed by many members of the Intergovernmental Panel on Climate Change in one form of another). The Gaia hypothesis became the Gaia theory by the 1990s.

2   Life sciences: this earth system is composed of a multiplicity of ecosystems of circles of participation and autopoiesis that sustain life. Lynn Margulis in biology (1998): symbiosis and symbiogenesis are the major factors in evolution, not competition. She also suggests that the Gaia hypothesis is just symbiosis on a planetary scale: an emergent property of ecosystems' interaction.

3   Ethnobotany: symbiosis and symbiogenesis are the same phenomenon as gift-reciprocity and gift-gratitude-reciprocity cycles in Traditional ecological knowledge and wisdom: Nancy Turner (2005) and Robin Wall Kimmerer (2013).

4   The ecological sciences and especially deep ecology: Arne Naess (2008), Stephen Harding (2013), a student of Lovelock's at Schumacher College who draws the parallel with traditional Indigenous knowledge.

5   Psychology, cognitive science, and social ecology: the gift-*gratitude*-reciprocity relationship explains virtuous relationships and cycles of *mutual*

aid between humans and non-humans and humans and humans (not obligation, command, and coercion: power-over). It is gratitude (and compassion) that move humans to reciprocate with their gifts of caring for the systems that sustain and care for them and all forms of life in turn and thus sustain the virtuous cycles of life: Evan Thompson (2010) and Joanna Macy and Chris Johnstone (2012).

6   The Kropotkin-Gandhi-Schumacher tradition of participatory cooperation and mutual aid: Paul Hawken (2007), Ellen LaConte (2012), Vandana Shiva (2005), Elinor Ostrom (1990).

7   The new field of eco-phenomenology, rediscovering Merleau-Ponty: David Abram (1997), and the lived experience of reconnecting with the animacy of the world through learning from Indigenous peoples.

8   The remarkable turn to ecological or steady-state economics, Herman Daly and John Cobb (1994); ecological law or green legal theory, Fritjof Capra and Ugo Mattei (2015); ecological technology and urban planning, William McDonough and Michael Braungart (2010); "reconnection with nature" education movements, Richard Louv (2011).

9   The remarkable convergence of many of the world's religious leaders on this: for example, Pope Francis's encyclical (2015), Thich Nhat Hanh (2013).

In summary, Fritjof Capra, in *The System View of Life*, converges with Indigenous earth teachings:

> The key to an operational definition of ecological sustainability is the realization that we do not need to invent sustainable human communities from scratch but can model them after nature's ecosystems, which are sustainable communities of plants, animals, and micro-organisms. Since the outstanding characteristic of the Earth household is its inherent ability to sustain life, a sustainable human community is one designed in such a manner that its ways of life, businesses, economies, federations, physical structures, and technologies do not interfere with nature's inherent ability to sustain life. Sustainable communities and networks evolve their patterns of living over time in continual interaction with other living systems, both human and non-human.
>
> (Capra 2002, 230)

There is not only a *convergence* between Traditional ecological knowledge and wisdom and these Western sciences. There is also collaboration and cooperation between them in academic work and in engaged activism of countless kinds around the world (IPWGCC, for example). This workshop is an example.

And, as we will see in the last part of the lecture, these networks of collaboration and cooperation are the groundwork of transformative reconciliation of the dominant, vicious, and unsustainable relationships to the living earth and to each other. However, before we turn to that, I want to try to explain what is wrong with our current relationship to the living earth and to each other.

The Vicious and Unsustainable Relationship: The Earth Belongs to Us

The unsustainable relationship to the living earth developed first in Europe and was spread around the globe by European imperial expansion and modernisation. And it was imposed over the co-evolving lifeways of Indigenous peoples (as Franz Boas argued in 1911).

The ecological crisis of the very conditions of life on earth is also beyond reasonable doubt. Since the early reports on climate change, global warming, pollution, and the limits to growth in the 1960s to endless studies and reports of the leadings earth scientists in the world and the IPCC, we have known that our dominant way of life is overshooting the carrying capacity of the earth and destroying the conditions that sustain life.

Climate change, non-renewable and renewable resource depletion, species and ecosystems extinction, the melting of glaciers and the polar ice cap, the acidification of the oceans and desertification of former agricultural and forest lands are not only past the tipping point to unsustainable warming and a possible sixth mass extinction. They are already bringing about horrendous social effects: mass starvation and migration, social divisions and a planet of slums and gated communities, wars over resources and water, and failed states. The ruthless race among states and corporations for the resources that are left is accelerating climate change and other factors in a vicious, cascading, and runaway spiral.

The conditions that sustain life on earth, as Lester Brown (2011) puts it in his latest report, are "on the edge." And, the intensified race to control the world's remaining resources has increased intervention and exploitation of the territories and resources of Indigenous peoples, drawing them into the spiralling social and economic consequences (Klare 2012).

I do not think we can respond effectively to this problem unless we understand the roots of it. I think the attempts to address it are failing because they do not address the underlying, modern ways of production and consumption that cause and reproduce it. This unsustainable way of relating to the living earth and each other is captured in the Indigenous mantra for it: "the earth belongs to us." I think we are in position to see what is wrong with it by examining it from the contrastive perspective of the alternative Indigenous worldview that I have just summarised.

The Great Disembedding and Reembedding

I think one of the best analyses is the analysis of the great disembedding and transformation brought about by modernisation by Karl Polanyi in *The Great Transformation* (2001). He was a student of both the dominant system of production and of the Indigenous systems it displaced.

In brief, Polanyi argued that during this great transformation humans have been disembedded from participation in the interdependent ecological and social relationships that sustain life and reembedded in abstracted and competitive economic, political, and legal relationships that are dependent on, yet destructive of, the underlying interdependent ecological and social relationships. I have also learned an enormous amount about the "great disembedding" through years of conversation with Robert Nichols and Glen Coulthard on primitive accumulation and settler colonialism.

This "great disembedding" and reembedding takes place in the following three steps:

First, the peoples who are embedded in symbiotic ecological and social relationships are dispossessed of this way of life and the territories in which it is carried on; in Europe, and then around the world by various forms of ongoing colonisation and neocolonialism.

The *second step* is to impose an ownership relation to the land by the spread of Western legal systems of private property and so to transform "earth into property," including the patenting and commodification of life processes, as Vandana Shiva has shown.

Polanyi describes the privatisation of land as a "fictitious commodity" because land is not a commodity produced for sale on the market. What we now call commodifiable and exchangeable "natural resources" are, as we have seen, *interdependent co-participants* in the symbiotic webs and cycles of life that sustain life on earth.

Relating to the living earth as a storehouse of commodifiable resources disembeds them from these interdependent ecological relationships and then re-embeds them in the abstract and competitive relations of the global market system. The ecosystems in which resources are embedded are then treated as "external" to the global system of commodification.

The natural world is radically transformed by continuous processes of competitive commodification, sale and use, and re-commodification. The result of "development" under this linear system is the destruction of the webs of interdependent ecological relationships and cycles that sustain the natural and human world, giving rise to the environmental crisis and climate change.

Once the means of the reproduction of human life are placed under the ownership of corporations, the *third step* is to treat the productive capabilities of human beings as commodities for sale on the labour market by the spread of Western contract, labour, and corporate law. This kind of commodification disembeds human producing and consuming capabilities and activities from the surrounding gift-reciprocity, social, and ecological relationship in which they take place and re-embeds them in abstract, competitive, and non-democratic global market relationships.

Polanyi describes the commodification of the productive capabilities of individual humans as the second "fictitious commodity" of modernisation. It is fictitious because abilities to work together and sustain ourselves are not commodities made for the market. These capabilities are, as we have seen in the previous section, the cooperative response-abilities and sustain-abilities through which we humans participate in the social and ecological systems that conciliate and sustain life on earth. They are the capabilities through which we "belong to the land" and are grounded in it. Yet, they are now treated as abstract capabilities that we as separate individuals "own" (self-ownership); and, by selling the use of these abilities to a corporation, they become the means by which we insert ourselves in the global competitive market system.

The result of "development" under this system is the destruction of the webs of interdependent social relations of mutual aid that sustain human communities, giving rise to the well-known forms of social suffering of modern life: alienation and anomie, the horrendous inequalities in life-chances, and the planet of slums and gated "communities" in which we find ourselves.

In 1944 Polanyi predicted that the result of this "great transformation" would be disastrous:

> To allow the market mechanism to be sole director of the fate of human beings and their natural environment...would result in the demolition of society... Robbed of the protective covering of cultural institutions, human beings would perish from the effects of social exposure; they would die as the victims of acute social dislocation through vice, perversion, crime, and starvation. Nature would be reduced to its elements, neighbourhoods and landscapes defiled, rivers polluted, military safety jeopardized, the power to produce food and raw materials destroyed.
>
> (Polanyi 2001, 76)

The Vicious Cycle

Despite Polanyi's warning and hundreds of others, this global system of double commodification in which the human species is reembedded continues to unfold as he predicted. It is now a deeply entrenched *vicious cycle*; what global systems theorists call a self-destructive "automaton."

If the real costs of this global system were taken into account it would collapse under its own economic irrationality. As Lester Brown points out,

> As the world economy expanded some 20-fold over the last century it has revealed a flaw – flaw so serious that if it is not corrected it will spell the end of civilization as we know it. The market, which sets prices, is not telling the truth. It is omitting indirect costs that in some cases now dwarf direct costs. Modern economic thinking and policymaking have created an economy that is so out of sync with the ecosystem on which it depends that it is approaching collapse.
>
> (Brown 2011, 8)

In summary, this global vicious system is a super-predatory system. It preys on the underlying gift-reciprocity ecosystems and informal social systems that sustain life; destroying them, but, at the same time, is dependent on them for the sustaining of life on earth. It is self-destructive, as Westerners from Polanyi, Schumacher, and Barry Commoner to E.O. Wilson and Craig Dilworth have argued, and as Indigenous knowledge keepers have been saying for much longer.

The Multiple Ways of Transformative Reconnection and Reconciliation Today: Gaia Citizenship

If this analysis is correct, then the way to transform this unsustainable system is to engage in what I called "transformative reconciliation." This is the Indigenous view that the way of transformation is to engage in a multiplicity of prefigurative gift-gratitude-reciprocity practices in relation to the living earth and in relations of mutual aid with other humans, within and against the dominant system. We have to begin to "be the change" by exercising and enacting our shared responsibilities if we wish to disclose and bring to self-awareness the underlying sustainable world we wish to re-inhabit.

This is how Robert Davidson describes the work of transformative reconciliation:

> We are now coming full circle, we are the fourth generation in which the white people have instilled their ideas and values, and denied our way of life, without any knowledge or concern of who we were and where we were coming from. It is our generation that is making the attempt to *bridge the gap*, to reclaim our identity, our cultural values, the philosophies developed by our ancestors for generations and generations. We are also making a great effort to *reconnect with the land*. The land is the very *foundation* of our culture. It is our homeland. We were born into it. We are the stewards: it is our right and *responsibility* to maintain, nurture, and preserve it for the future.
>
> (Davidson 1992, 9–10 emphasis added)

The exercise of shared responsibilities in practices of decolonisation, resurgence, and reconciliation can take place almost anywhere we find ourselves, as Val Napoleon and Hadley Friedland have shown in their on-the-ground training sessions in self-determination (Tully Wheel).

By self-organising and then beginning to join together, act together, and learn together in conciliatory and sustainable ways with Indigenous and non-Indigenous people and with the living earth, we begin to *reconnect* – and, in so doing, we sow the seeds of conciliatory and sustainable ways of life in the interstices of the unsustainable hegemonic way of life. As these seeds grow and spread their virtuous relationships and cycles of interdependency and symbiosis, they begin counter-acting the vicious relationships and cycles.

As these practices and networks of alternative modernities grow, they offer an alternative to the unsustainable relationships around them, others join in, and the momentum towards reconciliation and transformation on a larger scale increases. The logic of this mode of transformation is, if you live your life in such a way that it sustains yourself, and, also, at the same time and place, also co-sustains all your interdependent living neighbours, they will be moved to do the same in gratitude and reciprocity. This is the virtuous gift-gratitude-reciprocity cycle of life sustaining life. One of the great features of *Kaswentha* Two Row Wampum treaty relationships among diverse partners is that it allows for both independence and interdependence (self-rule and shared rule, or federalism).

In many cases and at different times, as Audra Simpson and Johnny Mack argue, it is crucial for Indigenous peoples to engage in grass-roots resurgence practices and networks among themselves, without entering into relationships with settlers. In other cases and times, it is just as important to be able to enter into relationship of peace and friendship with settlers, link arms, and coordinate their activities. As Paul Hawken argues, there are millions of people engaged in such activities and networks around the world; and Indigenous peoples are the living heart of this uncoordinated movement of movements.

On the West coast, for example, there are Indigenous-settler, gift-reciprocity networks around the shared problems of violence against women, poverty, the environment, pipelines, fracking, local cooperative food production, land claims, fish farms, education, and so on. This careful extension of resurgent, gift-reciprocity relationships within groups to nearby groups follows from the basic premise that we are all connected (*Tsawalk*). And the non-subordination and non-domination of each member is reciprocally guaranteed by the "relative independence" dimension of two row relationships.

We are not only interdependent. We also share the same global problems. As we saw above, there is a remarkable convergence on both the problems we face and the general ways to address them in both Indigenous and Western traditions of knowledge.

The Great Challenge

Thus, the great challenge of the twenty-first century is, thus, not so much indifference, as some have argued; but, more importantly, the challenge of the democratic and federal coordination of a multiplicity of networks of horizontal and vertical organisations, Indigenous, settler, and immigrant peoples, and civil and civic citizens – and all this without subordination or assimilation. It is not an easy problem but it is not insoluble. In my opinion, the logic of coordination of this currently disconnected constituent power from local nodes to global networks is the same general logic as the gift-reciprocity logic that coordinates all forms of life on earth in mutually sustainable ways.

I realise that all this is very sketchy work in progress with all sorts of problems. However, I wanted to present it to you in hope that it may be of some interest to you and that you might help me with it in further conversations for the next twenty years, as many of you have so generously done during the last twenty years.

The Spirit of Haida Gwaii: Gift, Gratitude, and Reciprocity as Exercising Shared Responsibilities

I would like to conclude with a brief discussion of a representation of the conciliatory and sustainable social and ecological lifeworld we have to begin to re-connect with in order to transform the unsustainable way of life we have imposed over it. The picture is behind me: *The Spirit of Haida Gwaii*. The Haida artist, Bill Reid, and his Haida and non-Haida fellow crafts-people, gave this monumental Haida work of art to Canadians. They gave this gift to Canadians in the hopes that they would take up the responsibility of trying to understand its meaning. Then, as its meaning gradually came alive for them, that they would be moved in gratitude and reciprocity to let it influence their lives. For, it is a picture of Indigenous and non-Indigenous passengers exercising together their shared responsibilities of living in mutually conciliatory and sustainable ways (see Steltzer 1997).

The Spirit of Haida Gwaii Here and Now

Haida Gwaii is the "home" or "dwelling place" of the Haida. The "Haida" refers to the people who inhabit these beautiful islands. But, "Haida" also means "human being." Bill Reid put it this way:

> As for what constitutes a Haida – well, Haida only means human being, and as far as I'm concerned, a human being is anyone who respects the needs of his fellow man, and the earth which nurtures and shelters us all. I think we could find room in South Moresby [the largest island of Haida Gwaii] for quite a few Haida no matter what their ethnic background].
>
> (Reid 2009, 233)

> [He hoped that] these shining islands may be the signposts that point the way to a renewed harmonious relationship with this, the only world we're ever going to have. Without South Moresby and other places like it, we may forget what we once were and what we can be again, and lose our humanity in a world devoid of the amazing non-humans with whom we have shared it.
>
> (2009, 227–8)

The Spirit of Haida Gwaii, the title of the sculpture, is the spirit or breath or power that animates Haida Gwaii, the dwelling place and the people who dwell there. The Haida are in dynamic yet "harmonious relationships" with each other and the living earth. This spirit is not unique to them. It is, as he says, the spirit of human beings and the more-than-human beings with whom they share Haida Gwaii. So, what is this spirit?

The spirit of Haida Gwaii is fairly easy to see and experience by walking around the work of art, hugging the animals, sitting on the edge of the canoe, talking to them, and so on, just as walking in the woods brings the spirit of the forest to our senses and perception and we feel ourselves coming into attunement with it. Perhaps it is not so easy on the screen. But, if you focus on it, its spirit begins to come to light. The spirit is the gift-gratitude-reciprocity network and cycle we have been talking about all evening.

Peaceful and Friendly Conciliation in Action

The passengers embody this *conciliatory spirit* in two main ways. First, they are touching and responding to each other as they conciliate their dynamic, ongoing interactions as they paddle. Second, they are also telling each other their stories from the different perspectives of their different ways of life. These stories remind the speakers and listeners of the interdependency of their different ways of life; the shared ground of their reciprocal well-being. Reid and his co-workers spent months moving the passengers around until their interdependency stood out clearly. Next, the lifeways of the passengers are intertwined and entangled in such complex overlapping ways that they require continuous conciliation. Note that the passengers are animals, but also represent individual human character types, families, clans, and myth-creatures.

As Bill Reid stresses throughout his writings on Haida Gwaii, the passengers are Indigenous and non-Indigenous, humans and animals, and they are surrounded by the ecological diversity of Haida Gwaii. They bring forth and set out the unbelievably rich cultural and biological multiplicity of ways of being on Haida Gwaii and Turtle Island and let them be (Reid 2009, 222–9, 244–6; Steltzer 1997, 8–9).

We know the members are telling stories because the chief at the centre is holding the talking stick. We also know that one of the points of telling and listening to these stories is to *transform* themselves into the way of life of the story-teller so each can see how the relationships of mutual dependency sustain their unique lifeways from the perspectives of each other; so they are not one-eyed. The transformative power of storytelling is reinforced by placing Raven at the helm. Raven is the transformer. So, humans can only paddle together in sustainable ways that do not tip their canoe if they are constantly listening to and responding to the perspectives of all participants and adjusting themselves accordingly.

The passengers are also in a conciliatory relationship with the living earth. The canoe, made of red cedar, holds them all afloat. It represents mother earth, the ground of being Haida (human) that nurtures and shelters all life:

> Modern methods of logging mean not just cutting trees but murdering forests – those wonderfully complex organisms which once gone will never return in their ancient form. And in killing the forests, you also kill forever the only authentic link the Haidas still have with their past. You murder once more their symbolic ancestors. That is what I think the land claims are about.
>
> (Reid 2009, 233)

The canoe is located in the ocean as a further reminder of the depth of vision required to see the ecosystems that nurture and shelter. This is part of the stories as well. The talking stick represents all three types of dialogue: the verbal dialogues with each other, the ongoing perceptual and sensory, non-verbal dialogue of humans with the living earth, and the non-verbal communion with the myth-world and ancestors.

The canoe is everywhere humans and non-humans dwell together. Wherever we are, we are symbiotically interdependent in the ways the passengers are in the canoe. This is why we have responsibilities to respect each other and our diverse ways of living, because, as a matter of fact, they all support each other, like an old growth forest. But, in order to see this, we need to listen patiently to each other and see how the diversity looks from different perspectives, as they are doing.

Note that the chief has no authority to impose order. Authority to be heard and listened to goes with the talking stick. Whoever holds the stick has the authority to give the gift of their story to others, who listen, and then, on receiving the talking stick, reciprocate by telling their stories in turn. There is no other type of authority on the canoe than the shared authority that emerges out of talking together in peaceful and friendly ways and carrying on in exercising power-together and with-and-for each other in paddling. This is the authority-with and power-with that animates and sustains all forms of life, as we have seen. They learn this way of being-with-others from the world around them and replicate it in the canoe. It is same spirit manifest in peace and friendship treaty talks and in relationships between Indigenous and settler partners that replicate treaty talks.

We see all sorts of diversity in the canoe and passengers competing and contending for recognition and human forms of power. Yet, for all the fore-ground agonistics, the canoe does not tip. The paddles are in dynamic equilib-rium and the canoe is upright. *This is the miracle of life itself.*

Tipping and Reconciling the Canoe

As we have seen, this astonishing way of life is not always harmonious. It is as sharp as a knife. The struggles over power and recognition, domination and subordination, greed, and destruction, can always get out of hand and over-turn the canoe. The passengers know this from their stories. So, they need to know the arts of re-conciliation so things do not get out of hand.

This possibility of tipping points is signalled by the one, non-native crew member, the ancient reluctant conscript. He is the crew member who teaches humans how to survive. When conflict, aggressiveness, and voraciousness get out of hand, he refuses to paddle any more, and says "Enough!"

Here is our professional survivor, the ancient reluctant conscript: pre-sent, if seldom noticed, in all the turbulent histories of men on earth. When our latter-day kings and captains have joined their forebears, he will still be carrying on, stoically obeying orders and performing the tasks allotted to him, but only up to a point. It is also he who finally says "Enough!" After the rulers have disappeared into the morass of their own excesses, it is he who builds on the rubble and once more gets the whole thing going (Steltzer 1997, 9; Reid 2009, 245).

But, how does he get things going again? What are his skills of re-conciliation? There are no other skills available aboard *The Spirit of Haida Gwaii* other than the multiple skills of dialogical conciliation represented in the talking stick. There are no instruments of violence, command and obedience, or ruler and ruled. The only way to re-conciliate a tipping canoe and get a conciliatory, sustainable way of life going again is by means of conciliation – as with life itself. Wherever the breakdown occurs, out comes the talking stick and proto-symbiotic dialogue begins again. And so, as Reid concludes, "the canoe goes on, forever anchored in the same place" (Steltzer 1997, 9; Reid 2009, 246).

The spirit of Haida Gwaii is thus the spirit or animism of the living earth itself.

Breathing Meditation

Let's pause for one moment and get in touch with this *spirit* in a brief mediation. Look at *The Spirit of Haida Gwaii*. Now, focus on and bring yourself back to your breath and your heart. Feel your breath breathing and your heart beating, your whole body adjusting to the changes in the environment of the room. Now cast your mind's eye to everyone breathing in the room together. Now, cast your mind's eye to the trees and plants outside the room breathing in what you exhale and breathing out fresh air for you to re-breathe in turn. Now think of a native drummer beating a drum. The drum beat, as you know, is meant to be in tune with your heartbeat. It brings the drum and your heartbeat into mutual attunement. This is also the heartbeat of all living things, the heartbeat of mother earth. We *sense* ourselves as participants in this shared spirit. This is to *experience* the spirit of Haida Gwaii – of Gaia.

Note

1 Lecture delivered at Indigenous Studies and Anti-Imperial Critique for the 21st Century. A Symposium Inspired by the Legacies of James Tully, Yale University, October 2015.

12 Integral Nonviolence

Two Lawyers on Nonviolence: Mohandas K. Gandhi and Richard B. Gregg (2018)

Preface

Throughout the last century we have witnessed increasing violence, domination, and exploitation, both among human beings and against the living earth.[1] This "great transformation" and "acceleration" has led to horrendous inequalities, social dislocation, and enmity in human societies; and to climate change, a sixth mass extinction, and ecosphere degradation. These interconnected ecosocial cycles are vicious: they feed on each other and threaten to render life unsustainable for most *Homo sapiens* and millions of other species.

One response to this complex crisis has been a revival of interest in nonviolence in practice and academic research. In its most ambitious form, the hypothesis is that relationships of violence and domination are at the root of the crisis of social and ecological unsustainability. If this is the case, then the cultivation of relations of nonviolence and nondomination with each other and the living earth is the way to remediating and sustaining the damaged social and ecological conditions of cooperation and contestation that sustain all forms of life on earth. To borrow Karl Polanyi's famous phrase, the project is to transform and re-embed violent and dominative human relations into nonviolent and nondominative, sustainable ecosocial relationships, systems, and virtuous cycles; and to do this by nonviolent means.

The problem this project faces is that the most prominent tradition of nonviolence today was not designed for such a task and is not suited to it. After the assassination of Martin Luther King Jr., a pragmatic or instrumental understanding of "nonviolence" as "unarmed resistance" became paramount. Nonviolence is seen as an effective set of instrumental techniques to change legislation, overthrow unjust rulers, and gain political power.

My aim in this lecture is to retrieve another, *broader* tradition of nonviolence. This is the nonviolence of Mohandas Gandhi, Richard Gregg, and Martin Luther King Jr. On their view, nonviolence is not a technique to gain power over others, but an integrated way of life based on the exercise of another type of power – power-with-and-for each other and the living earth.

DOI: 10.4324/9781003227403-16

This tradition is designed to transform gradually the violence, domination, and unsustainable development of modern industrial civilisation into a non-violent and sustainable *countermodernity*. As Gregg put it in 1953:

> War is an inherent, inevitable and essential element of the civilization in which we live. Our aim can be nothing short of building an entirely new civilization in which domination and violence of all kinds play a small and steadily decreasing part. We must change nonviolently and deeply the motives, functions, and institutions of our whole culture.
>
> (Gregg 1953, 9)

Hundreds of millions of people continue to practice it today, but in dispersed and disintegrated ways; not in the *integrated* way Gandhi, Gregg, and King argue is essential to its long-term success as a "slow but sure" process of transformative social change. The task today is the *re-integration* of these disintegrated communities of practice.

Richard Gregg

Everyone knows about Gandhi and King. Richard Gregg is less well known. So, I will say a few words about him because my presentation is based on his writings. Gregg lived from 1885 to 1974. Like Gandhi, he was a lawyer. He graduated from Harvard Law in 1911. He practiced law at the National War Labor Board during the war and in law firms in Boston and Chicago during the great labour-capital conflicts 1919–1922, including for the railway unions during their huge strikes. Disillusioned by violence as a means to settle disputes, the violence of industrial capitalism, and the repression of the labour movement, Gregg came across Gandhi's writings and decided to move to India and learn from him.

He lived and worked with Gandhi in his Sabarmati ashram from 1925 to 1929. They became close friends. Under Gandhi's guidance, Gregg taught Gandhian economics and village-based self-government in different parts of India. He returned to the United States in 1930, but he and Gandhi continued to correspond with each other until 1947. Gregg returned to India during the Salt March and after Gandhi's death.

Gregg dedicated himself to explaining Gandhian nonviolence as an integrated way of life to Westerners in ten books and many articles. His book, *The Power of Nonviolence* ([1934] 2018), became the leading text of the non-violent movements in the United Kingdom, Europe, and North America from 1934 to the mid-1960s.

King read Gregg's book in 1956 and it became the manual of non-violent resistance for the African-American movement and the Civil Rights Movement. King and Gregg met, corresponded, and lectured together. King wrote the preface to the 1959 edition of *The Power of Nonviolence*.

In addition, Gregg participated in sustainable farming communities in Vermont and New York. He wrote several books on the superiority of Gandhian, cooperative, and village-based economics to large-scale capitalism, socialism, and communism. These had a large influence on E.F. Schumacher and the alternative economics movement in India and North America.

The Banyan Tree: Power-With *versus* Power-Over

For Gandhi and Gregg, nonviolence is a multifaceted alternative way of life or civilisation composed of many interdependent branches, analogous to a living banyan tree.

The power of nonviolence – *satyagraha* – is the persuasive kind of power that comes into being when people exercise power-with-and-for each other without coercion or domination. It is the "power-with" that animates all branches of a nonviolent way of life and brings a "new civilisation" into being.

Power-with is used in systems of cooperation and in nonviolent forms of contestation, social change, and conflict resolution with nonviolent and violent opponents. It is an effective substitute for war, violent revolution, and domination as the means of conflict and conflict resolution. In learning how to connect with, trust, exercise, and be empowered by this form of power, humans participate in "spiritual unity" or *anima mundi*; the more general form of symbiosis that animates and sustains life on earth.

In contrast, violence and domination are the types of power exercised in violent conflicts and unequal relationships of domination and subordination that are imposed and backed up by force, or the threat of force, and various types of legitimation. It is "power-over" in its many forms. It is based on the false presupposition that humans are basically independent, insecure, and incapable of organisation and dispute resolution without the exercise of violence and domination by a ruler. The violence and domination, and the exploitation they enable, give rise to increasing cycles of violent resistance, counter-violence, and domination. These cycles are justified by the assumption that violent and dominating methods bring about peaceful and nondominating ends.

But this is a false view of the relation between means and ends. The vicious cycles continue because means are *autotelic*. Gregg writes:

> Whether we are considering the life of an individual or of society, that life is a process, a series of successive stages or steps. The character of each stage forms the basis for the character of the following stage. So, the character of means qualifies and determines the end.
>
> (Gregg 1958, v)

Thus, nonviolent cooperation and contestation is the only way to a peaceful and democratic world; that is, *by being the change*.

Many forms of violent and nonviolent power relations exist in every society and criss-cross in complex ways. Violent power-over is "an inherent, inevitable, and essential element" in almost every branch of modern civilisation, shaping the "motives, functions, and institutions," as well as the values, assumptions, and forms of subjectivity of moderns (Gregg 1953, 9). From within the prevailing mindset, nonviolent power is overlooked or perceived, as subordinate, and ridiculed as the soft power of the weak. Moderns have a kind of "disintegrated" form of subjectivity: power-over in some spheres; power-with in others. It becomes difficult to see that the overlooked and misrepresented social and biological relationships of being-with, power-with, and cooperating-with are the background conditions that sustain all forms of life; and that the "civilisation in which we live" parasitically depends on and destroys them (ibid.).

Thus, to see the human condition from the nonviolent perspective and test its validity, it is necessary to move around and begin participating and experimenting in nonviolent constructive and agonistic ways of living and the corresponding ways of knowing these practices disclose to participants.

Constructive Programmes

There are four main features of the banyan tree of nonviolence: (1) the power of nonviolence that animates all branches, (2) the nonviolent ethics that make up the trunk of the tree, (3) constructive programmes that are the main branches, and (4) nonviolent contestation and conflict resolution *vis-à-vis* violent opponents that grow out of the constructive programmes, and which transform violent and dominating systems.

The "parent trunk" is nonviolent ethics manifest in the ethos of a nonviolent actor (*satyagrahi*). It is the actualisation of the power of nonviolence in human life. Gandhi refers to it as *swaraj* (self-governance) in its primary sense: the governance of the conduct of oneself by oneself in all relationships with others in all branches.

Next, *swaraj* or "self-government" in its second sense is the central branch. This is participation in "constructive programmes": collective self-government in nonviolent communities of participatory democracy and nonviolent dispute resolution. Democratic *swaraj* begins in everyday activities, ashrams, cooperatives, community-based organisations, and villages. It scales out in concentric circles or networks of delegated representation to global federalism from below (integrated *swaraj*). Participatory democracy is the people exercising the power of nonviolence together. These forms of local self-government in communities of various scales are also economically self-reliant (*swadeshi*). Sustainable economic self-reliance in turn is dependent on regenerative or cyclical resource use, human-scale, green technology, handicrafts, and waste recycling.

The ethical and legal norm of these communities is *sarvodaya*: working and governing *with* each other and *for* the health and well-being of each other, their communities, and the ecosystems on which they depend. *Sarvodaya* goes along with non-attachment to possessions and ends, and attachment to means. Another complementary branch is public education integrated with the branches it studies and for which it prepares students. The branch immediately available to everyone is to live lives of nonviolent "voluntary simplicity" in appropriate ways in the relationships one inhabits in modern civilisation here and now. These branches comprise the basic constructive programmes of a nonviolent civilisation.

Gregg lived, worked, and taught in nonviolent communities of practice in India and the United States. He wrote more books and articles on these topics than on nonviolent contestation. His pamphlet, *The Value of Voluntary Simplicity* (Gregg [1935] 1936), presents the health, well-being, moral, intellectual, and spiritual benefits of nonviolent ways of life – in contrast to the lives of competitive display and consumption that modern industrial civilisation promotes and depends upon for its wasteful and destructive linear development. Finally, citizens of constructive programmes work with citizens reforming modern institutions from within, and other social movements for change.

What are the values of the constructive programmes that provide the basis of a nonviolent countermodernity?

First, participants in agriculture and handicrafts connect with the ecological relationships and cycles that sustain the renewable resources on which humans depend. They learn to work and live in accord with their cyclical and regenerative slow temporality, in contrast to the linear and extractive, unsustainable fast temporality of modern civilisation. They become aware of their basic interdependency with other forms of life; what Arne Naess called our ecological self, rather than the priority of an independent or autonomous self in modernity. They see themselves as citizens of their bioregions.

Second, their handicrafts, human-scale technology, and ecological economics create a technosphere that respects and learns from the ecosphere on which it depends (biomimicry).

Third, in exercising nonviolent powers of self-government-with-and-for each other in their everyday activities, they develop the virtues of democratic citizenship. They learn the skills of nonviolent communication, contestation, and conflict resolution with partners of different genders, religion, races, and languages.

Fourth, constructive programmes are activities of non-cooperation with the dominant institutions and the cooperative exercise of human capacities in constructing nonviolent, alternative institutions. This famous "double movement" quietly weakens the dominant institutions and shows that another civilisation is not only possible but also actual. Constructive programmes manifest a better way of life for all to see. Gregg learned in the railroad strikes of the 1920s that people are unlikely to be persuaded to contest an unjust system on which they depend if there is no viable alternative.

Fifth, constructive programmes provide a solution to one of the central problems of nonviolent campaigns: the tendency of campaigners to lose their self-discipline, turn to anger and animosity, and engage in violence, flee, or surrender. Participation addresses this problem by cultivating an ethos of nonviolent self-discipline and concern for others that grounds resolute and effective nonviolent agonistics and civil defence. Gregg presented this argument in a book entitled *Discipline for Nonviolence* (1941). Gandhi wrote the preface.

Participation cultivates a fourfold nonviolent ethos of the physical body, emotions, mind, and spirit working together. It consists of the nonviolent virtues of courage, endurance, patience, self-reliance and mutual reliance, love of truth, and the creative energy needed to sustain nonviolence in the face of violence and gain the respect and trust of violent opponents. "All these activities together," Gregg concludes, "provide a greater variety, engage a wider range of human faculties and potentialities, reach deeper and loftier levels of being, and are more mutually consistent than are military exercises and military discipline" (1941, 27). Thus, constructive programmes are the necessary support system of nonviolent contestation and conflict resolution.

In contrast, violence and domination as the means of conflict and resolution are supported by large-scale, power-over, private and public institutions, and an ethos of aggressive, self-interested competition among individuals, groups, corporations, states, empires, and military-industrial complexes. These global systems are *claimed* to be the way to world peace. Nonviolent proponents reply that, because means prefigure the ends, these systems lead to more violence and domination. Cooperative programmes and nonviolent contestation are the only means to world peace and democracy.

Now, constructive programmes themselves have to be grounded in a yet more basic feature of the banyan tree: its trunk of nonviolent ethics, or *swaraj* in its primary sense of individual self-government.

Nonviolent Ethics: The Way

Nonviolent ethics comprise the virtues that constitute the character formation or ethos of a free, self-governing human being. A nonviolent ethos "realises" the persuasive power of nonviolence (power-with) by becoming aware of it, grasping and hanging on to it, being moved by and with it, exercising it well in all relationships and circumstances, continuously reflecting on its use and misuse, and beginning again. It is the *way* humans participate in the personal, social, ecological, and spiritual power or energy that animates all life. Gregg calls this "spiritual unity":

> A person does not create moral power. It comes to him [or her] only after he [or she] has complied with certain principles. This compliance enables them to tap the spiritual power pervading the entire world, just as one by suitable connections and switches can tap an electric current from a power circuit.

(Gregg 2018, 168)

This is Gregg's reformulation of Gandhi's hypothesis of the soul-power of nonviolence uniting all life.

The nonviolent virtues are the engaged dispositions of the body, emotions, mind, and spirit integrated into a nonviolent person's orientation and pattern of existence. They are manifest in their characteristic attitude and ways of feeling, thinking, and interacting in relationships with oneself and others. They are cultivated and integrated into a settled yet changeable ethos through examples, meditation, practice (*yoga*), discipline, and experimental trial and error.

Ethical self-awareness and self-formation take place in communities of practice and practices of the self, as in Gandhi's *karma yoga* tradition of selfless service with others. Gregg learned them in Gandhi's ashram beginning with morning group meditation on the central virtues. The way one works on one's ethical comportment is so closely interrelated to one's conduct and one's relationships with and responsiveness to others that a nonviolent ethos brings into being and sustains nonviolent ways of life.

The core nonviolent virtues from which all others derive are encapsulated in Gandhi's concept of *satyagraha*.

Satya (truth) refers to the virtue of forthright truthfulness and openness. It consists in the continuous search for truth. It involves asserting the truth courageously as one sees it to the powers-that-be, yet with the awareness that each person's view of the truth is partial and thus that it is necessary to enter into a dialogue with all-affected others to gain a many-sided understanding of the truth in any situation. Thus, the soft power *way* one asserts the truth openly as one sees it, yet with the virtue of epistemic humility, is of utmost importance, as it must bring others around to see they can trust you and so enter into a dialogue in which they will be listened to and treated with reciprocal respect.

The root of *satya* is *sat* (being). The ground of our being is the interdependent, life-sustaining relationships of mutual love (*ahimsa*). "If love or non-violence be not the law of our being," Gandhi states, "the whole of my argument falls to pieces, and there is no escape from a periodical recurrence of war, each succeeding one outdoing the preceding one in ferocity" (Gandhi 1999b, 400). The virtue of love (*ahimsa*) refers negatively to the "non-harm" of any living being, and positively, to active understanding, compassion, and cooperation with all living beings (*biophilia*). It is the virtue appropriate to the belief in the interconnectedness of all forms of life.

For Gregg this virtue of love is "the origin of all the others... Love involves the very principle and essence of continuity of life itself" (2018, 56–7). It entails respect for all life. Like Kropotkin, he often describes relations of love as mutual aid or symbiosis. The most important dimension of love in nonviolent contestation is its creative power (*agape*): the persuasive power that can motivate humans to reflect on and transform their violent and dominative habits into nonviolent ways. He suggests that if the word "love" seems too "sentimental," then "call it a sort of intelligence or knowledge" (2018, 56).

The *graha* of *satyagraha* refers to the virtue of nonviolent courage. It is the courage to grasp firmly and exercise the power of nonviolence in everything one does, including self-suffering in contestation and helping others in need. Whereas soldiers control their fear and are willing to die, they direct their disciplined anger and hatred at the enemy and kill them. Nonviolent actors learn to control fear and anger and are willing to suffer and die, yet they also take the next step in human evolution if the species is to survive. They learn to sublimate their anger into the more powerful emotion and trained disposition of non-harm and compassion for their opponents. The non-violent virtues form an experimental ethos: a life of "experiments with truth." Truthfulness, love, and courage are not only autotelic. They orient humans to sustaining their own well-being in ways that co-sustain the well-being of all interdependent others (*sarvodaya*). To discover these ways they enter into dialogues of mutual learning and cooperation in which each learns how things appear from the perspectives of others. Nonviolent virtues are the virtues of participatory democracy. Their exercise gives rise to a kind of knowing-with through working with each other in constructive programmes and campaigns. Each exercise is a test of one's knowledge of the virtues involved. By means of many trials and errors, participants and researchers slowly build up the arts and sciences of a nonviolent civilisation.

Violence and Self-Transformation

However, the cultivation of a nonviolent ethos takes place in a world in which a violent ethos is normal in many circumstances. For Gandhi and Gregg, violence does not begin when people employ weapons. It begins long before in violent dispositions and attitudes. Gandhi writes:

> The word *satyagraha* is often most loosely used and is made to cover veiled violence. But as the author of the word I may be allowed to say that it excludes every form of violence, direct or indirect, and whether in thought, word, or deed. It is a breach of *satyagraha* to wish ill to an opponent or to say a harsh word to him or of him with the intention of doing harm. And often the evil thought or the evil word may, in terms of *satyagraha*, be more dangerous than actual violence used in the heat of the moment. *Satyagraha* is gentle, it never wounds. It is never fussy, never impatient, never vociferous. It is the direct opposite of compulsion. It was conceived as a complete substitute for violence.
>
> (Gandhi 1999a, 381)

Gandhi calls these violent dispositions *duragraha*. It means being propelled by and subject to the charge of fear, anger, and animosity in response to a disturbance. For the ethical nonviolent tradition, this initial attitudinal violence is the root of all violence and domination. This is why nonviolent ethics is of fundamental importance.

When disputes arise in everyday interactions, humans usually pause, collect themselves, and draw on the taken-for-granted, intersubjective relationships and resources of trustful nonviolence to discover the source of the difference and work out mutually acceptable modes of conciliation. These are the background, being-with conditions of social life. Nonviolent conciliation preserves these life-sustaining conditions. If, in contrast, antagonism were the usual response, humans would have perished long ago.

With *duragraha*, individuals and groups allow the emotional propulsion of fear and anger to disconnect them, alienate themselves from, and override the background relationships of mutual trust, define themselves as separate, and evince an aggressive or submissive attitude of distrust towards others. With this often-involuntary movement, they move out of the world of power-with and into the world of power-over.

This outwardly directed attitude of distrustful separateness affects relational others and they tend to respond in kind. The initial attitudinal interactions tend to generate amplifying circular responses of mutual insecurity, ill will, and antagonism, as each tries to acquire the means to gain power over others. These competitions give rise to the violent military, political, and economic power-over systems and struggles of modernity, and these have blowback effects on all social relations. These systems appear autonomous, but they are the ongoing consequences of outwardly directed attitudes of separation, distrust, and insecurity, and the "impulse to dominate."

Without training in nonviolence, people who grow up in these social systems acquire the corresponding subject formation. Independence, insecurity, and antagonism now appear as the ground of being human; the natural condition of humankind. The prior step of alienation from being-with relations of interdependence and cooperation is overlooked and forgotten. The only way to peace and security appears to be to impose order and compliance to the institutions of aggressive competition in modern societies. Within this worldview, the focus is on victory over the opponent as success. The long-term destruction, domination, exploitation, and greed of the victors and the resentment and resistance of the victims are overlooked, yet they lead to further cycles of insecurity and struggle. If they are not transformed, these trends will lead to extermination by war or civilisational collapse by resource depletion.

Subjects of these systems are caught up in what Gregg calls "dual loyalty" (2018, 59). On the one hand, they are familiar with the power of nonviolence in everyday life and their spiritual and humanistic traditions teach these virtues. On the other, they participate in and depend on the dominant power-over systems and are constrained to set aside nonviolent virtues and act aggressively in order to survive. The resulting disintegrated personality of these shifting dual loyalties leads to pervasive "social neurosis" that further fuels the competitive cycles for power-over.

The primary role of nonviolent ethics, therefore, is to acquire the ability of "non-retaliation": to pause and resist the emotional charge of *duragraha*;

or to transform the violent habitus once formed. Like Greek, Christian, and Eastern ethics, the cultivation of this ability involves three standard steps of self-transformation. The first consists in becoming aware of the need to free oneself from the disposition to be motivated by fear, anger, and animosity in its undisciplined or disciplined forms. This is the step of non-attachment to retaliation and of remaining attached, or beginning to re-attach, to relationships and dispositions of mutual trust, care, and concern.

The first step of dawning self-awareness goes along with the second step of beginning to practice the nonviolent ethics that bring about the self-transformation of one's habitual dispositions. In Gregg's own life, step one was the experience of unequal capital-labour contests in the United States, his realisation of the structural power of capital over labour, and then reading Gandhi. The second was his move to India and his immersion in the constructive programmes of the Sabarmati ashram.

As they engage in practices of self-transformation in constructive programmes and voluntary simplicity, they also acquire the corresponding form of self-awareness. The underlying spiritual, social, and ecological relationships of nonviolent cooperation come to awareness as they interact in accord with them. This dawning spiritual unity dimension of existence enables them to appraise the values and assumptions of the dominant ethos in contrast and to free themselves from them.

At some stage in this process of self-transformation, they reconnect with and trust the intersubjective power of nonviolence and it animates their further efforts. This is the third step of reconnection, de-alienation, and empowerment with the animacy of life. It is called rebound, gift-gratitude-reciprocity, and grace in different traditions.

Gregg uses the analogy of learning to swim to elucidate all three steps of this moral conversion to nonviolence. At first he could not believe that water would buoy him up. He fought against it and sank. Yet, he gradually acquired the ability to swim by learning through practice to become aware of, trust, and work with the background power of buoyancy of water, and so acquire the self-awareness, virtues, and self-confidence of a competent swimmer. Analogously, the three transformative ethical steps bring about a moral conversion from an ethos of separation and power-over to interbeing and power-with.

The cultivation of a nonviolent ethos is thus the way humans connect with the power of nonviolence and exercise it in animating all branches of a nonviolent way of life. This self-transformation is the way to a nonviolent world. Constructive programmes provide the milieu in which it is cultivated.

Nonviolent Agonistics

Nonviolent contestation or "agonistics" is a branch that grows in every other branch of the *satyagraha* banyan tree. Disagreements and disputes arise in any human relationship, including in constructive programmes. Members learn the arts of nonviolent contestation and resolution with each other and in response to the impulse to dominate whenever it irrupts. They then take this nonviolent *savoir-faire* into their campaigns with violent actors and observers.

There are two phases of these campaigns. The first is to persuade violent contestants, their backers and observers to move to nonviolent ways of contestation and resolution. Gregg explicates this complex struggle with his analogy of moral jiu-jitsu. In the second phase contestants enter into nonviolent negotiations and reconciliation. He calls this integration.

The aim of nonviolent actors is to assert truthfully and openly the injustice in dispute as they see it, and, to persuade violent actors and observers to become aware of the superiority of nonviolent ways of contestation to their power-over ways, and join them in resolving their differences nonviolently. Gregg calls this process of self-awareness and self-change "moral conversion." The way they try to bring about moral self-conversion of violent opponents is by playing a nonviolent game of contestation with them, as if they were already partners in it.

They exercise the persuasive powers of nonviolent ethics. They courageously refuse to retaliate with anger or hatred when attacked and abused. They openly announce their plans and campaigns, and break off, apologise, and make amends whenever their individual *swaraj* fails. They present the truth as they see it from their limited social standpoint, listen to the views of all affected, offer to enter into negotiations, always act in trustworthy and humble ways, strive to accept denigration, beatings, imprisonment, torture, and death with good temper, and all the other modes of nonviolent ethical conduct. They explain why their protests, sit-ins, marches, boycotts, noncooperation, occupations, strikes, and other types of campaigns are not coercive and express their willingness to amend them if they are found to be.

They treat everyone as moral agents and members of the "we" of spiritual unity, never as enemies, and thus with the inner freedom to engage in ethical self-change, as they have done.

Their ethical exercise of nonviolence in the democratic way they organise and interact among themselves and engage with their violent contestants and observers enacts and "dramatises" the alternative nonviolent way of life for all to see (Gregg 2018, 52). It is the "persuasive assertion of the unity of the human species" (2018, 169).

The whole event is a public contest between two categorically different forms of contestation and their contrasting lifeways. On the one side, the exemplary, open exercise and offer of power-with. On the other, power-over organisation, secrecy, and the mobilisation of violence, domination, and deception. Their objective in this great contest of contests is to encourage all affected to reflect on the two contrasting ways of life on display and work through steps of self-transformation and moral conversion towards trusting nonviolence. As differently situated actors and observers begin to reflect on the dramatic contest and change their attitudes to the dispute, their silent or open withdrawal of support begins to undermine the social basis of support of the violent actors and the social system they are defending.

In this contest of contests, nonviolent actors are analogous to exemplary swimming instructors showing students how to trust and use the buoyant power of water. Exemplary nonviolent actors manifest the virtues required to trust and share in the power of nonviolence on display.

There are three main reasons "why" nonviolent contestation works. The first is the hypothesis that everyone "has in their hearts at least a spark of good spirit which can eventually be aroused and strengthened into action" (2018, 78). Nonviolent action can spark the "suggestion" that "there may be something in the world more powerful and desirable than physical force" (2018, 59). This "auto-suggestion" is the beginning of nonviolent self-change (2018, 57).

The second reason is that organised nonviolence is more powerful than violence. While courageous violent actors remain at the level of anger, hatred, and antagonism, courageous nonviolent actors enact and dramatise the higher power of uncoerced cooperation with and for fellow contestants. Rather than dissipating energy in struggling against each other, they gently guide their opponents towards freely combining their energy in uncoerced negotiations.

The third reason is that nonviolence tends to surprise and throw violent actors off balance. They are trained to anticipate and fight with opponents who fight, flee, or submit. When nonviolent actors refuse to respond in these familiar ways and act otherwise, the *savoir-faire* of violent actors does not work as expected. They, and the regime they uphold, tend to lose control of the situation as they "plunge forward, as it were, into a new world of values" (2018, 50).

This unique situation is the emergence of the transformative dynamic that Gregg calls "a sort of moral jiu-jitsu" (ibid.). It has the capacity to supersede war, violent revolution, and pragmatic civil resistance (*duragraha*); the three dominant, yet destructive and self-reproducing, means of social change for centuries.

Moral Jiu-Jitsu

Gregg constructed his metaphor of "moral jiu-jitsu" to translate specific dynamic features of the immensely creative power of *satyagraha* because the art of *physical* jiu-jitsu was familiar to audiences in India, the colonised world, and the West. Jiu-jitsu was seen as the appropriate means of engagement in two types of struggles: decolonisation and feminist movements against male power. Rather than mimicking the violent ways of Western colonisation and patriarchy, anti-colonial revolutionaries and feminists would engage in jiu-jitsu movements; causing their opponents to lose their balance and plunge into unfamiliar, nonviolent ways, enabling them to gain the stronger position.

Gregg realised that specific features of the general dynamic in jiu-jitsu are somewhat analogous to features of the transformative dynamic of nonviolence in the moral and psychological realm. Thus, the redescription of these features of nonviolent campaigns in terms of moral jiu-jitsu enables readers to see clearly how the moral dynamic works. His radical argument is that the transformative method anti-colonists and feminists are looking for in jiu-jitsu exists in Gandhian nonviolent agonistics.

Gregg compares and contrasts the dynamic features of physical jiu-jitsu and the analogous dynamic features of moral and psychological jiu-jitsu in the following ways. First, the violent aggressors begin by assuming the superiority of the power of violence. The moral jiu-jitsu practitioners surprise the aggressor by refusing to retaliate. They non-retaliate by the exercise of nonviolent ethics and good will in campaigns. The aggressor loses the moral and psychic support that predictable violent resistance normally provides. The *satyagrahis* use the nonviolent virtues of "kindness, generosity, and self-suffering" to pull violent opponents along. The attackers lose balance and their *savoir-faire* becomes ineffective, whereas the nonviolent actors retain their balance and *savoir-faire*. In the course of the interactions between violent action and moral jiu-jitsu, the violent actor and observers come to realise that the nonviolent contestant has a stronger character formation, position, and form of power than violence. Over time, the prevailing assumption and attitude that violence is strong and love is weak is reversed in practice for all to see.

Finally, the moral jiu-jitsu master does not use their superior position to "throw" their opponent and gain power over them, as in physical jiu-jitsu. The moral jiu-jitsu contestant knows better and offers a helping hand.

The contest continues until the violent actor and observer are persuaded of the superiority of nonviolence and agree to convert to its use in resolving the conflict. Since winning the struggle, transforming oppressive social systems and securing genuine and lasting peace require winning over the morale (hearts and minds) of all affected, this autotelic method is the only effective means.

As they are engaging in campaign manoeuvres and counter-manoeuvres, nonviolent actors also engage in public dialogue – presenting their arguments, asking others to present theirs, and offering to enter into negotiations. They do not attack, dismiss, or destroy the opposing views. Rather, they engage in nonviolent ways of arguing with their dialogue partners. They examine the components of their arguments to find values and assumptions with which they agree. Then they examine the values and assumptions they disagree with, give their reasons, present their alternatives, acknowledge their perspectival character, and request constructive responses. This way of "reasoning-with" their opponents ensures that each other's points of view, needs, and new ideas are taken seriously. Without this dialogue, any so-called resolution is just another power-over structure of domination.

The self-suffering of nonviolent campaigners shows their "sincerity" and deep "convictions." This resolute commitment to a nonviolent way of life, come what may, elicits admiration and awe. It moves violent actors and onlookers to reflect more deeply on the two contrastive ways of life being performed. If nonviolent ethics are absent, as in unarmed resistance or *duragraha*, resisters mobilise ill will and animosity, and engage in strategies to gain power over violent opponents, then both contestants are playing the same power-over game. It is war by other means. Such campaigns can replace power-holders and specific legislation. However, because there is no contrast between violent and nonviolent ways of life to reflect on, there is no possibility of transforming the power-over attitudes, struggles, and systems. Both contestants accept and re-enact them.

Whereas, with Gandhian agonistics and public dialogues, the comparative contrast between the two ways of life being enacted becomes increasingly clearer, deeper, and transformative.

Conversion and Integration

At the core of the power-over systems that nonviolent actors challenge is the presumption that these systems are the necessary means to peace, cooperation, and security. The soft power of moral jiu-jitsu exposes the falsity of this position.

The presumptive necessity of power-over rests on the "rabble hypothesis" that humans are incapable of settling disputes and cooperating without the coercive imposition of power-over. The moral jiu-jitsu campaigns and constructive programmes demonstrate that this is empirically false. Observers see ordinary humans engaged fairly consistently in nonviolent cooperation and contestation in all their activities, resolutely hanging on to it in the face of violence, giving their explanations of it, and offering it to others. This resonates with the observers' spark and experience of nonviolence and calls into question the need for dual loyalty.

Power-over is also claimed to be the necessary means to peace, security, and cooperation in the future. When observers turn and examine their own society in contrast, they see that the exercise of violent means undermines the ends that are used to justify them. Domination does not lead to democratic cooperation but to coercive compliance and resistance in the competitive economic institutions of modern civilisation. Hierarchically organised violence and inequality in wars, revolutions, and repression of dissent do not lead to peace and security but to increasingly destructive cycles of violent struggles and insecurity. The dominant responses to this performative contradiction are justifications of faith in progress "to come" by means of more "overpowering" war and domination, and the excuse that there is no alternative.

For Gregg and his generation of peace activists, this "security dilemma" is the fatal flaw in the global system of armed states and all power-over systems within them. The dilemma is that the means employed to resolve the initial insecurity and distrust reproduce them. In the course of moral jiu-jitsu campaigns, the futility of violence and domination and their justifying assumptions come into the space of questions and are exposed. And, the nonviolent alternative is enacted for all to see and share.

Gregg agrees that insecurity and distrust underlie the fear, anger, and antagonism that initiate the dilemma. Yet, unlike most modern theorists, he does not take this as given, as the initial condition. Rather, he argues that insecurity and distrust are brought into being by the initial step of separation and alienation from the given background intersubjective relationships of mutual trust and security. The objective of moral jiu-jitsu is to bring to consciousness this whole background that is overlooked in the modern worldview. Nonviolent actors then present the nonviolent way to dissolve the security dilemma.

When violent actors and the powers-that-be lose their equilibrium, as their local and global support declines, nonviolent actors refuse to "throw" their opponents, as is done in physical jiu-jitsu, bargaining, *duragraha*, revolution, and war. Instead, they offer the gift of an open and sincere helping hand to create together a new game of moral equilibrium in nonviolent relationships of contestation and cooperation (integration).

This helping hand is a radical offer of trust and security, backed up by the whole trustworthy pattern of conduct that precedes and supports it – because the way to generate trust in conditions of distrust is by being trustworthy and trusting, despite the vulnerability it entails. This gift of joining hands can also ignite recollection of the relationships of trust and cooperation they separated and alienated themselves from in their fear, anger, and animosity.

It can change the whole dynamics of circular responses between violent and nonviolent actors. To accept this offer, perhaps only tentatively at first, is the initial step of self-transformation and moral conversion. Barbara Deming, a feminist theorist and practitioner of nonviolence, argues that the moral jiu-jitsu double movement of asserting truth to the powerful and offering a helping hand combines masculine and feminine characteristics into a new, androgynous synthesis: "the very genius of nonviolence, *in fact*, is that it demonstrates them to be indivisible, and so restores human community" (Deming 1984, 230).

The aim of joining hands is to convert the opponent, to change their understanding and sense of values, so they will join wholeheartedly in seeking settlements that are amicable and satisfying to both sides. It helps to re-establish the violent attacker's moral balance at a higher and more secure level. The crucial point here is that "no conflict can be solved at the level of the conflict," yet this is what all violent methods try to do (2018, 68). The contestants have to move themselves into nonviolent relations of cooperation and contestation. This is the way consistent with human freedom.

The cumulative effects of all interactions in the complex field of circular responses gradually move the participants to accept the offer of negotiations: that is, integration.

Integration (or reconciliation) consists in exercising the nonviolent virtues in dialogue to find ways of combining the energy of all partners. It continues the public dialogues. Participants compare and contrast the values and assumptions of their conflicting views to search for shared or analogous aspects within them that can provide initial steps of common ground and agreement. These dialogues generate mutual understanding for the ways differently situated participants experience the injustice at issue. In the course of participation the contestants are transformed into partners in nonviolent relationships of working together and creating ways of living together that they could not imagine beforehand.

The most important feature of integrative negotiation is not the specific uncoerced agreement, which is always imperfect and open to nonviolent contestation in the future. Rather, in working towards agreement, they learn and acquire the virtues and arts of combining their energies and working with and for each other. In so doing, they bring an intersubjective nonviolent practice of contesting and conciliating into being among them without subordination. Human conflicts never end, but humans learn nonviolent ways of enacting, addressing and resolving them as they learn the broader nonviolent way of life in which integration has its home.

The Process of Change

Finally, Gregg argues that large-scale, nonviolent conversion and social change do not occur in "fast time." Rather, the process is "slow but sure" (2018, 146). It is sure because each step of the means embodies and carries forward the ends: peace by peaceful means and democracy by democratic means.

It is also immediate in the specific sense that each step in ethics, constructive programmes, voluntary simplicity, and agonistics involves withdrawing our capabilities from the violent and dominative system at hand and exercising them in nonviolent and nondominative communities of practice. This is the double movement of Gandhian non-cooperation.

The processes of social change by persuasion rather than force are also long-term. The cumulative effects of these virtuous steps and cycles gradually reach local tipping points that outgrow the declining violent and dominative system. This process of change is analogous to processes of ecological succession in the life sciences.

Conclusion

What light can this integral nonviolent tradition throw on nonviolence today? There has been impressive growth in the main branches of nonviolence over the last one hundred years. There is also a global network of research and teaching on nonviolent constructive programmes, campaigns, and reconciliation around the world. However, these experiments have not been transformative of the global systems of violence, domination, exploitation, inequality, and ecological destruction. The major reason for this is the disintegration of the ethical trunk and branches of the nonviolent banyan tree into separate practices, campaigns, movements, community-based self-government, cooperatives, and networks. Many of these employ the "veiled violence" (*duragraha*) of enmity and power-over. They remain alienated from the ethical and ecological ground of integral nonviolent power-with. This disintegration stems from the failure to understand the process of social change.

This process just *is* the slow but sure, step-by-step, integrated nonviolent way of life.

The way out of this disintegration and disempowerment is to exercise one's inner freedom in ethical steps of self-transformation with others in coordinated voluntary simplicity, constructive programmes, and nonviolent agonistics. These exemplary steps reconnect participants and observers with the integral power of nonviolence, the only power that can grow to become greater than, and transformative of, the power of violence and domination.

Note

1 Lecture delivered as the Center for Law and Society in a Global Context Annual Lecture, Queen Mary University of London, October 2018.

13 Sustainable Democratic Constitutionalism and Climate Crisis (2020)

Introduction: The Crisis of Sustainability and Response

The Sustainability Crisis

As we all know, we humans are entangled in a cluster of interconnected crises of social and ecological sustainability and well-being.[1]

Over the last four hundred years, the West has developed an assemblage of social systems of production, consumption, law, government, military, and education that is socially and ecologically unsustainable and self-destructive. It overreaches and undermines the social and ecological conditions that sustain life on earth for *Homo sapiens* and many other species and ecosystems. It is now the dominant global social system.

It is an assemblage of "vicious" social systems in the technical sense that the regular feedback loops within and between these social systems, and the *informal* social systems and ecosystems on which they depend, reproduce, and intensify the destructive effects of the systems on the ecological and social spheres.

We have known that this antisocial system is unsustainable socially and ecologically since the first meetings of scientists at the United Nations on the sustainability crisis in the 1950s and 1960s. The limits to growth were pointed out in the 1970s. The global norm of sustainability was introduced and expanded to sustainability and social well-being in the 1980s and 1990s. The Intergovernmental Panel on Climate Change and thousands of scientific studies track the growth of the crisis and suggest responses. National and international meetings and agreements take place every year. There also have been countless legal responses to climate change and its cascading effects (Caradonna 2014).

Yet the crisis continues despite best efforts so far to address it. We are already into a sixth mass extinction of biological diversity – and biodiversity is the necessary condition of life on earth. If the cascading destructive ecological and social effects of business-as-usual development continue apace, much of the earth may be less habitable, or uninhabitable, for *Homo sapiens*

DOI: 10.4324/9781003227403-17

and thousands of other species by the turn of the century. Moreover, the wealthiest people and countries are the major contributors to the crisis, while the poor and poorest countries are the major immediate victims (Wallace-Wells 2019).

Thus, the great question is: what have we learned over the last sixty years and how can we address the crisis most effectively today?

Three Phases of Ecosocial Systems

The first thing we have learned from the study of complex social and ecological systems is that they often become *vicious* in the way ours has. They develop in ways that use up the conditions that sustain them, degrading or destroying the interdependent life forms on which they depend, and thus destroying themselves. There are many examples in the history of life systems, both human and non-human.

Fortunately, there are also many examples of resilient members of vicious social and ecological systems changing their behaviour and transforming their vicious systems into virtuous and sustainable ones before collapse, and also examples of recovering from collapse and regenerating virtuous, self-sustaining systems.[2]

Thus, there are three possible phases of life systems. The first is the more or less virtuous and self-sustaining, or conciliatory phase. The second is the more or less vicious and unsustainable, or "crisis" phase. The third phase is the *way* in which unsustainable systems in a crisis phase learn how to change and regenerate the virtuous conditions of sustainability before they collapse. This is the third phase of ecosocial succession and transformation into a regenerated self-sustaining, virtuous system. The way a forest ecosystem recovers after clear-cutting is an example (Harding 2013, 231–49, 268–74).

From this perspective, we are in the second, unsustainable crisis phase. Thus, the third phase of a complex system is of immense importance for us – that is, of transformation of our vicious systems into virtuous systems. We can study examples of regeneration and think of how to apply them to our own situation.

The vicious social systems that are the cause of the crises of sustainability are not automatons, as the doomsayers claim (Dilworth 2010). They are very complex local and global social systems to which we are subject and on which most of us depend for our livelihood. Our daily productive and consumptive behaviour reproduces them. However, we are not so enslaved to them that we cannot think or act otherwise. We are free to reflect on them and to ask how to live and act differently to regenerate and transform our second-phase, vicious social systems into virtuous, self-sustaining systems. Millions of people are doing so today. I call these responses "Gaia citizenship" (Tully 2014a, 92–3).

In this lecture, I survey the relevant features of regenerative and transformative sustainability practices and explain how they apply to the practice of law. I call this integral, nonviolent, sustainable democratic constitutionalism, or, simply, Gaia law.

Misperceiving the Crisis

However, before we turn to regenerative responses, we need to understand how our vicious social systems cause both the crisis phase we are in *and* the misperception we have of it as subjects within it. For Gaia citizens, the reason we have difficulty responding effectively to the sustainability crisis is that we misperceive the crisis.

The reason we misperceive the crisis is that we view it from within the ways of thinking and acting that sustain the vicious social systems that are causing it. It is our self-formation as participants within these social systems that discloses the world around us and our relationship to the environment in a way that overlooks or distorts how they degrade life-sustaining conditions. Thus, even when we can no longer ignore or discount the damage we are doing, we respond in the standard problem-solving ways and means of the vicious systems, and thereby reproduce their positive feedback loops, rather than changing them. This is the "regulatory trilemma" I mentioned at the beginning.

Hence, the problem is one not only of misperception but also of being subjects of the social systems that generate the misperception. Barry Commoner first suggested this in 1971:

> To survive on the earth, human beings require the stable, continuing existence of a suitable environment. Yet the evidence is overwhelming that the way in which we now live on the earth is driving its thin, life-supporting skin, and ourselves with it, to destruction. To understand this calamity, we need to begin with a close look at the nature of the environment itself. Most of us find this a difficult thing to do, for there is a kind of ambiguity in our relation to the environment. Biologically, human beings *participate in* the environmental system as subsidiary parts of the whole. Yet, human society is designed to *exploit* the environment as a whole, to produce wealth. The paradoxical role we play in the natural environment—at once participant and exploiter—distorts our perception of it. [We] have become enticed into a nearly fatal illusion: that ... we have at last escaped from dependence on the natural environment.
>
> (Commoner 1971, 14–15)

In the first section, I discuss the vicious social systems that cause the crisis and generate this fatal illusion of independence from the ecosphere on which all life depends. In the second section, I examine the three phases of the life systems that sustain life on earth, yet that we misperceive from within our current social systems. In the third and longest section, I apply Gaia's teachings to the roles that the practice of law can play in transforming the unsustainable social systems into sustainable, conciliatory ecosocial systems.

The Vicious Social Systems that Cause the Crisis

Four Processes of Disembedding and Reembedding

Rather than building social systems that participate in and co-sustain the social and ecological relationships of reciprocal interdependence on which they depend, we have built social systems that prey on them. In 1944, Karl Polanyi initiated one of the best analyses of this global, super-predatory mode of extraction, production, consumption, and disposal that came to global hegemony over the last four centuries. He called it the "great trans-formation" and "disembedding" from life-sustaining ecological and informal social systems (Polanyi 2001; Dalton 1968). More recently, scientists call the period from World War II to the present the "great acceleration" of these anthropogenic processes because of their increasingly destructive effects on biodiversity (McNeill and Engelke 2014).

From this perspective, four major processes of modernisation and glo-balisation disembed humans from participation in the social and ecological systems that sustain life. These processes re-embed us in abstract and com-petitive economic, political, legal, and military systems that are dependent on, yet destructive of, the underlying interdependent ecosocial relationships.

The first process is the dispossession of peoples who live embedded in reciprocally sustained ecosocial relationships of their territories and lifeways. This includes enclosure movements in Europe and the worldwide disposses-sion of Indigenous peoples. They were then subjected to Western institutions and laws, such as the *Indian Act* and residential schools in Canada (Tully 2008a, 257–88; Greer 2018; Nichols 2020b).

It is important to see that Indigenous peoples were dispossessed not only of their traditional territories but also of their relationship to their territory. Indigenous people explain that the living earth does not belong to them as property. Rather, they belong to the living earth as their mother. She takes care of them with her gifts. In reciprocity, they take care of her by using her gifts in mutually sustainable ways. From their perspectives, colonisation refers to the dispossession of their ecosocial, participatory, cyclical, and sustainable ways of life with the living earth.

Aaron Mills explains that Anishinaabe peoples refer to these symbiotic ecosocial systems as gift-gratitude-reciprocity relationships with the living earth. Moreover, they learn how to live this way from how more-than-human animals, plants, and ecosystems live together (Mills 2016, 2018). Colonisation dispossesses and discredits this worldview as "primitive" and replaces it with the modern view that the earth belongs to humans as property. The following three processes of disembedding follow from this initial double dispossession.

The second process of disembedding is the cognising of the living earth as a storehouse of "natural resources" that become the property of humans, corporations, and states by reembedding them in systems of Western property law. What we now treat as extractable and commodifiable natural resources are interdependent co-participants in the ecological webs and cycles that sustain life on earth. Relating to the living earth as a storehouse of commodifiable resources disembeds them from these ecological relations and re-embeds them in the abstract and competitive relations of the global market system (Hall 2010).

The result of extraction and development under this system is the destruction of the webs of interdependent ecological relationships that sustain the natural and human world, giving rise to the environmental crisis and climate change, and the cascading social crises. Yet, the damage these processes cause to the ecosphere all along the chains of dispossession, extraction, finance, commodification, production, consumption, disposal, and resource and climate wars has been perceived until recently as "external" to the property system that causes it.

Once the means of the reproduction of human life are under the control of corporations within legal systems of competition, the third process is to treat the productive capabilities of human beings as commodified "human resources" for sale on the labour market. This process is legalised by the global spread of Western contract, labour, and corporate law. It disembeds human producing and consuming capabilities and activities from the surrounding, interdependent, informal social and ecological relationships in which they take place and re-embeds them in abstract, competitive, and non-democratic global market relations.

The productive capabilities of humans are not commodities. They are the cooperatively exercised abilities through which humans participate in the social and ecological systems that sustain life. They are the capabilities through which we belong to and participate in local ecosystems and communities. Yet, they are treated as abstract capabilities that we as separate individuals own; and, by selling the use of them to a corporation, they become the means by which we become subjects of the global market system. The damage that labour and corporate competition do to the informal social systems that producers and consumers live in and which sustain them – such as families, communities, First Nations, networks, and so on – is treated as another externality.

The result of development under this system is the erosion of the webs of interdependent social relations of mutual aid that sustain human communities, giving rise to the well-known forms of social suffering and degradation of modern life: alienation, horrendous inequalities, slums and gated communities, resource and climate wars, and the increasing violence of everyday life.

If the costs of facilitating and protecting this global system, and of remediating the damages it externalises, were internalised, the system would be economically irrational and would collapse. Yet, from within, it is perceived as the paradigm of economic rationality (Brown 2011).

The fourth process is the extraction of the intersubjective human powers and responsibilities of local self-government from their local practices and their alienation to centralised, representative governments, by means of competitive electoral systems in which political parties compete for votes. This fictitious transfer of powers of self-government atomises and reduces democratic citizen participation to the individual right to vote and express an opinion in the public sphere.

In these systems of representative democracy, representatives govern *for* the people. Yet, representatives are dependent on non-democratic corporations for taxes, jobs, donations, and thus for re-election. The damage this political system does to learning and exercising reciprocal responsibilities of participatory democratic self-government with fellow citizens in their social and ecological communities is yet another externality (Tully 2014a, 84–100; 2018b, 106–7). Yet, local participatory democracy is the permaculture of a healthy representative democracy.

Charles Taylor calls these disembedding processes of modernisation "excarnation" in *A Secular Age* (2007).

Polanyi predicted that the result of this great transformation would be the demolition of society and the destruction of the environment. Despite his warning and hundreds of others, this competitive assemblage of systems continues to expand.

It is a classic case of a self-destructive "super-predatory" system. It depends on, and is nested within, the informal social and ecological relationships that sustain life on earth. Yet, it preys on and destroys them in an extractive, non-reciprocal, linear, and unlimited way. Moreover, at the same time, it treats the damage it does to them as externalities, as if it were independent of them.

These are the main vicious systems that are creating and accelerating the crisis phase of the earth's life systems and rendering it uninhabitable.

The Picture of Law in These Vicious Systems

What is the paramount perception of law that goes along with participation in these vicious social systems? First, as Commoner argued (1971), the constitutive and regulative legal systems are misperceived as independent and autonomous from the ecological and informal social systems on which they depend.

Second, the constitutive role of law is the coercive imposition of a structure of laws that govern the four systems. Since the eighteenth century, the role of law has been to facilitate and regulate competition over the exploitation and use of these commodified, natural, and human resources for the sake of security, linear economic growth, profit, and comparative advantage, and to do so in accordance with the private and public freedoms and rights of modern subjects and corporations.

The rationale is that legally constrained competition among individuals, groups, corporations, unions, political parties, universities, states, and military-industrial complexes in these value spheres is the motor of human development and progress. Through the hidden hand of these dynamic social systems and the reflexive monitoring and regulation of law, these competitive, self-interested activities move the human species through developmental stages towards representative democracy, perpetual peace, global equality, and technological solutions to the climate crises in some future generation. The increasing wars, oligarchies, inequalities, and ecosocial destruction of the present are not evidence against this faith in further development, for these vicious means are presumed to lead to virtuous ends in some generation that is always said "to come" by more of the same.

Adam Smith, Immanuel Kant, G.W.F. Hegel, John Stuart Mill, Karl Marx, and Max Weber developed this background picture and it continues to shape perceptions today (Tully 2008a, 160–256).

In the 1970s, it became obvious that these so-called progressive systems are undermining the ecosocial sustainability conditions of life on earth. The response was to add the norm of "sustainability" onto the meta-norm of "competitive development": that is, "sustainable development." The great, ongoing legal struggles for regulation and limitation under the sustainable development norm have made important modifications to the four systems and their effects. However, these regulations have been captured – and often rolled back – by the overpowering dynamic of the vicious systems, and subordinated to it (Caradonna 2014). This is the trilemma of the present.

A third misperception is of a modern, constitutional legal system as the imposed basis of civility, sociality, and democracy, rather than one that is in concert with, or dependent on, other life-sustaining systems. Hence the uniquely modern term "constitutional [representative] democracy." Humans are portrayed as antisocial and incapable of self-organisation and self-government without it – in either an antagonistic state of nature without the rule of law (*terra nullius*) or a "failed state" today (Tully 1995, 2008b, 243–309; Sripati 2020).

Yet, despite this orthodoxy, there is considerable evidence for the contrary view that there are informal, everyday, local, and global social systems of cooperation and conciliation that precede historically and continue to underlie the formal competitive relationships of the dominant competitive social systems. These informal relationships of mutual aid are seen as the major factor in human evolution. *Homo sapiens* would have perished long ago if this were not the case.

The argument is that humans are able to survive the destructive competitiveness of modern life only in virtue of the continuing existence of such relationships of mutual aid within and around the formal, competitive systems in which we are constrained to inhabit. When these conciliatory relationships are noticed from within the dominant worldview, they are misperceived as "social capital" or a minor, volunteer sector. As the race for what's left of natural resources increases, climate and social crises and wars intensify, and antagonistic relations of organised anger become the norm, these intersubjective cooperative relationships become frayed and broken. Yet, even in the worst of cases, these informal relationships appear and enable the victims to survive.[3]

That is a very brief summary of the vicious social systems that are causing the crisis and three misperceptions of the roles of law that accompany them. While brief, it is enough, I hope, to indicate how state and international law have been radically transformed in the modern period to serve the development of the four vicious social systems and limit legal and governmental attempts to reform them in response to the crisis (Chapter 9).[4] I will now move around and describe our situation from the perspective of the surrounding, life-sustaining ecological and informal social systems.

Learning from Gaia

Convergence of Western and Indigenous Life Sciences

In this section, I discuss what the life sciences can teach us about how life systems have learned to sustain and complexify life and well-being over 3.8 billion years. I call this learning from Gaia. In the final section, I discuss lessons the legal profession can learn from Gaia in transforming our vicious social systems into virtuous systems.

Indigenous people have been learning from mother earth by trial and error for thousands of years and preserving this knowledge in their traditional ecological sciences, practices, laws, and stories of interdependency and gift-reciprocity relationships among all living beings. I have learned about this from Richard Atleo Sr. (2004), John Borrows (2018), Aaron Mills (2019), and Val Napoleon (2009a).

Ethno-ecologists argue that there is a convergence of Indigenous sciences of sustainability and the new, Western earth and life sciences. After centuries of dismissing Indigenous lifeways and promoting the misperceptions of independence, dominance, and exploitation, the Western life sciences are coming around to an interdependent, symbiotic, and co-sustaining picture of the place and role of humans in the living earth with our more-than-human relations. They are entering into a local and global dialogue with Indigenous peoples in research and practice (Turner 2005, 232; Kimmerer 2013).

Aldo Leopold, a forest ranger in the United States and Canada, foresaw this transformation in 1949. He argued that we have to move from seeing ourselves as the conquerors and controllers of nature, to seeing ourselves as "plain member[s] and citizen[s]" of the biotic communities in which we live. We need to learn and practise the primary responsibilities we have as co-sustaining citizens of the living earth (Leopold 1966, 217, 220).

Gaia Hypothesis, Symbiosis, Symbiogenesis

In the 1960s, James Lovelock, an earth systems scientist, discovered the Gaia hypothesis. Despite the vast changes in the solar energy coming to the earth over the last 3.8 billion years, and despite the vast changes in the forms and conditions of life on earth over the same period, the atmospheric conditions and the temperature of the earth have somehow remained in the range that sustains life on earth (Lovelock 1995).[5]

The Gaia hypothesis is that the ecosphere, and all the systems of life that compose it, somehow regulate the atmosphere and temperature to sustain life. The biotic and abiotic ecosphere as a whole is self-organising and self-sustaining (sympoietic). The hypothesis has survived a number of tests and is now classified as a theory. The reason Lovelock called it the Gaia hypothesis is that the Greeks also believed that the earth is alive. They called the spirit of earth *anima mundi* (the soul, energy, or animacy of earth). They took it to be a goddess – Gaia. The majority of scientists associated with the Intergovernmental Panel on Climate Change endorse it (Gribben and Gribben 2009).[6]

This discovery has led to attempts to explain how the systems that compose the ecosphere actually regulate the content and temperature of the atmosphere within a broad range of cycles that sustain most forms of life – from ice ages to warm periods, such as the Holocene and Anthropocene, in which we live.

For our purposes, the important insight comes from Lovelock's colleague, Lynn Margulis. She argued that the Gaia hypothesis is not based on the assumption that the assemblage of life systems that compose the ecosphere is itself a purposeful living being that regulates the climate and temperature to sustain life. Rather, the self-sustaining quality of Gaia is an emergent property of the life systems that compose the ecosphere. Some Gaia theorists explain that the Gaia hypothesis is just symbiosis and symbiogenesis on a planetary scale. Life sustains, develops, and complexifies through life systems living with each other in complex interdependent ways (symbiosis), and giving rise to new life systems (symbiogenesis) (Margulis 1998; Gribben and Gribben 2009, 155–6, 189, and 221).

Spatially, symbiosis refers to the immensely complex webs or networks that link all forms of life in relationships of reciprocal interdependence. Temporally, these networks are cyclical. They form cycles in which the "waste" of one interdependent member is used in some sustaining way by another member, so that nothing is wasted, and at a temporality that enables species and ecosystem renewal. Photosynthesis is the prototype of this spatio-temporal quality of reciprocal interdependency and cyclical renewability of life (Commoner 1971, 18–31).

Three Phases of Life Systems and Ecological Succession

The way life sustains life is not that the whole system regulates the conditions of life for its members. Rather, it is the other way round. The plain members and citizens of Gaia sustain it by means of their symbiotic participation in it. *Homo sapiens*, as one minor species among millions, are members and citizens just like all others, with ecological responsibilities to participate in ways that reciprocally sustain the networks that support them. Symbiosis and symbiogenesis are just technical terms for how forms of life live together in mutually supportive ways and, in so doing, give rise to new symbiotic forms of life.

These virtuous feedback relationships of mutual support and sustainability are the major factors in the evolution of life on earth. Life systems that sustain life symbiotically are "virtuous" life systems. Sustainable, conciliatory-phase life systems are not harmonious. They are often far from equilibrium, patchy, full of cheaters, and subject to perturbations that can cause the system to tip over into a second-phase, vicious system. Yet, for all that indeterminacy, their remarkable qualities of resilience enable them to sustain themselves over vast stretches of time.

Conversely, second-phase life systems that destroy the interdependent life systems on which they depend, and thus destroy themselves, are called "vicious" life systems. If vicious life systems were the major factor in evolution, life would have perished. The opposite is the case. Life has become more complex. Symbiosis and symbiogenesis have prevailed most of the time, even recovering from five mass extinctions and periodic ice ages.

Like virtuous systems, vicious systems are also far from equilibrium and subject to tipping points. Life has resilient powers of regeneration by producing networks of symbiosis within a vicious system, or within the ruins of a vicious system.

Regeneration or reconciliation work by being the change. Members of a vicious system begin to change and interact symbiotically and symbiogenetically within it, thereby transforming it step-by-step into a virtuous one. Regeneration or ecological succession is *autotelic*: the means prefigure and enact the end. This is the third phase of life systems in which the participants transform a vicious system into a virtuous or conciliatory one, by interacting symbiotically.

Take the example of the recovery of a forest from clear-cutting. Living plants and microorganisms that remain in the clear-cut forest do not only reproduce themselves. Their very life processes nourish their habitat and co-generate the conditions of life around them. These cycles of life creating the conditions for more life continue as a forest gradually grows back into a rich, biodiverse ecosystem. This is ecological succession. We humans can learn how to transform our own vicious social systems from the way in which ecological succession transforms a vicious ecosystem into a virtuous one (Faulseit 2016, 6–16; Tully 2018b, 113).

Transforming Ecosocial Systems

The human sciences have entered into a dialogue of mutual learning with the life sciences in three important ways. The first is over the terms symbiosis and symbiogenesis. They have a long history in the human sciences. They refer to how human beings and communities have lived together in interdependent relationships of mutual support, conflict, conciliation, and peace. Such informal symbiotic social relationships exist within and across every social system, even within the most vicious and damaging social systems. Like the clear-cut forest, they can provide the basis for initial, small steps of regeneration.

The second Gaia lesson is the realisation that we are not dealing with two independent paths of symbiotic evolution, one for non-human life and the other for human life. Rather, non-human symbiotic ecosystems and human symbiotic social systems are perceived as evolving interdependently and reciprocally. They are interdependent, strongly coupled, and co-evolving ecosocial systems. As a result, humans are perceived as co-evolving apprentice citizens within their interdependent ecosocial systems. As William Rees argues, "we can no longer understand the dynamics of either the natural system or the human subsystem in isolation without understanding the dynamics of the other component" (2010, 25, 32). This is a revolutionary transformation of the independence misperception.

The third lesson is how to transform vicious social systems so they interact symbiotically, rather than destructively, with the ecosocial systems that support them by learning from ecological succession. While recognising the unique features of human social systems, successful ecosocial transformation and reembedding of our four vicious systems require modelling on, or biomimicry of, ecological succession. This way of transformation goes beyond the modern models of reform and revolution, both of which are internal to the vicious systems and based on their legitimating misperceptions. This ecosocial way is to "be the change": to act and interact symbiotically and co-sustainably in and around the vicious social systems we inhabit.

This is how Fritjof Capra puts it:

> [W]e do not need to invent sustainable communities and ways of transformation from scratch but can model them after nature's ecosystems, which are sustainable and regenerative communities of plants, animals, and microorganisms. [A] sustainable human community is one designed in such a manner that its ways of life, businesses, economy, physical structures, and technologies do not interfere with nature's inherent ability to sustain life.
>
> (Capra 2002, 230)[7]

Rather, these communities of practice participate in this life-sustaining ability – the greatest power on earth.

The Ecology of Law

Transformative Ways of Ecosocial-Legal Succession

If Indigenous and Western life sciences are correct, then our damaged yet still life-sustaining ecosocial systems can be the permaculture of regeneration and transformation. The way of transformation of crises-ridden systems towards a self-sustaining future is to participate in, cultivate, expand, and scale out the symbiotic or being-with relationships of reciprocal interdependence in which we find ourselves in our everyday activities. At some locale and time, a critical mass of such communities of practice will reach a tipping point and transform the local unsustainable social systems. As these local initiatives are nurtured and grown, they interconnect with others and bring about larger transformations, as in ecological succession. Think globally, act locally (Rees 2010; Faulseit 2016).[8]

In this way of regeneration there is no privileged position or actor. It is applicable whenever and wherever we find ourselves, in every ecosocial footstep we take. It encompasses all the experiential, trial-and-error, reflexive, practical arts of being virtuous Gaia citizens. Millions of people are already engaged in them, in being the change (Hawken 2007; Tully 2014a).

As earth citizens reciprocate by taking care of the social and ecological systems that sustain their well-being and connect with others doing the same, something both miraculous and commonplace occurs. The ecosystems regenerate and reciprocate in turn, thereby further animating these fellow citizens and their sustainable social systems. This "rebound" is the sign of humans reconnecting with the animacy of the living earth: the cooperative power of life itself. It is pragmatic proof of the Gaia hypothesis (Macy and Johnstone 2012; Harding 2013).[9]

In this final section, I examine the roles that practitioners of common law can play in this way of succession and transformation. I am far from the first to do so. Two famous lawyers developed this whole way of transformation of Polanyi's four vicious systems in the first half of the twentieth century: Mahatma Gandhi and Richard Gregg. I refer to it as integral nonviolence.[10]

Four Seeds of Legal Transformation: Law and Society, Ecology, Indigenous Law, and Ethics

I believe we can perceive four legal seeds or movements of transformation that have been planted and cultivated in response to the climate crisis over the last seventy years. To use a mantra connected to McGill University, these are legal "seeds of a good Anthropocene."[11]

The first seed is the reconnection of law and society. The law and society revolution rejects the autonomy and priority of law and recognises its relational interdependency on the surrounding virtuous and vicious social systems. This includes the academic and practical work on law and race, gender, sexual orientation, class, language, religion, Indigeneity, and intersectionality. The objective is to bring the practice of law into dialogue with diverse citizens who are subject to it, so they can become active agents and citizens of it. This refers not only to dialogues between the courts and representative government and public spheres. It includes dialogues with the diverse citizens who are subject to the particular law in question, so they are active agents of it, having a democratic say, and even a hand, in the laws' life cycles of formulation, enactment, enforcement, review, challenge, and amendment (Nedelsky 2013; Starblanket and Kiwetinepinesiik Stark 2018, 175).

This social democratisation of lawmaking is enacted through countless practices of consultation in almost every area of law. Citizens have a say about it from their intersectional standpoint within the virtuous and vicious social relationships they inhabit. The law is required to understand them in their language and from their perspective (the duty to listen). It is justified by the democratic principle that "all affected" should have an effective say. This movement is based on the equiprimordiality of democracy and rule of law. Thus, it is called "democratic constitutionalism," in contrast to constitutional democracy, which is based on the priority of the constitution to representative democracy. A constitutive norm of democratic constitutionalism is the sustainability and well-being of all communities and members affected by it.[12]

The second seed is the reconnection of law and ecology or environment. Here, the law-and-society nexus is reembedded in the Gaia laws of the ecosystems and ecosphere that underlie and co-sustain all other *nomoi*.[13] It rejects the misperception that the earth is a legal vacuum prior to the imposition of human law and adopts the working hypothesis that the earth's systems constitute a plenitude of Gaia laws (Capra and Mattei, 2015).

Hence, a proposed law is tested on its ability to sustain both the ecosystems and the social systems it affects intergenerationally. Legal practitioners do this by dialogues with the humans who live there, and, as much as possible, with their fellow citizens of plants, animals, microorganisms, and ecosystems. Experts in various fields often perform this for the courts. However, it can also be done by means of perceptual dialogues of citizens with their bioregions and their members. These dialogues involve using all one's sense – synaesthesia. Deep ecologists, eco-phenomenologists, and eco-psychologists argue that human–nature dialogues reconnect us with the living earth, overcome our misperception of independency, and heal our nature deficit disorder (Abram 1997). Excellent examples of this movement are the Indigenous and non-Indigenous land-based legal courses in Canadian law schools.

The third seed is the beginning of just and democratic relationships of common and civil law with Indigenous legal systems. Settler law is moving ever so slowly towards the possibility of transforming and abjuring its colonial relation to Indigenous legal systems, recognising their priority and equality, and entering into dialogues of negotiation and reconciliation (Borrows 2010b, 124; 2016, 37–8).[14] This movement has the potential to effect a double decolonisation.

First, this seed works to uproot dispossession – the first step in the generation of the four systems that cause climate crises. This slow movement works in many ways. For example, Indigenous and non-Indigenous legal practitioners slowly persuade the Crown to recollect and acknowledge that whatever sovereignty it may possess, it is only de facto; and that it can be made de jure only by nation-with-nation treaty negotiations in accord with the Royal Proclamation of 1763, now in Section 25 of the *Canadian Charter of Rights and Freedoms*, and with the *United Nations Declaration on the Rights of Indigenous Peoples* (Nichols 2020b, 24; McNeil 2019, 293).

Second, Canadian courts are beginning to recognise that Indigenous legal systems are embedded in their enveloping social and ecological systems, and have been oriented to sustaining them over the last twelve thousand years. Consequently, Western legal practitioners can learn through comparative dialogues with Indigenous law keepers how to live in good, sustainable ways with mother earth. The Honourable Justice Grammond states,

> Indigenous legal traditions are among Canada's legal traditions. They form part of the law of the land. In a long line of cases, Canadian courts have recognized the existence of Indigenous legal traditions and have given effect to situations created by Indigenous law.[15]

This movement challenges and dismantles the superiority complex of modern Western law and goes beyond Capra's injunction to learn from Gaia. As the Honourable Chief Justice Finch argues, it enjoins lawyers to listen and learn from Indigenous people who have been learning from mother earth for millennia.[16]

The fourth seed is the connection of law and ethics. At the heart of this reembedding movement is the hypothesis that each of us has to be the change we wish to bring about, to be exemplars of a virtuous – sustainable and conciliatory – ethos in the way we teach, learn, and practise law. It rejects the adversarial-imposition view and adopts the view that law is a complex, difficult, and challenging dialogue of cooperation and contestation with all our interdependent relatives (Borrows 2019).[17]

In summary, these four seeds enable us to re-embed and reconnect ourselves as co-dependent members and citizens of the plenitude of ecological, social, and legal normative systems that sustain life, with responsibilities to sustain them in reciprocity. Common law is one interdependent *nomos* among many in the commonwealth of all laws. The very fact that these seeds exist and appear to be growing gives a glimmer of hope in our dark times.[18]

Six Common Law Tools of Transformation

Now, I would like to discuss six common law tools that can be used to cultivate these four seeds of transformative growth. Similar tools also exist in the civil law and other Western legal traditions. My argument is that they can be used in the ways I describe to decolonise the common law from its subservience to the unsustainable development of the four vicious systems and to take up a critical, constructive, and potentially transformative orientation of sustainable democratic constitutionalism within the law. They provide a toolkit to overcome the trilemma. Of course, these are not the normal ways of teaching and using these tools in the present age. If they were, we would not be in the climate crisis. They are standardly either not used or misused and abused in ways that serve further unsustainable development. Notwithstanding, they are being taught and used in the exceptional ways I described in the four constructive movements of the previous section. My aim is to explain how they are being used in these creative ways and how, taken together, they constitute the means of legal succession from our present crisis phase to a conciliatory and sustainable phase.[19]

The first tool is surely the realisation that private property is not the basis of common law or Western law. The basis is the norm that long use and occupation generate a right to continue use and occupation and a right to the fruits of use (usufruct). In the language of Roman law, *usus* gives rise to *ius*. Right or justice (*iustitia*) comes into being through long use and occupation. The norm of long use and occupation has been the basis of rightful use, occupation, and self-government for over two thousand years. In the common law, it is contrasted with feudal law imposed by the Norman Conquest (Pocock 1957).

Long use gives rise to right only if the users occupy the land, not if they simply claim to own it. Moreover, the right requires "long" use. Use has to be cyclical and sustainable or else it would not be "long use." Unsustainable misuse or abuse does not give rise to a right; it violates the right.

Classic examples of long use and occupation giving rise to right are common footpaths and gardens that are continuously used, cared for, and kept open by their fellow commoners. The right these activities bring into being is so strong it trumps enclosure and privatisation. On this view, justice does not come into practice through mine and thine, but rather through symbiotic relationships with each other and the living earth. The global commoning movements, such as food sovereignty, are contemporary examples.[20]

Long use and occupation have always been the basis of Aboriginal title in common law settler countries (McNeil 2019, 151). In the *Tsilhqot'in Nation* case, the Supreme Court defined Aboriginal title in terms of three features: (1) Aboriginal title is the proactive use and management of title territory for the benefit of the Tsilhqot'in Nation; (2) it inheres in the Tsilhqot'in people as a whole, not just this generation, but all future generations; and (3) each generation of Indigenous people must exercise this right in such a way that future generations will always be able to exercise the right as well. That is, they must exercise the right in ways that sustain the Tsilhqot'in people, their society, and the ecosystems that sustain them, forever.[21]

This remarkable decision defines the rightful use and occupation of mother earth in terms of sustaining the well-being of all affected. The Tsilhqot'in affirm this understanding of land use from within their own traditions of "belonging to the land." This definition of title reverses the first step of dispossession and colonisation in the imposition of unsustainable social systems. When it is applied to the legal systems of Indigenous peoples, it shows that many have rightful use and occupation of their traditional territories.

Moreover, recognition of the right of self-government of peoples historically and of self-determination more recently are often grounded in the prior long use, occupation, and governance of their territories. Finally, long use and occupation is evidently the norm manifest in the trial-and-error ways Gaia continues life on earth over billions of years.

If we judge our modern, unsustainable property systems by this basic norm, they appear to be unjust and in need of transformation. They violate and extinguish the Indigenous, social, and ecological social systems that sustain life through long use and occupation.

The second tool follows from the first: the precautionary principle of continuity. It enjoins courts to recognise and study existing "customs and ways." If they pass the long use and occupancy test, then the courts should support their continuance. If they are vicious and unsustainable systems, courts should work to discontinue or transform them, with the approval of the people subject to them (Tully 1995, 30, 116, 124–9, 154, 158, 161, 209; Chapter 5).

The continuity norm is based on the presupposition that the world in which humans and other animals have lived for millions of years cannot possibly be *terra nullius*. To have existed for so long it must comprise a plenitude of laws, and our first task is to recognise and learn our way around in this infinitely complex labyrinth that sustains us. Thus, the sustainable legal sphere is the mutual recognition, coordination, and continuity of the complex, symbiotic family of legal orders that pass the test of long use and occupancy. The common law recognised and linked arms with Indigenous laws in treaties based on the Royal Proclamation of 1763 and with the civil law in the *Quebec Act* of 1774 (Tully 1995, 117–24, 129, 145–9, 154–5; Chapter 5; Asch 2014, 101).

This legal pluralism of partners in treaty and constitutional federalism constitutes a commonweal. Its good coordination generates the commonwealth. The transformative role of the common law today is to correct past injustices, continue the negotiations, and extend the same principle of continuity to the surrounding ecological and social norms that constitute the commonwealth of all life. Here I am following the footsteps of Roderick MacDonald, Jeremy Webber, Alain Gagnon, and Charles Taylor, from whom I have learned so much.[22]

If these common law norms had been followed and improved over the centuries, we would not be in crises today. However, beginning with Thomas Hobbes, a right of unilateral discontinuity and extinguishment at the pleasure of the Crown was grafted onto the common law, against the objections of Sir Matthew Hale. This marked the assertion of the Crown as sovereign, rather than as a partner in relations of mutual subjection, and modern law as a system imposed over a customary yet lawless state of nature (Hobbes 2005, 26–7; Holdsworth 1937, 485).[23]

To transform this vicious juridical system, the first task is to show clearly that it is extinguishing the biodiverse systems that sustain life on earth – that it is engaging in ecocide. Then, the complementary task is to show that the common law presents a democratic and sustainable alternative in a world of biodiversity and legal diversity. The first two tools of long use and occupation and continuity begin to do this.

The third tool is the common and civil law norm of *q.o.t.*: *quod omnes tangit ab omnibus tractari et approbari debet* (what touches all must be approved by all). The modern legal norm of the equiprimordiality of democracy and the rule of law – democratic constitutionalism – is a redescription and updating of this ancient norm of Roman law. It extends "approved by all" to the democratic participation of the people who are subject to it, as well as to the sustainability and well-being conditions of more-than-human forms of life.[24]

These first three tools are the basis of the nation-with-nation treaty system of settler and Indigenous laws from the common law perspective.

The problem with the normative tools of long use and occupation and continuity on their own is that they do not provide a tool of dissent and contestation by human and non-human subjects oppressed by de facto forms of use and occupation. This is why the third tool of *q.o.t.* is required – the approval of those subject to it. Then, the question becomes, what is the best way of gaining the approval of all affected?

The fourth legal tool provides the answer: *audi alteram partem*, "always listen to the other side[s]." Aeschylus introduced this legal norm in *Eumenides*, the third play in the *Oresteia* trilogy. The Roman lawyer Cicero brought it to prominence in Roman law and the Western tradition (Manderson 2019; Skinner 1996, 138). The basic idea is that full understanding of the justice or injustice of a case can be acquired only by moving around and listening carefully to all affected explaining how the case affects them from their diverse standpoints and perspectives. Engaging in these intersectional dialogues, citizens and judges become aware of their parochial perspectives, provincialise them, and try to see the situation from the diverse perspectives of others. By these dialogues of mutual understanding and enlightenment, participants begin to see how they can negotiate a fair resolution acceptable to all. This crucial process is successful only if courts encourage participants to speak in their own customs and ways, show them due respect when they have the courage to do so, and really listen carefully to what is being said (Finch 2012). Although it is far from perfect in practice, *audi alteram partem* is now a convention of the European Union, the Supreme Court of Canada, and alternative dispute resolution practices.

The fifth tool is a distinctive, contextual form of common law legal reasoning that has been deeply shaped by the previous tools. It is the mode of reasoning appropriate for the complex, interdependent, multi-perspectival ecosocial-legal world in which we live. It is often overshadowed by an abstract and universalising form of legal reasoning that claims to be context-transcending. Nevertheless, the contextual approach continues to be taught and practised in the common law, especially in the four movements of the previous section. Its practitioners often argue that the interpretation and application of the presumptively transcendent rules are particular, situated judgements masquerading as universals.

The contextual and pragmatic mode of reasoning consists in embedding particular cases in their legal, social, intersectional, and ecological contexts; considering all sides and aspects carefully; acknowledging the indeterminacy of language use; generalising without universalising; proposing resolutions;

recognising their fallibility and pre-judgements; respectfully recording dissent; revisiting a judgment and its reasons as a precedent in future cases and contexts; and, thereby, locating it within the ongoing dialogue that is the common law. At the centre of this *audi alteram partem* mode of reasoning together is the demand of justice to learn how the case appears from the perspectives of all affected in order to acquire a many-sided view. This enables them to generate a fallible, situated legal judgment that is "even-handed," rather than abstract and independent, yet, for this very reason, always open to judicial and citizen dissent.[25]

This form of common law reasoning exhibits both similarities and dissimilarities with Indigenous traditions of legal reasoning. An example is the practice of passing around a "talking stick" to each party involved at a meeting called a potlatch (to give). A talking stick is passed to each in turn to give their story of the events in question from their perspectives. The listeners express their gratitude to each speaker for this gift that enables them to see aspects of the case they overlooked from their own perspective.

They reciprocate by telling their stories in turn. As they listen, speak, and learn, they begin to see pathways to good, even-handed resolutions.[26]

The sixth and final tool, perhaps the most important, is common law ethics. The dialogical abilities legal practitioners acquire through the integrated use of these six tools comprise a jurisprudential ethics and ethos that constitute a way of being in the world with others. Using these tools in these ways is how legal practitioners participate in transforming the vicious systems they adjudicate into virtuous and conciliatory ones. In so doing, they cultivate further the four seeds their predecessors sowed. It is the way of being the change within the law (Borrows 2019).

Conclusion: Common Law Contestation, Transformation, Reconciliation

In conclusion, I would like to address one objection to everything I have said. It is that the adversarial nature of legal practice is incompatible with the ethos of being the change I outline. On this polarised, us/them view of law, the role of lawyers is to try to defeat their adversary and win the case. It allows only for victory, defeat, or compromise. Lawyers acquire this competitive ethos in law school and in practice. Even when they fight for eco-social justice, they do so within this dichotomised, competitive, power-over and "winner take as much as possible" ethos and worldview. They thus become conscripts of the power-over and competitive-advantage ethos of the second-phase, vicious social systems they inhabit, whether they support or oppose them.

This may be the hegemonic practice of adversarial conflict, contestation, and conflict resolution. Nevertheless, the common law ethics I have described include an alternative adversarial practice that also exists in courts, consultation, negotiation, protests, alternative conflict resolution, and everyday disagreements. As Gregg explains, this nonviolent, common law ethos is

Gandhi's direct response to the colossal inability of us/them adversarial practices in law and elsewhere to lead to reconciliation and peace. Rather, they lead to the increasingly destructive vicious cycles of adversarial conflict and counter-conflict that engulf the present (Mishra 2017). The Gandhian alternative is based on the premise that means determine ends. It consists in the integrated, nonviolent application of the six tools in disputes and conflicts of all kinds. Gandhi called it *satyagraha* – the transformative power of non-violent contestation. Its telos is to transform the adversaries into partners in mutually sustaining relationships by being such a partner from the beginning. That is, they act in a way analogous to ecological succession.[27]

On one hand, practitioners (*satyagrahi*) present their views of the controversy as truthfully and openly as possible. On the other hand, they invite adversaries to do the same and enter into negotiations. They continue to do so in response to us/them counterattacks by adversaries, always offering an open hand rather than a closed fist, until adversaries realise they are trustworthy. At some phase in the negotiations, both practitioners and adversaries also come to realise that their adversarial mode of conflict resolution is the root of the conflict they are trying to address. They gradually shed this vicious relationship and regenerate being-with relationships that are the very condition of sustainable living.

They then begin to enter into negotiations based on the six tools of sustainable democratic constitutionalism. The critical dialogues that follow lift the initially adversarial dispute and disputants to a higher plane in which they can discover common ground. They literally discover a sustainable way of being-with each other – and of settling future conflicts – that they could not see from within their polarised, adversarial plane. Gregg famously calls this transformative succession "moral jiu-jitsu" (Gregg 2018, 50).[28]

In cases of disputes and conflicts over the climate crisis and sustainability, these truth-speaking and truth-seeking transformative dialogues free the norm of sustainability and well-being from its colonisation by the hegemonic norm of competitive development. This enables the participants to call the crisis-causing competitive developmental norm and the vicious systems it legitimates into the space of questions and responses.

In so doing, they experience the *animacy* of combining their energy and working with each other, rather than against each other, or over and under one another. This being-with experience has different names in different traditions, such as reconnection, de-alienation, compassion, spiritual unity, integration, *agape*, gift-gratitude-reciprocity, and *Tsawalk*.[29]

This unique, transformative practice is reconciliatory justice for both the participants *and* the conflict they are addressing. It is the nonviolent way of moving each other from a vicious adversarial relationship to a virtuous and conciliatory one. It could be called legal succession. Gandhi and Gregg argue that it can be practised in any human relationship when conflict arises. If it includes all affected, it reconnects us with the animacy of the crisis-ridden living earth – and Gaia reciprocates.

Notes

1 Lectured delivered as the McGill Law Journal Annual Lecture, McGill University, February 2020. I would like to express my gratitude to the members of the McGill Law Journal editorial board for the invitation to give this lecture and for their wonderful hospitality from the beginning right through to rewriting and publication. I owe special thanks to Aaron Mills for all his insight and help with these complex issues. I would also like to thank the Dean and the Faculty and students who engaged in the lecture and discussions that followed in ways that embody the best of the dialogical seeds and tools mentioned in the lecture. This lecture, rewritten for publication, is my small and inadequate gift in gratitude and reciprocity.

2 I develop this point in greater detail in Tully (2018b).

3 For the classic presentation of this argument, see Kropotkin (1902). See also Capra (2002), Macy and Johnstone (2012), Bowles and Gintis (2011).

4 For a devastating critique of this role of Western law in colonisation and modernisation from an Indigenous perspective, see Mills (2019).

5 For an introduction to Lovelock's Gaia theory, see Harding (2013, 68–91).

6 For an explanation and testing of the Gaia hypothesis (now classed as a theory), see Harding (2013).

7 For an example of implementing this biomimicry, see McDonough and Braungart (2010).

8 I discuss the history of this way of thinking about ecosocial change in Tully (2020b) and Chapter 10 in this volume.

9 For two of the most comprehensive accounts, see Capra and Luigi Luisi (2014), Esbjörn-Hargens and Zimmerman (2009).

10 Gandhi is well known. Richard Gregg (1885–1974) was a Harvard-educated lawyer who practised law during the great railway workers' strikes of the early 1920s, moved to India and lived and worked with Gandhi between 1925 and 1929, returned to the United States, yet continued to correspond, visit with, and write about Gandhi until 1947. He became friends with Martin Luther King Jr., and the civil rights movement of the 1950s and 1960s used his books extensively. See Gregg (2018) and Chapter 11 in this volume.

11 Seeds of Good Anthropocenes is a global network that has a major node at McGill University. It connects people around the world who are working to regenerate sustainable ecosocial systems. "About Us," Seeds of the Good Anthropocenes, accessed January 25, 2022, https://goodanthropocenes.net/om/.

12 For the emergence of democratic constitutionalism and its major features, see Tully (2008b). For a critical discussion of it from various perspectives, see Tully (2014a) and Nichols and Singh (2014). On sustainability as a constitutive norm of democracy, see Laden (2020, 205).

13 *Nomoi* is the plural of *nomos*. *Nomoi* refers to the plenitude of human and natural normative orders embedded in their broader cultures.

14 The University of Victoria joint common law and Indigenous law program (JID) that Borrows, Val Napoleon, and Jeremy Webber established, and which Sarah Morales and Robert Clifford joined, is exemplary. "Joint Degree in Canadian Common Law and Indigenous Legal Orders (JD/JID)," University of Victoria, accessed January 25th, 2022, www.uvic.ca/law/admissions/jidadmissions/index.php.

15 *Pastion v Dene Tha' First Nation*, 2018 FC 648 at para 8.

16 See Finch (2012). See also Turner and Spalding (2018, 265), Noble (2018, 315).

17 Borrows describes the seven grandparent ethical teachings or gifts of Anishinaabe legal practice (*Niizhwaaswi-Miigiwewinan*). He compares these with seven ethical virtues of the Western tradition and then shows the similar (and dissimilar) ways they are used in both legal traditions. See further on ethics in the part "Six Common Law Tools of Transformation," *below*.

18 For an excellent critical and constructive survey of these four seeds, see Zúñiga (2020). For a complementary study that integrates legal, social, ecological, and spiritual dimensions of Anishinaabe law, see Mills (2019).

19 I am indebted to the thoughtful way Joshua Nichols explains how using legal tools creatively can be transformative in the preface and introduction to *A Reconciliation without Recollection* (2020, xviiff).

20 The Nobel Prize–winning work of the late Elinor Ostrom has been instrumental in bringing this commoning world beyond state and market to a broader audience. See Bollier and Helfrich (2012), Parker (2017), Ostrom (1990).

21 See *Tsilhqot'in Nation v British Columbia*, 2014 SCC 44 at paras 73–74.

22 For an introduction, see Webber (2006, 2009). For a creative application of this deep legal pluralist approach to Canada's legal pluralism, see Cherry (2020).

23 Thomas Hobbes presents his theory of sovereignty in *Leviathan* (1996).

24 For the first seed, see the part "Four Seeds of Legal Transformation: Law and Society, Ecology, Indigenous Law, and Ethics," *above*. For democratic constitutionalism, see note 12.

25 This contextual form of legal reasoning is associated with Lon Fuller, Jeremy Webber, Roderick MacDonald, John Borrows, Val Napoleon, and many scholars and practitioners associated with the four seeds movements. See e.g. Napoleon (2009b), Webber (2009).

26 These diversity awareness dialogues with all human and more-than-human citizens are symbolized in the monumental work of art by the Haida artist Bill Reid and his diverse co-workers – *The Spirit of Haida Gwaii*. See Steltzer (1997). For some of the challenges of these dialogues among cultures, traditions, and civilizations, see Chapter 3 in this volume.

27 Gregg (2018) draws the analogy between transformative nonviolent contestation and ecological succession (cf. Borrows and Tully 2018).

28 Gregg (2018, 101) also argues that it is an effective substitute for war and revolution. This mode of conflict resolution is similar in many respects to the classic Greek practice of *parrhesia*, speaking truthfully to power (Chapter 3). I am grateful to Ryan Beaton for discussions of this connection and its importance for law students.

29 For some of these traditions, see Ricard (2013), Atleo (2004, xi), Way et al. (2018), King Jr (2015, 39–64, 75–96). "Spiritual unity" is Gregg's term.

14 An Interview with James Tully

Alexander Livingston: The chapters collected in this volume reflect important milestones and innovations in the development of the distinctive approach to political theory you call public philosophy. To set the stage, I want to begin by asking you how you understand the meaning of public philosophy today.

James Tully: Public philosophy is an attempt to bring political practice and political theory in dialogue with each other. It brings together two types of dialogues of reciprocal elucidation in response to political problems. By "political problems" I mean the issues that arise in the countless relationships, systems, and processes in which humans govern and are governed and exercise various modes of individual and collective freedom in and over them. This approach is based on the Aristotelian presupposition that political knowledge is practical, not theoretical. Practical knowledge (*phronesis*) is articulated creatively in everyday language, perspectival (contextual), the world it discloses is multivalent or aspectival, and it is acquired through practice with diversely situated humans. This is why dialogue is necessary to political thought and action.

The first type of dialogue is academics and students with intersectional civic and civil citizens engaged in political, social, and ecological problems in whatever subject positions they occupy. This involves listening to, learning from, and asking questions of clarification of the ways intersectional citizens problematise and address the problem in their own terms. The oppressed are given priority in these dialogues. They are pedagogy of, with, and for the oppressed oriented to transformation. For this very reason, these dialogues are not closed. They are open, in carefully constructed ways, to the participation of stakeholders on all sides, legal and governmental officials, and so on. As I discuss in Chapters 3, 11, and 13, they also include perceptual dialogues with animals, plants, ecosystems, and other life forms.

Everyone honestly engaged in dialogues of reciprocal elucidation is, by definition, a public philosopher, contributing their perspectival assessment of the problem and listening openly and responsively to others. Academic public philosophers respond by turning to a second type of dialogue of reciprocal elucidation to see what they can contribute. This is a dialogue of reciprocal

DOI: 10.4324/9781003227403-18

elucidation with academics from their own and other relevant disciplines, approaches, Western and non-Western traditions, and non-academic knowledge keepers that address similar problems in distinctive ways. The aim here is to bring the best of this academic and traditional knowledge to the dialogue with engaged citizens who may not have access to it. They draw on this knowledge to construct their sketch of the problem and possible responses to it in an understandable form that relates to the ways citizens articulate the problem. This is their initial contribution to the citizens' dialogue in gratitude and reciprocity for being invited to listen and learn from them.

The first, "diversity-awareness," phase of citizen dialogues is to co-generate comparative and critical dialogues of reciprocal elucidation of the problem that enable the diverse and differently situated participants to free each other to some extent from their customary opinions, background presuppositions and perceptions, and move around and see the problematic local/global/planetary field of practical systems of interdependent relationships they co-inhabit from the different subject positions of their dialogue partners. These dialogues take a wider variety of forms in different cultural contexts. In a similar way, the aim of the second, academic dialogue is to bring to light the diverse ways different political traditions disclose and orient themselves to this and similar problems. In both cases, the participants "elucidate" or "enlighten" each other about the diversity of the world they share. Thus, all participants become public philosophers. It is the dialogue tradition's alternative to monological enlightenment.

Grounded in these diversity-aware, nonviolent relationships of mutual learning with each other, the participants begin the second phase of dialogues of reciprocal elucidation. They begin to experiment with transformative ways of thinking, negotiating, *and* interacting with each other in response to the problems at hand. If this is successful, they move on to implementing resolutions, reflecting on, and learning from their experiment, and then starting another cycle of dual dialogues of reciprocal elucidation. In these practical, trial and error cycles of evolving mutual learning, they gradually acquire the practical knowledge and abilities to dialogue and interact with each other, deal with problems and conflicts over them as they arise, and pass their knowledge on to future generations. That is, they become enlightened participatory democratic citizens with each other as they go along.

Public philosophy thus aspires to be a pragmatic, participatory democratic mode of political philosophy and political change. It seeks to put the best of political theory and philosophy into dialogues of mutual learning with both civic and civil citizens by enacting its democratic ethos here and now, and learning from successive trials and errors around the world. Participants learn to think and act differently and democratically at the same time. As I explain in Chapter 1, I learned the academic dialogue from the Cambridge school and the civic and civil dialogues from the McGill and Victoria schools. In my experience, engaged students play a crucial role in public philosophy. They bring contemporary political problems into the classroom and curriculum.

They discuss and research how political theory and philosophy can help us understand them, write their essays and dissertations in response, and bring this knowledge back to their communities of practice. In so doing, they generate and continuously expand the relationships between the two types of dialogue.

AL: One striking feature of public philosophy, present from your very first publications onwards, is its stress on the affinity between Skinnerian contextualism and Foucaultian genealogy as resources for constructing critical histories of the present. How did you come to Foucault's work during your time at Cambridge?

JT: I read Foucault and Skinner in two undergraduate courses at the University of British Columbia. The initial connection was that they both present distinctive contextual approaches that helped me in my initial study of Locke in courses by Edward Hundert and Maurice Cranston. John Dunn was my supervisor at Cambridge (1974–1977). He was working closely with Skinner and co-developing their contextual approach. They are outstanding teachers and they taught me this approach with infinite patience and generosity. Dunn, Skinner, and Anthony Giddens discussed Foucault as a fellow historian or genealogist of political thought. The major discussions took place among graduate students, however. They interpreted him as contextualizing political thought in a structuralist or post-structuralist manner and challenging the standard periodization of the history of Western political thought. Thus, at Cambridge, Foucault's early and middle works helped to historicize political thought and they were read along with the works of Dunn and Skinner. Accordingly, during the Cambridge years, Skinner and Foucault provided two distinct yet complementary approaches to contextualizing political thought.

It was only after *Surveiller et punir* (1975) that Foucault turned to the complex question of the active agency of subjects in relations of power, knowledge, and subjectification. This evolving work provided the connections I was able to draw between Wittgenstein, Skinner, and Foucault on contextualism *and* agency. However, this did not begin until after 1977 at McGill University. Charles Taylor and I taught a number of courses together. His accounts of context and agency also had a large influence on my work (2008a, 39–70; 2018d). We disagreed in various specific ways in our interpretations of Foucault and Skinner, but not on their importance. These stimulating dialogues enabled me to articulate and defend my developing accounts of contextualism and agency.

AL: Rereading your early writings on Locke, I am struck with how many themes central to your recent work – the disembedding and commodification of human capacities, the ecological costs of modernity, and the displacement of the cooperative tradition – were already present. What initially brought you to studying Locke and how do you see the enduring impact of these writings on your current research?

JT: Yes, thank you for noticing that these themes are present in the early writings. I became interested in capitalist, socialist, and communist forms of property as an undergraduate during the Cold War and the Vietnam War. I also studied cooperatives and the early writings of the young Marx on participatory democracy. I decided to pursue a PhD on Locke on property in context to see the historical antecedents to the current contest between capitalism and communism. I also wanted to learn the Cambridge school approach of studying authors in their historical contexts in order to understand the history of the present and, thereby, to free myself to some extent from the parochial conventions of the present.

In the book based on my dissertation, *A Discourse on Property* (1980), I was struck by the complexity of Locke's writings on property, the governance of property relations, and the right of the governed to overthrow the government. The text in context did not seem to fit very well any of the scripts that were attributed to Locke in the secondary literature. I tried to explicate Locke's arguments in the context of early modern writings on property, exhibit their inconsistencies and complexities, and their differences from some of the standard interpretations. There is, for example, a labour theory of property that was used by "Lockean socialists" in the nineteenth century; a robust right of governments to govern property for the public good and the preservation of mankind; and a defence of the commons in England against enclosure. Of course, interlocutors have shown my own inconsistencies, errors, and complexities ever since. I am grateful for this long and edifying dialogue.

In my second book on Locke, *An Approach to Political Philosophy: Locke in Contexts* (1993), I took up the themes you mention. I continue to work on them. In particular, my research on the "second" or global enclosure of land into private property by colonisation and the dispossession and genocide of Indigenous peoples had a profound effect on me as a Canadian on unceded Indigenous land. I worked on exposing Locke's role in colonisation and especially in legitimating dispossession of Indigenous peoples of Turtle Island. This occurred when I was an advisor to the Canadian Royal Commission on Aboriginal Peoples (1991–1996). I had the opportunity to listen to and learn from Indigenous people who came from across Canada to tell their stories of colonisation and their struggles for decolonisation. I have worked ever since to do what they asked Canadians to do: to decolonise the relationship over Indigenous peoples and transform it into a treaty relationship of equal self-governing peoples by means of treaty negotiations (Chapters 5 and 11; 2008a 223–88; 2020a).

This dialogue experience also had a transformative effect on my understanding of property. Indigenous people explained to the Commission that they have a relationship to the land that is different from the main Western traditions of private, public, socialist, communist, and common property. They believe that the earth does not belong to humans. Rather, humans belong to the living earth and its diverse lifeways. She is our mother. Thus, humans have responsibilities to care for her well-being in gratitude and reciprocity for the life-sustaining gifts she gives to humans in every breath, step, and meal they take. Moreover, they learn how to be good, reciprocal citizens of their ecoregions by learning the ways she sustains life and using this knowledge in generating mutually sustaining interdependent social systems: that is, ecosocial systems (Chapter 10).

It dawned slowly on me that this is an effective response to the exploitation and ecological crises. At the same time, Indigenous knowledge keepers and Western ecologists, earth and ocean scientists were meeting on the West coast to work out together forest practices codes to sustain old-growth forests and regenerate those that have been clear cut. These events and this view of belonging to the living earth in interbeing relationships of mutual aid led to two research projects. The first is to learn more about how Indigenous peoples govern their traditional territories in practice with all their more-than-human kin (2020a). The second is to search for Western traditions and practices of earth and life sciences, economics, and ecology that are able to enter into dialogues of reciprocal elucidation with Indigenous peoples and join hands in responding to the ecosocial crises (Chapter 13, 2018b).

AL: This brings me to a major theme in our current work, the crisis of sustainability and regenerating ecosocial systems. How did you come to this way of reframing issues of civic freedom, democracy, and empire discussed in Public Philosophy in a New Key *(hereafter* PPNK)?

JT: I came to the topic in a number of steps. My father was an oceanographer so I grew up with the environmental crisis of the oceans and scientific responses to it (1988b). I began my undergraduate studies in the natural sciences thinking I would follow in his footsteps. When I transferred to the human sciences I continued to follow the climate crisis. In the 1990s I began to lecture on it. There were two major factors that moved me to research and write on it. The first was the protests on the West coast over the logging of old growth forests, the acidification of the Pacific Ocean and the overfishing of salmon. The second was the response of Indigenous peoples' to the environmental crisis, first at RCAP, and then on the Northwest coast when I moved to the University of Victoria in 1996 and began to work with Indigenous people here. Given my educational background I was able to understand and exhibit the complementarity between the remarkable advances in the earth, ocean, and life sciences over the last eighty years and Indigenous traditional sciences. In addition, given my education in the history of philosophy, I was able to suggest that there is an older Western philosophical tradition in Europe and North America that discloses the world as a living being, Gaia, in which life itself animates and sustains life (*anima mundi*). In the course of these studies I discovered the remarkable multidisciplinary research and practice on the similarities of these four types of living relationships and the sustainable (virtuous), unsustainable (vicious), and regenerative cycles they undergo, depending on how the members interact within them. This led to the discovery or recovering of a way of ecosocial transformation of the unsustainable relationships in which we find ourselves based on ecological succession in the life and earth sciences and Indigenous knowledge traditions. I had the great privilege of working with many others on these important connections, including invaluable collaborations with Nancy Turner and John Borrows (Chapter 11, 2020a), as well as Akeel Bilgrami and the late Jonathan Schell (Chapter 10, 2020b).

The question for me today is how can we overcome alienation and disintegration by transforming and co-generating dialogical relationships that co-sustain and enhance the well-being of all interdependent life forms in these complex relationships? The difficulties we face are not "problems" solvable *within* modernisation but, rather, are interconnected crises of sustainability *of* the dominant, gridlocked, anthropocentric, and contested relationships, systems, and processes of modern development. "Progress and Scepticism 1789–1989" (Chapter 8) was my initial attempt to articulate this change in orientation. My work on imperialism in *PPNK2* provided the basis for this turn from "problems" to interconnected local, global, and planetary crises of ecosocial sustainability and well-being (Chapter 9). These include: (1) massive inequalities in life chances between and within the Global North and South; (2) destructive cycles of militarism, war, violent conflict resolution and resistance, expanding military-technological complexes, and the boomerang effects of violence, distrust, insecurity, and paranoia onto everyday relationships; (3) ecological degradation, destruction, and the sixth mass extinction of the biodiverse relationships that sustain all life; and (4) the incapacity of modern, elite representative governments to respond effectively because they are dependent on the economic, social, and military systems that are causing the crises. I first presented my research in this way in my *Oxford Amnesty Lecture* (Chapter 7), "Global Disorder and Two Responses" (2013b), and in *Freedom and Democracy in an Imperial Context* (2014b).

The next task was to research how the processes of development of the contrapuntal ensemble cause the social and ecological crises. I found that the work of Karl Polanyi and his followers provides a good starting point for understanding the complex, non-linear causality of the interconnected crises. I began to lecture and write on this from 2012 to the present. If this analysis has some plausibility, then the major question for me is: what kind of response does not replicate the contrapuntal ensemble but, rather, transforms it?

As Indigenous peoples, ecologists, and life and earth scientists taught me, the first step is to free ourselves from our alienated and anthropocentric *misperception* of our relationship to the living earth as independent knowers and controllers and realise that we are "plain members and citizens" of the living earth. We are earth or Gaia citizens in the first instance in strongly coupled, interdependent ecosocial relationships of mutual aid that co-sustain all life. That is, our so-called social systems and social actions are always strongly coupled and co-dependent ecosocial systems and actions.

These relationships, and the living systems they comprise, exhibit the three main cycles mentioned above. In the first, sustainable or virtuous phase, members sustain themselves in ways that, *eo ipso,* co-sustain the well-being of their interdependent relatives and relationships. When they conflict, they find ways of resolving it within the mutually sustainable background conditions. Yet, the systems are often far from equilibrium. When some members continue to interact in unsustainable ways (taking without taking care and non-reciprocating rather than reciprocating, extractive rather than generative), this can lead to tipping points and the transformation of the system (and related systems) into an unsustainable or vicious phase. Unless this trend is transformed, it continues until the vicious systems destroy the life systems on which they depend and they collapse as well. This is common in the long evolution of life on earth but obviously not the dominant factor. As earth scientists have been reporting since the 1970s, our dominant, global social systems are in an unsustainable phase. It is the complex cause of the sixth mass extinction, climate change, cascading effects on all relationships, and the trend to an uninhabitable earth by the next century.

The third phase is the capacity of members of unsustainable systems to transform them back into a sustainable system before they collapse or to start again after collapse. The way of transformation, ecological succession, consists in interdependent members acting in co-sustainable ways in and around the vicious systems until they regenerate sustainable relationships that overcome and transform the unsustainable systems. That is, they succeed by "being the change" because in all life systems the means determine the ends. They are *autotelic.*

Ecological succession is the great recent discovery of the earth and life sciences, and it substantiates the teachings of Indigenous knowledge traditions. The lesson for the human and social sciences is that the way to transform our unsustainable social systems is by means of ecosocial succession – by being the change.

AL: This formulation brings me to another important innovation in your recent work, your focus on nonviolence. How did Gandhi become such an important interlocutor for you and how do you understand the connection between the modern tradition of nonviolence and the ecosocial perspective we've been discussing?

JT: I came to nonviolence in two stages. During the Vietnam War, the Cold War, and the peace movement, I turned to the history of political thought to try to understand what was going on. During the 1980s at McGill, I was involved in setting up the McGill Study Group on Peace and Disarmament and the McGill Employees for Nuclear Disarmament (MEND). MEND was one of the organisations awarded the Nobel Peace Prize under the auspices of Dr. Helen Caldicott. I lectured on peace and disarmament. One of my first publications was a review article of an edited volume on E.P. Thompson's

Exterminism in the anti-war journal *Our Generation* (1983b). I lectured on war and peace during these years. The second stage occurred in the early 2000s when I began to lecture on Gandhi in seminars on postcolonial ethics in 2001. He makes an appearance in the conclusion of *PPNK2* (2008b, 308–9). However, I did not see the full significance of this nonviolent tradition until I came across *The Power of Nonviolence* by Richard Gregg in 2010. Gregg provides a comprehensive account of Gandhi's theory and practice of nonviolence as a "way of life" or what I call "integral nonviolence" (Chapter 12).

Gregg presents three theses to be tested in practice: Gandhi's critique of modern civilisation, his alternative nonviolent, co-sustainable and ecosocial countermodernity, and his nonviolent, transformative *way* from the present unsustainable contrapuntal ensemble to a nonviolent, sustainable future (Tully 2018a, 2019). The way of transformation is ecosocial succession and it is based on Gregg's understanding of Gandhi's practice and his own knowledge of ecological succession. Integral nonviolence is like a banyan tree with many branches that include all four types of relationships: ethics; non-cooperation with unsustainable systems; constructive sustainable communities of ecosocial practice; training in nonviolent conflict resolution; discussions of the various perspectives on spiritual unity in different religious traditions; and, on this countermodernity permaculture, *satyagraha*.

Satyagraha is the nonviolent way of transformation of the dominant violent and unsustainable social systems to which we are subject. It is based on the autotelic relation of means to ends, and thus on the necessity of change by nonviolent, democratic, dialogical, and sustainable means of cooperation and contestation by persuasive words and deeds. It employs a distinct form of power-and-knowledge-with-each-other rather than the predominant power-and-knowledge-over-others.

Thus, as I suggest in Chapter 12, integral nonviolent cooperation and contestation is a distinct mode of transformative agonistics. It consists in participatory democratic cooperation in constructive programmes and then in the organisation of *satyagraha* campaigns. On this basis, *satyagrahis* engage in nonviolent, truth-seeking, and justice-seeking contestation *with* their opponents, by means of non-coercive words and deeds, to persuade them to enter into dialogues of reciprocal elucidation, negotiations, and transformation of the unjust relationships in question. The resolution is put to the experimental test of implementation to see if it is acceptable to all affected, and another round of cooperation and contestation begins. The difference in successive rounds is that the participants have acquired the skill set to cooperate, contest, and resolve conflicts nonviolently. This is called democratic "transformative justice" because the participants co-construct the new relationships of interdependency they agree to share. In contrast, the prevailing "civil" model of regime change and conflict resolution, "transitional justice," constrains participants to transition to a predetermined set of civil social and economic relationships (Chapter 9; 2012a).

AL: PPNK *offered a bracing account of how contemporary critical and democratic theory have implicitly presumed and effectively promoted forms of imperial domination. In what ways has this expanded vision ecosocial or "Gaia citizenship" informed this critique of normative theories of democracy and your vision of public philosophy as a genuinely democratizing and de-imperializing alternative?*

JT: One of the many constructive criticisms of *PPNK* by academics, students, and engaged citizens is that its account of movements of local and global civic citizenship (Chapter 6; 2008b, 243–309) is interesting yet scarcely transformative of the massive processes that are causing the urgent crises (2011, 2014a, 2014b). I agree. In response, I have worked on finding examples of and showing how reforming civil citizens working within the dominant civil systems and civic citizens working outside and around them can "join hands" and coordinate their projects, as Gandhi tried with the Congress Party. This consists in linking together the critical practices of civil citizens surveyed in *PPNK1* (2008a, 291–316), and the critical practices of civic citizens in *PPNK2* (2008b, 243–309). I set this out in *On Global Citizenship* (2014a) and subsequent writings (Chapter 7; 2013a; 2022a). Chapter 13 is an example of how civil and civic actors can join in potentially transformative ways. More recently, I have pursued these questions further in *Democratic Multiplicity* (Tully et al. 2022) and *Dialogue and Decolonization* (Tully 2022b).

One of the most influential and well-researched examples of joining hands is the long historical attempt to decolonise the colonial relationships of the dominant settler systems over Indigenous peoples by means of "linking arms" together through nation-with-nation resurgent, transformative, and reconciliatory treaty relationships. It was at the heart of *Strange Multiplicity* (1995) and the politics surrounding it. The great symbol of it was the nonviolent mode of dialogical cooperation and contestation among diverse humans and more-than-human relatives in Bill Reid's monumental sculpture *The Spirit of Haida Gwaii.*

The Spirit of Haida Gwaii continues to function as a motivating symbol for many. However, the result of the dialogues of reciprocal elucidation since *PPNK* is that we can now see that there are many other similar joining hands traditions. Integral nonviolence is an example. It comprises a multiracial, multidisciplinary, and multi-continent network of traditions oriented to deparochialisation, decolonisation, and transformation since formal decolonisation and throughout the present neo-colonial period. Its multiracial members debate and experiment with violent and nonviolent means of change, constructive programmes and cooperatives, and they have developed intergenerational dialogues of reciprocal elucidation with engaged academics and students in universities throughout the world, and especially since the 1950s (2020b). University of Victoria is an exemplar of these dialogues of reciprocal elucidation. I see my public philosophy as one small member of this family of traditions of dialogues of reciprocal elucidation oriented to thinking and acting differently.

In an article entitled "Why Did Gandhi Fail?," Kenneth Boulding proposed that the failure of the Gandhian movement was not a failure of nonviolence (*ahimsa*) but, rather, of the failure of the social and human sciences to contribute their engaged research and dissemination networks to the practices of constructive programmes and experiments with truth (*satyagraha*):

> Nonviolence indeed is only effective when it is aligned with truth — *ahimsa* and *satyagraha* must go hand in hand. When truth is rejected, and when an illusory view of the world clouds the judgement, as it seems to me is true of India today, of course nonviolence will be rejected. The critical problem then, comes down to how we learn to test the reality of our images of social and political systems, for the greatest enemy of nonviolence is the lack of "reality testing."
>
> Thus, the failure of Gandhiism is not a failure of *ahimsa* but a failure of *satyagraha*. The modern world is so complex that the truth about it cannot be perceived by common sense or by mystical insight, important as these things are. We must have the more delicate and quantitative sampling and processing of information provided by the methods of the social sciences if we are really to test the truth of our images of social and political systems. The next logical step, therefore, for the Gandhian movement would seem to be in the direction of the social sciences, in peace research, and in the testing of all our images of society by the more refined means for discovering truth which are now available to us. I am not suggesting, of course, that the social sciences produce "absolute" truth, or indeed that much valid perception is not achieved through common sense and insight. What I do suggest, however, is that the problem of truth is so difficult that we cannot afford to neglect any means of improving the path towards it, and that without this, nonviolence will inevitably be frustrated.
>
> (Boulding 1967, 133)

I came across this article when I was researching for my edition of Gregg's *The Power of Nonviolence* (Tully 2018a). I think it is worthy of serious consideration and thus being put to the test of practice. If it is accurate, then perhaps the slow but sure ecosocial steps of these traditions are regenerating the groundwork of unsustainable to sustainable transformations at the local and eventually global levels. I now see public philosophy as one example of the kind of truth-seeking social science, as Boulding describes.

AL: Describing the impetus of your early work as an attempt to move beyond the reified ideological battles of capitalism versus socialism places it within a current moving through political theory in the 1980s that looked to radical democracy as an emancipatory alternative to a Marxism discredited by actually existing state socialisms. Fellow travelers along this current include William

Connolly, Sheldon Wolin, and Ernesto Laclau. Standing where we do today on the other side of the Cold War amidst intertwined global ecological and political crises have you reconsidered your evaluation of the socialist tradition? Have your recent studies of the "contrapuntal ensemble" of capitalist modernization and traditions of cooperative citizenship offered new insights into the kinds of reciprocal elucidation public philosophy and socialism can offer one another?

JT: These are two complex questions. I recognize the current you mention and I have learned from these major theorists. I would add Chantal Mouffe, Joe Parker, Boaventura de Sousa Santos, Arturo Escobar, Carole Pateman, Jane Mansbridge, Dimitrios Roussopoulos, Noam Chomsky, and Elinor Ostrom. In my case, the turn to radical or participatory democracy is based in part on a criticism of specific, authoritarian strands of Marxism and of some features of socialist governments. My response was not a rejection of socialism but to dialogically reevaluate the socialist tradition. The initial step of this re-evaluation was to turn to the early, humanist, and democratic Marx that Herbert Marcuse, Angela Davis, Lucio Colletti, and others brought to our attention. The objective here was to ground socialism more concretely in practices of democracy in the workplace, participatory self-government, and everyday relationships. The "Democratizing Work" movement is a current example.

It also involves a turn to Peter Kropotkin for his criticism of authoritarian and deterministic trends in Marxism, and his historical and conceptual argument that "mutual aid" is a better description of economic democracy than "socialism." Mutual aid is an ecosocial relationship. It ties economic relationships of sharing directly to democratic relationships among workers and all affected, on the one hand. It discloses a wide variety of forms of participatory democracy historically and globally underlying the dominant political and economic formations, on the other hand. It presents an alternative to the competitive developmental meta-narratives of Kant, Darwin, and Marx. My concept of civic and cooperative citizenship derives in part from the mutual aid tradition and its diverse instantiations in countless communities of practice. The works of Elinor Ostrom on the commons and Boaventura de Sousa Santos on globalisation from below have been formative. It also derives from the non-state, Indigenous peoples' traditional forms of self-government on Turtle Island (North America). The forthcoming co-edited volume entitled *Democratic Multiplicity: Perceiving, Enacting and Integrating Democratic Diversity* (Tully et al. 2022) surveys a plenitude of ways of enacting and coordinating ecosocial democracies today.

The second re-evaluation of socialism in my work is the attempt to understand how democratic socialism was defeated by the United States and its allies during the Cold War. For my generation, the Cold War refers to the Vietnam War, the rise of US, military and economic global hegemony, the defeat of the Non-Aligned Movement and the New International Economic Order at the United Nations (1974), the defeat of socialist parties in Europe, and the implementation of a global system of "informal imperialism" or neo-colonialism after decolonisation. This led me to turn to the history of imperialism before and after decolonisation in *An Approach to Political Philosophy* (1993), *Strange Multiplicity* (1995), *Imperialism and Civic Freedom* (2008b), "Lineages of Contemporary Imperialism" (2009b), "Reconciliation Here on Earth" (2018b), and some chapters in this volume. This is my contribution to the study of the "contrapuntal ensemble" that Edward Said diagnosed in *Culture and Imperialism*.

The third re-evaluation is of the top-down, reform and revolutionary models of decolonisation and state-building. They did not bring about democracy, socialism, or peace but, rather, inequality, militarisation, indebtedness, and competitive dependency on the great powers. They became unequal participants in the contrapuntal ensemble of competing states, corporations, and military-industrial complexes. Gandhi, Gregg, Martin Luther King Jr., Barbara Deming, and others argued that this means of change will lead to increasing inequality, wars, and chaos within and among states. The reason is that the means of change prefigure and shape the ends. Violence, authoritarian rule, and inequality do not lead to peace, democracy, and equality but to counter-violence, authoritarian organisation, and inequality. Because means are autotelic, the only way to peace, democracy, and equality is by nonviolent, democratic, and egalitarian forms of organisation.

The consequence of this third re-evaluation is that transformative change has to begin by decolonising our everyday relationships with each other and transforming them into the kind of nonviolent, democratic, and egalitarian relationships we wish to bring about in the larger society. We have to be the change. This revolutionised the way we think about decolonisation and revolutionary change. It begins in the everyday relationships of participatory democracy brought to light in the first re-evaluation above: for example, in Gandhi's constructive programmes, King's beloved cooperative communities, Thich Nhat Hanh's *sanghas*, food sovereignty, and nonviolent democratic community-based organisations throughout the Global South. These nonviolent communities of democratic practice then provide the basis of *satyagraha* campaigns and transformative negotiations and reconciliation. Moreover, this multiracial movement led to the emergence of a multiplicity of democratic, "decolonial praxes" here and now, in everyday unequal and undemocratic relationships of class, race, Indigeneity, LGBTQ2S+, and BIPOC in all spheres of modern societies. The outstanding scholarship of Dennis Dalton, Karuna Mantena, and yourself has enabled me to appreciate the depth and importance of this third re-evaluation. I discuss these decolonial praxes with Charles Mills, Sudipta Kaviraj, Sor-Hoon Tan, Garrick Cooper, and Monika Kirloskar-Steinbach in *Dialogue and Decolonization* (2022b).

The fourth re-evaluation is of human relationships *to* the environment. Ecologists and earth scientists have shown that the climate crisis is caused by the dominating, power-over, extractive, and exploitive relationship to the living earth of our dominant social systems. We need to free ourselves from this form of subjectivity and move around and see ourselves as plain members and citizens *within and with* the biodiverse webs of interdependent relationships that co-sustain all life, as Aldo Leopold put it in 1949, E.F. Schumacher in 1971, and Vandana Shiva in the 1990s. We then have to transform our social systems, so they co-sustain us in ways that reciprocally sustain the life forms and relationships that sustain us. That is, we need to extend the democratic principle of "all affected having and say and a hand" to all our human and non-human relatives. In so doing, we re-integrate humans into the larger "earth" or "Gaia" democracy of life-sustaining relationships of mutual aid. Indigenous peoples call these "gift-gratitude-reciprocity" relationships. Due to the autotelic character of means, this transformation has to take place by democratic and ecologically sustainable means: that is, step-by-step ecosocial succession modelled on ecological succession.

Thus, these are four re-evaluations that I continue to learn from "my studies of the contrapuntal ensemble of capitalist [and communist] modernization and traditions of cooperative [or civic] citizenship." Participatory democratic, ecosocial everyday relationships of mutual aid are the permaculture of healthy delegative and accountable representative democratic governments. Subjects become democratic citizens through participating in them. Linking them to reforming civil citizens in representative institutions can be mutually enhancing and overcome democratic deficits and disconnections. As we have seen in the third re-evaluation, the biggest problem is the tendency of political movements oriented to gaining state power to mobilise participatory communities to win elections, and to treat them as subaltern means to their legislative ends. It is self-defeating. For joining hands relationships between civic and civil citizens to be successful and transformative, they must be democratic, egalitarian, and mutual aid. This is one of the great lessons we can learn from the horrors of the last century.

Works Cited by James Tully

Tully, James. 1980. *A Discourse on Property: John Locke and His Adversaries.* Cambridge: Cambridge University Press.

Tully, James, ed. 1982. *John Locke. A Letter Concerning Toleration.* Indianapolis, IN: Hackett Publishing Company.

Tully, James. 1983a. "The Pen Is Mighty Sword: Quentin Skinner's Analysis of Politics." *British Journal of Political Science* 13: 489–509.

Tully, James. 1983b. "Complex Issues: E.P. Thompson and the Peace Movement." *Our Generation* 16(1): 60–7.

Tully, James, ed. 1988a. *Meaning and Context: Quentin Skinner and His Critics.* Princeton, NJ: Princeton University Press.

Tully, James. 1988b. "John Patrick Tully: 1907–1987." *Transactions of the Royal Society of Canada* 5(3): 206–8.

Tully, James. 1993. *An Approach to Political Philosophy: Locke in Contexts.* Cambridge: Cambridge University Press.

Tully, James. 1994a. "Diversity's Gambit Declined." In *Constitutional Predicament: Canada after the Referendum of 1992*, edited by Curtis Cook, 149–99. Montreal: McGill Queen's University Press.

Tully, James. 1994b. "Multirow Federalism and the Charter." In *Protecting Rights and Freedoms: Essays on the Charter's Place in Canada's Political, Legal, and Intellectual Life*, edited by Phil Bryden, Steven Davis, and John Russell, 178–205. Toronto: University of Toronto Press.

Tully, James. 1994c. "Aboriginal Property and Western Theory: Recovering a Middle Ground." In *Property Rights: A Publication of Social Philosophy and Policy*, edited by Jeffrey Paul, Ellen F. Paul, and Fred Miller, 153–80. Cambridge: Cambridge University Press.

Tully, James. 1995. *Strange Multiplicity: Constitutionalism in an Age of Diversity.* Cambridge: Cambridge University Press.

Tully, James. 1996. "The Principles of a Renewed Relationship." In *Report of the Royal Commission on Aboriginal Peoples*, Volume 1. Ottawa: Canadian Communication Group.

Tully, James. 2003. "Diverse Enlightenments." *Economy and Society* 32(3): 485–505.

Tully, James. 2008a. *Public Philosophy in a New Key. Volume 1, Democracy and Civic Freedom.* Cambridge: Cambridge University Press.

Tully, James. 2008b. *Public Philosophy in a New Key. Volume 2, Imperialism and Civic Freedom.* Cambridge: Cambridge University Press.

Tully, James. 2009a. "The Crisis of Global Citizenship." *Radical Politics Today* (July): 1–31.

Tully, James. 2009b. "Lineages of Contemporary Imperialism." In *Lineages of Empire: The Historical Roots of British Imperial Thought*, edited by Duncan Kelly, 3–30. Oxford: Oxford University Press.

Tully, James. 2011. "Dialogue." *Political Theory* 39(1): 145–60.

Tully, James. 2012a. "Middle East Legal and Governmental Pluralism: A View of the Field from the Demos." *Middle East Law and Governance* 4(2–3): 225–63.

Tully, James. 2012b. "On the Global Multiplicity of Public Spheres: The Democratic Transformation of the Public Sphere?" In *Beyond Habermas: From the Bourgeois Public Sphere to Global Publics*, edited by David Midgley and Christian Emden, 169–205. New York, NY: Berghahn Books.

Tully, James. 2013a. "Two Ways of Realizing Justice and Democracy: Linking Amartya Sen and Elinor Ostrom." *Critical Review of International Social and Political Philosophy* 16(2): 220–32.

Tully, James. 2013b. "Global Disorder and Two Responses: Keynote Address." *Journal of Intellectual History and Political Thought* 2(1): 35–64.

Tully, James. 2014a. *On Global Citizenship: Dialogue with James Tully*, edited by David Owen. London: Bloomsbury Academic.

Tully, James. 2014b. "Responses." In *Freedom and Democracy in an Imperial Context*, edited by Robert Nichols and Jakeet Singh, 223–72. London: Routledge.

Tully, James. 2016. "Deparochializing Political Theory and Beyond: A Dialogue Approach to Comparative Political Theory." *Journal of World Philosophies* 1(1): 51–74.

Tully, James, ed. 2018a. *The Power of Nonviolence*. Cambridge: Cambridge University Press.

Tully, James. 2018b. "Reconciliation Here on Earth." In *Resurgence and Reconciliation: Indigenous-Settler Relations and Earth Teachings*, edited by Michael Asch, John Borrows, and James Tully, 83–129. Toronto: University of Toronto Press.

Tully, James. 2018c. "Rediscovering the World of Franz Boas: Anthropology, Equality/ Diversity and World Peace." In *Indigenous Visions: Rediscovering the World of Franz Boas*, edited by Ned Blackhawk and Isaiah Wilner, 111–46. New Haven, CT: Yale University Press.

Tully, James. 2018d. "Dialogical Animals." *Philosophy and Social Criticism* 44(7): 754–5.

Tully, James. 2019. "The Power of Integral Nonviolence: On the Significance of Gandhi Today." *Politika* (April 23). www.politika.io/en/notice/the-power-of-integral-nonviolence-on-the-significance-of-gandhi-today.

Tully, James. 2020a. "On Resurgence and Transformative Reconciliation." In *Plants, People, and Places: The Roles of Ethnobotany and Ethnoecology in Indigenous Land Rights in Canada and Beyond*, edited by Nancy J. Turner, 402–19. Montreal: McGill-Queens University Press.

Tully, James. 2020b. "Life Sustains Life 1." In *Nature and Value*, edited by Akeel Bilgrami, 163–205. New York, NY: Columbia University Press.

Tully, James. 2022a. "On Gaia Democracies." In *Democratic Multiplicity: Perceiving, Enacting, and Integrating Democratic Diversity*, edited by James Tully, et al., 524–62. Cambridge: Cambridge University Press.

Tully, James. 2022b. *Dialogue and Decolonization: Dialogues with James Tully*, edited by Monika Kirloskar-Steinbach. Bloomington, IN: Indiana University Press.

Tully, James. 2022c. "Trust, Mistrust and Distrust in Diverse Societies." In *Trust and Distrust in Political Theory and Practice: The Case of Diverse Societies*, edited by Dimitrios Karmis and Francois Rocher. Montreal: McGill-Queens University Press.

Asch, Michael, John Borrows, and James Tully, eds. 2018. *Resurgence and Reconciliation: Indigenous-Settler Relations and Earth Teachings*. Toronto: University of Toronto Press.

Borrows, John, and James Tully. 2018. "Introduction." In *Resurgence and Reconciliation: Indigenous-Settler Relations and Earth Teachings*, edited by Michael Asch, John Borrows, and James Tully, 3–25. Toronto: University of Toronto Press.

Gagnon, Alain-G, and James Tully, eds. 2001. *Multinational Democracies*. Cambridge: Cambridge University Press.

Simpson, Michael, and James Tully. 2012. "The Unfreedom of the Moderns in the Post-9/11 Age of Constitutionalism and Imperialism." In *Federalism, Plurinationality and Democratic Constitutionalism*, edited by Ferran Requejo and Miquel Caminal, 51–84. London: Routledge.

Tully, James, Pablo Ouziel, Fonna Forman, Keith Cherry, David Owen, Jeanne Morefield, Joshua Nichols, and Oliver Schmidtke, eds. 2022. *Democratic Multiplicity: Perceiving, Enacting, and Integrating Democratic Diversity*. Cambridge: Cambridge University Press.

Additional Works Cited

Abram, David. 1997. *The Spell of the Sensuous: Perception and Language in a More-than-Human World*. New York, NY: Vintage Books.

Ackerman, Peter, and Robert DuVall. 2000. *A Force More Powerful: A Century of Nonviolent Conflict*. New York, NY: St. Martin's Press.

Aeschylus. 2009. *Orestia*, translated by Alan Sommerstein. Cambridge: Cambridge University Press.

Allen, Amy. 2016. *The End of Progress: Decolonizing the Normative Foundations of Critical Theory*. New York, NY: Columbia University Press.

Amoore, Louise. 2005. *The Global Resistance Reader*. New York, NY: Routledge.

Anghie, Antony. 2004. *Imperialism, Sovereignty and the Making of International Law*. Cambridge: Cambridge University Press.

Arendt, Hannah. 1970. *On Violence*. New York, NY: Harcourt.

Arendt, Hannah. 1977. "What is Freedom?" In *Between Past and Future*, 143–72. Harmondsworth: Penguin.

Arendt, Hannah. 1990. *On Revolution*. New York, NY: Viking.

Arendt, Hannah. 1998. *The Human Condition*. Chicago, IL: University of Chicago Press.

Armitage, David. 2011. "Probing the Foundations of Tully's Public Philosophy." *Political Theory* 39(1): 124–30.

Asch, Michael. 2014. *On Being Here to Stay: Treaties and Aboriginal Rights in Canada*. Toronto: University of Toronto Press.

Atleo, E. Richard (Umeek). 2004. *Tsawalk: A Nuu-chah-nulth Worldview*. Vancouver: UBC Press.

Ayers, Alison. 2006. "Demystifying Democratization: The Global Constitution of Neo-Liberal Polities in Africa." *Third World Quarterly* 27: 312–38.

Bailey, Saki, and Ugo Mattei. 2013. "Social Movements as Constituent Power: The Italian Struggles for the Commons." *Indiana Journal of Global Legal Studies* 20(2): 965–1013.

Bandarage, Asoka. 2013. *Sustainability and Well-Being: The Middle Path to Environment, Society and the Economy*. London: Palgrave.

Bardi, Ugo. 2011. *The Limits to Growth Revisited*. New York, NY: Springer.

Barker, Andrew W. 1986. "Nestroy and Wittgenstein: Some Thoughts on the Motto to the Philosophical Investigations." *German Life and Letters* 39(2): 161–7.

Bell, Duncan. 2014. "To Act Otherwise: Agonistic Republicanism and Global Citizenship." In *On Global Citizenship*, edited by David Owen, 181–206. New York, NY: Bloomsbury.

Bellamy, Richard, and Dario Castiglione. 1998. "Between Cosmopolis and Community: Three Models of Rights and Democracy within the European Union." In *Re-Imagining Political Community: Studies in Cosmopolitan Democracy*, edited by Daniele Archibugi, David Held, and Martin Köhler, 138–51. Cambridge: Polity Press.

Benhabib, Seyla. 1992. *Situating the Self: Gender, Community, and Postmodernism in Contemporary Ethics*. New York, NY: Routledge.

Benhabib, Seyla, ed. 1996. *Democracy and Difference: Contesting the Boundaries of the Political*. Princeton, NJ: Princeton University Press.

Benson, Bruce. 2003. *The Improvisation of Musical Dialogue: A Phenomenology of Music*. Cambridge: Cambridge University Press.

Bilgrami, Akeel. 2014. *Secularism, Identity, and Enchantment*. Cambridge: Harvard University Press.

Boas, Franz. 1911. *The Mind of Primitive Man*. New York, NY: Macmillan.

Bohm, David. 2014. *On Dialogue*. London: Routledge.

Bollier, David, and Silke Helfrich, eds. 2012. *The Wealth of the Commons: A World Beyond Market and State*. Amherst, MA: Levellers Press.

Borrows, John. 2002. *Recovering Canada: The Resurgence of Indigenous Law*. Toronto: Toronto University Press.

Borrows, John. 2010a. *Drawing Out Law: A Spirit's Guide*. Toronto: University of Toronto Press.

Borrows, John. 2010b. *Canada's Indigenous Constitution*. Toronto: University of Toronto Press.

Borrows, John. 2016. *Freedom and Indigenous Constitutionalism*. Toronto: University of Toronto Press.

Borrows, John. 2018. "Earth-Bound: Indigenous Resurgence and Environmental Reconciliation." In *Resurgence and Reconciliation: Indigenous-Settler Relations and Earth Teachings*, edited by Michael Asch, John Borrows, and James Tully, 49–82. Toronto: University of Toronto Press.

Borrows, John. 2019. *Law's Indigenous Ethics*. Toronto: University of Toronto Press.

Boulding, Kenneth E. 1967. "Why Did Gandhi Fail?" In *Gandhi: His Relevance for Our Times*, edited by G. Ramachandran and T.K. Mahadevan, 129–34. Berkeley, CA: World without War Council.

Bowles, Samuel, and Herbert Gintis. 2011. *A Cooperative Species: Human Reciprocity and Its Evolution*. Princeton, NJ: Princeton University Press.

Brodie, Janine. 2004. "Introduction: Globalization and Citizenship beyond the Nation State." *Citizenship Studies* 8(4): 323–32.

Brown, Lester R. 2011. *World on the Edge: How to Prevent Environmental and Economic Collapse*. London: W.W. Norton.

Brown, Peter G., and Geoffrey Garver. 2008. *Right Relationship: Building a Whole Earth Economy*. San Francisco, CA: BK Currents Book.

Buber, Martin. 1970. *I-Thou*, translated by Walter Kaufmann. New York, NY: Simon & Shuster.

Buber, Martin. 1993. *Between Man and Man*. London: Routledge.

Capra, Fritjof. 1983. *The Turning Point*. New York, NY: Bantam Books.

Capra, Fritjof. 2002. *The Hidden Connections: A Science for Sustainable Living*. New York, NY: Anchor Books.

Capra, Fritjof, and Pier L. Luisi. 2014. *The Systems View of Life: A Unifying Vision*. Cambridge: Cambridge University Press.

Capra, Fritjof, and Ugo Mattei. 2015. *The Ecology of Law: Toward a Legal System in Tune with Nature and Community*. Oakland, CA: Berrett-Koehler Publishers.

Caradonna, Jeremy L. 2014. *Sustainability: A History*. New York, NY: Oxford University Press.

Carson, Rachel. 1962. *The Silent Spring*. Boston, MA: Houghton Mifflin Company.

Cassidy, Frank, ed. 1992. *Delgamuukw v. the Queen: Aboriginal Title in British Columbia*. Montreal: Institute for Research on Public Policy.

Chakrabarty, Dipesh. 2000. *Provincializing Europe: Postcolonial Thought and Historical Difference*. Princeton, NJ: Princeton University Press.

Cherry, Keith. 2020. *Practices of Pluralism: A Comparative Analysis of Trans-Systemic Relationships in Europe and on Turtle Island*. PhD Dissertation: University of Victoria. https://dspace.library.uvic.ca/handle/1828/11677.

Chin, Clayton. 2018. *The Practice of Political Theory: Rorty and Continental Thought*. New York, NY: Columbia University Press.

Clutesi, George. 1969. *Potlatch*. Sidney: Gray's Publishing.

Commoner, Barry. 1971. *The Closing Circle: Nature, Man, and Technology*. New York, NY: Knopf.

Connolly, William E. 1995. *The Ethos of Pluralization*. Minneapolis, MN: University of Minnesota Press.

Conway, Janet. 2004. "Citizenship in a Time of Empire: The World Social Forum as a New Public Space." *Citizenship Studies* 8(4): 367–81.

Cooke, Maeve. 1997. "Authenticity and Autonomy: Taylor, Habermas, and the Politics of Recognition." *Political Theory* 25(2): 258–88.

Crutzen, Paul, and Hans Günter Brauch, eds. 2016. *Paul J. Crutzen: A Pioneer on Atmospheric Chemistry and Climate Change in the Anthropocene*. New York, NY: Springer.

Cullinan, Cormac. 2011. *Wild Law: A Manifesto for Earth Justice*, 2nd edition. Cape Town: Green Books.

Cutler, Claire. 2013. "Legal Pluralism as the 'Common Sense' of Transnational Capitalism." *Oñati Socio-Legal Series* 3(4): 719–40.

Dalton, George, ed. 1968. *Primitive, Archaic, and Modern Economies: Essays of Karl Polanyi*. Garden City, NY: Anchor Books.

Dalton, Dennis. 2012. *Mahatma Gandhi: Nonviolent Power in Action*. New York, NY: Columbia University Press.

Dalton, Dennis. 2016. "Gandhi's Significance at the Center of Indian Political Discourse." Lecture Delivered at the Gandhi Workshop, Reed College, Portland, OR, April.

Daly, Herman, and John Cobb, Jr. 1994. *For the Common Good: Redirecting the Economy Toward Community, the Environment, and a Sustainable Future*, 2nd edition. Boston, MA: Beacon Press.

Darwin, Charles. 2003. *On the Origin of Species by Means of Natural Selection, or the Preservation of Favoured Races in the Struggles for Life*, edited by Joseph Carroll. Peterborough: Broadview Press.

Davey, Nicholas. 2006. *Unquiet Understanding: Gadamer's Philosophical Hermeneutics*. Albany, NY: State University of New York Press.

Davidovic, George. 1967. *Towards a Cooperative World: Economically, Socially, Politically*. Antigonish: St. Francis University Press.

Davidson, Robert. 1992. *Robert Davidson Exhibit: A Voice from Inside*. Vancouver: Derek Simpson Gallery.

Davis, Wade. 2009. *The Wayfinders: Why Ancient Wisdom Matters in the Modern World.* Toronto: House of Anansi Press.

Dean, Mitchell. 1999. *Governmentality: Power and Rule in Modern Society.* London: Sage.

Deffeyes, Kenneth S., 2005. *Beyond Oil: The View from Hubbert's Peak.* New York, NY: Hill and Wang.

Deming, Barbara. 1984. *We Are All Part of One Another: A Barbara Deming Reader,* edited by Jane Meyerding. Philadelphia, PA: New Society Publishers.

Descartes, René. 1985. "Discourse on the Method." In *The Philosophical Writings of Descartes,* Volume 1, translation by John Cottingham, Robert Stoothoff, and Dugald Murdoch, 111–51. Cambridge: Cambridge University Press.

Dewey, John. 1980. "The Need for a Recovery of Philosophy." In *The Middle Works of John Dewey,* Volume 10, edited by Jo A. Boydston, 3–48. Carbondale: Southern Illinois University Press.

Dhamoon, Rita. 2009. *Identity/Difference Politics: How Difference is Produced and Why It Matters.* Toronto: UBC Press.

Dilworth, Craig. 2010. *Too Smart for Our Own Good: The Ecological Predicament of Humankind.* Cambridge: Cambridge University Press.

Dower, Nigel. 2003. *An Introduction to Global Citizenship.* Edinburgh: Edinburgh University Press.

Dower, Nigel, and John Williams. 2002. *Global Citizenship: A Critical Introduction.* New York, NY: Routledge.

Drury, Maurice. 1984. "Some Notes on Conversations with Wittgenstein." In *Recollections of Wittgenstein,* edited by Rush Rhees, 76–96. Oxford: Oxford University Press.

Emmott, Stephen. 2013. *Ten Billion.* New York, NY: Vintage.

Engler, Mark, and Paul Engler. 2016. *This Is an Uprising: How Nonviolent Revolt Is Shaping the Twenty-First Century.* New York, NY: Nation Books.

Esbjorn-Hargens, Sean, and Michael E. Zimmerman, eds. 2009. *Integral Ecology: Uniting Multiple Perspectives on the Natural World.* Boston, MA: Integral Books.

Escobar, Arturo. 2004. "Beyond the Third World: Imperial Globality, Global Coloniality and Anti-Globalisation Social Movements." *Third World Quarterly* 25(1): 207–30.

Evans, Peter. 2008. "Is an Alternative Globalization Possible?" *Politics and Society* 36(2): 271–305.

Evans, Tony, and Alison J. Ayers, 2006. "In the Service of Power: The Global Political Economy of Citizenship and Human Rights." *Citizenship Studies* 10(3): 289–308.

Falzon, Christopher. 1998. *Foucault and Social Dialogue: Beyond Fragmentation.* London: Routledge.

Fanon, Frantz. 1963. *The Wretched of the Earth.* New York, NY: Grove Press.

Faulseit, Ronald K., ed. 2016. *Beyond Collapse: Archaeological Perspectives on Resilience, Revitalization, and Transformation in Complex Societies.* Carbondale, IL: Southern Illinois University Press.

Finch, Lance S.G. 2012. "The Duty to Learn: Taking Account of Indigenous Legal Orders in Practice." Paper delivered at the Continuing Legal Education Society of British Columbia, Conference on Indigenous Legal Orders and the Common Law. www.cerp.gouv.qc.ca/fileadmin/Fichiers_clients/Documents_deposes_a_la_Commission/P-253.pdf.

Forst, Rainer. 2010. "The Justification of Human Rights and the Basic Right to Justification." *Ethics* 120(4): 711–40.

Foucault, Michel. 1966. *Les Mots et les choses*. Paris: Editions Gallimard.

Foucault, Michel. 1970. *The Order of Things. An Archaeology of the Human Sciences*. London: Tavistock Publications.

Foucault, Michel. 1975. *Surveiller et punir: Naissance de la prison*. Paris: Edition Gallimard.

Foucault, Michel. 1984. "Politics and Ethics: An Interview." In *The Foucault Reader*, edited by Paul Rabinow, 373–80. New York, NY: Pantheon.

Foucault, Michel. 1985. *The Use of Pleasure*, translated by Robert Hurley. New York, NY: Pantheon.

Foucault, Michel. 1988. "Truth, Power, Self: An Interview with Michel Foucault." In *Technologies of the Self: A Seminar with Michel Foucault*, edited by Luther H. Martin, Huck Gutman, and Patrick H. Hutton, 3–15. Amherst, MA: University of Massachusetts Press.

Foucault, Michel. 1997. *Ethics: Subjectivity and Truth*, edited by Paul Rabinow and translated by Robert Hurley, et al. New York, NY: The New Press.

Foucault, Michel. 2000. *Power*, edited by James D. Faubion. New York, NY: The New Press.

Foucault, Michel. 2001. *Fearless Speech*, edited by Joseph Pearson. Los Angeles: Semiotext(e).

Foucault, Michel. 2011. *The Courage of Truth*. New York, NY: Palgrave Macmillan.

Gadamer, Hans-Georg. 1999. *Truth and Method*. New York, NY: Continuum.

Gandhi, Mahatma. 1949. "Letter to the Director-General of UNESCO." In *Human Rights: Comments and Interpretations*, edited by UNESCO, 3–4. New York, NY: Columbia University Press.

Gandhi, Mohandas. 1961. *Satyagraha: Non-Violent Resistance*. Boston, MA: Shocken.

Gandhi, Mohandas. 1999a. "An Impatient Worker" In *Collected Works of Mohandas Gandhi*. Electronic edition, 60: 381–2. New Delhi: Publications Division Ministry of Information and Broadcasting Government of India.

Gandhi, Mohandas. 1999b. "The Law of Our Being." In *Collected Works of Mohandas Gandhi*. Electronic edition, 69: 399–401. New Delhi: Publications Division Ministry of Information and Broadcasting Government of India.

Gandhi, Mohandas. 2008. *The Essential Writings*, edited by Judith M. Brown. Oxford: Oxford University Press.

Gandhi, Mohandas K. 2009. *Hind Swaraj and Other Writings*, centenary edition. Cambridge: Cambridge University Press.

Gandhi, Mohandas K. 2011. *My Experiments with Truth*. London: Fitzhenry & Whiteside.

George, Susan. 2015. *Shadow Sovereigns: How Global Corporations Are Seizing Power*. Cambridge: Polity Press.

Getty, Ian A.L, and Antoine S. Lussier. 1983. *As Long as the Sun Shines and Water Flows: A Reader in Canadian Native Studies*. Vancouver: University of British Columbia Press.

Gill, Stephen, and A. Claire Cutler, eds. 2015. *New Constitutionalism and World Order*. Cambridge: Cambridge University Press.

Gills, Barry K., Joel Rocamora, and Richard Wilson, eds. 1993. *Low Intensity Democracy: Political Power in the New World Order*. Boulder, CO: Pluto Press.

Gisday Wa, and Delgam Uukw. 1992. *The Spirit in the Land: Statements of the Gitksan and Wet'suwet'en Hereditary Chiefs in the Supreme Court of British Columbia, 1987–1990.* Gabriola: Reflections.

Grandin, Greg. 2007. *Empire's Workshop: Latin America, the United States, and the Rise of the New Imperialism.* New York, NY: Owl Records.

Greer, Allan. 2018. *Property and Dispossession: Natives, Empires and Land in Early Modern North America.* Cambridge: Cambridge University Press.

Gregg, Richard. 1936. *The Value of Voluntary Simplicity.* Wallingford: Pendle Hill.

Gregg, Richard. 1941. *Discipline for Non-Violence.* Ahmedabad: Navajivan Publishing House.

Gregg, Richard. 1953. "The Structure of a Nonviolent Society." *Fellowship* 19(5): 9–12.

Gregg, Richard. 1958. *A Philosophy of Indian Economic Development.* Ahmedabad: Navajivan Publishing House.

Gregg, Richard. 2018. *The Power of Nonviolence*, edited by James Tully. Cambridge: Cambridge University Press.

Gribbin, John, and Mary Gribbin. 2009. *He Knew He Was Right: The Irrepressible Life of James Lovelock and Gaia.* London: Allen Lane.

Grossman, Zoltán, ed. 2012. *Asserting Native Resilience: Pacific Rim Indigenous Nations Face the Climate Crisis.* Portland, OR: Oregon State University Press.

Gutmann, Amy, ed. 1994. *Multiculturalism: Examining the Politics of Recognition.* Princeton, NJ: Princeton University Press.

Habermas, Jürgen. 1995. *Moral Consciousness and Communicative Action*, translated by Christian Lenhardt and Shierry Weber Nicholsen. Cambridge: MIT Press.

Habermas, Jürgen. 1996. *Between Facts and Norms: Contributions to a Discourse Theory of Law and Democracy*, translated by William Rehg. Cambridge: MIT Press.

Hall, Tony. 2010. *Earth into Property: Colonization, Decolonization, and Capitalism.* Montreal: McGill-Queen's University Press.

Hanh, Thich N. 2013. *Love Letter to the Earth.* Berkeley, CA: Parallax Press.

Harding, Stephan. 2013. *Animate Earth: Science, Intuition and Gaia.* Cambridge: Green Books.

Hawken, Paul. 2007. *Blessed Unrest: How the Largest Movement in the World Came into Being and Why No One Saw It Coming.* New York, NY: Viking.

Heidegger, Martin. 2008. *Being and Time*, translated by John Macquarrie and Edward Robinson. New York: Harper Perennial.

Heinberg, Richard, and Daniel Lerch, eds. 2010. *The Post Carbon Reader: Managing the 21st Century's Sustainability Crises.* Berkeley, CA: University of California Press.

Held, David. 1995. *Democracy and the Global Order: From the Modern State to Cosmopolitan Governance.* Stanford, CA: Stanford University Press.

Held, David. 1998. "Democracy and Globalization." In *Re-Imagining Political Community*, edited by Daniele Archibugi, David Held, and Martin Köhler, 11–28. Cambridge: Polity Press.

Held, David. 2006. *Models of Democracy.* Cambridge: Polity Press.

Held, David, and Anthony McGrew, eds. 2002. *The Global Transformations Reader: An Introduction to the Globalization Debate.* Cambridge: Polity Press.

Hénaff, Marcel. 2010. *The Price of Truth: Gift, Money, and Philosophy.* Stanford, CA: Stanford University Press.

Henderson, James (Sa'ke'j) Youngblood. 2007. *Indigenous Diplomacy and the Rights of Peoples: Achieving UN Recognition.* Saskatoon: Purich Publishing.

Henry, Alexander. 1809. *Travels and Adventures in Canada and the Indian Territories between the Years 1760 and 1776.* New York, NY: I. Riley.

Hilmy, Stephen. 1987. *The Later Wittgenstein.* Oxford: Blackwell.

Hobbes, Thomas. 1996. *Leviathan.* Cambridge: Cambridge University Press.

Hobbes, Thomas. 2005. *Writings on Common Law and Hereditary Right: A Dialogue between a Philosopher and a Student, of the Common Laws of England,* edited by Alan Cromartie. New York, NY: Oxford University Press.

Holdsworth, W.S. 1937. *A History of English Law,* Volume 5. London: Methuen & Co.

Honig, Bonnie. 2011. "'[Un]Dazzled by the Ideal?' Tully's Politics and Humanism in Tragic Perspective." *Political Theory* 39(1): 138–44.

Honneth, Axel. 1995. *The Struggle for Recognition,* translated by Joel Anderson. Cambridge: Polity Press.

Huizinga, Johan. 1955. *Homo Ludens: A Study of the Play Element in Culture.* Boston, MA: Beacon Press.

Intergovernmental Panel on Climate Change. 2014. *Climate Change 2014: Synthesis Report. Contribution of Working Groups I, II, and III to the Fifth Assessment Report of the Intergovernmental Panel on Climate Change.* Geneva: IPCC.

Ishay, Micheline. 2004. *The History of Human Rights: From Ancient Times to the Globalization Era.* Berkeley: University of California Press.

Ivison, Duncan. 1997. *The Self at Liberty: Political Argument and the Art of Government.* Ithaca, NY: Cornell University Press.

Ivison, Duncan. 2008. *Rights.* Stocksfield: Acumen.

Ivison, Duncan. 2011. "'Another World Is Actual': Between Imperialism and Freedom." *Political Theory* 39(1): 131–7.

Jobin, Shalene, Hadley Friedland, Renee Beausoleil, and Tara Kappo. 2021. "Wahkohtowin: Principles, Process, and Pedagogy." *Canadian Legal Education* 71: 75–109.

Johnson, Chalmers. 2004. *The Sorrows of Empire.* New York, NY: Metropolitan Books.

Johnson, Sir William. 1853. "To the Lords of Trade, November 13, 1763" and "To the Lords of Trade, n.d." In *Documents Relative to the Colonial History of the State of New York; Procured in Holland, England, and France,* edited by John Romeyn, Berthold Fernow, and E.B O'Callaghan. Albany, NY: Weed, Parsons, and Company.

Jonsen, Albert R. and Stephen Toulmin. 1988. *The Abuse of Casuistry: A History of Moral Reasoning.* Berkeley, CA: University of California Press.

Khan, Irene. 2009. *The Unheard Truth: Poverty and Human Rights.* New York, NY: W. W. Norton.

Kant, Immanuel. 1991. *Kant: Political Writings,* edited by Hans Reiss and translated by H.B. Nisbet. Cambridge: Cambridge University Press.

Kimmerer, Robin W. 2013. *Braiding Sweetgrass: Indigenous Wisdom, Scientific Knowledge, and the Teaching of Plants.* Minneapolis, MN: Milkweed Productions.

Kimmerer, Robin W. 2014. "Retuning the Gift." *Minding Nature* 7(2): 18–24.

King Jr., Martin Luther. 2015. *The Radical King,* edited by Cornel West. Boston, MA: Beacon Press.

Kirloskar-Steinbach, Monika. 2019. "Diversifying Philosophy: The Art of Non-Domination." *Educational Philosophy and Theory* 51(4): 1490–503.

Klare, Michael. 2012. *The Race for What's Left: The Global Scramble for the World's Last Resources.* New York, NY: Picador.

Kompridis, Nikolas. 2006. *Critique and Disclosure: Critical Theory between Past and Future.* Cambridge: MIT Press.

Korten, David C. 2007. *The Great Turning: From Empire to Earth Community.* Oakland, CA: Berrett- Koehler Publishers.

Kropotkin, Peter. 1902. *Mutual Aid: A Factor of Evolution.* London: William Heinemann.

LaConte, Ellen. 2012. *Life Rules: Nature's Blueprint for Surviving Economic and Environmental Collapse.* Gabriola Island: New Society.

Laden, Anthony S. 2011. "The Key to/of Public Philosophy." *Political Theory* 39(1): 112–17.

Laden, Anthony S. 2012. *Reasoning: A Social Picture.* Oxford: Oxford University Press.

Laden, Anthony S. 2020. "The Value of Sustainability and the Sustainability of Value." In *Nature and Value*, edited by Akeel Bilgrami, 205–23. New York, NY: Columbia University Press.

Lasch, Christopher. 1987. "The Idea of Progress in our Time." Lecture delivered at McGill University, QC, November.

Leopold, Aldo. 1966. *A Sand County Almanac with Essays on Conservation from Round River.* New York, NY: Oxford University Press.

Linklater, Andrew. 1998. *The Transformation of Political Community: Ethical Foundations of the Post-Westphalian Era.* Cambridge: Polity Press.

Loader, Ian, and Neil Walker. 2007. *Civilizing Security.* Cambridge: Cambridge University Press.

Lovelock, James. 1995. *The Ages of Gaia: A Biography of Our Living Earth.* New York, NY: W.W. Norton & Company.

Lovelock, James. 2000. *Gaia: A New Look at Life on Earth*, 3rd edition. Oxford: Oxford University Press.

Lovelock, James. 2014. *The Rough Ride to the Future.* London: Allen Lane.

MacIntyre, Alasdair. 1988. *Whose Justice? Which Rationality?* Notre Dame: University of Notre Dame Press.

Macy, Joanna, and Chris Johnstone. 2012. *Active Hope: How to Face the Mess We're in Without Going Crazy.* Novato, CA: New World Library.

Magnusson, Warren. 1996. *The Search for Political Space.* Toronto: University of Toronto Press.

Mamdani, Mahmood. 2001. "Beyond Settler and Natives as Political Identities: Overcoming the Legacy of Colonialism." *Comparative Studies in Society and History* 43(4): 651–64.

Mander, Jeremy, and Victoria Tauli Corpuz, eds. 2004. *Paradigm Wars: Indigenous Peoples Resistance to Economic Globalization.* San Francisco, CA: International Forum on Globalization; Committee on Indigenous People.

Manderson, Desmond. 2019. "Athena's Way: The Jurisprudence of the Oresteia." *Law, Culture, and the Humanities* 15(1): 253–76.

Margulis, Lynn. 1998. *Symbiotic Planet: A New Look at Evolution.* Amherst, MA: Basic Books.

Marshall, John. 1839. *The Writings of Chief Justice Marshall on the Federal Constitution.* Boston, MA: James Monroe and Company.

Marx, Karl. 1853. "The British Rule in India." *New York Daily Tribune*, June 25, 1853. www.marxists.org/archive/marx/works/1853/06/25.htm.

Maybury-Lewis, David. 1992. *Millennium: Tribal Wisdom and the Modern World.* New York, NY: Penguin.

McDermott, Rachel F., Leonard A. Gordon, Ainslie T. Embree, Frances W. Pritchett, and Dennis Dalton, eds. 2013. *Sources of Indian Traditions*, Volume 2. New York, NY: Columbia University Press.

McDonough, William, and Michael Braungart. 2010. *Cradle to Cradle: Remaking the Way We Make Things*. New York, NY: North Point.

McNally, David. 2006. *Another World Is Possible: Globalization and Anti-Capitalism*. Winnipeg: Arbeiter Ring Publishing.

McNeil, Kent. 2019. *Flawed Precedent: The Saint Catherine's Case and Aboriginal Title*. Vancouver: UBC Press.

McNeill, J.R., and Peter Engelke. 2014. *The Great Acceleration: An Environmental History of the Anthropocene Since 1945*. Cambridge: Harvard University Press.

Meadows, Donella H., Dennis Meadows, Jørgen Randers, and William W. Behrens III. 1972. *The Limits to Growth: A Report for the Club of Rome's Project on the Predicament of Mankind*. New York, NY: Universe Books.

Mercant, Carolyn. 1980. *The Death of Nature: Women, Ecology, and the Scientific Revolution*. San Francisco, CA: Harper and Row.

Mignolo, Walter. 2000. *Local Histories/Global Designs: Coloniality, Subaltern Knowledges, and Border Thinking*. Princeton, NJ: Princeton University Press.

Mill, John S. 1991. *Considerations on Representative Government*. In *On Liberty and Other Essays*, edited by John Gray, 205–470. Oxford: Oxford University Press.

Mills, Aaron. 2016. "The Lifeworlds of Law: On Revitalizing Indigenous Legal Orders Today." *McGill Law Journal* 61(4): 847–84.

Mills, Aaron. 2018. "Rooted Constitutionalism: Growing Political Community." In *Resurgence and Reconciliation: Indigenous-Settler Relations and Earth Teachings*, edited by Michael Asch, John Borrows and James Tully, 133–74. Toronto: University of Toronto Press.

Mills, Aaron (Waabishki Ma'iingan). 2019. *Miinigowiziwin: All That Has Been Given for Living Well Together; One Vision of Anishinaabe Constitutionalism*. PhD Dissertation: University of Victoria. https://dspace.library.uvic.ca/handle/1828/10985

Mishra, Pankaj. 2017. *Age of Anger: A History of the Present*. New York, NY: Farrar, Strauss & Giroux.

Mitchell, Grand Chief Michael. 1989. "Akwesasne: An Unbroken Assertion of Sovereignty." In *Drumbeat: Anger and Renewal in Indian Country*, edited by Boyce Richardson, 105–36. Toronto: The Assembly of First Nations, Summerhill Press.

Mommsen, Wolfgang J. 1976. "The End of Empire and the Continuity of Imperialism." In *Imperialism and After*, edited by Wolfgang Mommsen, 333–58. London: Allen & Unwin.

Mommsen, Wolfgang. 1977. *Theories of Imperialism*. Chicago, IL: Chicago University Press.

Monk, Ray. 1990. *Ludwig Wittgenstein: The Duty of Genius*. London: Cape.

Montagu, Ashley. 1952. *Darwin: Competition and Cooperation*. New York, NY: Henry Shuman.

Montesquieu, Charles de Secondat. 1989. *The Spirit of the Laws*, translated and edited by Anne M. Choler, Basia Carolyn Miller, and Howard Samuel Stone. Cambridge: Cambridge University Press.

Moran, Emilio F. 2006. *People and Nature: An Introduction to Human Ecological Relations*. Oxford: Blackwell Publications.

Morefield, Jeanne. 2022. "For a Politics of Exile: Criticism in an Era of Global Liberal Decline." In *Democratic Multiplicity*, edited by James Tully et al., 167–88. Cambridge: Cambridge University Press.

Mountz, Alison, Anne Bonds, Becky Mansfield, Jenna Loyd, Jennifer Hyndman, Margaret Walton-Roberts, Ranu Basu, Risa Whitson, Roberta Hawkins, Trina Hamilton, and Winifred Curran. 2015. "For Slow Scholarship: A Feminist Politics of Resistance through Collective Action in the Neoliberal University." *ACME: An International E-Journal for Critical Geographies* 14(4): 1235–59.

Naess, Arne. 2008. *The Ecology of Wisdom: Writings by Arne Naess*, edited by Alan Drengson and Bill Devall. Berkeley, CA: Counterpoint.

Napoleon, Valerie R. 2009a. *Ayook: Gitksan Legal Order, Law, and Legal Theory*. PhD Dissertation: University of Victoria. https://dspace.library.uvic.ca:8443/handle/1828/1392

Napoleon, Valerie R. 2009b. "Living Together: Gitksan Legal Reasoning as a Foundation for Consent." In *Between Consenting Peoples: Political Community and the Meaning of Consent*, edited by Jeremy Webber and Colin M. Macleod, 45–76. Vancouver: UBC Press.

Napoleon, Val, and Hadley Friedland. 2014. "Accessing Tully: Political Philosophy for the Everyday and for Everyone." In *Freedom and Democracy in an Imperial Context*, edited by Robert Nichols and Jakeet Singh, 202–19. New York, NY: Routledge.

Nedelsky, Jennifer. 2013. *Law's Relations: A Relational Theory of Self, Autonomy, and Law*. Oxford: Oxford University Press.

Nestroy, Johann. 1962. *Der Schiltding*. Vienna: Verlag von Anton Schroll and Co.

Nichols, Joshua B.D. 2020. *A Reconciliation without Recollection? An Investigation of the Foundations of Aboriginal Law in Canada*. Toronto: University of Toronto Press.

Nichols, Robert. 2020a. "Context, Violence, and Methodological Drift in the Study of Empire." *Contemporary Political Theory* 19(2): 295–301.

Nichols, Robert. 2020b. *Theft is Property! Dispossession and Critical Theory*. Durham: Duke University Press.

Nichols, Robert, and Jakeet Singh. 2014. "Editor's Introduction." In *Freedom and Democracy in an Imperial Context*, edited by Robert Nichols and Jakeet Singh, 1–12. New York, NY: Routledge.

Nietzsche, Friedrich. 1974. *The Gay Science*, translated by Walter Kaufman. New York, NY: Vintage Books.

Nietzsche, Friedrich. 1986. *Human, All Too Human: A Book for Free Spirits*. Cambridge: Cambridge University Press.

Noble, Brian. 2018. "Treaty Ecologies: With Persons, Peoples, Animals, and the Land." In *Resurgence and Reconciliation: Indigenous-Settler Relations and Earth Teachings,* edited by Michael Asch, John Borrows, and James Tully, 315–42. Toronto: University of Toronto Press.

Normand, Roger, and Sarah Zaidi. 2008. *Human Rights at the UN: The Political History of Universal Justice, United Nations Intellectual History Project Series*. Bloomington: Indiana University Press.

Norval, Aletta. 2007. *Aversive Democracy: Inheritance and Originality in the Democratic Tradition*. Cambridge: Cambridge University Press.

Ostrom, Elinor. 1990. *Governing the Commons: The Evolution of Institutions for Collective* Action. New York, NY: Cambridge University Press.

Ouziel, Pablo. 2015. *Vamos Lentos Porque Vamos Lejos: Towards a Dialogical Understanding of Spain's 15Ms.* PhD Dissertation: University of Victoria. https://dspace.library.uvic.ca/handle/1828/6734

Owen, David. 1994. *Maturity and Modernity: Nietzsche, Weber, Foucault and the Ambivalence of Reason.* London: Routledge.

Owen, David. 1995. *Nietzsche, Politics and Modernity.* London: Sage.

Owen, David. 1999. "Orientation and Enlightenment." In *Foucault contra Habermas*, edited by David Owen, 21–44. London: Sage.

Owen, David. 2012. "Tully, Foucault and Agonistic Struggles over Recognition." In *Recognition Theory and Contemporary French Moral and Political Philosophy*, edited by Miriam Bankovsky and Alice Le Goff, 133–65. Manchester: Manchester University Press.

Owen, David. 2016. "Reasons and Practices of Reasoning." *European Journal of Political Theory* 15(2): 172–88.

Paine, Thomas. 1987. The Rights of Man. In *The Thomas Paine Reader*, edited by Michael Foot and Isaac Kramnick, 201–364. Harmondsworth: Penguin.

Paley, Julia. 2002. "Towards an Anthropology of Democracy." *Annual Review of Anthropology* 31(1): 469–96.

Parker, Joe. 2017. *Democracy beyond the Nation State: Practicing Equality.* New York, NY: Routledge.

Parker, Arthur C., and Seth Newhouse. 1916. *The Constitution of the Five Nations or the Iroquois Book of the Great Law.* Albany, NY: The University of the State of New York.

Paxton, Marie. 2019. *Agonistic Democracy: Rethinking Political Institutions in Pluralist Times.* New York, NY: Routledge.

Phillips, Anne. 1997. "Why Worry about Multiculturalism?" *Dissent Magazine* Winter: 57–63.

Pitts, Jennifer. 2005. *A Turn to Empire: The Rise of Imperial Liberalism in Britain and France.* Princeton, NJ: Princeton University Press.

Plato. 1956. *Protagoras*, edited by Gregory Vlastos. Indianapolis, IN: Bobbs-Merrill.

Pocock, J.G.A. 1957. *The Ancient Constitution and the Feudal Law: A Study of English Historical Thought in the Seventeenth Century.* Cambridge: Cambridge University Press.

Pocock, J.G.A. 2003. *The Machiavellian Moment: Florentine Political Thought and the Atlantic Republican Tradition.* Princeton, NJ: Princeton University Press.

Polanyi, Karl. 2001. *The Great Transformation: The Political and Economic Origins of Our Times.* Boston, MA: Beacon Press.

Pope Francis. 2015. *Encyclical on Climate Change and Inequality: On Care for Our Common Home.* London: Melville House.

Potter, David, David Goldblatt, Margaret Kiloh, and Paul Lewis, eds. 1997. *Democratization.* Cambridge: Polity Press.

Powers, Roger, ed. 1997. *Protest, Power, and Change: An Encyclopedia of Nonviolent Action from ACT-UP to Women's Suffrage.* New York, NY: Garland Press.

Prashad, Vijay. 2007. *The Darker Nations: A People's History of the Third World.* New York, NY: The New Press.

Rahnewa, Majid, ed. 2006. *The Post-Development Reader.* London: Zed Books.

Rajagopal, Balakrishnan. 2004. *International Law from Below: Development, Social Movements and Third World Resistance.* Cambridge: Cambridge University Press.

Rawls, John. 1993. *Political Liberalism.* New York, NY: Columbia University Press.

Rawls, John. 2001. *Justice as Fairness: A Restatement*. Cambridge: Belknap Harvard University Press.

Rees, William E. 2010. "Thinking 'Resilience.'" In *The Post Carbon Reader: Managing the 21st Century's Sustainability Crises*, edited by Richard Heinberg and Daniel Lerch, 25–42. Healdsburg: Watershed Media.

Reid, Bill. 2009. *The Essential Writings of Bill Reid*, edited by Robert Bringhurst. Vancouver: Douglas and McIntyre.

Restakis, John. 2010. *Humanizing the Economy: Co-operatives in the Age of Capital*. Gabriola Island: New Society Publishers.

Ricard, Matthieu. 2013. *Altruism: The Power of Compassion to Change Yourself and the World*, translated by Charlotte Mandell and Sam Gordon. New York, NY: Little, Brown & Company.

Rist, Gilbert. 1997. *The History of Development: From Western Origins to Global Faith*. London: Zed Books.

Rorty, Richard. 1989. *Contingency, Irony, and Solidarity*. Cambridge: Cambridge University Press.

Rorty, Richard. 1991. "The Priority of Philosophy to Democracy." In *Objectivity, Relativism and Truth*, 175–96. Cambridge: Cambridge University Press.

Rorty, Richard. 1998. "The Role of Philosophy in Human Progress." In *Truth and Progress*, 274–350. Cambridge: Cambridge University Press.

Rosenau, James N. 1998. "Governance and Democracy in a Globalizing World." In *Re-Imagining Political Community*, edited by Daniele Archibugi, David Held, and Martin Köhler, 28–57. Cambridge: Polity Press.

Rousseau, Jean-Jacques. 1994. *Discourse on the Origin of Inequality*. Oxford: Oxford University Press.

Royal Commission on Aboriginal Peoples. 1993. *Partners in Confederation: Aboriginal Peoples, Self-Government, and the Constitution*. Ottawa: Minister of Supply and Services.

Sahle, Eunice N. n.d. "Global Citizenship and Transnational Civil Society: Theory and Practice." Unpublished manuscript on file with author.

Sahle, Eunice N. 2010. *World Orders, Development and Transformation*. London: Palgrave Macmillan.

Sahle, Eunice N. 2014. "Spaces of Freedom, Citizenship and State in the Context of Globalization: South Africa and Bolivia." In *Freedom and Democracy in an Imperial Context*, edited by Robert Nichols and Jakeet Singh, 147–73. London: Routledge.

Said, Edward W. 1989. "Representing the Colonized: Anthropology's Interlocutors." *Critical Inquiry* 15(2): 205–25.

Said, Edward W. 1993. *Culture and Imperialism*. New York, NY: Knopf.

Said, Edward W. 2004. "The Public Role of Intellectuals and Writers." In *Humanism and Democratic Criticism*, 119–43. New York, NY: Columbia University Press.

Santos, Boaventura de Sousa. 2005. "The Future of the World Social Forum: The Work of Translation." *Development* 48(2): 15–22.

Santos, Boaventura de Sousa. 2006. *The Rise of the Global Left: The World Social Forum and Beyond*. New York, NY: Zed Books.

Santos, Boaventura de Sousa, ed. 2007. *Democratizing Democracy: Beyond the Liberal Democratic Canon*. New York, NY: Verso.

Santos, Bernard de Sousa. 2014. *Epistemologies of the South: Justice against Epistemicide*. London: Routledge.

Santos, Bernard de Sousa, and César A. Rodríguez-Garavito, eds. 2005. *Law and Globalization from Below*. Cambridge: Cambridge University Press.

Scheppele, Kim L. 2006. "The International State of Emergency: Challenges to Constitutionalism After September 11." Unpublished manuscript on file with author.

Schumacher, E.F. 1973. *Small Is Beautiful: A Study of Economics as if People Mattered*. London: Blond and Briggs.

Seabrook, Jermey. 2003. *The No Nonsense Guide to World Poverty*. London: Verso.

Sharp, Gene. 2005. *Waging Nonviolent Struggles: Twentieth-Century Practice and Twenty-First Century Potential*. Boston, MA: Horizons Books.

Shiva, Vandana. 2005. *Earth Democracy: Justice, Sustainability, and Peace*. Cambridge: South End Press.

Simpson, Leanne, and Kiera L. Ladner, eds. 2010. *This is an Honour Song: Twenty Years since the Blockades*. Winnipeg: Arbeiter Ring Publishing.

Six Nations. 1924. *The Redman's Appeal for Justice: The Position of the Six Nations that they Constitute an Independent State*. Brantford, ON: Six Nations.

Skinner, Quentin. 1978. *The Foundations of Modern Political Thought, Volume 1: The Renaissance*. Cambridge: Cambridge University Press.

Skinner, Quentin. 1996. *Reason and Rhetoric in the Philosophy of Hobbes*. Cambridge: Cambridge University Press.

Skinner, Quentin. 1998. *Liberty before Liberalism*. Cambridge: Cambridge University Press.

Skinner, Quentin, and Bo Strath, eds. 2003. *States and Citizens: History, Theory, Prospects*. Cambridge: Cambridge University Press.

Sripati, Vijayashri. 2020. *Constitution-Making under UN Auspices: Fostering Dependency in Sovereign Lands*. New Delhi: Oxford University Press.

Starblanket, Gina, and Heidi K. Stark. 2018. "Towards a Relational Paradigm – Four Points for Consideration: Knowledge, Gender, Land, and Modernity." In *Resurgence and Reconciliation: Indigenous-Settler Relations and Earth Teachings*, edited by Michael Asch, John Borrows, and James Tully, 175–208. Toronto: University of Toronto Press.

Stears, Marc, and Bonnie Honig. 2014. "James Tully's Agonistic Realism." In *On Global Citizenship*, edited by David Owen, 131–52. New York, NY: Bloomsbury.

Steltzer, Ulli. 1997. *The Spirit of Haida Gwaii: Bill Reid's Masterpiece*. Vancouver: Douglas & McIntyre.

Stiglitz, Joseph. 2002. *Globalization and Its Discontents*. New York, NY: W.W. Norton.

Szakolczai, Arpad. 1998. *Max Weber and Michel Foucault: Parallel Life-Works*. London: Routledge.

Taylor, Charles. 1986. "Overcoming Epistemology," In *After Philosophy: End or Transformation?*, edited by Kenneth Baynes, James Bohman, and Thomas McCarthy, 464–88. Cambridge: MIT Press.

Taylor, Charles. 1994. "The Politics of Recognition." In *Multiculturalism: Examining the Politics of Recognition*, edited by Amy Gutmann, 25–74. Princeton, NJ: Princeton University Press.

Taylor, Charles. 2007. *A Secular Age*. Cambridge, MA: Harvard University Press.

Temelini, Michael. 2015. *Wittgenstein and the Study of Politics*. Toronto: University of Toronto Press.

Thompson, Evan. 2010. *Mind in Life Biology, Phenomenology, and the Sciences of Mind*. Cambridge: Belknap Harvard University Press.

Tilly, Charles. 2007. *Democracy*. Cambridge: Cambridge University Press.

Tuck, Eve, and K. Wyane Yang. 2012. "Decolonization Is Not a Metaphor." *Decolonization: Indigeneity, Education, Society* 1(1): 1–40.

Turner, Nancy J. 2005. *The Earth's Blanket: Traditional Teachings for Sustainable Living*. Seattle, WA: University of Washington Press.

Turner, Nancy J., and Pamela Spalding. 2018. "Learning from the Earth, Learning from Each Other: Ethnoecology, Responsibility and Reciprocity." In *Resurgence and Reconciliation: Indigenous-Settler Relations and Earth Teachings*, edited by Michael Asch, John Borrows, and James Tully, 265–92. Toronto: University of Toronto Press.

United Nations Alliance of Civilizations. 2006. *Report of the High-Level Group* (November 13).

United Nations General Assembly. 1960. *Resolution 1514 (XV): Declaration on the Granting of Independence to Colonial Countries and Peoples*, A/REST/1514(XV) (December 14).

United Nations General Assembly. 1974. *Resolution 3201 (S-VI): Declaration for the Establishment of a New International Economic Order*, A/RES/S-6/3201 (May 1).

United Nations General Assembly. 2007. *Resolution 61/295: Declaration on the Rights of Indigenous Peoples*, A/61/295 (September 13).

United Nations Security Council. 2001. *Resolution 1373*, S/RES/1373 (September 28).

Vasquez-Arroyo, Antonio Y. 2014. "At the Edges of Civic Freedom: Violent, Power, Enmity." In *Freedom and Democracy in an Imperial Context*, edited by Robert Nichols and Jakeet Singh, 48–70. New York, NY: Routledge.

Volk, Christian. 2021. "On Radical Democratic Theory of Political Protest: Potentials and Shortcomings." *Critical Review of International Social and Political Philosophy* 24(4): 437–59.

Wackernagel, Mathis, and William Rees. 1996. *Our Ecological Footprint: Reducing Human Impact on the Earth*. Gabriola: New Society Publications.

Walker, Neil. 2002. "The Idea of Constitutional Pluralism." *Modern Law Review*, 65(3): 317–59.

Wallace-Wells, David. 2019. *The Uninhabitable Earth: Life after Warming*. New York, NY: Tim Duggan Books.

Walton, Douglas. 1998. *The New Dialectic: Conversational Contexts of Argument*. Toronto: University of Toronto Press.

Ward, Peter. 2009. *The Medea Hypothesis: Is Life on Earth Ultimately Destructive?* Princeton, NJ: Princeton University Press.

Way, Niobe, Alisha Ali, Carol Gilligan, and Pedro Noguera, eds. 2018. *The Crisis of Connection: Roots, Consequences, and Solutions*. New York, NY: New York University Press.

Webber, Jeremy. 2006. "Legal Pluralism and Human Agency." *Osgoode Hall Law Journal* 44(1): 167–98.

Webber, Jeremy. 2009. "The Grammar of Customary Law." *McGill Law Journal* 54(4): 579–626.

Webber, Jeremy. 2021. *The Constitution of Canada: A Contextual Analysis*, 2nd edition. New York, NY: Hart Publishing.

Weber, Thomas. 2004. *Gandhi as Disciple and Mentor*. Cambridge: Cambridge University Press.

Wenman, Mark. 2013. *Agonistic Democracy: Constituent Power in the Era of Globalization*. Cambridge: Cambridge University Press.

Wiener, Antje. 2008. *The Invisible Constitution of Politics: Contested Norms and International Encounters.* Cambridge: Cambridge University Press.

Wiener, Antje. 2014. *A Theory of Contestation.* New York, NY: Springer.

Wilde, Ralph. 2008. *International Territorial Administration: How Trusteeship and the Civilizing Mission Never Went Away.* Oxford: Oxford University Press.

Willinsky, John. 2017. *The Intellectual Properties of Learning: A Prehistory from Saint Jerome to John Locke.* Chicago, IL: University of Chicago Press.

Wilner, Isaish. 2013. "A Global Potlatch: Identifying Indigenous Influence on Western Thought." *American Indian Culture and Research Journal* 37(2): 87–114.

Wilson, Vernon. 2015. "A Post-Delgamuukw Philosophical Feast: Feeding the Ancestral Desire for Peaceful Coexistence." MA Thesis: Trinity Western University.

Wittgenstein, Ludwig. 1972. *The Blue and Brown Books: Preliminary Studies for the 'Philosophical Investigations.'* Oxford: Basil Blackwell.

Wittgenstein, Ludwig. 1974. *On Certainty*, translated by Denis Paul and G.E.M. Anscombe. Oxford: Blackwell.

Wittgenstein, Ludwig. 1980. *Culture and Value*, edited by G.H. von Wright and Heikki Nyman and translated by Peter Winch. Oxford: Blackwell.

Wittgenstein, Ludwig. 1993. *Philosophical Occasions 1912–1951*, edited by James Klage and Alfred Nordmann. Indianapolis, IN: Hackett Publishing.

Wittgenstein, Ludwig. 2009. *Philosophical Investigations*, 4th edition, translated by G.E.M. Anscombe, et al. and edited by P.M.S. Hacker and Joachim Schulte. Chichester: Wiley-Blackwell.

Wollstonecraft, Mary. 2010. *The Vindication of the Rights of Woman*, edited by Nina Power. London: Verso.

Young, Iris M. 1996. "Communication and the Other: Beyond Deliberative Democracy." In *Democracy and Difference*, edited by Seyla Benhabib, 120–36. Princeton, NJ: Princeton University Press.

Young, Iris M. 1997. "The Complexities of Coalition." *Dissent* 44(1): 64–9.

Zamagni, Stefano and Vera Zamagni. 2010. *Cooperative Enterprise.* Cheltenham: Edward Elgar.

Zerilli, Linda. 2005. *Feminism and the Abyss of Freedom.* Chicago, IL: University of Chicago Press.

Zinn, Howard. 2007. *A Power Governments Cannot Suppress.* San Francisco, CA: City Lights.

Zúñiga, Didier. 2020. *Relational Ethics for a World of Many Worlds: An Ecosocial Theory of Care, Vulnerability and Sustainability.* PhD Dissertation: University of Victoria. https://dspace.library.uvic.ca/handle/1828/11959

Index

Note: References to notes are provided as the page number followed by 'n' and the note number, e.g. 48n2.